Therapeutic Paradox

EDITED BY
L. Michael Ascher
Temple University Health Sciences Center

The Guilford Press
New York London

A Division of Guilford Publications, Inc.
72 Spring Street, New York, NY 10012

Printed in the United States of America

This book is printed on acid-free paper.

Last digit is print number: 9 8 7 6 5 4 3 2 1

Library of Congress Cataloging-in-Publication Data

Therapeutic paradox / edited by L. Michael Ascher.
p. cm.
Includes bibliographies and index.
ISBN 0-89862-393-6
1. Behavior therapy. 2. Paradox. I. Ascher, L. Michael.
[DNLM: 1. Behavior Therapy. WM 425 T3976]
RC489.B4T55 1989
616.89'142—dc20
DNLM/DLC
for Library of Congress 89-11999
CIP

*In loving memory of my father,
who first introduced me to the concept
of paradoxical intention. And in fond
remembrance of my mother, who had to
live with the results.*

Contributors

L. Michael Ascher, Ph.D. *Department of Psychiatry, Temple University Health Sciences Center, Philadelphia, Pennsylvania*

Philip H. Bornstein, Ph.D. *Private practice, Missoula, Montana*

June Chiodo, Ph.D. *Weight Management Program, Temple University Medical Practices, Philadelphia, Pennsylvania*

Kenneth Cogswell, Ph.D. *Department of Psychology, University of Montana, Missoula, Montana*

Joseph Cools, M.S. *Department of Psychology, University of Health Sciences/The Chicago Medical School, North Chicago, Illinois*

James C. Coyne, Ph.D. *Department of Family Practice, The University of Michigan Medical Center, Ann Arbor, Michigan*

Robert A. DiTomasso, Ph.D. *West Jersey Health System Family Practice Residency, Tatem-Brown Family Practice Center, Voorhees, New Jersey*

Barry L. Duncan, Psy.D. *The Dayton Institute for Family Therapy, Centerville, Ohio*

Ruth L. Greenberg, Ph.D. *Center for Cognitive Therapy, University of Pennsylvania, Philadelphia, Pennsylvania*

Steven C. Hayes, Ph.D. *Department of Psychology, University of Nevada–Reno, Reno, Nevada*

Holly K. Krueger, Ph.D. *Department of Psychology, University of Montana, Missoula, Montana*

Marsha M. Linehan, Ph.D. *Department of Psychology, University of Washington, Seattle, Washington*

Susan M. Melancon, M.S. *Department of Psychology, University of Nevada–Reno, Reno, Nevada*

David Morris Schnarch, Ph.D. *Sex and Marital Health Clinic, Department of Urology, Louisiana State University Medical Center, New Orleans, Louisiana*

David E. Schotte, Ph.D. *Department of Psychology, University of Health Sciences/The Chicago Medical School, North Chicago, Illinois*

Edward N. Shearin, B.S. *Department of Psychology, University of Washington, Seattle, Washington (Present address: Department of Psychiatry, Medical College of Pennsylvania at EPPI, Philadelphia, Pennsylvania)*

Steven A. Szykula, Ph.D. *Departments of Psychiatry and Psychology, The University of Utah College of Medicine, and The Western Institute of Neuropsychiatry, Salt Lake City, Utah*

Preface

Although therapeutic paradox has appeared in the psychotherapy literature on a consistent basis since the 1950s, interest in the concept has increased markedly in the last 10 years. And, although therapeutic paradox can be identified with nearly all methods of psychotherapy, it is most closely associated with the broad and loosely confederated area of family therapy. Consequently, while the family therapy literature incorporates some excellent, even classic, books and articles that can provide valuable assistance to any psychotherapist, most of the available information on therapeutic paradox appears in publications that adhere to the tenets and practices of the family approach. The purpose of the present book is to supplement this literature by investigating the topic from an alternative perspective, that of a broadly based cognitive-behavioral approach.

The presentation of therapeutic paradox within a cognitive-behavioral context can provide a number of advantages for the reader. First, after the family literature, that of behavior therapy offers the most extensive, systematic treatment of the topic. This material can be useful to those wishing to expand their knowledge of clinical and theoretical alternatives incorporated by therapeutic paradox. Second, throughout its development, behavior therapy, in contrast to other psychotherapeutic orientations, has been uniquely associated with the experimental validation of clinical procedures. A complete understanding of therapeutic paradox is impossible without knowledge of the relevant empirical literature from the standpoint of what data have been collected, methods for evaluating these data, ways of applying this information to the clinical setting, and procedures helpful in conducting research in this difficult area. Third, behavior therapy incorporates principles that have been used as the bases of effective programs for the treatment of specific behavioral problems and for common adjustment difficulties of major segments of the population. The chapters in the last section of this book illustrate the enhancement generated by the synergy resulting from the association of cognitive-behavior therapy with therapeutic paradox.

Therapeutic paradox is a relatively recent addition to the literature of behavior therapy, but here also, interest has accelerated in the last decade. During this time, behavior therapists have explored utilization of the concept in several ways: in its traditional manner of enhancing cooperation; in directly treating a major focus of behavior therapy—ameliorating anxiety (e.g., see Ascher, Chapter 4, this volume); and even in a guiding role, supplementing a behavioral position (e.g., see Shearin & Linehan, Chapter 9, this volume). As a group, the chapters in this book constitute a broad survey of the operations of therapeutic paradox in behavior therapy by including a wide range of populations, target problems, and ways of formulating and administering an extensive variety of procedures.

Contributors to the book have sought to provide the latest information on the application of therapeutic paradox to specialized areas in a manner that would be useful both to the behavioral and to the nonbehavioral professional interested in clinical and/or research aspects of the area. The book benefits from the varied orientations of the authors, including cognitive-behavior therapists, behaviorally oriented family therapists, therapists affiliated with alternative schools of psychotherapy, and eclectic therapists whose clinical methods are congruent with the principles and procedures of behavior therapy.

The impetus for the project that culminated in this volume resided in an interest that I have pursued for some years. During that time I have had the good fortune to have been associated with a number of colleagues who have been valuable in stimulating my thoughts and in suggesting interesting and rewarding directions for investigation. Among these individuals, I would particularly like to acknowledge Professor Viktor Frankl, who is always generous in sharing his time and his thoughts with me. The critical comments of Joseph Wolpe served as a beacon in a potentially foggy area. Conversations over the years with my friends Joseph Cautela, Jay Efran, and Alan Goldstein have been important in my considerations of paradox in psychotherapy.

Elsa Efran contributed her editorial expertise to earlier drafts of Chapters 1 and 4. Seymour Weingarten, Editor-in-Chief of The Guilford Press, was helpful and encouraging in every stage in the production of this book. And the efforts of his colleague Judith Grauman smoothed the impediments of what might otherwise have been a difficult undertaking. Finally, Heather's support in this and in all of my endeavors is gratefully acknowledged.

L. Michael Ascher

Contents

Therapeutic Paradox

Introduction

Chapter 1

Therapeutic Paradox: A Primer

L. Michael Ascher

Most of the authors of the chapters in this book have assumed that the reader is fairly sophisticated with respect to the concept of therapeutic paradox and its role in behavior therapy. This may not in fact be the case, since the *concept* of therapeutic paradox has been most closely associated with the family therapy literature. Those who are not acquainted with this orientation may be relatively unfamiliar with the topic. The purpose of this section is to introduce the reader to some of the questions and issues in the domain of this topic and to describe the manner in which paradoxical procedures have been employed in behavior therapy.

Behavior Therapy and Therapeutic Paradox

Therapeutic paradox and the behavioral tradition have a long, if spare, relationship. As might be expected, the nature of this association has been colored by the behavior therapist's insistence on operational descriptions of the procedures, and that treatment of the behavioral complaints be subjected to systematic series of studies.

Dunlap (1928) was the first to systematically employ, within a behavioral context, what might be classified as a paradoxical technique. Negative practice was initially directed toward relatively simple motor responses whose frequency the individual wished to reduce. Although common sense might dictate that one should attempt to limit such behavior directly, Dunlap suggested that the unwanted response must be practiced in a specifically prescribed manner with the aim of bringing it under the individual's control.

Dunlap's interest seemed to focus on the nature of the learned motor behavior; although he believed anxiety to be an important factor, it typically played an ancillary role in his considerations. Viktor Frankl (1939, 1947, 1955, 1975), who first began exploring paradox in 1925 in connection with his clinical practice in Vienna, was primarily concerned with the role of anticipatory anxiety in producing and exacerbating a variety of behavioral complaints. Using a procedure that he labeled "paradoxical intention," he suggested that individuals actively court the very behavior of which they wished to rid themselves. Accordingly, a person who remained at home fearing a possible heart attack would be encouraged to travel far from home, to increase cardiac rate, and to "provoke a heart attack."

An important component of paradoxical intention, as practiced by Frankl, is humor. It is employed in the service of assisting the individual to obtain some necessary distance from his or her problems. When an individual is able to employ the procedure in the recommended fashion, anticipatory anxiety is reduced, as are its deleterious effects on behavior.

A third example of the convergence of paradox and general behavioral principles in the history of behavior therapy occurred in the work of Stampfl and Levis (1967, 1968). During a time when the major behavioral approach to the amelioration of anxiety disorders was systematic desensitization, these authors proposed the antithesis—implosion. Whereas systematic desensitization requires the gradual hierarchical exposure of the client to discomforting stimuli, keeping anxiety level at a minimum, implosion—or "flooding"—involves the presentation of fearful stimuli at the highest possible levels so as to elicit strong client responses. The client is then encouraged to remain in the presence of these stimuli until he or she no longer experiences anxiety. The recent consideration that paradox has received in behavior therapy (see, e.g., Schotte, Ascher, & Cools, Chapter 2, this volume) is perhaps a realization of the implied promise that these earlier exploratory studies and reports suggested.

These three examples illustrate the way in which therapeutic paradox has been adapted to the postulates of the behavioral tradition. Ascher (Chapter 4) and Chiodo (Chapter 5), in their respective chapters, demonstrate the continued development of the role of therapeutic paradox within a relatively traditional behavioral context. Focusing on anxiety disorders, Ascher uses paradoxical intention as a central procedure around which auxiliary behavioral and paradoxical methods are administered. This may be contrasted with Chiodo, who highlights eating disorders and supplements behavioral treatment programs designed for this class of difficulties by incorporating paradoxical strategies on an ancillary, *ad hoc* basis.

Recently, behavior therapists have become more interested in employing therapeutic paradox in the manner that is customarily associated with this category of procedures. Thus, rather than utilizing traditional behavioral problem-oriented treatment programs, behavior therapists are using paradoxical procedures to address general issues of therapy. The most salient of these considerations is client resistance to behavioral treatment programs (e.g., Dowd & Milne, 1986). For example, reframing (Watzlawick, Weakland, & Fisch, 1974) and similar procedures have been employed by behavior therapists to help clients obtain maximum benefits from behavioral procedures. In defining the process of reframing, Watzlawick et al. (1974) state that it "means to change the conceptual and/or emotional setting or viewpoint in relation to which a situation is experienced and to place it in another frame that fits the 'facts' of the same concrete situation equally well or even better, and thereby changes its entire meaning" (p. 95). The adaptive role of reframing is illustrated by Tom Sawyer, who—when required to undergo the ordeal of whitewashing a fence on a hot summer day—convinced his friends to do the work for him by changing its context from something unenjoyable to something desirable. Instances of the use of reframing in a supplementary capacity or as the central component of a treatment program are replete in cognitive therapies, particularly in those associated with Beck and Ellis. The more traditional approaches to behavior therapy also incorporate reframing, again particularly in preparing the client to engage in the *in vivo* use of behavioral techniques.

In the practice of behavior therapy, clients' explanations of troubling experiences often serve to exacerbate their difficulties. As part of the initial phase of treatment, the therapist is involved in assisting clients to reclassify their experiences. Many agoraphobics who experience panic attacks report that these attacks, having no apparent external cause, seemed to them to indicate psychosis—they feared that they were "going crazy." Subsuming these aspects of anxiety under the aegis of "symptoms of serious mental illness" serves to magnify the discomfort that agoraphobics experience. By placing these symptoms into a logical context (e.g., in terms of conditioning theory and the normal physiological process of anxiety, anticipatory anxiety, and consequent avoidance behavior), the explanation of the therapist (e.g., Barlow & Cerny, 1988, pp. 88–93) can be interpreted as a reframe that assists the client to shift from an anxiety-provoking explanation to one that is more comforting.

Therapeutic Paradox as a Category of Behavioral Techniques

A principle coming from any subdivision of psychology, or any cohesive system of behavior change, can form the basis of a clinical procedure. In order for that technique to be appropriately placed under the "behavioral" aegis, it must reliably produce clinically significant results that are consistently verified by controlled experimental investigation. It is this tenet that provides behavior therapy with its unique place among schools of psychotherapy.

Although a myriad of uncontrolled case reports have been available for many years, as is fully detailed by DiTomasso and Greenberg (Chapter 3), systematic clinical investigations of paradoxical techniques have been undertaken only in the last decade. These studies, most of which employ paradoxical intention, have been critically evaluated by Ascher, Bowers, and Schotte (1985). In the present volume, Schotte et al. (Chapter 2) evaluate a more selected set of experiments. Several conclusions may be drawn from these and other reviews (e.g., Hampton, 1987; Hill, 1987; Shoham-Salomon & Rosenthal, 1987). First, controlled research in this area is in a preliminary stage. Therefore, data sufficient to support incontrovertible conclusions do not exist. Second, most studies are flawed—some more seriously than others. Third, the data that do exist suggest that paradoxical intention is an effective clinical procedure for certain kinds of behavioral complaints. It therefore appears that paradoxical intention has—on a preliminary basis—met the empirical requirement necessary for inclusion in the behavior therapist's repertoire of techniques (Ascher, 1989).

Aspects of Definition

The great diversity of paradoxical techniques and their labels can obscure common characteristics that themselves serve to define the compass of therapeutic paradox. Among these are two significant features. First, the procedures are designed to be surprising. They are contrary to the expectations of clients with respect to their view of the nature and conduct of therapy. (In this regard, humor that is to some extent based on confounding the expectations of the audience is often associated with paradoxical directives.) Second, rather than providing suggestions that would be congruent with the goal of directly changing an offending behavior, the character of the contradiction requires that the therapist unexpectedly recommend that the client maintain the particular response at its most uncomfortable level. In other words, the client is enjoined from making changes relevant to the presenting complaint. The client's emotional response to paradox (e.g., shock, surprise, confusion) may serve as a positive therapeutic experience.

Does the term "paradox" in therapeutic paradox refer to logical paradox? The answer to this depends on one's definition of logical paradox. For example, those who ascribe to the "double-bind" hypothesis in explaining the operation of paradoxical procedures (e.g., Haley, 1973) can support the contention that their paradoxical directives employ logical paradox on the basis of Whitehead and Russell's theory of logical types.

On the other hand, Hughes and Brecht (1975) require that a statement incorporate three criteria in order to qualify properly for the label "logical paradox": self-reference, contradiction, and vicious circularity. Most paradoxical directives fulfill only the first two; the third is not typically achieved except by hypothetical explanation. In this sense, then, most paradoxical directives are merely ironic—that is, "the use of words to express a meaning which is different from, and often the direct opposite of, the literal meaning" (*Random House Dictionary of the English Language*, 1967, p. 753).

A divergent position comes from Dell (1981), who suggests that paradox is not a natural phenomenon and that its recognition rests entirely with the perceiver. To the extent that it must be the client who is affected by the paradox, then it may be that the issue of definition is academic and that Dell offers a useful alternative in examining therapeutic paradox.

The chapters in the clinical section of this book demonstrate the ways in which the authors have based their approaches to therapeutic paradox on differing definitions. For example, although Schnarch (Chapter 8) does not explicitly define paradox, his presentation is congruent with that of the systems position (e.g., Watzlawick, Beavin, & Jackson, 1967). This background readily lends itself to Schnarch's categorization of therapeutically relevant paradox. His classification consists of "constructed paradox," which is therapist-generated (e.g., the use of paradoxical procedures to neutralize resistence to the therapeutic program), and "inherent paradox," referring to phenomena that are embedded in interpersonal interactions and engender paradox (e.g., conflicting messages, inconsistencies in communication). The latter are often targets of the former.

Dialectics

A number of writers have examined the potentially significant role of dialectics in therapeutic paradox. In their chapter, Shearin and Linehan

(Chapter 9) discuss the implications of this concept for the behavioral treatment of a notoriously refractory clinical population—namely, borderline personality disorder. The modern concept of dialectics is derived from Hegel, who considered the dialectic to be the logical model that guides thought. To Hegel, thought proceeded from contradiction to reconciliation (Flew, 1984). Weeks and L'Abate (1982) emphasize opposition, conflict, and dynamic change in dialectics and suggest that therapeutic paradox may serve to maintain constructive cognitive activity when impediments arise.

Historically, symptoms have been viewed as problems that impede the individual's adjustment. The anxiety that is assumed to maintain this behavior may, for example, be exacerbated by explanations that suggest that symptoms are signs of negative personality characteristics or serious underlying pathology. Dialectics introduces the possibility that symptoms can have a constructive role in adaptive change. Applying a positive meaning or label to a behavior can serve to reduce associated anxiety and thereby assist the individual in gaining control. Certainly, the explanation of reframing developed by Watzlawick et al. (1974) as a shift in classification is quite similar to the concept of dialectics. In a variety of ways, paradoxical directives support this positive alternative to the individual's typically pernicious interpretation of symptoms (see Ascher, Chapter 4, this volume, for illustrations).

Theory

The confusion resulting from the diverse labels given to paradoxical procedures in the many psychotherapeutic approaches that incorporate them has produced a divergent array of theoretical explanations. Hypotheses that may be useful to therapists working with one set of circumstances usually are of less assistance to other therapists applying paradox in different situations. The range sampled in the second section of this book illustrates the difficulty that confronts individuals who want to develop a useful metatheory of paradox. As a result, few have accepted the challenge.

The most comprehensive attempt to explain paradoxical approaches is described in an article by Omer (1981). He considers three alternative hypotheses for the efficacy of paradoxical techniques: Frankl's logotherapeutic concept of anticipatory anxiety, the double-bind assumption associated with systems theory, and the learning concept of conditioned inhibition. However, none of these hypotheses clarifies the *modus operandi* of therapeutic paradox in all schools of psychotherapy.

Omer presents an overarching hypothesis entitled "symptom decontextualization." It is based on his understanding that in each paradoxical procedure the symptom is not prescribed as it is typically exhibited by the client but always in a different form and context. He proposes that the context of a symptom supports the behavior by providing it with meaning that is significant to the client. When the symptom is dislodged from its meaningful framework, it loses its role in the client's life. He concludes that "in paradoxical treatments the change producing factor may not be the paradoxical directive as such, but the decontextualization of symptomatic behavior" (Omer, 1981, p. 322).

Although this is an interesting proposition. Omer's presentation encounters a number of difficulties. First, as Seltzer (1986) points out, Omer does not consider therapeutic paradox as conceptualized and employed by a variety of psychotherapeutic approaches including psychoanalysis, gestalt, and methods based on Eastern philosophies (e.g., Watts, 1961). Second, it is not always the case that the symptom is prescribed in this disjointed manner, and applying Omer's hypothesis in such cases sometimes requires an unrealistic extension. Third, it is easily possible to apply his principle to nonparadoxical therapeutic procedures. For example, the act of complaining represents a central feature of the difficulties of many clients. When clients exhibit such behavior to Carl Rogers or to Albert Ellis, or to any therapist for that matter, the context will be very different from that to which they have grown accustomed. That is, the reaction of the therapist will represent a significant contrast to the responses that the clients typically elicit from friends, relatives, and other acquaintances. To the extent that Omer's concept can be applied similarly to paradoxical and to nonparadoxical procedures without differentiating between the two, it becomes less helpful in explaining the effectiveness of therapeutic paradox.

Several other investigators have proposed similarly inclusive hypotheses intended to account for the entire domain of therapeutic paradox (e.g., Fay, 1978; Seltzer, 1986). Every hypothesis is forced to become so encompassing that, as with Omer's, each applies to both paradoxical and nonparadoxical procedures—without accounting for the apparently unique characteristics of the former. Here again, Dell's (1986) position offers some assistance, since he suggests that paradox is not a natural classification but rather is the reified result of a conflict that exists between our theories of therapeutic behavior change and clinical data that fail to confirm them. When our theories are reconstituted to accommodate such data, there will be no need for the term "paradox," because events bearing this label will at that juncture be incorporated into a comprehensive theory.

The great amount of pivotal information and conceptual writing on therapeutic paradox that continues to be produced by those ascribing to the systems (Watzlawick et al., 1974) and strategic (Haley, 1963) approaches to family therapy has led professionals to associate paradoxical strategies closely with these areas of psychotherapy. In light of the ease with which paradoxical procedures have been merged with behavioral techniques, it is interesting that a comparison of systems and strategic principles with those of behavior therapy reveals a number of significant similarities. Foremost among these is their problem-focused orientation. The three approaches tend to discount the role of such traditional factors as history, problem etiology, underlying theoretical constructs, and client insight. Instead, they emphasize the formulation of programs that are specifically tailored to the clinical profile and the presenting complaint of the client.

The similarities that exist between the systems approach and behavior therapy, particularly with respect to therapeutic paradox, are emphasized in the chapter by Duncan (Chapter 11). In addition, his presentation incorporates a concept toward which some of the systems therapists have been progressing for some time—that is, "invented reality" (Watzlawick, 1984). This principle suggests that a single objective reality for all individuals does not exist but is constructed by each person and is, therefore, different for each.

In contrast, Coyne (Chapter 6) and Szykula (Chapter 12) take the strategic approach to family therapy as a point of departure. Each emphasizes the affinity of behavior therapy, strategic family therapy, and therapeutic paradox, discussing how an integration of the three can be applied to the respective domains of their clinical interests. As is the case with strategic and systems approaches, Hayes and Melancon (Chapter 7) also consider the social and communication context within which problem behaviors develop and are maintained. However, in their chapter they analyze this context from what is basically an empirically based human learning perspective. Within this framework, they demonstrate how the concepts associated with therapeutic paradox can be generated and employed in therapy.

Perhaps the most influential hypothesis of therapeutic paradox is the "double-bind" postulate that is associated with systems theory. It is attributed to Bateson (Bateson, Jackson, Haley, & Weakland, 1956), who was engaged in the study of families of individuals diagnosed as schizophrenic. Contrary to the dominant intrapsychic hypotheses of the day, Bateson et al. (1956) focused on disturbed interpersonal communication as an important factor in the generation and maintenance of the pathology. Briefly, the "pathogenic double-bind" refers to a communication in which simultaneous mutually exclusive messages are presented. Although similar in many respects to the pathogenic double-bind, the "therapeutic double-bind" is constructed and administered with the goal of producing an adaptive behavioral change (Watzlawick et al., 1967). Whereas both double-binds can explain a variety of communications, the therapeutic double-bind has been employed as a guide in the formulation and administration of paradoxical therapeutic procedures.

Another interesting concept from systems theory that appears in several of the clinical chapters to follow is a method for classifying transformational communications into those related to "first-order" change and those associated with "second-order" change (Watzlawick et al., 1974). Based, to some extent, on the theory of logical types (Whitehead & Russell, 1910), first-order operations occur within the rules of the system, whereas second-order processes breach system rules. Second-order solutions are often viewed from within the system as unpredictable, amazing, and surprising, since they are not necessarily based on the rules and assumptions of that system. Therapeutic paradox represents a category of second-order solutions.

In the treatment of insomnia, first- and second-order operations can be contrasted. First-order procedures include teaching the individual some type of relaxation technique that he or she is to practice at bedtime and prescribing a sedative. On the other hand, instructing the person to remain awake through the night, as is the case with paradoxical intention, is a second-order operation, since it violates many of the client's assumptions regarding psychotherapeutic approaches to the treatment of insomnia.

Ethics

Ethical considerations are dependent on the perspective that one takes with respect to therapeutic paradox. In the present volume, this viewpoint is significantly influenced by the nature of the relationship between therapeutic paradox and behavior therapy. Three types of associations are illustrated in the clinical chapters to follow. In the first, represented in the chapter by Ascher (Chapter 4), paradoxical techniques are transformed into behavioral procedures. That is, they are subjected to the same criteria (e.g., empirical tests of efficacy, administered in the context of a behavioral treatment program, incorporated into an overall cohesive theory of behavior change) as are all behavioral methods. Once this transformation has been achieved, ethical concerns are then identical to those of any behavioral technique (e.g., the most appropriate procedure based on the client's profile and goals, administered in the correct manner). In other words, when considered from a behavioral perspective, ethical considerations regarding the use of paradoxical intention are no different from those of any behavioral procedure such a systematic desensitization or flooding.

A second relationship between therapeutic paradox and behavior therapy treats paradox as a model within which to apply behavioral procedures. This has been accomplished by Shearin and Linehan (Chapter 9), who have used dialectic principles, a position closely related to therapeutic paradox, as a guiding structure in their approach to a specific clinical population. Again, ethical standards seem to be similar to those employed for any therapeutic approach.

The third method of associating behavior therapy with therapeutic paradox involves employing each in its respective, traditional way. The organizing principle is that each position should complement the other. Thus, by combining the two, a superior psychotherapeutic product will result. From this position, therapeutic paradox is seen as a related body of techniques that are employed to enhance conventional behavioral programs by reducing client resistance. This stance forms a component of the approaches taken by Chiodo and Szykula in their respective chapters (Chapters 5 and 12). Of the three relationships described, only this last would seem to warrant the traditional caveats uniquely associated with paradox.

Introduction to the Chapters

The book is divided into two sections. The first consists of reviews of the literature. The review of Schotte, Ascher and Cools (Chapter 2) is representative of the typical methods used to investigate paradox experimentally. Because of the relative preponderance of research, focus of the evaluation is on paradoxical intention in the treatment of primary insomnia and anxiety disorders. The comprehensive review of case studies that was conducted by DiTomasso and Greenberg (Chapter 3) indicates the range of behavioral complaints that have been exposed to a wide variety of paradoxical techniques.

The second section is composed of clinically oriented chapters designed to illustrate the array of methods by which therapeutic paradox can be associated with behavior therapy. The specific behavioral problems or treatment groups selected were those with which therapeutic paradox presently plays a significant role in treatment, as in the case of Duncan's chapter on therapy with families (Chapter 11), or with which these procedures appear to have considerable potential for treatment, which is Chiodo's suggestion with respect to eating disorders (see Chapter 5).

References

Ascher, L. M. (1989). Paradoxical intention: Its clarification and emergence as a conventional behavioral procedure. *the Behavior Therapist, 12,* 23–28.

Ascher, L. M., Bowers, M. R., & Schotte, D. E. (1985). A review of data from controlled case studies and experiments evaluating the clinical efficacy of paradoxical intention. In

G. R. Weeks (Ed.), *Promoting change through paradoxical therapy*. Homewood, IL: Dow Jones-Irwin.

Barlow, D. H., & Cerny, J. A. (1988). *Psychological treatment of panic*. New York: Guilford Press.

Bateson, G., Jackson, D. D., Haley, J., & Weakland, J. H. (1956). Toward a theory of schizophrenia. *Behavioral Science, 1*, 251-264.

Dell, P. F. (1981). Paradox redux. *Journal of Marital and Family Therapy, 7*, 127-134.

Dell, P. F. (1986). Why do we still call them "paradoxes"? *Family Process, 25*, 223-234.

Dowd, T., & Milne, C. R. (1986). Paradoxical interventions in counseling psychology. *The Counseling Psychologist, 14*, 237-282.

Dunlap, K. (1928). A revision of the fundamental law of habit formation. *Science, 67*, 360-362.

Fay, A. (1978). *Making things better by making them worse*. New York: Hawthorn.

Flew, A. (1984). *A dictionary of philosophy* (2nd ed.). New York: St. Martin's Press.

Frankl, V. E. (1939). Zur memischen Bejahung und Vermeinung. *Internationale Zeitschrift fuer Psychoanalyse, 43*, 26-31.

Frankl, V. E. (1947). *Die Psychotherapie in der Praxis*. Vienna: Deuticke.

Frankl, V. E. (1955). *The doctor and the soul: From psychotherapy to logotherapy*. New York: Knopf.

Frankl, V. E. (1975). Paradoxical intention and dereflection. *Psychotherapy: Theory, Research, and Practice, 12*, 226-237.

Haley, J. (1963). *Strategies of psychotherapy*. New York: Grune & Stratton.

Haley, J. (1973). *Uncommon therapy: The psychiatric techniques of Milton H. Erickson, M.D.* New York: Norton.

Hampton, B. (1987, August). *Paradoxical approaches to psychotherapy, do they work?* Paper presented at the American Psychological Association, New York.

Hill, K. A. (1987). Meta-analysis of paradoxical interventions. *Psychotherapy, 24*, 266-270.

Hughes, P., & Brecht, G. (1975). *Vicious circles and infinity: An anthology of paradoxes*. New York: Penguin.

Omer, H. (1981). Paradoxical treatments: A unified concept. *Psychotherapy: Theory, Research, and Practice, 18*, 320-324.

Random House dictionary of the English language. (1967). New York: Random House.

Seltzer, L. F. (1986). *Paradoxical strategies in psychotherapy: A comprehensive overview and guidebook*. New York: Wiley.

Shoham-Salomon, V., & Rosenthal, R. (1987). Paradoxical interventions; a meta-analysis. *Journal of Consulting and Clinical Psychology, 55*, 22-28.

Stampfl, T. G., & Levis, D. J. (1967). Essentials of implosive therapy: A learning theory-based psychodynamic behavioral therapy. *Journal of Abnormal Psychology, 72*, 496-503.

Stampfl, T. G., & Levis, D. J. (1968). Implosive therapy—A behavioral therapy? *Behaviour Research and Therapy, 6*, 31-36.

Watts, A. W. (1961). *Psychotherapy east and west*. New York: Pantheon.

Watzlawick, P. (1984). *The invented reality*. New York: Norton.

Watzlawick, P., Beavin, J. H., & Jackson, D. D. (1967). *Pragmatics of human communication*. New York: Norton.

Watzlawick, P., Weakland, J., & Fisch, R. (1974). *Change: Principles of problem formulation and problem resolution*. New York: Norton.

Weeks, G. R., & L'Abate, L. A. (1982). *Paradoxical psychotherapy: Theory and practice with individuals, couples, and families*. New York: Brunner/Mazel.

Whitehead, A. N., & Russell, B. (1910). *Principia mathematica* (Vol. I). Cambridge: Cambridge University Press.

Reviews of the Literature

Chapter 2

The Use of Paradoxical Intention in Behavior Therapy

David E. Schotte
L. Michael Ascher
Joseph Cools

In recent years, behavior therapists have shifted from an exclusive focus on treatment techniques derived from models of human and animal learning (e.g., operant or respondent conditioning) or skills training (e.g., assertion) to a more eclectic utilization of empirically tested procedures developed within alternative areas of psychological research (e.g., cognitive psychology, social psychology) or of therapeutic practice. The incorporation of the techniques of other schools of psychotherapy into the repertoire of behavioral clinicians appears to be determined increasingly by demonstrations of clinical efficacy rather than concordance with orthodox behavioral theories. The growing use of paradoxical intention by behavior therapists represents one example of this shift toward a broader empiricism.

Paradoxical intention was originally developed in logotherapy during the 1920s as a technique for circumventing the maladaptive consequences of anticipatory anxiety (Frankl, 1984). The procedure consists of instructing clients "to do, or wish for, the very things they fear, albeit with tongue in cheek" (Frankl, 1984, p. 102). Thus, the client is encouraged, usually in a humorous vein, to court his or her worst fears by attempting to increase exposure to that which he or she had previously sought to avoid. Although the client's hypothesized disastrous consequences are usually associated with signs of sympathetic arousal (e.g., tachycardia → heart attack), they can also be linked to specific phobias, such as the fear of contamination.

The review in the present chapter is focused on behavioral outcome studies of the efficacy of paradoxical procedures in the treatment of both sleep-onset insomnia and anxiety disorders. Although paradoxical intention has been applied to the treatment of a wider variety of disorders (e.g., urinary retention, encopresis, anorexia, depression, procrastination), this literature is extremely limited. As a result, there are not at present sufficient data from well-controlled studies to support the efficacy of paradoxical intention in the treatment of these disorders. Reviews of the role of paradox in the treatment of these disorders have been published by Ascher, Bowers, and Schotte (1985), Michelson and Ascher (1984), Jacob and Moore (1984), Wilson and Bornstein (1984), and Dowd and Swoboda (1984), among others.

Sleep-Onset Insomnia

Research on the treatment of sleep-onset insomnia provides the best example of the systematic advances in the experimental evaluation of paradoxical intention. Here one can observe the utilization of increasingly sophisticated research methods that support the efficacy of paradoxical intention as a treatment for sleep-onset insomnia. Thus, there is progression from claims based on uncontrolled case studies (e.g., Ascher, 1975) through single-case experimental designs of varying degrees of sophistication (Ascher & Efran, 1978; Relinger & Bornstein, 1979; Relinger, Bornstein, & Mungas, 1978) to experiments incorporating random assignment of subjects to groups that contrast the effects of paradoxical intention to those of other behavioral treatments, placebo, and no-treatment control procedures (Ascher & Turner, 1979; Lacks, Bertelson, Gans, & Kunkel, 1983; Turner & Ascher, 1979).

Descriptions of the use of paradoxical intention in clinical settings characterize the procedure as a dynamic, complex approach to problems that are refractory to other psychotherapeutic efforts. As such, it is difficult to accommodate the procedure to the exigencies of experimental investigation. Attempts to satisfy the requirements of behavioral research and still retain the essence of paradoxical intention have resulted in several methods of presentation. Many of the early studies have employed an "assessment" rationale as the context for paradoxical instructions. In using this approach, the therapist may discuss with the client the importance of being able to obtain information on "the upper limits" of the sleep problem and on "any disturbing thoughts that may occur while you lay awake in bed" (Ott, Levine, & Ascher, 1983, p. 29). In accord with this rationale, the client is requested to lie quietly in bed with open eyes and to try to remain awake as long as possible, paying close attention to whatever thoughts come to mind. To bolster this rationale, the client is further instructed to make note of these thoughts when completing his or her sleep log the following morning. Thus, the pressure to fall asleep is removed by the request to remain awake. In a similar fashion, "counter-demand" instructions incorporated into procedural instructions (e.g., Lacks et al., 1983) suggest to the client that he or she is not to expect any change in sleep during this assessment period. Later studies (e.g., Ascher & Turner, 1980) have used a more veridical method of administration in which the dynamics of the client's presenting complaint are described, and the role of a treatment program utilizing paradoxical intention as a central feature is detailed.

The earliest claim for the efficacy of this type of procedure with sleep-onset insomnia within a behavioral context was made in a paper presented at the annual meeting of the Association for Advancement of Behavior Therapy (Ascher, 1975). In his presentation, Ascher (1975) reported on the successful application of paradoxical intention to the treatment of a small series of clients with sleep-onset insomnia who had proven refractory to a behavioral program consisting of systematic desensitization and relaxation-training procedures. Unfortunately, the majority of the cases were uncontrolled, and no systematic outcome data were collected.

Based on this initial positive experience with the technique, Ascher and Efran (1978) applied paradoxical intention in the treatment of five sleep-onset insomniacs who had not responded to a 10-week behavioral treatment program that included systematic desensitization, relaxation training, covert conditioning, and stimulus-control procedures. Client self-monitoring was used to obtain a variety of data (e.g., mood when retiring, time of retiring, latency to sleep onset, number of awakenings, restfulness of sleep) during a 1-week pretreatment baseline period and throughout the treatment program itself. Paradoxical intention instructions were presented using either the assessment rationale or a variation that attempted to involve the client in voluntarily lengthening sleep-onset latency. In accord with the assessment rationale, three of the clients were told to try to remain awake as long as possible so that the therapist could gain detailed descriptions of the clients' thoughts prior to falling asleep. The deceptive treatment rationale used with the two remaining clients involved asking the clients to lengthen the period of bedtime relaxation, even if this meant resisting the urge to fall asleep.

Descriptive analyses of the self-report data showed that within 2 weeks of treatment, self-reported sleep-onset latency decreased from a pretreatment mean of 48.6 minutes to less than 9.8 minutes. As a further test, one of the "assessment rationale" clients was requested to resume the initial behavioral treatment assignments for an additional 3 weeks. During this period, his self-reported sleep-onset latency increased from 6 to 28.3 minutes. Subsequent readministration of paradoxical instructions resulted in substantial reductions in the sleep-onset latency of this client.

Relinger et al. (1978) reported on the use of a similar assessment rationale in combination with counterdemand instructions in the use of paradoxical intention to treat a 31-year-old woman with chronic sleep-onset insomnia. In this case, the client was encouraged to remain awake as long as possible in order that she identify thoughts to be used in planning systematic desensitization. Time series analysis of self-report data over 3 weeks of treatment indicated improvement on a number of sleep parameters, including sleep-onset latency (from 65 to 15 minutes), degree of restfulness, daytime functioning, and frequency of falling back to sleep with difficulty. At 1-year follow-up, the self-report data suggested excellent maintenance of treatment gains, with a mean sleep-onset latency of slightly under 11 minutes and a posttreatment improvement in the number of nighttime awakenings.

Relinger and Bornstein (1979) replicated these findings (i.e., the use of an assessment rationale and counterdemand instructions) using a multiple-baseline design with a series of four additional clients. Sleep-onset latency was decreased by 50%, and statistically significant improvements were obtained on self-report measures of restfulness, difficulty falling asleep, and number of awakenings. Three-month follow-up data suggested that self-reported treatment gains were maintained.

These case reports (Ascher, 1975; Ascher & Efran, 1978; Relinger et al., 1978; Relinger & Bornstein, 1979) suggest that paradoxical directives can be effective in the treatment of sleep-onset insomnia. Despite the use of procedures intended to minimize demand characteristics (i.e., "assessment" rationales and counterdemand instructions), however, these reports suffer from a number of methodological shortcomings, including the use of single-case designs that have relatively low levels of internal validity, the lack of untreated or placebo control groups, and exclusive reliance on self-report outcome measures.

In the first study of paradoxical intention to incorporate the random assignment of subjects to groups, Turner and Ascher (1979) assigned clients with clinically significant levels of sleep-onset insomnia to one of five conditions: paradoxical intention, stimulus control, relaxation training, an attention-placebo condition, or a no-treatment control group. Thus, paradoxical intention was compared to alternative behavioral treatments of choice, to a treatment designed to focus on nonspecific therapeutic factors, and to a waiting-list condition. In addition, Turner and Ascher (1979) supplemented client self-monitoring data with ratings of sleep behavior from spouses or roommates. Statistical analysis of both self-report sleep data and sleep ratings made by client cohabitants (i.e., spouses or roommates) demonstrated that whereas clients receiving active treatments improved more than those in the two control conditions, the paradoxical and behavioral interventions did not differ in efficacy. Thus, paradoxical intention was more effective than no treatment, but it was no more effective than alternative behavioral aproaches.

In a partial replication of the Turner and Ascher (1979) study, Ascher and Turner (1979) randomly assigned clients with clinically significant levels of sleep-onset insomnia to paradoxical intention, credible placebo (i.e., a quasidesensitization procedure), or no-treatment conditions. Clients in the paradoxical intention group were instructed to darken their bedroom when retiring and then to lie still and keep their eyes open for as long as possible. The clients in the paradoxical condition reduced their sleep-onset latency by over 50% during the 4-week treatment program and showed greater improvements on all but one self-reported sleep measure (restedness) than did those in the placebo and no-treatment conditions.

Ladouceur and Gros-Louis (1986) obtained similar results in a study contrasting paradoxical intention, stimulus-control procedures, an educational control condition, and no treatment. Although both stimulus control and paradoxical intention produced results superior to educational or no-treatment controls, the two behavioral treatments were equally effective.

Ott et al. (1983) reported on the first evaluation of paradoxical intention using both self-report information and (possibly more objective) data obtained with a sleep-monitoring unit. Clients with sleep-onset insomnia were randomly assigned to paradoxical intention, paradoxical intention plus sleep-monitor feedback, feedback only, or no-treatment and no-feedback conditions. Thus, this design allowed for assessment of the main effects for paradoxical intention and for the sleep monitor, as well as for the interaction between the two. To offset demand characteristics, an assessment rationale and counterdemand instructions were used in all conditions. Interestingly, whereas decreases in sleep-onset latency were observed in clients who received either paradoxical intention alone or feedback alone, clients who received a combination of the two displayed increases in the time required to fall asleep. There was no change in sleep-onset latency among the no-treatment controls. With respect to clients in the paradoxical intention plus feedback condition, Ott et al. (1983) suggest that use of the recording device may have facilitated their literal adherence to the therapist's request to "remain awake as long as possible" (p. 29)

Lacks et al. (1983) controlled for self-reported symptom severity by randomly assigning clients matched for varying levels of sleep-onset latency to paradoxical intention, progressive relaxation, stimulus control, or credible placebo conditions. All treatment procedures included counterdemand instructions. Unlike previous researchers (i.e., Ladouceur & Gros-Louis, 1986; Turner & Ascher, 1979), Lacks et al. found stimulus control to be more effective at all levels of symptom severity than was paradoxical intention. In fact, the Lacks et al. (1983) results suggested that paradoxical intention was no more effective than a credible placebo. These findings are in stark contrast to those of other investigations with similar treatment procedures and comparison groups.

In attempting to explain this difference, Ascher et at. (1985) focused on the counterdemand instructions and on the subjects used. They suggested that these instructions could be considered to be a separate paradoxical intention component appended to each treatment condition. Further, they pointed out that whereas most studies used clients with clinically significant levels of sleep-onset insomnia, the subjects of Lacks et al. (1983) varied from mild through moderate to severe. Thus, with respect to sleep disturbance, the subjects utilized by Lacks et al. (1983) could be considered to be more heterogeneous than were those in other studies. Finally, Ascher et al. (1985) concluded that it was not surprising that a treatment package consisting of stimulus control plus paradoxical intention should be more effective than paradoxical intention alone in such a heterogeneous sample.

Another possible reason for this discrepancy, however, is variability in client response to treatment, a possibility highlighted by the findings of Espie and Lindsay (1985). In their study, Espie and Lindsay (1985) reported on the treatment of a series of six clients with chronic sleep-onset insomnia. Treatment was divided into two phases, the first of which incorporated counterdemand instructions. Espie and Lindsay (1985) noted that although three patients showed rapid positive responses to paradoxical intention, one progressed more slowly, and two actually evinced exacerbations of their sleep disorder. These latter two clients benefited from subsequent treatment with an alternative procedure (i.e., relaxation training). Thus, their report underscores the potential variability in response to paradoxical treatment across clients.

Research by Ascher and Turner (1980) further complicates the interpretation of studies contrasting paradoixcal intention to alternative behavioral treatments for insomnia. In this study, Ascher and Turner (1980) compared two methods for administering paradoxical instructions: the frequently used "assessment" rationale and a veridical rationale concerning the role of performance anxiety in the maintenance of sleep-onset insomnia.

Clients receiving the veridical rationale showed greater improvements on all sleep parameters than did those receiving the assessment rationale. Thus, studies using an assessment rationale may underestimate the efficacy of paradoxical intention in the treatment of sleep-onset insomnia. Overall, the studies reviewed above suggest that in most cases, paradoxical intention is more effective than either a credible placebo treatment or no treatment in reducing sleep-onset insomnia. In addition, it appears that paradoxical intention may, in some cases, be more effective than alternative behavioral procedures such as relaxation training or stimulus-control procedures. In fact, paradoxical intention may benefit clients who have not responded to prior behavioral treatments for their insomnia.

It also appears, however, that paradoxical intention may, in some cases, be less effective in alleviating insomnia than are alternative behavioral procedures (Lacks et al., 1983; Espie & Lindsay, 1985). Indeed, whereas some clients demonstrate rapid improvements in initiating sleep under paradoxical directives, others may actually experience a worsening of their condition (Espie & Lindsay, 1985). These latter clients may, in turn, respond more favorably to an alternative treatment approach such as training in progressive relaxation (Espie & Lindsay, 1985).

Obviously, the data from the studies reviewed here suggest that there is variability among clients in their responses to paradoxical intention. Unfortunately, little attention has been devoted to elucidating the individual difference variable(s) responsible for this varied response to treatment. Espie and Lindsay (1985) have suggested that the best candidates for paradoxical intention may be "patients who can readily identify with experiencing 'effort to sleep' and who experience considerable anxiety regarding the negative consequences of sleep loss" (p. 709). As we discuss below, we concur with this opinion and suggest that paradoxical approaches are indicated only in cases where cognitions centering on the potential consequences of symptom occurrence (e.g., the effects of not falling asleep or of experiencing anxiety) play a role in maintaining the targeted behavior.

Finally, the method used to administer paradoxical instructions may influence their efficacy (Ascher & Turner, 1980). It appears that a veridical treatment rationale may yield stronger treatment effects than the more commonly applied "assessment" rationale. In addition, the similarity between counterdemand instructions and paradoxical directives may serve to confound further comparisons between paradoxical intention and alternative treatment procedures (Ascher et al., 1985; Kendall & Norton-Ford, 1982). Thus, further research on the effects of instructional manipulations is warranted.

Anxiety Disorders

Although Frankl (1984) originally developed paradoxical intention as a treatment for anxiety disorders, behavioral research on paradox in the treatment of these disorders has been somewhat less systematic than has research on sleep-onset insomnia. Nevertheless, several studies suggest that paradoxical intention may be an effective technique in the treatment of a number of disorders in which maladaptive behaviors are maintained by anxiety.

Ascher (1981) conducted the first controlled study of paradoxical intention in the treatment of agoraphobia. Using a crossover design, he randomly assigned 10 travel-restricted agoraphobic clients to one of two treatment conditions: six sessions of graded *in vivo* exposure followed by six sessions of paradoxical intention, or six sessions of paradoxical intention followed by six sessions of *in vivo* exposure.

Prior to treatment, a behavioral approach test was developed in which each client selected two maximally difficult travel goals and these goals were then divided into 10 relatively equally spaced intervals. Completion of each interval was assigned one point, and clients could, therefore, achieve as many as 20 points for successfully completing the behavioral approach test. The resulting weekly scores were used to provide an objective behavioral outcome measure.

Graded *in vivo* exposure followed the model of Emmelkamp's (1974) self-observation technique. Thus, the therapist assisted the clients in planning self-exposure assignments, and clients were instructed that each time they attempted a travel assignment they were to proceed as far as they could without experiencing anxiety. As soon as they began to feel anxious, they were to return home immediately. Clients were requested to attempt at least one travel assignment a day for 5 days each week and could undertake as many as two per day if desired. Weekly sessions focused on discussing completed travel assignments and planning subsequent exposure.

Paradoxical intention was conducted in a similar fashion, except that clients were instructed to focus on the most prominent aspect of physiological arousal during travel assignments and to try to increase this experience and thereby court their anticipated disastrous consequences. Thus, clients who experienced tachycardia associated with fears of having a heart attack were instructed to try to increase their heart rate even further and to have as many heart attacks as possible during their exposure assignments.

Pretreatment behavioral travel scores were comparable across the two conditions. Unlike clients who received paradoxical intention instructions at the outset of treatment, clients who were exposed only to the graded *in vivo* exposure assignments showed no significant improvement over baseline assessment in achieving their travel goals during the first 6 weeks of treatment. Clients in this group did improve, however, when paradoxical intention was added to their treatment program.

Mavissakalian, Michelson, Greenwald, Kornblith, and Greenwald (1983) have also demonstrated the efficacy of paradoxical intention in the treatment of travel-restricted agoraphobia. These investigators randomly assigned 26 medication-free clients to group treatments using either a paradoxical-intention procedure similar to Ascher (1981) or a self-statement training approach derived from Meichenbaum (1977). Although analysis of data obtained with multiple outcome measures (e.g., frequency and intensity of panic attacks, self-reported anxiety and depression, global severity ratings, and behavioral approach test scores) suggested that paradoxical intention was more effective then self-statement training at the end of treatment, continued improvements among clients in the self-statement condition resulted in a lack of significant differences between the treatments at 6-month follow-up.

In a subsequent investigation, Michelson and his colleagues (Michelson, 1986; Michelson, Mavissakalian, & Marchione, 1986; Michelson, Mavissakalian, Marchione, Dancu, & Greenwald, 1986) randomly assigned 39 agoraphobics to one of three treatments: therapist-assisted graduated exposure, a comprehensive relaxation program that included training in diaphragmatic breathing, or paradoxical intention. Clients in all three treatments were instructed in self-exposure procedures and were encouraged to engage in regular self-exposure between treatment sessions. Weekly sessions were conducted in small groups of four to five clients.

Although clients receiving paradoxical intention demonstrated significant posttreatment improvements and maintenance of gains at 3-month follow-up on a wide variety of self-report, therapist-rated, behavioral, and physiological indices, treatment results in this group were not achieved as rapidly as in the other conditions and were not as great on some measures as those obtained with graduated exposure or training in diaphragmatic breathing and relaxation techniques. In particular, it appeared that clients exposed to paradoxical intention, in contrast to those in the other treatment conditions, required more time to demonstrate improvements on physiological indices (i.e., heart-rate variables) and were more likely to be classified as low responders at follow-up. This latter finding suggested greater variability among clients in their response to paradoxical intention than to exposure or training in diaphragmatic breathing and relaxation techniques.

In their most recent paper, Michelson, Mavissakalian, and Marchione (1986) offer a final appraisal of the completed investigation. They indicate an inability to observe consistent differences among the three treatment groups at any point during the course of the study from pretreatment to follow-up. As was the case with the insomnia research, these data support the conclusion that in a subgroup of clients paradoxical intention can be as effective as, or more effective than, conventional behavioral techniques in the amelioration of a variety of cognitive-behavioral aspects of agoraphobia. Of more general interest, however, was their conclusion that each procedure in isolation was capable of only incomplete treatment of the discomforts of agoraphobia; satisfactory behavior therapy, they suggested, involves a multitechnique program.

Data from a study by Ascher, Schotte, and Grayson (1986) support this position by demonstrating that paradoxical intention, when supplemented with adjunctive treatment components designed to augment the client's ability to employ the procedure, produces results superior to those observed in clients treated with paradoxical intention alone. In this latter study, 15 travel-restricted agoraphobics were randomly assigned to one of three treatments: paradoxical intention in the manner described by Ascher (1981), an enhanced paradoxical-intention treatment that incorporated ancillary techniques (e.g., imaginal and self-directed *in vivo* exposure, and cognitive therapy to reduce negative self-statements) intended to maximize clients' ability to use paradoxical intention, or the enhancement procedures alone. Clients in all three conditions completed weekly behavioral approach tests similar to those used by Ascher (1981). Analysis of approach test scores indicated that the clients receiving the enhancement procedures alone did not improve with treatment. Although both paradoxical-intention methods resulted in significant improvements in comparison to the enhancement procedure, those who received the enhanced paradoxical-intention treatment package improved more rapidly than did those who received standard paradoxical intention.

Michelson (1986), in a reanalysis of the data from his outcome project, described an interaction between client and treatment variables: clients whose treatment was consonant with their symptom profile had better outcomes than did those whose treatment was dissonant. Thus, clients with a preponderance of cognitive symptoms (i.e., high fears of disastrous consequences with lower behavioral impairment and less physiological arousal) fared best with paradoxical intention, whereas those whose predominant symptoms were behavioral (i.e., high behavioral impairment with lower physiological arousal and fewer fears of disastrous consequences) did best with graduated exposure, and clients whose symptoms were predominantly physiological (i.e., high physiological arousal with less behavioral impairment and fewer fears of disastrous consequences) benefited most from progressive relaxation and diaphragmatic breathing.

These latter analyses suggest that paradoxical intention is most useful for clients whose complaints include marked cognitive components (e.g., fears of the potential disastrous consequences of anxiety). We suggest that these findings parallel those of Espie and Lindsay (1985) and provide further support for the need to match clients to treatments on the basis of their unique clinical profiles, including the way in which they use their cognitive systems to interpret reality.

Ascher and Schotte (1988) have conducted pilot research to test this hypothesis with individuals complaining of public-speaking phobia. In this study, interviews were conducted with a series of professionals who reported clinically significant anxiety and avoidance behavior associated with employment-related public speaking. Based on these clinical interviews, clients were classified as either reporting or not reporting cognitions describing hypothesized disastrous consequences associated with experiencing anxiety in public-speaking situations.

Fulfilling the requirements of a 2 × 2 design, clients in each group were then assigned to one of two treatments, each composed of a comprehensive behavioral program for the amelioration of public-speaking anxiety (i.e., a treatment package including cognitive therapy, systematic desensitization, and skills training) but that either did or did not include paradoxical intention instructions. Thus, in the 2 × 2 factorial design, one-half of the clients in each classification were matched to treatment (e.g., clients concerned about possible catastrophes associated with anxiety experienced during public speaking who received paradoxical intention), and one-half of the clients were mismatched to treatment (e.g., clients without such cognitions who received paradoxical intention).

In accord with the hypotheses, no main effects were observed for treatment approach (i.e., clients improved regardless of treatment) or for classification (i.e., clients improved regardless of the presence or absence of hypothesized disastrous consequences), but a significant interaction effect was obtained: that is, clients who were matched to treatments improved more rapidly and completely than did those who were not.

The studies reviewed here support the efficacy of paradoxical intention as a treatment for both agoraphobia and social phobia. Case reports (e.g., Gerz, 1962, 1966; Lamontagne, 1978) suggest that paradoxical intention may also be effective in the treatment of a wider variety of disorders (e.g., psychogenic urinary retention, obsessive-compulsive disorder) in which anxiety and avoidance behavior serve to maintain maladaptive behavior.

This conclusion is further confirmed by three meta-analyses (Hampton, 1987; Hill, 1987; Shoham-Salomon & Rosenthal, 1987) that have included data from the studies described above as well as additional investigations whose behavioral targets fell outside the purview of the present chapter. Generally, these analyses suggest that paradoxical procedures are at least as effective, and are sometimes more effective, than are conventional behavioral procedures. The strength of the support that these meta-analyses can provide, however, is mitigated by certain procedural problems that each incorporates as well as by the small number of studies that met their criteria for review.

As with insomnia, however, the research on paradoxical intention in the treatment of anxiety disorders suggests that not all clients benefit equally. It appears that paradoxical intention is most appropriate for those clients who report cognitions centered on the potential negative consequences of symptom occurrence. Paradoxical intention appears to be less effective, and perhaps even irrelevant, in cases where such cognitive components are absent.

Issues in Research on Paradoxical Intention

The literature that we have reviewed on the efficacy of paradoxical intention suggests that investigators in this area may benefit from consideration of several pertinent issues. Indeed, failure to attend to these caveats may serve to attenuate estimates of the efficacy of paradoxical intention.

The first and perhaps most important of these considerations arises from the observation that certain client characteristics may predict treatment response to paradoxical intention. Specifically, we have asserted that paradoxical intention is most appropriate for those clients who report cognitions centered around the potential negative consequences of sympathetic arousal. Paradoxical intention appears to be less effective, and perhaps even irrelevant, for those clients who do not report such concerns. Thus, researchers should incorporate an assessment of the cognitive characteristics of clients in their samples into the design of studies on the effectiveness of paradoxical intention.

In addition, although counterdemand instructions and assessment rationales may help to mitigate against artifactual sources of client improvement (e.g., expectancy effects), these manipulations may, by reducing performance anxiety (e.g., the pressure to fall asleep that is commonly observed among those with insomnia), mimic the effects of paradoxical intention in some cases. We suggest that investigations of paradoxical intention rely instead on other control procedures for expectancy effects and demand characteristics, such as the use of credible placebos.

Finally, it may be more difficult to specify the components of paradoxical intention than those of other behavioral procedures, such as graded exposure or covert positive reinforcement. For example, the frequent use of humor in the presentation of paradoxical directives contributes to the difficulties inherent in delineating the procedure of paradoxical intention. In fact, it could be argued that studies purporting to test the efficacy of paradoxical intention were actually using symptom prescription (Ascher, 1989). We suggest that studies of paradoxical intention, therefore, may require more careful training, monitoring, and, perhaps, more experienced clinicians than would be the case with some alternative behavioral procedures.

Summary

The use of paradoxical intention by behavior therapists is but one example of a growing trend toward acceptance of therapy techniques developed by nonbehavioral clinicians. In general, it appears that behavior therapists are gradually shifting toward a broader-based clinical empiricism that is grounded less frequently in orthodox behavioral theory. We suggest that this trend is positive so long as behavioral clinicians cling firmly to their commitment to demonstrate the efficacy of the techniques they adopt in clinical practice (Ascher, 1989).

Paradoxical intention is a promising approach to the treatment of a surprising variety of disorders. Client responses to paradoxical intention, however, are mixed, and we suggest that the clients who respond best to paradoxical intention are those who report cognitions centered on the potential negative consequences of the symptoms for which they seek treatment. Such cognitions may serve to exacerbate and maintain the symptoms with which they are associated. Paradoxical intention can be an effective means for circumventing anticipatory anxiety and for disconfirming erroneous beliefs about the consequences of physiological sensations, thereby disrupting the recursive system that serves to maintain many patient complaints.

Ascher and Schotte (1988) have argued that clients with a number of disorders (e.g., public-speaking anxiety, panic attacks, sleep-onset insomnia) may share this recursive element in which discomforting physiological sensations (e.g., tachycardia) or other subjective occurrences (e.g., difficulty falling asleep) give rise to cognitions that result in further discomfort, thereby engendering a vicious circle. The presence of this recursive component delineates the individuals and disorders with which paradoxical intention is likely to be effective.

We hope that clinicians and researchers alike will extend the available data on paradoxical intention and help to further elucidate both the situations in which paradoxical intention is effective and the means by which these effects are obtained.

References

Ascher, L. M. (1975). *Paradoxical intention as a component in the behavioral treatment of sleep onset insomnia: A case study.* Paper presented at the meeting of the Association for Advancement of Behavior Therapy, San Francisco.

Ascher, L. M. (1981). Employing paradoxical intention in the treatment of agoraphobia. *Behaviour Research and Therapy, 19,* 533–542.

Ascher, L. M. (1989). Paradoxical intention: Its clarification and emergence as a conventional behavioral procedure. *the Behavior Therapist, 12,* 23–28.

Ascher, L. M., & Bowers, M. R., & Schotte, D. E. (1985). A review of data from controlled case studies and experiments evaluating the clinical efficacy of paradoxical intention. In G. R. Weeks (Ed.), *Promoting change through paradoxical therapy.* Homewood, IL: Dow Jones-Irwin.

Ascher, L. M., & Efran, J. S. (1978). Use of paradoxical intention in a behavioral program for sleep onset insomnia. *Journal of Consulting and Clinical Psychology, 46,* 547–550.

Ascher, L. M., Schotte, D. E. (1988). *Paradoxical intention and recursive anxiety: A preliminary examination of the importance of matching clients to treatments.* Unpublished manuscript.

Ascher, L. M., & Schotte, D. E., & Grayson, J. B. (1986). Enhancing effectiveness of paradoxical intention in treating travel restriction in agoraphobia. *Behavior Therapy, 17,* 124–130.

Ascher, L. M., & Turner, R. M. (1979). Paradoxical intention and insomnia: An experimental investigation. *Behaviour Research and Therapy, 17,* 408–411.

Ascher, L. M., & Turner, R. M. (1980). A comparison of two methods for the administration of paradoxical intention. *Behaviour Research and Therapy, 18,* 121–126.

Dowd, E. T., & Swoboda, J. S. (1984). Paradoxical interventions in behavior therapy. *Journal of Behavior Therapy and Experimental Psychiatry, 15,* 229–234.

Emmelkamp, P. M. G. (1974). Self observation versus flooding in the treatment of agoraphobia. *Behaviour Research and Therapy, 12,* 229–237.

Espie, C. A., & Lindsay, W. R. (1985). Paradoxical intention in the treatment of chronic insomnia: Six case studies illustrating variability in therapeutic response. *Behaviour Research and Therapy, 23,* 703–709.

Frankl, V. E. (1984). Paradoxical intention. In G. R. Weeks (Ed.), *Promoting change through paradoxical therapy.* Homewood, IL: Dow Jones-Irwin.

Gerz, H. (1962). The treatment of the phobic and obsessive-compulsive patient using paradoxical intention. *Journal of Neuropsychiatry, 3,* 375–387.

Gerz, H. (1966). Experience with the logotherapeutic technique of paradoxical intention in the treatment of phobic and obsessive-compulsive patients. *American Journal of Psychiatry, 123,* 548–553.

Hampton, B. (1987, August). *Paradoxical approaches to psychotherapy: Do they work?* Paper presented at the American Psychological Association convention, New York.

Hill, K. A. (1987). Meta-analysis of paradoxical interventions. *Psychotherapy, 24,* 266–270.

Jacob, R. G., & Moore, D. J. (1984). Paradoxical interventions in behavioral medicine. *Journal of Behavior Therapy and Experimental Psychiatry, 15,* 205–213.

Kendall, P. C., & Norton-Ford, J. D. (1982). Therapy outcome research methods. In P. C. Kendall & J. N. Butcher (Eds.), *Handbook of research methods in clinical psychology.* New York: Wiley.

Lacks, P., Bertelson, A. D., Gans, L., & Kunkel, J. (1983). The effectiveness of three behavioral treatments for different degrees of sleep onset insomnia. *Behavior Therapy, 14,* 593–605.

Ladouceur, R., & Gros-Louis, Y. (1986). Paradoxical intention vs stimulus control in the treatment of severe insomnia. *Journal of Behavior Therapy and Experimental Psychiatry, 17,* 267–269.

Lamontagne, Y. (1978). Treatment of erythrophobia by paradoxical intention: Single case study. *Journal of Nervous and Mental Disease, 166,* 304–306.

Mavissakalian, M., Michelson, L., Greenwald, D., Kornblith, S., & Greenwald, M. (1983). Cognitive-behavioral treatment of agoraphobia: Paradoxical intention versus self-statement training. *Behaviour Research and Therapy, 21,* 75–86.

Meichenbaum, D. H. (1977). *Cognitive-behavior modification.* New York: Plenum.

Michelson, L. (1986). Treatment consonance and response profiles in agoraphobia: The role of individual differences in cognitive, behavioral, physiological treatments. *Behaviour Research and Therapy, 24,* 263–275.

Michelson, L., & Ascher, L. M. (1984). Paradoxical intention in the treatment of agoraphobia and other anxiety disorders. *Journal of Behavior Therapy and Experimental Psychiatry, 15,* 215–220.

Michelson, L., Mavissakalian, M., & Marchione, K. (1986). Cognitive, behavioral, and psychophysiological treatments of agoraphobia: A comparative outcome investigation. *Behaviour Research and Therapy, 24,* 263–274.

Michelson, L., Mavissakalian, M., Marchione, K., Dancu, C., & Greenwald, M. (1986). The role of self-directed *in vivo* exposure in cognitive, behavioral, and psychophysiological treatments of agoraphobia. *Behavior Therapy, 17,* 91–108.

Ott, B. D., Levine, B. A., & Ascher, L. M. (1983). Manipulating the explicit demand of paradoxical intention instructions. *Behavioural Psychotherapy, 11,* 25–35.

Relinger, H., & Bornstein, P. H. (1979). Treatment of sleep onset insomnia by paradoxical instruction. *Behavior Modification, 3,* 203–222.

Relinger, H., Bornstein, P. H., & Mungas, D. M. (1978). Treatment of insomnia by paradoxical intention: A time-series analysis. *Behavior Therapy, 9,* 955–959.

Shoham-Salomon, V., & Rosenthal, R. (1987). Paradoxical interventions: A meta analysis. *Journal of Consulting and Clinical Psychology, 55,* 22–28.

Turner, R. M., & Ascher, L. M. (1979). Controlled comparison of progressive relaxation, stimulus control, and paradoxical intention therapies for insomnia. *Journal of Consulting and Clinical Psychology, 47,* 500–508.

Wilson, G. L., & Bornstein, P. H. (1984). Paradoxical procedures and single-case methodology: Review and recommendations. *Journal of Behavior Therapy and Experimental Psychiatry, 15,* 195–203.

Chapter 3

Paradoxical Intention: The Case of the Case Study

Robert A. DiTomasso
Ruth L. Greenberg

Our aim in this chapter is to review case studies describing the use of paradoxical psychotherapeutic techniques for diverse clinical problems. In doing so, we have lent careful attention to the merits of the case study as a methodology in clinical psychology. We are aware of the limitations of the case method, and in fact our review highlights some of its shortcomings. Still, we have come to share a premise that underlies our considerations in these pages. Our premise is that clinical researchers who assume that no useful information can be extracted from a case study can be likened to practitioners who renounce the results of a well-controlled outcome study. There are philistines in both camps, and we do not wish to be among them.

Case study refers to the intensive study of an individual. It would be an understatement to point out that the case-study method has played a major role in the development of clinical psychology. As Kazdin (1980) observed, the history of a variety of therapeutic techniques is rooted in case information that adumbrated their potential efficacy.

Kazdin (1980) noted that case studies have a number of functions. They are a source of ideas or hypotheses about possible psychotherapeutic techniques and their application to particular disorders. Second, they may be the only available resource for the study of unusual or rare phenomena. Third, a case study may illustrate the "exception to the rule" and thereby make known the one instance that calls into question a universally accepted idea. Finally, case studies may serve a persuasive or motivational purpose by providing preliminary information about the potential value of a technique.

Trouble arises, of course, when the case study is used to draw firm conclusions about cause-and-effect relationships: in general, there is little reason to invest the method with that sort of power or responsibility. Still, there are instances in which a case study could lead to information that is somewhat comparable to experimentally derived data. Kazdin (1981) has identified some major dimensions that influence the extent to which valid inferences may be drawn from a case study. These dimensions include the type of data reported, the number of measurement occasions, the availability of past and future performance projections, immediacy and magnitude of the observed effect, and number and heterogeneity of subjects.

The type of data collected in a case study is an important factor determining whether one can legitimately conclude that change has occurred as a result of an intervention. Case studies vary with regard to the subjectivity of the information used to "demonstrate" an effect. The "data" may range from impressionistic, anecdotal accounts to standardized objective measures. When change is assessed with a device of demonstrated reliability and validity, the outcome is simply more convincing.

The number and timing of measurement occasions are also essential factors. In the typical pre–post measurements, there are a number of potential threats to internal validity (Campbell & Stanley, 1963). Events occurring between pretest and posttest can legitimately compete with the treatment alone as the agent responsible for observed change. Using a number of measurement occasions provides a basis for projecting performance levels and minimizes the likelihood that extraneous factors were responsible for change. Similarly, the availability of historic and prognostic information that supports the stability and resistance of the problem increases the likelihood of inferring correctly that treatment is responsible for the observed change.

The immediacy and magnitude of an observed effect are also worthy of note. The more immediate the effect, the larger the observed change, the greater one's confidence that treatment caused change. Finally, greater number and heterogeneity of subjects provide a stronger case that the treatment is potentially efficacious, since the effect is replicated with individuals of varying demographic characteristics.

In this chapter, we have kept Kazdin's (1981) criteria in mind in presenting our sampling of the case-study literature on paradoxical intervention. We have tried to convey the character of each paradoxical intervention in order to dramatize the rich diversity of clinical lore in this area. But we have also analyzed each case according to a variety of relevant demographic and methodological dimensions and attempted to draw conclusions about this body of literature. The ultimate question we wish to address is "To what extent can valid inferences be drawn about the efficacy of paradoxical intention from this literature?" In Table 1, we

TABLE 1
Characteristics of Case Studies of Paradoxical Intention

Source	Problem	Age	Sex	Duration of condition	Additional treatments	Orientation	Type of data	Frequency of measurement	Type of effect	Outcome	Follow-up
					Anxiety disorders						
Salter (1949)	Social phobia (erythrophobia)	45	M	?	Express feelings as much as possible; fight for own beliefs	Behav	SR	PP	D	Felt better than ever; referred other cases to therapist	Y, ?
Lamontagne (1978)	Erythrophobia	25	M	12 yr	None	?	SM BO	MM	I	Reduction from 28 episodes at baseline to 3 per mo during treatment; reduction in duration	Y, 6 mo
Boeringa (1983)	Erythrophobia	27	M	L	Discussion of relationship problems	Trad	RT	MM	D	No incidents by wk 5	N
Goldstein (1978)	Agoraphobia (fear of leaving home)	32	F	9 yr	Discussions of current life situation; relaxation training; assertiveness training	Behav	SR	PP	D	Reduced anxiety and avoidance; free travel maintained but some depression, anxiety, insomnia	Y, 7 mo
Ascher (1981)	Agoraphobia (driving phobia)	?	M	?	Exposure	Behav	SR	PP	D	Rapid progress	N
Sargent (1983)	Snake phobia	?	F	L	Progressive desensitization; *in vivo* desensitization; training in appropriate expression of anger	Behav	SR	PP	D	Could come within 3 ft. of live snake; cessation of anxiety attacks	Y, 2 yr

Domangue (1985), Case 2	Insect phobia	38	F	?	Discussion of fears regarding pregnancy, life situation; systematic desensitization; hypnotic suggestion	Eclec	SR	PP	?	Reduced anxiety	Y, 2 yr
Gerz (1966), Case 1	Multiple phobias	29	F	10 yr	Logotherapeutic dereflection and deconditioning; Valium 15 mg daily	Exis	SR	PP	I	Overcame phobias	Y, 2 yr
Gerz (1966), Case 2	Multiple obsessions, compulsive checking, fear of being sued	56	M	17 yr	Logotherapeutic dereflection and deconditioning	Exis	SR	PP	D	Only occasional worries	N
Lamb (1980)	Test-taking phobia	19	F	L	None	?	SR BO	MM	I	Completed all exams; received 3 B's	N
Dalton (1983)	Compulsive handwashing and checking; daydreaming, academic underachievement	9	M	?	Reinstate normal family hierarchy, chart behavior, deemphasize dysfunctional behavior	Fam	SR BO	MM	D	Compulsive behavior reduced, schoolwork and family structure improved; child taking increased responsibility	Y, 1 yr
					Compulsive gambling						
Victor & Krug (1967)	Compulsive gambling	36	M	22 yr, exacerbated past several years	None	Psych	SR	PP	D	Stopped gambling, but felt restless; quarrels with wife increased	N

(*continued*)

TABLE 1 (Continued)

Source	Problem	Age	Sex	Duration of condition	Additional treatments	Orientation	Type of data	Frequency of measurement	Type of effect	Outcome	Follow-up
					Eating disorders						
Hsu & Lieberman (1982)	Chronic anorexia nervosa	24 26 34 26 27 22 22 21	M F F F F F M F	6 yr 5 yr 9 yr 5 yr 9 yr 7 yr 8 yr 6 yr	Prior inpatient feeding, intensive individual psychotherapy, family therapy	?	SR RT Phys	PP	D	One-half of P's at normal weight (within 15% of average); only 1 P at very low weight (below 75% of average)	Y, 2–4 yr
					Substance abuse						
Morelli (1978)	Obesity and polydrug and alcohol abuse	18	F	2 yr	Behavior modification; verbal positive reinforcement when patient showed change	Behav	SR	PP	D	Lost 14 lb. over 4 mo and regained weight plus 2.5 lb.; reenrolled in college and obtained B+ average	Y, 1.5 mo and 3 mo
					Psychosexual disorders						
Vandereycken (1982)	Secondary impotence; persistent belief that cause is physical problem	?	M	L	Sensate focus; combined tranquilizer with antidepressant (low dose)	Sex	SR	PP	I	For first time in several mo P attained an erection	N

	Preorgasmic woman; passivity in sexual encounter	?	F	L	Once-a-wk sensate focus	Sex	SR	PP	I	Therapy was unblocked, and wife became more active	N
de Shazer (1974)	Wife's lack of sexual enjoyment	??	MF	3 yr	Sharing hunches with them to facilitate progress by changing the destructive pattern	Fam	SR	PP	D	By 4th wk wife enjoyed sex a little once; by 5th session she enjoyed sexual involvement over a weekend; for first time in 3 yr they had intercourse	
Relationship and family problems											
Mandel & Cooper (1980)	Obsessional ruminations about partner	19	F	T	Hypnotic suggestion not to think of partner so much	Gest	SR	PP	D	No disturbing thoughts or fantasies about partner; no contact with him or time spent with him	Y, 3 and 6 mo
Gilewski, Kuppinger, & Zarit (1985)	Marital dysfunction (tension in relationship)	65 63	M F	L	Prior marital/sex therapy; husband prior individual therapy; wife, psychodynamic therapy (33 hr)	Mar	SR	PP	D	Improved relationship	N

(*continued*)

TABLE 1 (Continued)

Source	Problem	Age	Sex	Duration of condition	Additional treatments	Orientation	Type of data	Frequency of measurement	Type of effect	Outcome	Follow-up
Relationship and family problems											
Crane & Taylor (1983)	Headaches	17	M	L	Join with mother to provide alternative source of support; encourage mother to meet female friends and also to date more often; have identified patient conduct baseball coaching sessions with brother	Fam	A	MM	I	Identified P found a job and discontinued therapy; rapid and dramatic reductions in prescription filling for identified P during treatment; no change in prescription filling for other members of family except for younger son whose rate increased	Y, 3 mo
Hyer (1983)	Chronic pain; dysfunctional family	65	M	20 yr	N	Fam	BO	PP	D	Family changed behavior; P discharged and doing well	Y, 6 mo
Sluzki (1985)	Severe hypertension; multiple somatic complaints	56	F	L	N	?	A	PP	D	Chart review 18 mo later revealed that 2 wk post-interview blood pressure returned to normal; no substantial changes in dose or type of medication	Y, 18 mo

Coyne & Biglan (1984)	Adolescent rebelliousness; argumentativeness; out of control; runaway behavior	15	F	?	N	Fam	SR	PP	D	By session 3, daughter frustrated by inability to argue with parents; by sessions 4 and 5 problem behavior decreased and daughter apologetic; parents took vacation alone; daughter's grades improved from F's and D's to B's and C's	Y, 3 mo
Gaines (1978)	Mother's obsessions, fears, and overinvolvement with son who was mildly oppositional with tantrums and considered normal except by mother	?	F	L	Father instructed to take reponsibility to direct child to complete chores as way of controlling tantrums which only occurred to mother's demands of child	Fam	SR	PP	D	Resolution of obsession about son; realized silliness of fears; ready to approach feeling that life was meaningless since children did not need her anymore; began to explore other areas of her life; at follow-up, job searching and active in church and social activities with husband	Y, several mo

(*continued*)

TABLE 1 (Continued)

Source	Problem	Age	Sex	Duration of condition	Additional treatments	Orientation	Type of data	Frequency of measurement	Type of effect	Outcome	Follow-up
Relationship and family problems											
Weeks & Wright (1978)	Disruptive, combative, overactive child at home and school; marital dysfunction	6	M	T	N	Fam	SR	PP	D	Child's behavior improved dramatically at school; parents were able to admit that their marriage was a major problem and were willing to work on it	N
Bergman (1983)	School refusal; also grandfather very critical of patient's mother	14	F	3 mo	Grandfather was asked to take child to school each day	?	SR	PP	I	2 wk later, prescription kept grandfather from criticizing; at 1-yr follow-up, child was going to school, mother pursuing career, and grandfather politically active	Y, 1 yr
	Fused family with mutual criticism of parents and children	30	F	L	N	Fam	SR	PP	I	No criticism for 2 wk; allowed parents to address their conflicts; other family members doing well	Y, 1 yr

Breit, Gi Im, & Wilner (1983)	Depressed wife; tried to talk herself out of it, and husband did same	?	F	L	Prior individual therapy and behaviorally oriented parent counseling	Fam	SR	PP	D	By wk 3, P reported that she was sick and tired of being miserable	N
	Wife abused by husband in extramarital affair; trying to get him back by pursuing, clinging, and trying to please him	in 50s	F	L	N	Fam	SR	PP	D	Spending more time together	Y, 18 mo
	School-phobic girl who remained at home for months; severely distressed	12	F	T	N	Fam	SR	PP	I	Living with grandmother and returned to school in another neighborhood with no recurrence of school phobia	N
Sleep disorders											
Riverose-de-Carbone (1984)	Sleep-onset insomnia	?	M	1.5 mo	15 sessions of therapy	?	FMSR	MM	I	15 min after going to bed child was asleep; tried to remain awake three more nights without success	Y, 2 mo

(*continued*)

TABLE 1 (Continued)

Source	Problem	Age	Sex	Duration of condition	Additional treatments	Orientation	Type of data	Frequency of measurement	Type of effect	Outcome	Follow-up
					Sleep disorders						
Ascher & Efran (1978)	Sleep-onset insomnia	32 27 41 23 25	M M F F M	5 yr 12 yr 21 yr 3 yr 4 yr	Relaxation therapy, stimulus control, systematic desensitization, and covert conditioning	Behav	RT	MM	D	After standard behavioral program, change was not sufficient; average min to sleep onset reduced from 49.8 to average range of 6–14.5 min with paradoxical intention	Y, 1 yr
Relinger, Bornstein, & Mungas (1978)	Chronic insomnia	31	F	20 yr	N	Behav	RT SM	MM	I	Significant improvement in sleep-onset latency, number of times difficulty experienced falling asleep, degree of restlessness, personal functioning	Y, 1, 3, 12 mo
Gall (1983)	Sleep-onset insomnia	44	F	L	1–2 Faustan pills per night; subsequently instructed to take meds every other day; autogenic training	Logo	SR	PP	D	P well and sleeping normally without sleep medication	Y, 3 yr

Psychogenic genitourinary problems											
Ascher (1979)	Psychogenic urinary retention	19 43 38 47 41	M F M F M	5 yr 21 yr 23 yr 25 yr 10 yr	8 sessions including covert positive reinforcement, thought stopping, and other procedures to alter the cognitive component	Behav	SR	MM	D	Relatively rapid reduction of discomfort related to urination following the use of paradoxical intention; within 6 wk all cases reported little or no anxiety in public restrooms	Y, 6 mo
Mozdzierz (1985)	Psychogenic urinary retention	43	F	40 yr	N	?	SR	PP	D	After 20 sessions 60% success in urinating in unfamiliar restrooms; no longer preoccupied with success ("If it happens, it happens, if it doesn't, it doesn't")	Y, 1 yr
Psychotic disorders											
Davis (1965)	Paranoid schizophrenic; legally insane	30 50 30	F F F	L L L	Thorazine or Librium daily; prior shock treatment	?	SR	PP	D	P 1 discharged after 7 mo on convalescent status in her own custody; P 2 released after 9 mo on convalescent status to a nursing home job; P 3 released in 10th mo of therapy to nursing home job	N

(continued)

TABLE 1 (Continued)

Source	Problem	Age	Sex	Duration of condition	Additional treatments	Orientation	Type of data	Frequency of measurement	Type of effect	Outcome	Follow-up
					Psychotic disorders						
Bergman (1982)	Schizophrenic resistant to participation in day activity program	28	M	T	Prior use of positive reinforcement, extinction, and time out	?	SR BO	PP	I	Returned immediately to day activities and participated in all aspects of program	N
	Schizophrenic with incessant complaining	25	F	T	N	?	SR BO	PP	D	1 wk later 95% decrease in complaining	N
	Schizophrenic with urination and defecation all over bathroom	48	M	T	N	?	SR BO	PP	I	Within 1 day behavior changed	N
	Schizophrenic who would speak nothing but gibberish in Italian; pacing for hours; incessant whining	30	M	T	N	?	SR BO	PP	D	Within 2 days stopped pacing; within 2 wk stopped his whining and gibberish	N

	Schizophrenic who resisted using a regular bathroom as opposed to a commode	73	F	T	N	?	SR BO	PP	I	Within 20 min behavior changed	N
	Schizophrenic exhibiting helplessness; laid in bed 23 hr a day	39	M	L	N	?	SR BO	PP	D	4 days later P began participating in program; refused to sleep or remain in room for more than 7 hr; began dating; began doing his own cooking and laundry	Y, 2 yr
Rosen (1946), Case 1	Acute catatonic excitement	15	M	L	Inpatient treatment followed course of shock treatments	Psych	SR	PP	D	Paroled from hospital; able to maintain himself	N
Fay (1976)	Paranoid schizophrenic with obsessive ruminations about his mental health	30	M	15 yr	Phenothiazines; prior course of ECT and pharmacotherapy	?	SR	PP	?	P's ruminative tendency decreased significantly	N
	Paranoid schizophrenic with resistance to half-way house and other problems	22	M	13 yr	Previous psychotherapy and full range of psychotropic drugs without success	?	SR	PP	D	Working full time	N
	Paranoid psychosis	61	M	40 yr	N	?	SR	PP	D	In 1 wk P feeling much better; at follow-up in remission	Y, 6 mo

(continued)

TABLE 1 (Continued)

Source	Problem	Age	Sex	Duration of condition	Additional treatments	Orientation	Type of data	Frequency of measurement	Type of effect	Outcome	Follow-up
Malingering, dependency, and uncooperativeness in prison inmates											
Chase, Shea, & Dougherty (1984)	Malingering; complaints of weakness, partial paralysis with no organic lesion	?	M	T	N	?	SR	PP	D	Within 2 days, P was demanding to leave, demonstrated that he was feeling better, and was discharged the next day	Y, 2 yr
	Depression and suicidal ideation as means to avoid being placed with prison population	20	M	T	N	?	SR	PP	I	Insisted on being released	Y, ?
	Dependent and irresponsible behavior	26	M	T	N	?	SR	PP	D	Patient became more dependable and responsible	N
	Manipulation and refusal to cooperate in obtaining necessary surgery	?	M	T	N	?	SR	PP	I	Allowed physician to perform surgery	N

Childhood disorders											
Erikson (1954)	Enuretic couple	Early 20s	M F	L	N	Hyp	SR	PP	D	No wetting of bed	Y, 1 yr
Propp (1985)	Encopresis and enuresis	8	M	5 yr	Praise and encouragement for chart completion	?	SM	PP	D	Average of seven soilings at baseline dropped to none	Y, 6 mo
		8	F	L	Praise and encouragement for chart completion	?	SM	PP	D	Seven during baseline and reduced to none	Y, 6 mo
Hare-Mustin (1975)	Temper tantrums	4	M	T	N	Fam	FMSR	PP	D	Tantrums resolved	Y, 9 mo
Zarske (1982)	Temper trantrums	5	M	T	N	?	FMSR	MM	I	During wk 1, dramatic decrease in frequency and duration (average decrease from 6 to 1.4 per day and 11.1 min to 2.2 min; in phase 2, decrease to 0.57 per day for 40.4 sec on average); follow-up: total absence of tantrums	Y, 1 and 2 mo
Yoder (1983)	Thumb sucking	7	F	L	Father instructed to arrange to take child out to dinner when she quit	Logo	SR	MM	D	Stopped sucking her thumb	N

(continued)

TABLE 1 (Continued)

Source	Problem	Age	Sex	Duration of condition	Additional treatments	Orientation	Type of data	Frequency of measurement	Type of effect	Outcome	Follow-up
Childhood disorders											
Hoffman & Laub (1986)	Elective mutism toward adults except parents, grandparents, and school children	4½	F	2½ yr	Reinforcement; counterconditioning; successive approximations	Fam Behav	SR	PP	D	Began speaking to adults; stopped using pacifier; increased number of adults to whom she spoke; increased circle of friends; more indepenent, age-appropriate behavior	Y, 2 mo
Baideme, Kern, & Taffel-Cohen (1979)	School phobia	9	F	7 wk	Reinforcement of responsible behavior; asked to join an ongoing children's therapy group; mother instructed to tell child, "It's O.K. for you to go to school"	Fam	FMSR	PP	D	Attending school on regular basis; planning to spend night away from home with friend	Y, 2 and 10 mo
Jessee & L'Abate (1980)	Hospitalized following accidental shooting of brother; began having accidents involving himself and others when angry	11	M	T	Individual and group therapy	?	SR	PP	D	Within 3 days, accidents completely disappeared; only two more accidents happened during the remaining mo of hospitalization; began responding to tasks to help him verbalize his anger appropriately	Y, 1 mo

	Repeated stealing resulting in hospitalization	11	M	T	N	?	SR	PP	I	Never stole again	Y, several mo
	Hyperactiveness, inattentiveness at school, defiance in speech and behavior	10	M	L	Several wk	?	SR	PP	I	Behavioral problems discussed on the unit and at home	N
Kolko & Milan (1983)	School discipline problems; academic performance problems, drug/alcohol abuse	15	M	L	Ongoing contingency contracting	Behav	BO SR	MM	D	Class attendance improved during paradoxical intervention and was sustained at follow-up; received 2–3 times as many satisfactory grades during intervention and follow-up relative to baseline	Y, 6 mo
	Stealing, lying, failure to follow instructions; excessive school tardiness or absences; misconduct, poor academic performance	14	M	L	Ongoing contingency contracting	Behav	BO SR	MM	I	Class attendance improved during paradoxical intervention and was sustained at follow-up; received 2–3 times as many satisfactory grades during intervention and folow-up relative to baseline	Y, 6 mo

(continued)

TABLE 1 (Continued)

Source	Problem	Age	Sex	Duration of condition	Additional treatments	Orientation	Type of data	Frequency of measurement	Type of effect	Outcome	Follow-up
						Childhood disorders					
	Truancy; conflicts with mother about hygiene, work habits, social life, sexual practices, and late hours	14	F	L	Ongoing contingency contracting	Behav	SR	MM	I	Class attendance improved during paradoxical intervention and was sustained at follow-up; received 2–3 times as many satisfactory grades during intervention and follow-up relative to baseline	Y, 6 mo
Arnesen, Libby, & Miller (1973)	Aggression	15	M	7 yr	N	?	BO A	MM	D	Released and discharged to half-way house; exhibited no problems requiring institutionalization or incarceration	Y, 16 mo
						School problems					
Williams & Weeks (1984)	Two 7th graders fighting in school; blaming teacher for picking on them	12	M	T	N	Fam	SR	PP	I	Neither boy was referred to the In-School Suspension Program for the next several months	Y, several mo

A 7th grade girl leaving class because she felt upset	12	F	T	Behavior modification program (setting up rules)	Fam	SR	PP	D	Improved grades	Y, first half of school yr
An 8th grade overly dependent girl with problem of need for acceptance	13	F	T	N	Fam	SR	PP	I	Did not go on trip; never mentioned again; made new friends	Y, several mo
A 9th grader in conflict with parents and angry with them	14	F	T	N	Fam	SR	PP	I	Family outbursts ceased	Y, 6 mo
"Fuss fighting" between two 8th graders	13	F	T	N	Fam	SR	PP	D	No more fuss fighting; became friends again	Y, 2 wk
Sadness and depression in overly dramatic 8th grader secondary to boyfriend breakup	13	F	T	N	Fam	SR	PP	D	Depression improved; met new boy, made better grades	Y, 1 yr
8th grader with anger and resentment toward teacher and friend and unable to express it; feeling dumb	13	F	T	N	Fam	SR	PP	D	Defied therapist and took friend to session	N

(*continued*)

TABLE 1 (Continued)

Source	Problem	Age	Sex	Duration of condition	Additional treatments	Orientation	Type of data	Frequency of measurement	Type of effect	Outcome	Follow-up
School problems											
Brown (1986)	Disruptive behavior in class; bugging others, poking at them, making noises	8	M	T	A number of other interventions	Fam	SR	PP	N	Problems continued for rest of yr	Y, remainder of term
	Oppositional child with mood swings; disruptive and aggressive behavior in class	8	M	T	N	Fam	SR	PP	I	Very few instances of aggressive behavior over few wk of treatment; change restricted to presence of teacher who implemented it	Y, 3 mo
	Aggressive behavior in school: hitting, kicking, punching peers	8	M	T	Ritalin	Fam	SR	PP	I	No further reports of aggression	Y, remainder of school yr
Stuttering											
Nystul & Muszynska (1976)	Ability to say only one coherent word a minute; severe body contortion in head and neck region	20	M	15 yr	Rational emotive therapy	Adler	BO	PP	D	Fluency increased from 8 in 10 words stammered to 1 in 10 words	N

					Tic/Tourette's syndrome						
Clark (1966)	Tourette's: frequent, jerky head and arm movements; incessant explosive repetitions of four obscenities	22	M	12 yr	Prior treatment by pediatrician, analytic therapist, eclectic psychiatrist using all available drug therapy	Behav	SR BO	MM	D	Symptom-free	Y, 4 yr
	Barking tic	17	M	L	Previous drug therapy	Behav	SR BO	MM	D	Symptom-free	Y, 4 yr
	Complex muscular spasm and explosive verbalizations of one word	47	F	L	N	Behav	SR BO	MM	D	P terminated after 10 sessions despite showing improvement	N
					Psychophysiological problems						
Gentry (1973)	Unrelieved migraine headaches	26	F	13 yr	Prior to treatment, had been using Stelazine and Darvon	?	SR	PP	D	By fifth session four headaches in 1 wk; by session 11, reported no headaches	Y, 12 mo

(continued)

TABLE 1 (Continued)

Source	Problem	Age	Sex	Duration of condition	Additional treatments	Orientation	Type of data	Frequency of measurement	Type of effect	Outcome	Follow-up
Miscellaneous											
Greenberg (1973)	Perfectionism and resistance as way of covering up sexual and aggressive impulses	31	F	L	N	Psych	SR	PP	D	Able to tell husband of her concerns and talk openly for first time in years	N
	Feeling tense, anxious, and dizzy with continual headaches	40	M	3 yr	1 yr of treatment with psychiatrist	?	SR	PP	D	First time no headache in 3 yr; when upset and anxious, his fantasy became so exaggerated he started laughing, and tension disappeared	N
Fish (1973)	Fused identity in three college freshmen	?	M	T	N	?	SR	PP	I	Spending less time together; did not feel that they were the same person any longer	N

Lopez (1983)	Vocational indecision regarding college major; father overly involved in son's decision making	20	M	L	N	Career	SR	PP	D	Improved frequency of quality of father–son interaction versus 2–3 phone calls per wk from father about career matters	N
Greenberg & Pies (1983)	Hopelessness, depression, and suicidal ideation; borderline personality	22	F	L	Supportive, uncovering work	Psych	SR	PP	I	Self-mutilated, became increasingly suicidal	N
Fay (1976)	Jealousy; accusing husband of having extramarital affair	30	F	?	N	?	SR	PP	?	Opening of channels of authentic communication	N
	Poor academic performance	17	F	L	N	?	SR	PP	D	Passed all of her subjects	N

Note. Explanation of abbreviations: *Sex*: F = female; M = male; ? = not reported. *Duration*: L = longstanding problem; T = transient problem. *Orientation*: Adler = Adlerian; Behav = behavioral; Career = career counseling; Eclec = eclectic; Exis = existential; Fam = family; Gest = gestalt; Hyp = hypnosis; Logo = logotherapy; Mar = marital; Psych = psychodynamic; Sex = sex therapy; ? = not reported; Trad = traditional. *Additional treatment*: N = none. *Type of data*: A = archival; BO = behavioral observation; FMSR = family member self-report; RT = standardized rating; Phys = physiological; SM = self-monitoring; SR = subjective self-report. *Frequency of measurement*: MM = multiple measurements; PP = pretest–posttest. *Type of effect*: D = delayed/gradual; I = immediate; N = none. *Outcome*: P = patient. *Follow-up*: N = no; Y = yes; mo = month(s); wk = week(s); yr = year(s).

have systematically described each study according to a list of characteristics derived from Kazdin's criteria. In fact, as will become apparent, very few of the studies actually meet Kazdin's criteria. We hope that aggregating the studies in this way will help the reader assess the validity of, and appreciate the variability in, this wide-ranging literature.

One cautionary note: although this review includes a rather large number of case studies, it is by no means exhaustive. We have concentrated on full case reports appearing in journals and have tended to exclude brief case descriptions intended chiefly to illustrate a point. These case descriptions typically provide only scanty details.

Anxiety Disorders

Anxiety disorders seem to invite experimentation with paradoxical methods. As Driscoll (1985) noted, some varieties of paradox specifically address conditions such as anxiety disorders in which preoccupation with symptoms, anticipatory worry about symptoms, or fearful avoidance of symptoms are an important focus of treatment. Paradoxical strategies, he notes, attempt to relieve the patient of the pressure to avoid symptoms, which itself seems to create autonomic arousal.

Erythrophobia

Erythrophobia—fear of blushing—is a condition clearly marked by fear and worry about a highly visible symptom and not so surprisingly has been the focus of a number of case studies. Salter (1949) sketched the case of the salesman who feared meeting people because of the blushing and sweating he experienced on these occasions. Presenting for treatment, he heard his symptoms explained as the result of poor treatment by his family of origin and of the habit of keeping his feelings to himself. He was instructed in Dunlap's beta hypothesis, namely, "that the occurrence of a response lessens the probability that on the recurrence of the same stimulus-pattern, the same response will recur" (Salter, 1949, p. 105), and was told that through practice in deliberate blushing, he would be able to bring the involuntary response under control. At the same time, he was exhorted to express his feelings as much as possible and, in fact, to fight for his beliefs. This case of "conditioned reflex therapy" has the best outcome for which a practitioner might hope: the patient claims he feels better than ever and refers other clients to the therapist. However, Salter's enthuiastic account clearly denotes treatment elements other than paradoxical intervention. The client was provided with a plausible explanation for his symptoms, fortified with new scientific knowledge, and directed to change his interpersonal behavior. Was paradox alone at work?

A far better detailed case of erythrophobia was presented by Lamontagne (1978). Here, a young man who had suffered for 12 years from frequent, severe blushing was asked to stop fighting his symptoms, escaping, or avoiding situations where he might blush. He was also instructed to practice blushing for three 10-minute periods a day, both at home and in situations where he would tend to be anxious, and to continue to keep a record of his blushing episodes, as he had done for the month prior to treatment. Further, during his weekly therapy sessions, he was to try to blush "to show the therapist that there was no improvement" (p. 305). Involuntary autonomic nervous system reactions, his therapist informed him, cannot be induced voluntarily—this is the principle that underlies the technique. The client's records revealed a decrease from 20 blushing episodes during the month preceding treatment to three episodes during treatment; he reported a further decrease during the 6-month follow-up. Lamontagne's report is unusual in that in his brief treatment (four half-hour sessions), paradoxical intention involving deliberate practice of symptoms as well as exposure appears to have been the main strategy. The inclusion of baseline data is also rare in this literature. From a design perspective, Lamontagne's study also benefits from continual measurement through self-monitoring, though a therapeutic contribution from self-monitoring cannot be ruled out.

In Boeringa's (1983) case study, another young male erythrophobic was given the paradoxical instruction to practice blushing at home. Further, when he found himself beginning to blush in public, he was to try blushing even harder. He was given Lamontagne's article to read and asked to keep a diary of blushing episodes, with each rated for intensity. By week 5 of an 8-week course of treatment, the client was reporting no blushing incidents.

To account for this client's happy outcome, we must consider the possible impact of other, traditional therapeutic elements with which paradoxical intention was admixed. The therapist attended to current problems, relationship issues, historical material, feelings of inferiority, repression of emotionally charged material; he related these discussions to the blushing problem. Further, as the author himself noted, the client had sought help only for a recent exacerbation of a longstanding tendency to blush easily. We cannot rule out the possibility that this acute flare-up might have resolved on its own.

Agoraphobia

Like erythrophobics, agoraphobics generally restrict their activities because of fear of anxiety symptoms. Goldstein (1978) rendered a sensitive case study of an agoraphobic woman who experienced anxiety on leaving home. Her longstanding problems of phobic anxiety and avoidance were substantially improved following several months of a multifaceted treatment. One element of this treatment involved paradoxical intention: the therapist instructed the client to practice trying to increase the intensity of her symptoms rather than fighting them—"because that contributes to spiraling anxiety and panic" (p. 47). Although there were no structured exposure exercises, therapist and client agreed that the client would place herself in situations where she would become anxious, with the goal of becoming more comfortable in handling anxiety. The treatment also involved discussion of her family background and current marital situation, training in assertiveness, and muscle relaxation.

Ascher's (1981) study shows how paradoxical interventions may be intertwined in a behavioral exposure program for agoraphobia. Treating the client's driving phobia, the therapist's initial intervention was to have the client make no effort to avoid symptoms or the consequences he feared—heart attack, fainting, etc. The client, a salesman, was to drive slowly but avoid his usual practice of stopping to allow anxiety to subside; instead, he was to let anxiety develop and subside while he was driving, so that he might learn that no disaster would occur. When, after several weeks, the client had been "too anxious" to comply with this program, the therapist modified the instructions. The client was then instructed not to drive at all when anxious but to drive until he experienced any anxiety, then park his car and perform "an imaginal anxiety-reducing technique" for 5 minutes. Each week, the duration of the imaginal exercise was increased by 5 minutes.

Although the client complained bitterly about these prescriptions, since it was now taking him an intolerably long time to complete his sales calls, the therapist responded by lengthening the procedure yet again. He suggested that since the car itself might be provoking anxiety, the client must leave the car when anxious and walk a distance, finally carrying out the imaginal procedure for 20 minutes. The client rejected this ordeal as impossible and volunteered to return to the original program, at which point he began to make rapid progress.

In Ascher's case, the initial "paradox" was essentially an instruction to engage in *in vivo* exposure. The more dramatic paradox was introduced only when the client was clearly "stuck." By agreeing that the salesman was "too anxious" to comply with the original program, the therapist gained the patient's cooperation. In this case, the combination of exposure and countertherapeutic instructions appears to have produced an immediate and clinically significant effect.

Snake Phobia

Sargent (1983) also integrated paradoxical intention into a behavioral program, again because the client had become "stuck" in her progress along a desensitization hierarchy. A newly divorced woman complained of snake phobia so intense that, when living with her family on a ranch, she had had difficulty leaving her house. In her current life, she would become terrified by images of snakes in the movies and in books. She could not draw a snake in her art class. When, after training in relaxation and focusing, the client failed to make much progress in an imaginal desensitization hierarchy, the therapist introduced a "paradoxical" technique.

The client was to designate a room in her house a "favorite snake room." There she was to go frequently to practice spending time with her "snake friends." She was also to read an imaginary book about snakes with great enjoyment. After four sessions of this fantasy exercise, the client was able to return to her hierarchy and eventually to *in vivo* work at the zoo. Anxiety attacks ceased, and she was able to come within 3 feet of a live snake.

Sargent's intervention essentially used humor and fantasy to change the client's attitude toward the feared object. Amused by the new notion of snakes as cherished intimates, she was able to flood herself with images of snakes and gradually to gain a sense of mastery over her fear. At the same time, Sargent notes, the client was beginning to meet with success in another problem area that was a focus of treatment—the appropriate expression of anger. It would be difficult to disentagle the effects of Sargent's "paradox" from those of desensitization or assertive communication.

Domangue (1985) reported on the treatment of a 38-year-old insect phobic with hypnotic regression and reframing. The treatment also included a discussion of relevant issues in the patient's life as well as systematic desensitization.

Obsessive-Compulsive Disorder

Gerz (1966) describes a number of successful cases using paradoxical intention in treating phobic and obsessive-compulsive patients. He reports that of 51 patients treated over a 6-year period for phobias, obsessive-compulsive neurosis, or pseudoneurotic schizophrenia, 88.2 % "recovered or made considerable improvement" (p. 548). These patients had been ill for as long as 24 years and had received many forms of therapy. Gerz notes that his group always uses "a combination of PI, logotherapeutic dereflection, and reconditioning therapy, which are embedded in existential psychotherapy. In other words, *we do not merely use the technique of PI, but intensive efforts are made to understand the patient and his symptoms. . . . Paradoxical intention is to supplement dynamic therapy, not to replace it*" (p. 551, italics in original). He also advocates the use of medication, suggesting that drug therapy may have been employed in the case histories he reports. Although Gerz presents an impressive overview of his group's success rate, he cautions us explicitly about attributing therapeutic power to a single technique.

In one of Gerz's case descriptions, a 56-year-old lawyer was treated for multiple obsessions and compulsions that revolved around an intense fear of being sued. The illness was of 17 years' duration and had had ruinous effects on his life and career. He had been hospitalized, given extensive psychotherapy and also electoconvulsive treatment, and had been forced to give up his law practice and find work as a court clerk. When logotherapy began, he was instructed not to "give a damn" anymore about the mistakes he feared might lead to lawsuits, but to *hope* to get sued as soon and as often as possible, and in fact to "try to show his secretary he was the greatest mistake maker in the world" (p. 551). The therapist carried the ploy further by claiming to be waiting to read news of his patient's scandals in the newspapers. According to Gerz's account, the patient eventually adopted a nonchalant attitude toward errors and lawsuits, apparently influenced by the therapist's relaxed, humorous posture. A year after this 4-month treatment, the patient reported he was a "new person," worried only occasionally, and was able to cope with worries when they came. Of course, the case history depicts only the paradoxical elements in an avowedly complex treatment approach.

Dalton (1983) provides a richly detailed case study of family treatment provided for an obsessive-compulsive child. Because Dalton's account describes the progression of the treatment on a nearly session-by-session basis, it alows the reader a good look at an intricate fabric of interventions that once again included, but was not limited to, paradoxical techniques.

Dalton's 9-year-old patient was referred for treatment of compulsive rituals such as frequent handwashing and checking behind doors and generally poor academic behavior involving daydreaming, disorganization, and lack of progress in his studies. The therapist observed that the mother was overinvolved with the boy, whereas the father was underinvolved. Initially, then, the therapist worked to normalize the family hierarchy through straightforward directives. Paradox entered the treatment in session 2, when, having worked with the family to define initial goals for the child, the therapist expressed doubt that the child could manage all the mandated changes; the child protested that indeed he could! She then devised a chart on which the mother was to record the child's behavior ("paradoxical charting" of functional behaviors).

Another paradoxical intervention was used when the mother failed to comply precisely with one of the directives. Here, rather than criticizing her, the therapist "praised her for her ingenuity" (p. 103). Later, when the child relapsed after initial gains, the therapist reframed his behavior, calling the relapse "an experiment to see how many different ways he could be in order to compare them." She instructed the child "to finish up the experiment by washing his hands and checking behind doors even more the next week" (p. 105). In the next session (the 13th), she gave a specific directive for the child to wash hands for 10 minutes each morning "so he would not forget how to do it" (p. 105). According to the mother, the child became "bored" with the assignment and apparently returned to normal behavior. Treatment was terminated after 15 sessions.

Dalton's chronicle exemplifies particularly well how paradoxical intention may be embedded in a complex treatment program. The therapist modeled a healthy interaction with a 9-year-old, reassured the parents about the meaning of the child's symptoms, and legitimized and pursued each family member's individual goals. She identified desired behavior and conveyed confidence in the family's capacity for change. Although treatment appears to have been successful, we have no way to isolate the effectiveness of its paradoxical elements.

Test Anxiety

Paradoxical interventions have also been applied to the treatment of evaluative anxiety. In educational settings, such anxiety not only impairs academic performance but is associated with anticipatory anxiety related to testing situations. In one such instance, Lamb (1980) reported the case of a 19-year-old female student suffering from test anxiety who reported fainting between one and three times per day. Her fear of fainting was so severe that she had asked to take exams alone rather than with her classmates. In this case, the therapist encouraged the student to practice passing out three times a day. The therapist also described her own history of seizures in a humorous, exaggerated fashion. The client eventually passed all of her exams with acceptable grades.

Compulsive Gambling

Victor and Krug's (1967) intriguing treatment of compulsive gambling is a good example of a paradoxical intervention based on the expectation that the paient will defy the therapist's directives. (For further discussion of so-called "defiance-based" interventions, see Tennen, Rohrbaugh, Press, & White, 1981.) Beginning in the third session, the patient was instructed to gamble each day at specified hours, then to write in detail about feelings he had experienced while gambling. By the next interview, the patient was describing a reluctance to gamble: "I cannot stand being controlled, and now you are trying to control me" (p. 811). Because he lost a substantial amount of money during this period of therapeutic gambling, the patient was forced to admit the problem to his family; they loaned him money but put him under strict financial control. The therapist, however, maintained his posture, remarking that the patient should let him know when he had money again to gamble and suggesting he sell personal property to make this possible. When the patient rebelled and refused to gamble any more, the therapist insisted he "could not really be permitted to stop gambling in this fashion" (p. 812).

Victor and Krug's (1967) account is one of the very few to describe undesirable effects of paradoxical intention. Although the patient's 11-year gambling compulsion went into remission, they noted, the patient was unhappy and restless, sought sexual excitement, and argued with his wife. Still, the history lacks important detail. We are not told how long the patient attended weekly sessions, nor do the authors relate what else was discussed.

Eating Disorders

Eating disorders comprise a group of problems that are, relatively speaking, difficult to treat. The question of what to offer those patients who do not benefit from traditional therapy is important. In an uncontrolled, multiple-case study, Hsu and Lieberman (1982) studied the results of a paradoxical intervention in eight chronic anorexics. The patients' problems had endured for 5 or more years with no remission lasting more than 4 months. Each patient had previously been treated with inpatient feeding, individual psychotherapy, and family therapy. The paradoxical intervention involved telling the patients, sometimes in the presence of their families, that they should keep their anorexia, since previous attempts to treat them had failed. The benefits of the illness (based on the individual case) were also explained. At follow-up, half of the patients were at normal weight (within 15% of average). However, social and sexual adjustment did not appear to be improved at follow-up. Because paradoxical interventions are typically not considered to be total treatment programs, it is not surprising that the use of such procedures, when focused on a specific behavioral problem, may leave other aspects of the client's life unaffected.

Substance Abuse

Morelli (1978) applied paradoxical therapy in the treatment of an 18-year-old obese female with a 2-year history of drug and alcohol abuse. Although her presenting complaint was obesity, this young woman drank about a pint of hard liquor daily and ingested a considerable quantity of marijuana, cocaine, amphetamine, depressants, and LSD. Not surprisingly, her academic performance was poor—despite her having been valedictorian of her high school class. In phase 1 of a two-part treatment, a standard behavioral weight-control treatment was conducted. Subsequently, a paradoxical intervention was introduced. In response to the patient's reports of excessive alcohol and drug use, the therapist "expressed surprise that that was all she had." She was instructed that she could have much more; large quantities of different drugs were suggested. When the patient described some of the possible academic consequences of such behavior, the therapist told her that he did not expect her to submit any reports or attend classes and that she could even drop out. The patient was surprised, but the therapist continued to advocate the use of more drugs. Whenever the patient exhibited more desirable academic behavior, the therapist provided verbal positive reinforcement. However, whenever she mentioned substances, he told her she could have more. Whereas the patient initially had failed all of her classes, she reenrolled in school, and at 1.5 and 3 months later, the patient had reduced alcohol intake to about one or two beers on a weekend. All drug usage except occasional marijuana had stopped. She achieved a B+ average.

Psychosexual Disorders

The treatment of sexual dysfunctions has traditionally been an area where paradox has been employed. Vandereycken (1982) employed paradoxical interventions in two cases of sexual dysfunction. In the first case, a man suffering from secondary impotence persisted in believing his problem was physically caused despite the fact that repeated exams had ruled out an organic basis. During sensate focus treatment, he consistently monitored his penis for signs of an erection. The wife, fearful of a recurrence of her husband's "nervous breakdown," advocated an interruption of treatment. To the standard Masters and Johnson treatment was now added a low dose of a combination tranquilizer and antidepressant to prevent the "breakdown." The therapist informed the patient that the drug produced sexual impotence as a major side effect but that he should nevertheless enjoy caressing his wife and giving her an orgasm. Attributing the patient's impotence to the medication apparently helped. The patient returned to report that for the first time in several months he had attained an erection. He was warned that the effect was probably an accident, and the dose of medication was increased (although still low); the therapist then predicted complete impotence. Once again the patient attained an erection. According to the author, this intervention became the turning point in a treatment that subsequently proved successful. Relabeling the symptom as a drug-caused side effect apparently alleviated self-observation. However, once again disentangling the effects of paradox in the midst of other interventions is impossible.

In Vandereycken's (1982) second case, a preorgasmic wife was passive in her marriage and in sexual encounters. Therapy became blocked when, despite instructions to take the active role in sensate focus exercises assigned as homework, she remained passive. The husband was instructed to continue initiating sensate focus except for one randomly selected day. On that day, he was to remain passive and his wife would be active; however, the wife was not to know which day was the "test day." The wife then began to engage actively in sexual encounters. The standard Masters and Johnson therapy continued with success.

de Shazer (1974) described a case in which a paradoxical intervention was added to a family therapy technique (sharing "hunches"). The presenting complaint was the fact that the wife did not enjoy sex and had not allowed her husband to complete intercourse for the past 3 years, although she was able to achieve orgasm manually. The therapist instructed the couple to have sex three times within the following week; he shared a "hunch" that the wife might begin "enjoying sex one of these days." He also told her that if she began to enjoy sex she might be more comfortable if she denied any pleasure until she became acclimated to enjoying it. The effect of the task was simple: if she was not enjoying sex, her husband would not know for sure, so that the couple might be able to relax. Another intervention was based on the wife's remark that she "bought" her husband through her control of sex; ther therapist suggested that she pay her husband $5.00 for each sexual episode! By the fourth week, the wife admitted that she had enjoyed sex a little on one occasion. By the fifth week, she indicated that she had enjoyed sex and for the first time in 3 years had had intercourse.

In the cases reviewed above, paradox was implemented in situations where barriers to therapeutic progress were evident. Under such circumstances, the therapist presented a paradoxical intervention to break a pattern of resistance and eliminate a therapeutic impasse. Perhaps such situations may provide the setting conditions for a paradoxical shift to have an impact.

Relationship and Family Problems

Paradoxical techniques may also be used to deal with resistance in the treatment of relationship and family problems. In fact, family therapy is the modality most closely associated with the development of paradoxical techniques.

Mandel and Cooper (1980) presented a case of a 19-year-old woman who was involved in an affair with a married man almost 30 years her senior. The patient was experiencing considerable frustration; she realized that the relationship could not develop further, yet she felt compelled to maintain the relationship and was obsessed with thoughts of her lover. She received about 13 counseling sessions, which incorporated a combination of hypnosis and paradox. The paradoxical strategy involved instructing the patient to focus her thoughts on this man for specific 5-minute periods throughout the course of the day. Within the context of a posthypnotic suggestion, the patient was told that these 5-minute periods would allow her to "soak up" enough of her lover and thereby reduce her obsessions for the remainder of the day. At the 12th session, she announced that her condition had gotten worse. She was told that her observation was correct and that the hypnosis and suggestions would not really work. She was instructed to stop all exercises because they would not help and was told that the best thing to do was to try to enjoy the thoughts and be thankful for them. At her final session, a week later, she reported that she was better. At 3- and 6-month follow-up, she had no obsessions or worries. She now fantasized about the man very little and had no contact with him.

Gilewski, Kuppinger, and Zarit (1985) describe a case of marital dysfunction in a geriatric couple. Despite a long history of problems and considerable tension, their expressed goal was to spend more time together. The therapist instructed them to spend less time and also expressed doubts that they would succeed. Over the course of several sessions the couple received other paradoxical interventions as well as communication training. Ultimately their relationship improved with the realization that they could be happy and different. However, the previous history of marital, sex, and individual therapy as well as the role of communication training cannot easily be discounted from the outcome in this instance.

Crane and Taylor (1983) provide a case of a family in which each member had a number of physical complaints. The identified patient, age 17, suffered from headaches that had resulted in serious academic difficulties. Local pharmacies provided records of medication obtained for each family member; prescription filling served as a dependent measure.

In the context of family therapy, major therapeutic interventions were made to attempt to normalize family structure. The paradoxical intervention involved prescribing the symptom of overdependency in the identified patient. This patient was told to "notice even the slightest sign of pain or dizziness" and to take appropriate precautions by immediately lying down on his bed until he was totally recovered. The mother was encouraged to provide care by taking his temperature and bringing juice every quarter-hour until he left the bed. The identified patient showed a rapid and marked decrease in prescription filling during treatment, although results were mixed for other family members. On follow-up, the patient showed 2 months of low rates interspersed with a month when rates reached pretreatment levels. The authors note that lack of both stability in baseline measures and replication preclude the inference that treatment alone caused the change. Although the use of an objective measure was creative, it was obtrusive and subject to falsification by the patients.

Hyer (1983) treated the family of a 65-year-old male with low-back pain who lived as an invalid despite the absence of medical data to support his complaints. The identified patient constantly complained of being tired, in pain, and did very few things for himself. His family exhibited a dysfunctional pattern with the wife doing essentially everything in the house and the patient receiving support from his children. This situation made the wife angry, frustrated, and depressed. Eventually, the patient was admitted to a psychiatric inpatient unit and treated with antidepressants and a variety of techniques to reduce his pain and pain behaviors. Within a 2-week period, he was spending only 5% of his time in bed. However, the real question was whether these changes would be maintained when he was discharged home to his family. A number of paradoxical strategies were implemented at this time. For example, the wife was told that things would take a turn for the worse on her husband's discharge and that she should work on getting herself strong because of her likely depression. She was also instructed to communicate frustration and pessimism (symptom prescription). Also, paradoxical letters were mailed to the wife and distributed to the children during hospitalization and follow-up. The patient was discharged and 6 months later was doing well.

Sluzki (1985) employed paradoxical treatment with a severe hypertensive woman with multiple physical complaints who was a chronic worrier. Her blood pressure had been controlled with medication, but during some recent stress, it became refractory. The patient was a worrier in a family where mother worried and children placated her worry, which in turn generated more worrying on her part. The therapist informed the family that they should simply tell mother to increase her worrying. Despite some reluctance, the family complied, and within 2 weeks her blood pressure was within normal limits.

Paradoxical therapy has also been used with a variety of other problems in dysfunctional families. In one such instance, Coyne and Biglan (1984) treated a family in which a rebellious 15-year-old persisted in demands for money and privileges until her parents gave in. The therapists reframed her behavior to the parents as "breaking down the door with unreasonableness" and recommended that they provide unreasonable explanations for their refusals of her requests. The therapist then told the girl that he needed her assistance in training the parents to tolerate her behavior. She should, for example, counter refusals by asking, "Why not?" Later, the parents were asked to state, "We cannot force you to do this," whenever they demanded things of her. If the daughter stayed out late, parents were to lock the house, turn the lights off, delay in letting her into the house, and then apologize for their forgetfulness. Another intervention included having the father pay the daughter a penny whenever she argued with or was disrespectful to her mother. By sessions 4 and 5, there was a dramatic improvement in the adolescent's behavior with maintenance of results at follow-up.

Gaines (1978) treated the obsessional mother of a 6-year-old boy with "behavioral problems." Although the father and professionals viewed the child as normal, the mother believed that his tantrums and oppositional behavior were abnormal and, if left untreated, would lead to injury or to life as a criminal. A behavioral analysis was conducted and revealed that tantrums were more likely to occur when the mother told the child to perform chores; thus, the father was encouraged to make these requests. Although this strategy was effective, the mother continued to be overinvolved with the boy and to express many fears and worries about him. Her worries continued even when she had achieved an intellectual understanding of the problem. Consequently, the therapist instructed the patient to "write all her worries" about her child when they came to mind and to fill up a notepad. During the next session, the therapist read out loud the patient's worries. As he did this, the patient interrupted and reported that she realized how "silly" her fears were. She was then ready to deal with concerns about interests outside home and family. On follow-up several months later, the mother reported that she was searching for a job and was involved in more social activities.

A disruptive, combative 6-year-old child was the focus of family treatment described by Weeks and Wright (1979). The parents described the child as the cause of serious marital problems, whereas the therapist believed the parents had labeled him the problem in order to avoid examining their own problems. Therapy involved helping the child to engage in appropriate behavior while simultaneously working on the marriage. A paradoxical intervention facilitated this process. Since parents and child believed the youngster was "bad," the therapists did not argue this point. Instead, they informed the child that things would be better if he could just pretend to be good in order to fool his teachers. The parents were also asked to pretend he was good. In fact, they were instructed to compete and determine which of them could find more positive things to say about the child. According to the parents, the child's behavior changed dramatically. After several weeks of therapy the parents were able to admit that the problem was actually in their relationship.

Bergman (1983) describes a family treatment in which the identified patient was a 14-year-old girl who refused to attend school. The therapist developed the view that problems derived from the mother's dependency on her own overly critical father; as long as the mother looked to him for approval, she would remain a child and be unable to parent her own child. Thus, grandfather was told to triple his criticism so that ultimately his daughter would not care about it anymore. Two weeks later, the prescription had kept him from criticizing her. The daughter felt relieved and dealt more firmly with the child, who returned to school.

Further work in a family context is found in Breit, Gi Im, and Wilner (1983) and is described in a later section.

Sleep Disorders

Anticipatory anxiety about sleeping is sometimes thought to disrupt the normal sleep process and to create a self-perpetuating pattern of insomnia. Paradoxical intention, then, may be used in an attempt to interrupt this vicious cycle (Ascher, 1975; Gall, 1983).

Paradoxical techniques were applied with a 7-year-old boy who was experiencing sleep-onset problems at night (Riveros-de-Carbone, 1984). At the time of consultation, the child had apparently developed anticipatory anxiety and was very frightened that he would be unable to fall asleep. The problem had persisted for 1½ months. After 15 days, the author introduced paradoxical intention in the form of a game called "touch last with Mr. Sleep." The child was allowed to do whatever he wanted when he went to bed except to fall asleep. According to the rules of the game, if the child fell asleep, Mr. Sleep would touch him and win the game. On the first evening, the child fell asleep 15 minutes after he had gone to his bedroom. He attempted to remain awake for two to three more nights without success. At 2-month follow-up, the improvement was still maintained.

Some of the sleep-onset studies are among the most successful in satisfying Kazdin's (1981) criteria. Ascher and Efran (1978) conducted a multiple-case study of five insomniacs with protracted sleep-onset latency. These patients had been unusually unresponsive to a standardized behavioral program that incorporated a 2-week baseline and a 10-week treatment phase that included systematic desensitization, progressive muscle relaxation, covert conditioning, and stimulus-control instructions. Since clinically significant improvement was not obtained, the patients were then paradoxically instructed to increase their sleep-onset time. This phase resulted in an average sleep-onset latency of only 10 minutes. Treatment was terminated for four of the subjects. However, for one subject, the baseline phase was reinstituted, which resulted in a worsening of the problem. Afterward, the presentation of paradoxical treatment resulted in improvement.

Following the lead of Ascher (1975), Relinger, Bornstein, and Mungas (1978) treated a 31-year-old chronic insomniac with a 20-year history of sleep-onset problems. During baseline and treatment phases, the patient provided data on several self-report variables: sleep-onset latency, frequency of falling back to sleep, difficulty falling back to sleep, restfulness, number of awakenings, and personal functioning on the previous day. The paradoxical treatment involved providing a bogus rationale for the patient to try to remain awake as long as possible. A counterdemand instruction was also employed: she was instructed not to expect change until the end of treatment. The patient showed significant improvement on all dimensions except number of awakenings, which did eventually improve at follow-up.

Finally, Relinger and Bornstein (1979) obtained significant positive effects using a multiple-baseline design across subjects to study the effects of a similar paradoxical intervention.

Psychogenic Genitourinary Problems

Urinary retention of psychogenic origin or paruresis is characterized by the inability to urinate in public restrooms or in the homes of other individuals and, particularly, when others are present. In an early multi-case report, Ascher (1979) treated five patients with long-term functional urinary retention. All of the patients had been exposed to a standard behavioral program of eight sessions that included systematic desensitization, covert positive reinforcement, thought stopping, and cognitive interventions. According to Ascher (1979), these patients constituted the small percentage of the cases treated with the behavioral program who were not satisfied with their progress. Consequently, following the eighth week, a paradoxical treatment was instituted. The patients were instructed to practice entering uncomfortable bathrooms over the next 2 to 3 weeks and to engage in all of the usual activities associated with urination, but they were prohibited from urinating. After a reasonable period of time, the patient was to readjust his anatomy, flush the urinal, wash his hands and leave. It was hypothesized that when urgency was high and performance anxiety low the patient would violate the prohibition. When patients reported violating the instruction not to urinate, they were told to inhibit the flow of urine for as long as possible. Within a 6-week period, each patient reported little or no anxiety in public bathrooms. All reported that their latency to onset of urination was satisfactory. Of course, paradoxical treatment had been preceded by a number of standard behavioral interventions that may actually have set the stage for it.

More recently, Mozdzierz (1985) used a combination of Eriksonian hypnosis and paradox in the successful treatment of a woman with a 50-year history of "bashful bladder."

Psychotic Disorders

Paradoxical strategies have been creatively applied to resistances typically encountered in the treatment of psychotic patients. Davis (1965) reported on a modification of short-term psychoanalytic therapy with hospitalized schizophrenics in which the analyst joins or supports the patients' resistance as opposed to making interpretations of them. He found it successful in five of six cases, four of whom were improved enough to be released. Davis (1965) reports in depth on three of these cases. All six patients had been in the hospital from 6 months to 10 years, had been previously diagnosed as schizophrenic, and had been declared legally insane. Symptoms ranged from delusions of persecution to delusions of being controlled and auditory hallucinations. All patients had continued to receive daily doses of thorazine or lithium during the paradoxical intervention.

Some other interesting applications of paradoxical intention to schizophrenics are also described in case studies by Fay (1976), Rosen (1946), and Bergman (1982).

Malingering, Dependency, and Uncooperativeness in Prison Inmates

The use of paradoxical treatment has found its way into work with special problems of prison inmates such as malingering, difficulty adjusting to prison life, and resistance to obtaining necessary medical attention (Chase, Shea, & Dougherty, 1984). These problems typically provide the secondary gain of avoiding placement with the regular prison population.

In one interesting example, a prison inmate was in need of surgery after inserting a piece of wire in his arm. Despite infection and attempts to persuade him, he resisted having the surgery. The psychologist then informed the patient that no one cared whether or not he had surgery or whether his arm was amputated. He was asked to sign a form stating that he refused treatment and was releasing the prison from any liability. The staff members were also instructed not to allow him to sign a consent form for surgery. The next day, the inmate consented to surgery.

Childhood Disorders

Functional Enuresis

In a rather unusual and intriguing case, Erikson (1954) used indirect hypnotic therapy in the treatment of a married couple in their early 20s, each of whom suffered longstanding enuresis. Neither of them had admitted the problem to the other. They had simply pretended to ignore the wet bed each morning for over 9 months until each surprisingly discovered that the other was a bed-wetter. As the couple had limited financial resources, Erikson informed them that they would be accepted as patients on a "purely experimental basis" and that they would be obliged to pay only in the event that they did not benefit from the therapy. The patients were instructed to ingest fluids freely and 2 hours prior to bedtime to drink water and lock the bathroom door. At bedtime, they were to put on their pajamas, kneel by the side of the bed, face their pillows and "deliberately, intentionally and jointly" wet the bed. They were told that they must do it and afterwards should go to sleep and be done with bed-wetting for the night.

They were instructed to follow this routine every night for 2 weeks. On a specified date, they were to take a rest from the task, lie down, and sleep in a dry bed (which they did). They were told that "only as you see a wet bed and only then" would they then have another 3 weeks of kneeling and wetting the bed. Erikson then dismissed them and asked them to return in 5 weeks, at which time they would give him a "full and amazing account." The couple improved and maintained improvement at 1-year follow-up.

Encopresis

Fecal incontinence, or encopresis, refers to a repeated lack of bowel control that results in the passing of feces in inappropriate places. Performance anxiety may play a major role in maintaining and worsening this problem when more traditional treatment approaches have been unsuccessful (Bornstein, Sturm, Retzlaff, Kirby, & Chong, 1981).

Bornstein et al. (1981) treated a 9-year-old male with a 4-year history of encopresis in an ABAB design with follow-up. He had been unsuccessfully treated with a number of therapies during the preceding 4 years, including laxatives, enemas, and hypnosis. At the time treatment was being sought, he was soiling on a daily basis and was having an appropriate bowel movement once a week. His peer relationships and social interactions were negatively affected by this problem. The therapists hypothesized that performance anxiety played a critical role in the case as evidenced by the amount of anxiety associated with toileting as well as the behavior of the parents who, in seeking to help the child, were in all likelihood exacerbating the problem. Throughout baseline and treatment phases, the parents maintained weekly data on bowel movements and soilings. The paradoxical instructions involved four aspects by instructing the child to go to the bathroom every hour, pull down his pants, sit on the toilet for 5 minutes, and to behave as if he had to have a bowel movement but not to allow it to occur. During the first treatment phase, the average number of soilings during the week dropped from a baseline of 7 to 0, whereas bowel movements increased from less than one to approximately four. The reversed baseline was associated with a deterioration in performance, whereas the reintroduction of treatment (with fading instructions regarding trips to the bathroom) was associated with approximately five bowel movements per week with no soiling. Follow-up at 12 months revealed that the changes had been maintained.

Propp (1985) describes the treatment of two encopretic and enuretic boys in whom organic causes were ruled out. Case 1 was an 8-year-old male with a 5-year history of encopresis who had never been bowel trained. He had been treated with medication, laxatives, and enemas, all of which had provided transitory effects. Prior to treatment, he was soiling on a daily basis. The second case was a 6-year-old male who also soiled daily and had never been bowel trained. He had had a history of receiving verbal and physical punishments from his father whenever he soiled. His mother, on the other hand, was lax about training. The paradoxical intervention was made during the first session and comprised two instructions. The first was designed to involve the children in charting. Each child was instructed not to change his behavior but simply to record soilings and appropriate bowel movements. According to Propp (1985), the second intervention reminded the children not to be anxious about toileting and was designed to reduce performance anxiety only. In subsequent sessions, praise was given to reinforce chart completion, but again the patients were told not to worry about changing anything. If any change in soiling occurred, they were told not to worry about it. They were also told that soiling might return to its previous level. Treatment was discontinued when no soiling occurred for a 2-week period or after two consecutive weekly sessions.

The results of therapy in both instances were associated with improvement. For case 1, there was a mean of seven soilings during baseline, which dropped to one; subsequently the patient never had more than three soilings a week. Soilings dropped to two per week at week 9 and then to zero. For case 2, the mean number of seven soilings during baseline dropped to one after treatment was initiated and then to zero by the next week until treatment terminated. During follow-up at 6 months, the soiling rate remained at zero for both clients, and both were reported to continue to have appropriate bowel movements.

Temper Tantrums

The display of temper tantrums in a child is often a source of embarrassment to parents who may inadvertently contribute to maintaining them. Hare-Mustin (1975) reported on an application of paradoxical intention to the problem of temper tantrums in a 4-year-old named Tommy. This child, who was immature and overprotected, was exhibiting tantrums on a daily basis totaling as many as 10 per week. Family treatment was provided over eight weekly sessions, with the tantrums being the focus of treatment during the first three sessions. The paradoxical treatment was a symptom prescription in which the therapist instructed Tommy to continue to have tantrums in a specifically designated place. One week later the number of tantrums decreased to one. Next, a tantrum time was designated, which was the time tantrums had previously occurred with the greatest frequency. If

Tommy were to begin to have a tantrum at another time, he was to be reminded to wait until the specified time. By week 3, there were no tantrums, and Tommy was given the choice to select a tantrum day and still maintain the tantrum place and time. A 9-month follow-up with Tommy's mother revealed that the improvement was maintained.

Following the lead of Hare-Mustin (1975), Zarske (1982) applied paradoxical intervention to the case of a 5-year-old cerebral palsied child with a 6-month history of tantrums that comprised crying and screaming loudly with occasional projectile vomiting. The tantrums were usually handled by talking with the child and encouraging his cooperation. During a 1-week baseline period, there were an average of six daily tantrums with an average duration of about 11 minutes. Treatment was delivered in two phases and incorporated the child's parents and his live-in aide. In phase 1, the child was told by his parents that it was all right for him to have tantrums, but they could only occur in a predetermined location of his choice (bedroom). The adults were instructed to remain with the child during a tantrum and to encourage it. During this phase the child's tantrums decreased dramatically from an average frequency of six tantrums per day lasting more than 11 minutes to one and one-half per day with an average duration of 2.2 minutes. In phase 2 of treatment, the child was encouraged to have his tantrums in the absence of the adults. The frequency and duration of tantrums dropped to 0.57 per day and to 40 seconds per episode. At 1- and 2-month follow-up, there was no evidence of tantrums.

Thumb Sucking

Another childhood habit that typically concerns parents and may adversely affect dental cosmetics is thumb sucking. Yoder (1983) described the treatment of a 7-year-old female referred by an orthodontist for a long-standing problem with thumb sucking. The logotherapist described the child as clearly motivated to stop sucking her thumb but simply "could not." Treatment was conducted within three sessions plus one follow-up meeting and involved having the child select a date after which she would no longer need to engage in the habit (4 weeks later). The child was then instructed to suck her thumb as much as she needed as well as to establish practice times. She was explicitly encouraged to practice thumb sucking for 12 minutes a day in the same place and at the same time. Thumb-sucking practice over the next 2 weeks was reduced to 9 minutes per day and then 5 minutes. Also, a contingency contract was set up such that the child's father would take her to dinner when she quit. Within 3 days after the third session the child stopped sucking her thumb.

Elective Mutism

In contrast to thumb sucking, elective mutism is a rare problem with considerable potential for impairment in social and school functioning. Hoffman and Laub (1986) present the successful family treatment of a 4½-year-old child with a 2½-year history of speaking only to her parents, grandparents, and children at school. The mutism had begun during the time the child had been hospitalized for ataxia at 2 years of age. The authors enlisted the assistance of the family and teacher, all of whom were asked to stop "pressuring" the child to speak. The therapists then arranged to split the roles of good and bad therapist: the former was supportive of the child; the latter attempted to provoke defiance in the child in relation to her symptoms. This defiance-based approach also included a bet by the "bad therapist" that the child could only make infant-like sounds, whereas the "good therapist" insisted she was capable of mature speech. After 18 sessions of therapy, the child began speaking to adults, stopped using a pacifier, and increased her circle of friends. A 2-month follow-up revealed that the change was sustained.

School Phobia

Another disorder with great potential for creating childhood impairment is school refusal. For this reason, prompt treatment is essential.

Baideme, Kern, and Taffel-Cohen (1979) treated a 9-year-old school-phobic girl who had displayed irregular school attendance and fear of attending school over the previous 7 weeks. Treatment was delivered in the context of Adlerian family therapy, as the child was an overprotected girl whose role in the family was that of the "helpless and sickly one." The parents were instructed to return the child to school immediately and every day afterward. Phone contact was used to provide support to the parents, principal, and teacher. The child was instructed to be fearful and to scream and cry every morning before her parents took her to school. To disengage overinvolvement of the parents, they were encouraged to participate in some fun activities together. By session 3, the child had attended school every day except for 1 day when she was hysterical. Paradoxical antisuggestion was again employed by instructing the child to spend 15 minutes every morning on her way to school telling her father her worries. Also, her mother was instructed to develop a list of ways the daughter could be less dependent and was instructed to tell the child that it was all right for her to go to school. Further, the child was encouraged to join a children's therapy group. Following a relapse of 1 day when the child would not go to school, the parents were instructed that if the child reported she was ill, she had to have a fever in order to stay home and then must remain in bed. On follow-up at 2 months, the child was attending school regularly and was planning to spend a night away from home with a friend. At 10-month follow-up, the child was experiencing no problems at home or in school. She was regularly attending school with no relapses.

Breit et al. (1983) successfully employed the paradoxical technique of "illusion of alternatives" in the treatment of a 12-year-old school phobic to overcome her resistance to returning to school. The focus was shifted from whether the girl would return to school to how and when she would return.

Delinquency

A far more serious problem is a pattern of repeated delinquent acts in children and adolescents. Jessee and L'Abate (1980) describe the use of paradoxical therapy with three children in an inpatient treatment facility. The children ranged in age from 10 to 11 and had been hospitalized for a variety of reasons including repeated stealing, misbehavior, defiance, and accidents involving both self and others when angry. The first case was an 11-year-old boy with a history of repeated delinquent acts of theft. The second case was a 10-year-old boy with a history of hyperactivity, inattention, mischief at school, and peer aggression and defiance. His family was simply unable to deal with him any longer. All three children exhibited positive changes in behavior following paradoxical treatment.

In one of the best designed and implemented studies, Kolko and Milan (1983) evaluated the effects of reframing and paradoxical instruction superimposed on a contingency contract with three youths in outpatient treatment, using a multiple-baseline design across subjects with follow-up. Alphonse was a 15-year-old boy with school discipline problems, academic performance problems, and drug and alcohol abuse. Benny, a 14-year-old with a history of unsuccessful counseling, was referred for a number of problems including stealing, lying, failure to follow instructions, misconduct, poor academic performance, and excessive lateness and school absences. Cleona, a 14-year-old girl, was referred for truancy and conflicts with her mother about her hygiene, work habits, social life, sexual practices, and the hours she kept. Outcome was assessed through two means: class attendance and academic grades. During baseline, the three youths were seen with their parents to assess their individual problems. School-related problems were chosen as primary targets for treatment. Also, contingency contracts were established to reinforce academic performance and school attendance and were in effect throughout the course of the study.

Paradoxical intervention involved two components: reframing and paradoxical directive. The reframing component was designed to increase opposition, whereas the paradoxical directive involved prescribing the symptoms. For example, Alphonse's behavior was interpreted as indicating that he was "immature, impulsive, and childish" and that he should not attend school. This procedure was gradually eliminated to allow improvements to be maintained by the contingency contract. The findings revealed that the introduction of paradoxical procedures was associated with clinically significant changes in all three youths. Relative to baseline, class attendance showed a marked improvement ranging from 300% to 450%, which was essentially maintained at follow-up except for a slight deterioration by the end of school. On academic performance overall, the youths achieved two to three times as many satisfactory grades during treatment and follow-up.

Aggression

Arnesen, Libby, and Miller (1973) provide an interesting case study of a 15-year-old male with a history of fire setting, slashing furniture, aggression, and defecating wherever he wanted. He exhibited a vast array of severe behaviors and challenged staff and peers. He self-mutilated, attacked staff, set fires, and destroyed property. His behavior provided reinforcement for him through the status he gained among his peers. Numerous techniques were tried to bring his behavior under control, including individual, group, and community therapy, drugs, isolation, restraint, wet pacs, operant conditioning, and a peer-pressure program. Finally, a paradoxical intervention was devised. The paradoxical treatment program involved encouraging the boy's symptoms by telling him to continue what he was doing. Records indicated a dramatic drop in number of isolation episodes and number of hours in isolation per week following the paradoxical intervention. During the latter part of the program, the boy required no isolation for many weeks. He was eventually sent to a halfway house with success maintained at 16-month follow-up.

School Problems

Paradoxical strategies have also been applied to the treatment of behavioral difficulties in the classroom setting with preadolescents and adolescents.

Williams and Weeks (1984) described a series of such cases. Most of the children were treated in the absence of their families. In the first case, two seventh graders were referred to the In-School Suspension Program (ISSP) for fighting, and both blamed their teacher for picking on them since they "weren't really fighting." The therapist suggested an experiment whereby the boys were given the prescription to do the very same thing that had gotten them into trouble in order to discover whether other teachers would take disciplinary action against them. If no other teacher "wrote them up," the therapists would agree that it was their original teacher who was the "one with the problem." Following this reframing strategy, neither boy was referred to the ISSP during the next several months.

The second case involved a seventh grade girl whose problem entailed her leaving her classroom in tears when upset with a teacher whom she perceived as mean and scary. A behavior modification program in the form of setting up explicit family rules was arranged to deal with the child's desire to change class, her acting "sick," and calling home to have someone come to pick her up at school. The rules were very explicit and entailed a number of contingencies. For example, if Ann went home from school or stayed home, she would be required to remain in bed with no TV, radio, calls, visitors, or discussion with her parents about the school problem. Although this program resulted in behavioral change, the author reported that there was no "attitudinal change." To facilitate such change, the child was then informed that she had improved too quickly, was going to have a relapse, and that she should not have changed her behavior so quickly. She was then told to have a "big upset" during the next 2 to 3 weeks to practice her control over these upset feelings. Follow-up over the first half of the school year revealed no further incidents of being upset and improved school grades.

Other cases treated included an overly dependent eighth grader, a ninth grader with school and family problems, two girls in conflict, and an eighth grader with difficulty expressing anger and resentment.

In another series of cases, Brown (1986) discussed three instances of oppositional behavior in the classroom. In the first case, an 8-year-old boy was referred for disruptive classroom behavior including bothering other children. The second 8-year-old boy was referred for disruptive and aggressive behavior. He apparently had mood swings during which he became very oppositional. The third case involved an 8-year-old boy who was hitting, pinching, and kicking his peers in the classroom. Treatment involved having each child practice the behavior in question outside of the classroom whenever the behavior occurred. Two of the three cases exhibited improvement. However, the first case did not improve, which may have possibly been related to the fact that the child was allowed to practice in the classroom. Also, lack of commitment by the principal and the failure of the teacher to consistently supply the paradoxical instructions may have been detrimental to the treatment. Interestingly, in the second case, the child's improvement occurred only in the presence of the teacher who implemented the treatment.

Stuttering

The role of performance anxiety in exacerbating speech dysfluency is clear and often creates a vicious cycle. In this vein, paradoxical treatment was applied in the treatment of a 20-year-old male with a 15-year history of stuttering (Nystul & Muszynska, 1976). Prior to treatment he could only say one coherent word a minute, and his efforts to speak were accompanied by severe contortions of his head and neck. The Adlerian therapist made a contract with the client that he was to do no talking but just stuttering and that if he wanted to communicate with the therapist he must do so by writing notes. Dereflection was used by having the patient shift attention from speech fluency to speech volume. Rational-emotive strategies were employed as well as *in vivo* exposure and homework assignments during which the patient spent 2 hours a week over a 2-month period with a female friend. At the conclusion of treatment, the average number of stammered words was 1 in 10, and there was a dramatic increase in fluency.

Tics

Clark (1966) employed massed practice of tics in three patients diagnosed as Gilles de la Tourette's syndrome, all of whom suffered longstanding problems. Case 1 was a 22-year-old male who exhibited frequent jerky head movements and incessant repetitions of obscenities. Case 2 was a 17-year-old male with a barking tic. Case 3 had muscular spasms associated with explosive verbalizations of one word. Clark (1966) conceptualized a tic as a learned neuromuscular habit that could be unlearned. In a massed practice paradigm all patients were asked to repeat the obscenity as frequently and as loudly as possible to the criterion of being unable to say the word even once a minute. Cases 1, 2, and 3 were treated for 49, 25, and 10 sessions, respectively. Two of the three improved, and one terminated.

Psychophysiological Problems

The relationship between stress and tension and the development of physical symptoms is well documented. Chronic headache is one such example. Gentry (1973) treated a 26-year-old female with chronic migraine headaches occurring three to four times daily. Prior to treatment, she had had a number of neurological tests and had been placed on Stelazine® and Darvon®. Therapy, conducted in 11 weekly 1-hour sessions, consisted of asking the patient to continue her symptoms. By the fifth session, the patient's headaches had decreased to four per week, and by the 11th session, she was experiencing no headaches. A 12-month follow-up indicated that improvement was maintained.

Miscellaneous

Resistance

We have noted above that paradoxical techniques are frequently implemented when more direct approaches have met an impasse. Greenberg (1973) incorporated "antiexpectation" techniques in dynamic psychotherapy to decrease patient resistance and assist patients in overcoming symptoms. The first case was a 31-year-old mother suffering from perfectionistic tendencies. She apparently believed that she must have control over her entire life and that everything in her life must be perfect. Attempts to encourage the patient to examine other issues beyond the need for perfection were met with resistance. Paradoxical techniques were introduced at different times and involved the therapist agreeing with the patient's need to be perfect and encouraging her to spend *more* time cleaning each day.

In the second case, a 40-year-old male with a 3-year history of tension, anxiety, dizziness, and headaches was treated. The patient was encouraged to get worse and to become a failure. He was instructed to talk himself into getting a severe headache each day. As expected, he was unable to talk himself into a headache and obtained relief for the first time. Whenever he began to feel upset, he began to try to feel worse and exaggerated his fantasies until they became humorous.

Fused Identity

Perhaps one of the most unusual applications of paradoxical treatment is Fish's (1973) report on three female university freshmen who sought psychological consultation for "fused identity." The clients started the session by complaining that they had lost their identities and that they were the "same" person. The therapist immediately responded that he could differentiate among the three of them. Their response revealed a number of facts that the therapist interpreted more as a sign of friendship than of fused identity. This observation was met repeatedly with resistance. The women also described an incident the previous evening in which they had spent time with the same boy alternating kissing him on the same bed. Assuming that they may have been concerned about homosexuality, the therapist reassured them. He hypothesized that, as college freshmen, they were lonely and therefore spent considerable time together, relying on each other for support. He then used an opportunity to demonstrate how, when asked a question, they "smoothed over" any initial disagreement so that it appeared as if they had agreed from the outset.

When the "controlling" member of the three expressed resentment at this notion, he suggested an experiment. They were asked to plan when they would be together and what they would do. After a complete list of activities was obtained, they were instructed to follow it to the letter. At the next appointment the "controlling" person was absent. The others reported that they had begun following the list but had given up. Once they were spending less time together, they no longer felt as if they were the same person. This upset the controlling one, who demanded more time together and even threatened to take drugs. The therapist then offered individual counseling to the "dependent" and "depressed" members of the triad. No follow-up data were collected, although the "controlling" member did return to another therapist for an unrelated problem.

Vocational Indecision

Career development is an important task for the college student and may be impeded by any number of factors. Lopez (1983) employed a paradoxical approach in counseling a vocationally indecisive 20-year-old college student who was having much difficulty selecting a major. The problem appeared to be related to his father's overinvolvement in his affairs. The father's interference had created a number of intense conflicts about vocational issues. Analysis of the situation revealed a pattern: when the client attempted to discuss an important decision, the father would exhibit an aggressive, opinionated reaction, after which the client would change his opinion, reject his father's view, and feel confused. In five sessions of therapy, the counselor reframed the father's overinvolvement in a positive way and informed the client that he must be willing to comply with the counselor's instructions before learning what he would be asked to do. He was given a week to think about this, and when he returned he had agreed to comply. At this point the counselor gave the client a letter that the counselor had composed and that was to be given to the client's father—either read aloud or hand delivered by the client in a face-to-face meeting. The letter included the paradoxical demand that both of them continue to respond in the same manner. It pointed out that the client usually presented underdeveloped ideas and that his father was prudent in not supporting him; moreover, it predicted that the client would continue to act confused, whether or not he was confused, as a means of helping himself to become confident in his ideas. Further, the father was asked to continue questioning the son about his career plans at least twice a week. In the next session the client reported that his relationship with his father was on a more equal basis and that the frequency and quality of their interactions had changed. For example, during the week following delivery of the letter, the client had spoken briefly with his father once about an issue unrelated to career issues, in comparison to the two to three weekly phone calls about career matters that had constituted the previous pattern. Further, the client reported that his father's ideas were now being presented more as suggestions than as directives.

Severe Depression, Borderline Personality

A case by Greenberg and Pies (1983) is perhaps the only published instance in which paradoxical techniques were shown to have produced deleterious effects alone. The patient was a 22-year-old woman with borderline personality disorder. She had spastic paralysis, exhibited a tendency to self-mutilate, and showed depression and suicidal ideation. In the course of psychodynamically oriented inpatient treatment, the therapist attempted to alleviate the patient's hopelessness by agreeing with and exaggerating the patient's prediction that she would never get well: "I'd say that the chances of your getting well are about 1 in 100" (p. 68). Following this intervention, the patient became increasingly anxious, sullen, withdrawn, and suicidal, and she self-mutilated. The authors present the case report specifically to correct the impression that the technique is risk-free and that failure is only a remote possibility.

Conclusion

Despite the remarkable diversity of these applications of paradoxical intention (see Table 1), a number of generalizations can be made. First, paradoxical therapy has been applied to a wide variety of clinical problems and to patients of all ages ranging from pediatric to geriatric populations. Paradoxical strategies have been particularly applied to habits and autonomic reactions over which the patient experiences a lack of voluntary control. Paradox is frequently employed when resistance or barriers to further progress in therapy are encountered. Second, paradoxical interventions are often embedded in a program of treatment that includes nonparadoxical elements. For example, Kolko and Milan (1983) combined paradoxical therapy with contingency contracting. Similarly, in many instances, paradoxical treatment is preceded by other interventions. These additional treatment elements preclude generalizing to situations where paradox is not preceded by or combined with other therapies. Campbell and Stanley (1963) have termed this threat to generalizability "multiple treatment interference." Third, paradoxical interventions are flavored by the theoretical orientation of the therapist as well as by the nature of the problem treated; widely varying rationales have been provided by writers of different schools (Rohraugh, Tennen, Press, & White, 1981; Riebel, 1984). In our sample of case studies, paradoxical interventions were delivered within the context of several major therapeutic orientations: for example, behavior therapy, family therapy, logotherapy, and psychodynamic therapy. The presumed mechanism of action differs according to the therapist's persuasion.

A fourth generality about these interventions can be made. Paradoxical treatment typically encompassed the actual prescription of the symptom itself with or without the reinterpretation (reframing) of the meaning of the symptom by the clinician. Patients are generally instructed to do the direct opposite of what they might have expected, much to their surprise.

However, one generalization that cannot be drawn is that paradoxical interventions are as successful as this case-study literature might lead the uncritical reader to suspect. After carefully cataloguing the case studies according to four of Kazdin's (1981) criteria for drawing valid inferences from such studies, we are forced to conclude that the present literature falls short of the mark. Despite the overwhelming number of positive outcomes, we must be cautious in interpreting these findings. We examined Kazdin's (1980) criteria *across* all studies (Table 2) and *within* each study. This analysis allowed us to answer two key questions: (1) How frequently are each of the four criteria met across the studies in this literature? (2) How many (0 through 4) of these criteria are achieved within these case studies? In response to the first question, the types of measurement methods employed in the majority of the case studies reviewed were either patient or therapist self-report, which are clearly subjective in nature and prone to bias. In only exceptional instances were standardized rating forms, be-

TABLE 2
Frequency of Kazdin's (1981) Criteria Satisfied across Studies

Criteria[a]	Frequency (N = 88)
Problem duration	
Transient	30
Longstanding	53
?	5
Type of data	
Self-report	61
Other	26
?	1
Frequency of measurement	
Pre–post	70
Multiple	18
Type of effect	
Gradual/delayed	56
Immediate	28
?	3
None	1

[a]Kazdin's criteria are italicized.

havioral observations, self-monitoring, or a physical measure used. The duration of problems treated in these studies was also examined. Problems of longstanding duration were treated more often than transient problems, making alternative hypotheses for change less viable. However, the majority of the cases described employed a before–after format as opposed to systematically obtained measurements across multiple occasions. Reliance on this pre–post measurement approach leaves open numerous threats to valid inference. Also, there were almost twice as many delayed effects as immediate effects observed. Immediate effects of the slam-bang variety (Kazdin, 1981) can more easily be attributed to treatment.

Our within-case analysis revealed that 19 of the 88 case studies met none of Kazdin's criteria, 37 met one criterion, 19 met two criteria, 8 met three criteria, and only 5 met all of Kazdin's criteria. Assuming the most conservative perspective, then, in only five cases was there enough experimental control to warrant a firm conclusion that paradoxical treatment was responsible for change. When we couple this finding with the well-known bias for publishing positive outcomes in the clinical literature, we must become even more critical. As Rosenthal (1979) has noted in regard to meta-analysis, the "file drawer" problem looms large here. We may legitimately ask how many cases with no change or negative outcome are tucked away in the file drawers of clinicians.

The case studies themselves suggest that the outcome of paradoxical interventions may be strongly influenced by therapist factors and patient factors. Variations among the interventions can be subtle, and outcome may depend on the therapeutic relationship as a whole and on precisely how the technique is implemented. Does the therapist acknowledge that a paradoxical effect is intended, provide a rationale for the intervention, use humor, drop the ploy when initial effects are achieved? On what basis do therapists decide whether to use specific elements such as these in treatment? Whereas some paradoxical interventions seem unlikely to backfire on the therapeutic relationship, others require that the therapist invite rebellion while retaining status as a helping confidante. Common sense suggests that this feat is more likely accomplished in some therapeutic relationships than in others.

These studies are even further from clarifying the mechanisms through which paradoxical methods achieve change when they are successful, but they do permit speculation. Although it may be partisan for cognitive-behavioral therapists to say so, in virtually all of these interventions, the therapist adopts a surprising stance in order to effect a change in the patient's attitude about key symptoms, behaviors, or relationships. In fact, change of attitude was the goal Frankl (1960) posited for his own work with paradox; he argued that neurotic symptoms could best be resolved by using humor to facilitate a sense of detachment from the problem.

The attitude-changing property of paradoxical interventions seems most obvious in those techniques in which the patient is explicitly invited to take a new look at symptoms—for example, urged to welcome panic attacks rather than avoid them (e.g., Goldstein, 1978). It is less apparent when a therapist asks a patient to spend longer and longer periods of time sitting in a parked car to avoid feelings of anxiety, as in the report by Ascher (1981); yet it seems clear that this strategy may have worked by exaggerating the implications of the patient's premises until he was forced to reevaluate them. When anorexics or enuretics are asked deliberately to perform a dysfunctional habit, when impotent men are forbidden to have intercourse, it is even less evident that the therapist may be provoking changes in the set of entrenched meanings associated with problematic interactions, behaviors, and situations (Beck, 1976). However, in these interventions, the therapists can be viewed as using cognitive dissonance created by their own behavior to modify the belief that dysfunctional symptoms or behaviors are empowering, intolerable, or grossly unacceptable to others. The key question, from our point of view, is whether, and under what circumstances, paradoxical techniques can *reliably* produce beneficial changes without placing the therapeutic relationship at risk.

In conclusion, paradoxical strategies represent a rather intriguing approach to treatment. However, if case studies are expected to provide valid and useful information about the efficacy of paradoxical treatment, clinicians must incorporate more careful controls into future case studies. The selection of valid, reliable outcome measures, the collection of data across a number of measurement occasions, and the more frequent use of single-case experimental designs (see Hersen & Barlow, 1976) would help to achieve a useful end. This is the case of the case study in the paradoxical intention literature.

References

Arnesen, R. B., Libby, R., & Miller, P. H. (1973). Altering the behavior of an aggressive institutionalized boy through paradoxical communication. *Journal of Nervous and Mental Disease, 157,* 63–65.

Ascher, L. M. (1975). *Paradoxical technique in behavior therapy: Single case studies in the treatment of insomnia.* Paper presented at the meeting of the Association for Advancement of Behavior Therapy, San Francisco, CA.

Ascher, L. M. (1979). Paradoxical intention in the treatment of urinary retention. *Behaviour Research and Therapy, 17(3),* 267–270.

Ascher, L. M. (1981). Application of paradoxical intention by other schools of therapy. *International Forum for Logotherapy, 4,* 52–55.

Ascher, L. M., & Efran, J. S. (1978). Use of paradoxical intention in a behavioral program for sleep onset insomnia. *Journal of Consulting and Clinical Psychology, 46 (13),* 547–550.

Baideme, S. M., Kern, R. M., & Taffel-Cohen, S. (1979). The use of Adlerian family therapy in the case of school phobia. *Journal of Individual Psychology, 35(1),* 58–69.

Beck, A. T. (1976). *Cognitive therapy and the emotional disorders.* New York: International Universities Press.

Bergman, J. S. (1982). Paradoxical interventions with people who insist on acting crazy. *American Journal of Psychotherapy, 36(2),* 214–222.

Bergman, J. S. (1983). Prescribing family criticism as a paradoxical intervention. *Family Process, 22(4),* 517–522.

Boeringa, J. A. (1983). Blushing: A modified behavioral intervention using paradoxical intention. *Psychotherapy: Theory, Research, and Practice, 20,* 441–444.

Bornstein, P. H., Sturm, C. A., Retzlaff, P. D., Kirby, K. L., & Chong, H. (1981). Paradoxical instruction in the treatment of encopresis and chronic constipation. *Journal of Behavior Therapy and Experimental Psychiatry, 12,* 167–170.

Breit, M., Gi Im, W., & Wilner, R. S. (1983). Strategic approaches with resistant families. *American Journal of Family Therapy, 11(1),* 51–58.

Brown, J. E. (1986). The use of paradoxical intention with oppositional behavior in the classroom. *Psychology in the Schools, 23,* 77–81.

Campbell, D. T., & Stanley, J. (1963). *Experimental and quasiexperimental designs for research.* Chicago: Rand McNally.

Chase, J. L., Shea, S. J., & Dougherty, F. I. (1984). The use of paradoxical intervention within a prison psychiatric facility. *Psychotherapy, 21(2),* 278–281.

Clark, D. F. (1966). Behaviour therapy of a Gilles de la Tourette's syndrome. *British Journal of Psychiatry, 112,* 771–778.

Coyne, J. C., & Biglan, A. (1984). Paradoxical techniques in strategic family therapy: A behavioral analysis. *Journal of Behavior Therapy and Experimental Psychiatry, 15(3),* 221–227.

Crane, D. R., & Taylor, V. L. (1983). Prescription-filling as a dependent variable in the study of psychosomatic families: A demonstration. *Family Systems Medicine, 1(2),* 73–76.

Dalton, P. (1983). Family treatment of an obsessive-compulsive child: A case report. *Family Process, 22,* 99–108.

Davis, H. L. (1965). Short-term psychoanalytic therapy with hospitalized schizophrenics. *Psychoanalytic Review, 52,* 421–448.

de Shazer, S. (1974). On getting unstuck: Some change-initiating tactics for getting the family moving. *Family Therapy, 1(1),* 19–26.

Domangue, B. B. (1985). Hypnotic regression and reframing in the treatment of insect phobias. *American Journal of Psychotherapy, 39,* 206–214.

Driscoll, R. (1985). Commonsense objectives in paradoxical interventions. *Psychotherapy, 22,* 774–778.

Erickson, M. H. (1954). A clinical note on indirect hypnotic therapy. *Journal of Clinical and Experimental Hypnosis, 2,* 171–174.

Fay, A. (1976). Clinical notes on paradoxical therapy. *Psychotherapy: Theory, Research, and Practice, 13,* 118–122.

Fish, J. M. (1973). Dissolution of a fused identity in one therapeutic session: A case study. *Journal of Consulting and Clinical Psychology, 41,* 462–465.

Frankl, V. E. (1960). Paradoxical intention: A logotherapeutic technique. *American Journal of Psychotherapy, 14,* 520–535.

Gaines, T. (1978). A technique for reducing parental obsessions in family therapy. *Family Therapy, 5(1),* 91–94.

Gall, H. (1983). Logotherapeutic treatment of neurotic sleep disturbances. *International Forum for Logotherapy, 6(2),* 92–94.

Gentry, D. L. (1973). Directive therapy techniques in the treatment of migraine headaches: A case study. *Psychotherapy: Theory, Research, and Practice, 10,* 308–311.

Gerz, H. O. (1966). Experience with the logotherapeutic technique of paradoxical intention in the treatment of phobic and obsessive compulsive patients. *American Journal of Psychiatry, 123,* 548–553.

Gilewski, M. J., Kuppinger, J., & Zarit, S. H. (1985). The aging marital system: A case study in life changes and paradoxical intervention. *Clinical Gerontologist, 3(3),* 3–15.

Goldstein, A. J. (1978). Case conference: The treatment of a case of agoraphobia by a multifaceted treatment program. *Journal of Behavior Therapy and Experimental Psychiatry, 9,* 45–51.

Greenberg, R. P. (1973). Anti-expectation techniques in psychotherapy: The power of negative thinking. *Psychotherapy: Theory, Research, and Practice, 10,* 145–148.

Greenberg, R. P., & Pies, R. (1983). Is paradoxical intention risk-free?: A review and case report. *Journal of Clinical Psychiatry, 44,* 66–69.

Hare-Mustin, R. T. (1975). Treatment of temper tantrums by paradoxical intervention. *Family Process, 14,* 481–486.

Hersen, M., & Barlow, D. H. (1976). *Single case experimental designs: Strategies for studying behavior change.* New York: Pergamon.

Hoffman, S., & Laub, B. (1986). Paradoxical intervention using a polarization model of cotherapy in the treatment of elective mutism: A case study. *Contemporary Family Therapy, 8(2),* 136–143.

Hsu, L. G., & Lieberman, S. (1982). Paradoxical intention in the treatment of chronic anorexia nervosa. *American Journal of Psychiatry, 139(5),* 650–653.

Hyer, L. A. (1983). Case history: Paradoxical letters in family therapy. *Clinical Gerontologist, 2(2)*, 58–61.

Jessee, E., & L'Abate, L. (1980). The use of paradox with children in an inpatient treatment setting. *Family Process, 19*, 59–64.

Kazdin, A. E. (1980). *Research design in clinical psychology*. New York: Harper & Row.

Kazdin, A. E. (1981). Drawing valid inferences from case studies. *Journal of Consulting and Clinical Psychology, 49*, 183–192.

Kolko, D. J., & Milan, M. A. (1983). Reframing and paradoxical instruction to overcome "resistance" in the treatment of delinquent youths: A multiple baseline analysis. *Journal of Consulting and Clinical Psychology, 51(5)*, 655–660.

Lamb, C. S. (1980). Use of paradoxical intention: Self management through laughter. *Personnel and Guidance Journal, 59(4)*, 217–219.

Lamontagne, Y. (1978). Treatment of erythrophobia by paradoxical intention. *Journal of Nervous and Mental Disease, 166*, 304–306.

Lopez, F. G. (1983). A paradoxical approach to vocational indecision. *Personnel and Guidance Journal, 61*(7), 410–412.

Mandel, H. P., & Cooper, I. J. (1980). Paradoxical intention and hypnosis in brief psychotherapy: A case report. *Ontario Psychologist, 12(1)*, 6–12.

Morelli, G. (1978). Paradoxical intention: A case study of an effective method of treating alcoholism and drug abuse. *Psychology, 15(1)*, 57–59.

Mozdzierz, G. J. (1985). The use of hypnosis and paradox in the treatment of a case of chronic urinary retention/"bashful bladder." American Journal of Clinical Hypnosis, *28(1)*, 43–47.

Nystul, M. S., & Muszynska, E. (1976). Adlerian treatment of a classical case of stuttering. *Journal of Individual Psychology, 32*(2), 194–202.

Propp, L., (1985). A self-control treatment for encopresis combining self-charting with paradoxical instructions: Two case examples. *Journal of Child and Adolescent Psychotherapy, 2*(1), 26–31.

Relinger, H., & Bornstein, P. H. (1979). Treatment of sleep onset insomnia by paradoxical instruction: A multiple baseline design. *Behavior Modification, 3*, 203–222.

Relinger, H., Bornstein, P. H., & Mungas, D. M. (1978). Treatment of insomnia by paradoxical intention: A time-series analysis. *Behavior Therapy, 9(5)*, 955–959.

Riebel, L. (1984). Paradoxical intention strategies: A review of rationales. *Psychotherapy, 21*, 260–272.

Riveros-de-Carbone, J. (1984). Maurice and Mr. Sleep. *International Forum for Logotherapy, 7(1)*, 55–56.

Rohrbaugh, M., Tennen, H., Press, S., & White, L. (1981). Compliance, defiance, and therapeutic paradox: Guidelines for strategic use of paradoxical interventions. *American Journal of Orthopsychiatry, 51*, 454–467.

Rosen, J. N. (1946). A method of resolving acute catatonic excitement. *Psychiatric Quarterly, 20*, 183–198.

Rosenthal, R. (1979). The "file drawer problem" and tolerance for null results. *Psychological Bulletin, 86*, 638–641.

Salter, A. (1949). *Conditioned reflex therapy: The direct approach to the reconstruction of personality*. New York: Creative Age Press.

Sargent, G. (1983). Treatment of snake phobia: Combining paradoxical intention with behavior modification. *International Forum for Logotherapy, 6*, 28–30.

Sluzki, C. E. (1985). Family consultation in family medicine: A case example. *Family Systems Medicine, 3(2)*, 160–170.

Tennen, H., Rohrbaugh, M., Press, S., & White, L. (1981). Reactance theory and therapeutic paradox: A compliance-defiance model. *Psychotherapy: Theory, Research, and Practice, 18,* 14–22.

Vandereycken, W. (1982). Paradoxical strategies in a blocked sex therapy. *American Journal of Psychotherapy 36(1),* 103–108.

Victor, R. G., & Krug, C. M. (1967). "Paradoxical intention" in the treatment of compulsive gambling. *American Journal of Psychotherapy 21,* 808–814.

Weeks, G., & Wright, L. (1979). Dialectics of the family life cycle. *American Journal of Family Therapy 7,* 85–91.

Williams, J. M., & Weeks, G. R. (1984). Use of paradoxical techniques in a school setting. *American Journal of Family Therapy 12(3),* 47–57.

Yoder, J. D. (1983). A child, paradoxical intention, and consciousness. *International Forum for Logotherapy, 6(1),* 19–21.

Zarske, J. A. (1982). The treatment of temper tantrums in a cerebral palsied child: A paradoxical intervention. *School Psychology Review, 11(3),* 324–328.

Clinical Applications

Chapter 4

Paradoxical Intention and Recursive Anxiety

L. Michael Ascher

Paradoxical procedures have traditionally been employed in a primary or ancillary capacity to facilitate clients' cooperation with therapeutic objectives (e.g., Weeks & L'Abate, 1982). Although behavior therapists have also utilized paradox in this manner (e.g., Ascher, 1980; Dowd & Milne, 1986), they have more characteristically used paradoxical techniques to treat anxiety disorders or other anxiety-based problems (e.g., sexual dysfunction, sleep-onset insomnia). For behavior therapists, paradoxical intention (Frankl, 1955) has been the most frequently used paradoxical procedure, perhaps because it is easily incorporated into behavioral treatment programs (Ascher, 1980), and it can be conceptualized in learning terms (e.g., Ascher & Schotte, 1987; Frankl, 1975; Omer, 1981). Further, it has been described throughout its history as a method for ameliorating anxiety disorders (Ascher, Bowers, & Schotte, 1985; Frankl, 1955). The present chapter is devoted exclusively to the application of paradoxical intention as the cognitive-behavioral treatment of choice for certain aspects of anxiety disorders and anxiety-based difficulties. Cognitive-behavior therapy, the orientation taken in this chapter, involves the use of traditional behavioral procedures whose efficacy in ameliorating anxiety has been empirically validated. Supplementary cognitive strategies are employed to systematically guide the therapist in responding to the client's maladaptive thoughts and statements.

For some years, clinicians have been engaged in exploring, in both research and clinical contexts, the efficacy of paradoxical intention in the treatment of behavioral problems resulting from excessive anxiety. Initially they found, as would be the case with any behavioral procedure, that paradoxical intention seemed to be useful for some clients but unproductive for others. This variability of effect could, of course, be attributed to a number of phenomena that constitute the behavior-therapy situation. However, as data have accumulated, it has become clear that one of the most influential factors determining the efficacy of the technique is the relationship between paradoxical intention and an aspect of the client's problem that I have labeled "recursive anxiety" (Ascher, 1984; Ascher & Schotte, 1987). I have used that term, based on my observations, to describe what has otherwise been called the "second fear" (Weekes, 1976), "anxiety phobia" (Ascher, 1980), "fear of fear" (Evans, 1972; Goldstein & Chambless, 1978), and "anxiety sensitivity" (Reiss, 1987). The phenomenon was first systematically reported by Frankl (1955) in association with his early papers on paradoxical intention and anticipatory anxiety.

Recursive anxiety refers to the discomfort that the person experiences regarding the consequences of his or her fear reaction. That is, the affected person is concerned that currently experienced anxiety (or anxiety anticipated to occur under specific circumstances) will reach a level (that may or may not be perceived as a panic attack) at which he or she imagines losing control and being exposed to disastrous consequences. The hypothesized catastrophe may be life-threatening in nature (e.g., cardiac arrest, loss of consciousness, inability to breathe or swallow), or it may be fear of loss of control over physical or psychological processes (e.g., vomiting, incontinence, emitting word salad or profane language, "going crazy"). Sometimes the person is worried about symptoms that are natural components of sympathetic activity, for example, blushing, perspiration, tremors, or increased cardiac and respiratory activity.

Because recursive anxiety seems to be exhibited invariably by agoraphobic clients, it is sometimes considered to be exclusively associated with that disorder (Reiss, Peterson, Gursky, & McNally, 1986). However, this does not appear to be the case. Thus, recursive anxiety is frequently present in connection with driving difficulties, particularly when the focus is on tunnels, bridges, traffic jams, or minimum-access highways. Difficulties that may not be classified as anxiety disorders but that can have anxiety-based variants also may be associated with recursive anxiety. For example, this is now an accepted variety of sleep-onset insomnia and of sexual dysfunction (Masters & Johnson, 1970).

However, of more significance to the present discussion is the association of recursive anxiety with conditions of social difficulty. Social anxiety refers to general discomfort in the presence of others. Social phobia concerns fear of scrutiny; the discomfort implies that such close observation will result in negative evaluation. Although social anxiety and social phobia are independent phenomena, social phobics often exhibit social anxiety. Recursive anxiety is hypothesized to be a variant of social phobia and to represent for the phobic the mechanism by which the negative evaluation of others will be engendered. This connection is corroborated, to some extent, by characterizations of a process similar to recursive anxiety presented in both DSM-III and its revised form (DSM-III-R). The following statement appears as part of the description of social phobia (300.23).

> The essential feature of this disorder is a persistent fear of one or more situations (the social phobic situations) in which the person is exposed to possible scrutiny by others and fears that he or she may do something or act in a way that will be humiliating or embarrassing. . . .
>
> Marked anticipatory anxiety occurs if the person is confronted with the necessity of entering into the social phobic situation, and such situations are therefore usually avoided. Less commonly, the person forces himself or herself to endure the social phobic situation, but it is experienced with intense anxiety. Usually the person fears that others will detect signs of anxiety in the social phobic situation. A vicious cycle may be created in which the irrational fear generates anxiety that impairs performance, thus increasing the motivation to avoid the phobic situation. Invariably the person recognizes that his or her fear is excessive or unreasonable. (American Psychiatric Association, 1987, pp. 241–242)

Exclusive of agoraphobia, recursive anxiety is not invariably found in any anxiety disorder or anxiety-based complaint. Moreover, cases in which recursive anxiety is a complicating factor occur in virtually all categories of anxiety disorder or anxiety-based complaints.

The possibility that recursive anxiety is associated with nonagoraphobic anxiety disorders and a wide range of anxiety-based complaints suggests the need to review another closely held belief—the reportedly close relationship of this process to panic attacks. Although some have argued that recursive anxiety is a fear of panic attacks and develops as the result of these attacks (e.g., Goldstein & Chambless, 1978), Reiss and his associates (Reiss, 1987; Reiss et al., 1986) have made an interesting case for the position that recursive anxiety need not be based on panic attacks but may result from the fear of a variety of consequences learned in a diversity of ways. Clinical observations also support a number of factors in the initiation of recursive anxiety; thus, the experience of panic need not be present in the history of affected individuals.

I have hypothesized that paradoxical intention (among other exposure-based procedures) is a necessary component of a treatment program when recursive anxiety is present and may not be helpful—may perhaps even be detrimental—when recursive anxiety does not form a part of the anxiety profile. If this hypothesis is correct, and preliminary data appear to support it (Ascher, 1984, 1985; Ascher & Schotte, 1987), then determination of the status of the individual with respect to recursiveness would have significant treatment implications. However, it is common that the recursive-anxiety component can remain obscured by the more salient aspects of the presenting complaint during the initial stages of therapy and sometimes throughout the entire course of treatment. Thus, a person with a specific anxiety-based complaint—for example, acrophobia—complicated by a recursive anxiety component might initially appear indistinguishable from an acrophobic individual who was unencumbered by recursive-anxiety factors. Although the use of imaginal systematic desensitization with the latter client would result in neutralizing the phobic discomfort, it would not generally produce satisfactory results with the acrophobia complicated by a recursive element.

Difficulty in differentiating the presence or absence of this component continues, even though several inventories (Chambless, Caputo, Gallagher, & Bright, 1984; Reiss et al., 1986) have been developed specifically to identify recursive anxiety. At the present time, in clinical practice with clients complaining of anxiety disorders, the behavior therapist must depend largely on careful questioning during the behavioral analysis to resolve the issue of recursive anxiety.

Before I discuss methods for identifying this aspect of anxiety in the therapeutic setting, I should mention certain observations and hypotheses relating to the dynamics of this phenomenon. First, a basic illustration: contrast clients who have a clinically significant level of discomfort that is associated with some environmental stimulus complex and that is complicated by recursive anxiety with clients having the same presenting complaint but who have not demonstrated the recursive element. For example, people reporting simple public-speaking phobia typically avoid public-speaking assignments whenever possible, anticipate discomfort when it is necessary to speak to an audience, are uncomfortable throughout the presentation, and look forward to and are greatly relieved at the conclusion of the address. Clients with public-speaking phobia that is accompanied by a recursive element experience all this and more. The additional concern is the hypothesized loss of control and consequent embarrassing circumstances following peak levels of anxiety. For example, such individuals might fear that—once in front of an audience—the anxiety with which they began their presentation will increase and will be incapacitating. They fear standing for a long period of time silently frozen before the assemblage, or they may fear vomiting or losing bladder or bowel control. Some anticipate emitting word salad or merely blushing or perspiring. Others are certain that in the midst of their presentation their anxiety will cause them to run from the room. During the period preceding public-speaking events, these individuals experience anticipatory anxiety and, as seems to be the case with most of those who exhibit recursive anxiety, focus on a specific aspect of sympathetic activity.

This response acquires the property of signaling that they are in a dangerous situation and are potentially at risk for losing control; it becomes the presenting complaint or at least a central aspect of the presenting complaint. Thus, clients who tend to perspire when under stress may notice slight perspiring as they approach the auditorium. The perspiration, their interpretation of it, and their failing attempt to control it all serve to exacerbate the total complex of sympathetic activity that led to perspiring initially. This, of course, results in further perspiration in a self-maintaining, circular fashion. The term "recursive" was chosen as the label for this process because the definitions of recursion, "the determination of a succession of elements . . . by operation on one or more preceding elements," and of recursive, "constituting a procedure that can repeat itself indefinitely or until a specified condition is met" (*Webster's New Collegiate Dictionary,* 1977, p. 967), highlight this dynamic.

No matter what the initial content may be, the basis of the hypothesized disastrous consequence is typically the performance of some behavior that may receive negative social evaluation. The focus might be on behavior typically associated with disapproval—for example, responses resulting from mental disorders, the effects of narcotics, or the excessive use of alcohol. However, even behavior that is normally considered to be harmless or socially neutral (e.g., cardiac arrest, stroke, loss of consciousness caused by illness, observable sympathetic nervous system activity) may be interpreted by the individual in a manner that generates concerns about negative social evaluation. For example, a member of a college faculty was concerned that if she blushed when presenting a lecture, this would be interpreted by her students as indicating that she lacked sufficient familiarity with her material.

The ensuing two cases illustrate the social focus of the recursive syndrome. The first example refers to a 37-year-old married woman who complained of symptoms of agoraphobia. Exploration of the recursive element of her concerns produced a typical response. (The case material used in the present chapter is modified to disguise any identifiable details about the individual and to emphasize the most relevant content while abbreviating less important transitional or contextual information.)

CLIENT: I will be some place, and I'll have a stroke.
THERAPIST: And then . . .
CLIENT: . . . or a seizure, or something.
THERAPIST: And then what?

CLIENT: I'll fall down.

THERAPIST: Yes. And then what will happen?

CLIENT: I don't know. I guess I would fall down and people would begin to look and come over.

THERAPIST: And, what do you feel would be the problem with that?

CLIENT: I would be surrounded by all those people.

THERAPIST: Looking to help you, I suppose. You don't like to be surrounded by people.

CLIENT: No, it's not just being surrounded by people.

THERAPIST: What else?

CLIENT: I'm not sure.

THERAPIST: What would they be thinking?

CLIENT: They might not know what's wrong and think I was drunk or crazy. Somebody might say, "What's wrong with her, is she crazy?" The others might start to wonder.

It is common that such individuals fear that their behavior will be misinterpreted by witnesses and labeled as socially inappropriate. As mentioned previously, the recursive factor may be a variant of—or a component of—social phobia. This hypothesis relates to another that explains the comfort many agoraphobic clients experience when they are accompanied by others in their travels to potentially dangerous places. It is assumed, and is often reported, that such companions are enlisted to provide assistance in case disaster should strike. That is, if the agoraphobic person suffers the feared cardiac arrest, he or she knows that the friend or relative will have more interest in obtaining proper emergency aid than a stranger would. Further questioning often indicates that the assistance the agoraphobic individuals would require should they lose control would be that of having their companion intercede for them with observers and explain that the person was not crazy, drunk, or behaving in an otherwise inappropriate manner.

Individuals who exhibit recursive anxiety maintain an unrealistically elevated regard for the opinions of others, associated with their propensity toward low self-esteem and flagging self-confidence. In fact, it is the predicted disapproval of significant others that appears to form the core around which the vortex of recursive anxiety is organized. Affected individuals thus assume that they are the object of constant detailed scrutiny by others, and they invest certain of their own behaviors with a disproportionate amount of social significance.

In the second example, a 26-year-old man with a promising career as a corporate executive complained that he experienced discomfort during interactions associated with professional activities as well as during certain other interpersonal exchanges. In fact, clinical interviews established the existence of generalized social anxiety in the presence of all but a few very close relationships as well as considerable social phobia. The degree of anxiety was correlated with his desire to appear calm. The more important the person and/or the circumstances of the interaction, the greater would be his desire to look comfortable, and, consequently, the greater would be his experience of anxiety. The following material was taken from our first session.

THERAPIST: Now we see the wide variety of people and circumstances that are discomforting. What is different about those conditions that are uncomfortable as compared with those that are not?

CLIENT: It's just that some are more important than others.

THERAPIST: In what way?

CLIENT: I don't know. For different reasons.

THERAPIST: Give me some examples.

CLIENT: At work, the more important the person, the more anxious I am.

THERAPIST: O.K., let's stay with the work situation for now. Why is a more important person less comfortable for you to speak with than a less important person?

CLIENT: I guess because they're more important.

THERAPIST: Well, O.K. then, what makes a person more important?

CLIENT: If they supervise me or my supervisors I suppose.

THERAPIST: If they evaluate you and have some control over your future at XYZ, Inc.?

CLIENT: Yes, I suppose so.

THERAPIST: So, perhaps you wish to impress them?

CLIENT: Definitely.

THERAPIST: How do you do that?

CLIENT: I don't know, I guess the usual ways . . .

THERAPIST: And, how else?

CLIENT: I don't know.

THERAPIST: How about feeling comfortable with them?

CLIENT: Yes, that too.

THERAPIST: Why is that important?

CLIENT: Well, you want to appear calm, cool, and collected.

THERAPIST: What if you don't?

CLIENT: Then they think there's something wrong.

THERAPIST: What could be wrong, what do "they" think?

CLIENT: That you don't feel comfortable with them, you don't belong, you don't fit in, you don't have confidence, you can't do the work.

THERAPIST: How would they know that you don't feel comfortable with them?

CLIENT: Because I'm anxious.

THERAPIST: How can they tell?
CLIENT: Sometimes I have tremors.
THERAPIST: Often?
CLIENT: Only when I get very anxious.
THERAPIST: And, how often does that happen?
CLIENT: Well, I've been getting very anxious more often recently.
THERAPIST: And the tremors?
CLIENT: Not as much of an increase.
THERAPIST: When you have tremors, what are your concerns?
CLIENT: I think that now everyone can tell I'm anxious.
THERAPIST: So you try not to have these so that people do not get the wrong idea.
CLIENT: Right.
THERAPIST: How do you keep from having them at times when you ordinarily might?
CLIENT: I tell myself not to be nervous. I try to distract myself by thinking of other things; things I enjoy away from work.
THERAPIST: Do these things work?
CLIENT: Sometimes.
THERAPIST: When?
CLIENT: When I'm less anxious. When it's less important.
THERAPIST: But these are times when you probably don't have tremors anyway.
CLIENT: I suppose.
THERAPIST: Have you ever been successful in ending tremors once they began other than by leaving the situation or by spontaneously calming down?
CLIENT: Not usually. Occasionally. I guess not.

In this example, the client displays social phobia complicated by a recursive element—the need to appear to be calm and to suppress tremors—a difficult task at best. He enters situations with anxiety and perhaps the slightest of tremors. The tremors are associated with anxiety that he attempts to control. His inability to regain a feeling of calmness increases the experience of anxiety and exacerbates the tremors. They become more noticeable to him and are accompanied by increasing discomfort. In addition, because of the offensive meaning with which the tremors are labeled, they become a font of negative self-statements, images of catastrophe, and further anxiety. He thinks that if his anxiety is noticed then higher-ranking executives will draw unfavorable conclusions regarding his place in the firm. This will lead to major difficulties in his life. The resulting motivation to reduce anxiety and tremors serves only to intensify this recursive process. In the case of this client, loss of control and panic were not issues, merely the experience of signs of discomfort that might be discerned by others.

To summarize, the recursive-anxiety component is composed of two major factors. The first highlights activity of the sympathetic nervous system in a self-maintaining circular process. The threat is that individuals will be forced to endure high levels of anxiety and lose control. The total experience involved in their awareness of this discomforting physiological response, and their apparent inability to maintain control, intensifies anxiety. Perception of increased levels of anxiety serves to augment each of the physical components of sympathetic arousal, including those that specifically function as danger signals. Recognition of the elevated magnitude of the danger signal results in the increase of general anxiety. The second factor details the nature of the disaster that the danger signal purportedly predicts. That is, at high levels of anxiety experienced in difficult social situations, individuals fear that they will lose control and will exhibit inappropriate behavior resulting in negative social evaluation. This in turn will lead to generalized deleterious effects on their lives, presently and in the future.

The presence of a recursive-anxiety component suggests important implications for the composition of the treatment program of any anxiety-based complaint or anxiety disorder. Chief among these is its hypothesized close association with social phobia. A preponderance of individuals who seek psychotherapy suffer some level of interpersonal discomfort. However, in most cases (e.g., simple phobias), this can be ignored, at least initially, in favor of focusing on the presenting complaint. In contrast, the appearance of a recursive-anxiety complex typically suggests a clinically significant level of social phobia that must be addressed as a pivotal component of the clinical profile in any complete program of behavioral treatment.

Some Comments on Assessment

Although inventories that attempt to highlight recursive anxiety have been published, there are problems with each that limit their effectiveness both in research and in clinical settings. Thus, because of incomplete validation, the questionnaires developed by Chambless et al. (1984) have not been shown to be more useful than measures of general anxiety. In her most recent paper (Chambless & Gracely, 1989), Chambless mitigates this criticism of her questionnaires to some extent by obtaining promising psychometric results using samples that include a range of nonagoraphobic anxiety disorders.

Reiss et al. (1986) attempted to distinguish their Anxiety Sensitivity Inventory (ASI) from general procedures for the assessment of anxiety.

They hypothesized that individuals exhibiting anxiety sensitivity would experience a greater magnitude of fear and that this would, in turn, be related to conditioned reactions to a wide variety of environmental stimuli. They were able to demonstrate a stronger relationship between the ASI and the Fear Survey Scale II (a list of commonly observable stimuli that the individual rates with respect to degree of discomfort) than between this specific measure of fearfulness and the frequency of occurrence of anxiety symptoms.

Although this represents a successive approximation to their intent of producing an inventory that differentiates general anxiety from anxiety sensitivity, Reiss et al. (1986) are yet some distance away from satisfactorily achieving their goal. This is because the Fear Survey Scale and their measure of frequency of occurrence of anxiety symptoms are limited in scope. An additional problem incorporated into their validating procedures and that of Chambless et al. (1984) remains the heavy, if not sole, reliance on data from agoraphobic individuals. The difficulty with this approach is the extremely high correlation (and consequent lack of variance) between agoraphobia and recursive anxiety. This obscures the ability of any questionnaire to differentiate high elevations of anxiety from recursiveness. In order for an inventory to prove itself as a valid measure of the recursive process, it must be able to distinguish between those who exhibit recursive anxiety and those who do not. This requires the selection of clients presenting with nonagoraphobic anxiety disorders, since it is only in these cases that there is sufficient variance in recursive anxiety to test the sensitivity of recursive-anxiety questionnaires. Chambless and Gracely (1989) show the promise of the Chambless et al. (1984) questionnaires in this regard, since their data do tend to verify the variable relationship between recursive anxiety and agoraphobia versus nonagoraphobic anxiety disorders.

The final criticism of these questionnaires is more subjective, since it relates to my conception of the phenomenon of recursive anxiety. The questionnaires emphasize affected clients' attention to the physiological components of anxiety. From my perspective, the recursive-anxiety syndrome is a multifaceted phenomenon with a significant social phobic element. To the extent that this view is supported by subsequent data, then these questionnaires, by virtue of the stress they place on one aspect of recursive anxiety, may not be shown to be useful in diagnosing this facet of anxiety disorders. Similarly, if social phobia is a basic factor in the maintenance and treatment of recursive anxiety, then a useful measure of the existence of this syndrome must include this significant interpersonal component.

The concern of individuals who exhibit recursive anxiety is the effect of the experience of fear on their behavior, particularly with respect to the possibility of loss of control. Therefore, although a client may have discomfort regarding an external stimulus complex (e.g., driving across bridges), his or her attention is quickly drawn back to himself or to herself. Thus, in attempting to ascertain whether or not a recursive component is complicating an anxiety-based presenting complaint, one line of questioning that has been helpful focuses on individuals' expectations of involuntary sustained exposure to fear-associated circumstances. That is, clients are asked what it is that they think would happen if they were to be required, by forces beyond their control, to remain in a difficult setting for an indefinite period of time. The purpose of such questions is to explore concerns regarding the consequence that follows the hypothesized loss of control.

If clients do experience recursive anxiety, then it is very possible that the dynamics have been incorporated into a well-rehearsed story. The presentation of recursive-anxiety concerns early in the course of therapy is fortunately a common occurrence and allows clinicians to plan in advance for the additional problems generated by this process. Sometimes, however, clients do have recursive concerns, but, as a result of motivation to avoid anxiety, they have not fully formulated or thought through the details of the consequences of "dangerous" situations. Under these circumstances, the clinician must encourage clients to remain with the anxiety-provoking images that have been presented in an effort to ascertain the details of the hypothesized disaster. Clients who do not have a recursive element to their anxiety profiles will, of course, also fail to report such consequences, but in these cases, they will be quite forthright in indicating to the clinician that no further investigation need be undertaken. In contrast, the previously described individuals whose complaints are complicated by recursive anxiety (but who fail to report well-constructed disastrous consequences) typically provide some clue suggesting the need for additional inquiry on the part of the clinician.

The previous example involving a 32-year-old agoraphobic woman depicted presentation of the dynamics of recursive complications in a straightforward manner. In the following instance, a 29-year-old single woman complained of generalized social discomfort in addition to specific low-level phobic complaints. She required some assistance in disclosing her recursive concerns.

THERAPIST: What is your experience of anxiety in these situations?
CLIENT: I get a funny feeling in my stomach and chest.
THERAPIST: What happens as you become more anxious?
CLIENT: I get warm; my heart beats faster.
THERAPIST: And then what happens?
CLIENT: If I get too frightened I leave.

THERAPIST: What happens that indicates to you that you are "too frightened" and must leave?

CLIENT: I think when I get to the point that I feel warm and my heart beats so loud and fast that I think people can hear it.

THERAPIST: Can they?

CLIENT: No, but you know, you think they can.

THERAPIST: Have you ever continued to remain in a situation beyond the point at which you feel warm and notice your heart beating?

CLIENT: No. Sometimes I leave before, but I never stay longer.

THERAPIST: Have you never been in a situation where you could not leave, something involving work for example?

CLIENT: I always leave, I make some excuse. I can always find some way of getting out. After all this time you get good at it.

THERAPIST: Well, suppose you couldn't get out?

CLIENT: I can't.

THERAPIST: Have you never thought of what might happen if you were caught in some social situation and you could not leave?

CLIENT: No. I always manage to get out, even when I might imagine it. I sometimes try to imagine the worst thing that could happen. You know, before a party or a meeting, to try to calm down. I always imagine leaving when I get too anxious.

THERAPIST: But, what if you couldn't. What would happen if you were trapped some place and were unable to leave. Suppose, for example, that you were in an elevator at work. You had stepped into the elevator with several important people. Who might they be? (*She names several individuals.*) You are riding in the elevator, perhaps engaged in conversation, and without warning the elevator stops. What would happen?

CLIENT: I would be very frightened. In the first place, I would not have gotten onto the elevator with them but would've made an excuse and taken another one.

THERAPIST: But, imagine the situation that I have suggested.

CLIENT: I would be very scared.

THERAPIST: As time went on what would happen?

CLIENT: I would just be very scared.

THERAPIST: Try to imagine that you are actually in the situation that I have described. Close your eyes and imagine it. Tell me when the scene is clear.

CLIENT: O.K.

THERAPIST: Now imagine that you are quite anxious. You have been in the elevator for some time. There is some difficulty in repairing the problem. You are told that it may take a while before they can get it to operate. You are becoming increasingly anxious. You feel warm, the sound of your heartbeat seems to echo from the walls of the elevator. What is happening now?

CLIENT: I would get so anxious I wouldn't know what would happen.

THERAPIST: You would not know what would happen, or you would not know what was happening?

CLIENT: Both . . . what would happen and what was happening.

THERAPIST: Well, by not knowing what was happening does that mean that you would be so anxious that you would not know what was happening to you?

CLIENT: Yes, I think so. It's never happened, but I think that if I hung around long enough I would get very frightened and not know what I was doing. I might not pay attention to what was going on around me; lose control of myself.

THERAPIST: Could anybody else in the elevator know that you had lost control?

CLIENT: Yes.

THERAPIST: How?

CLIENT: I might go crazy and scream and tell them to get me out of here, or bang on the walls. I don't know—go crazy.

THERAPIST: I see. I suppose that *would* be discernible to others.

In this instance, the client had a recursive concern but had never formally constructed the specific circumstances of events following the experience of peak anxiety levels. She probably had a vague understanding that dire social consequences would result, but the mere thought of remaining in a discomforting situation beyond the point at which she felt that she could maintain control was too anxiety-provoking to consider. There is a quality about such individuals' presentations that suggests that even though they initially deny consequences to increasing levels of anxiety, further exploration is warranted.

On the other hand, anxiety-based problems and anxiety disorders other than agoraphobia are more commonly unencumbered by a recursive element. Here individuals clearly indicate that the presenting complaint is devoid of recursive complexity. The conviction that they display in this regard further reinforces the uncomplicated status of their behavioral concerns. A 40-year-old married male security guard reported anxiety in elevators. The presence or absence of others did not seem to influence his level of discomfort. The following conversation was extracted from the second session.

THERAPIST: Imagine that you were in the small service elevator with the building manager, your supervisor, and Mr. ______ [the director of the security firm]. Has this ever occurred?

CLIENT: As a matter of fact, this or something like this comes up from time to time.

THERAPIST: Do you get more upset when these particular people are on the elevator with you than when you are there alone, or with people whom you may not know, or with friends?

CLIENT: No. Unless they are there because of me, as I told you.

THERAPIST: But then that has less to do with the elevator. So, suppose that you are in the elevator with these people, and it stops between floors. Has this every happened to you?

CLIENT: No.

THERAPIST: Well suppose that it did happen, how would you feel?

CLIENT: Very anxious.

THERAPIST: What would your experience be like?

CLIENT: As I said, I start to sweat, my stomach gets butterflies. I would think, "I wonder when this thing is going to start? Can I get out the trap door?"

THERAPIST: And then what?

CLIENT: What?

THERAPIST: What would happen if you were unable to get out for several hours?

CLIENT: It would be murder. I would sweat like a pig.

THERAPIST: Go on.

CLIENT: I would keep on being anxious and hoping to get out.

THERAPIST: What would happen if the anxiety became very intense? Could you lose control of yourself, do something embarrassing?

CLIENT: Like what?

THERAPIST: I don't know, think about it. Close your eyes and imagine the scene: you are in the elevator with the manager, your supervisor, and Mr. Big; the elevator stops between floors; the maintenance crew tells you it will take several hours before they can free you. Imagine that you are actually in that situation, and tell me when you can feel the experience, see the people.

CLIENT: O.K.

THERAPIST: Now what will happen?

CLIENT: As I said, I would be very uncomfortable there.

THERAPIST: You are very anxious, you have already been in the situation for several hours. You cannot hold on any longer. What would you do?

CLIENT: What could I do? I would stay until I could get out.

THERAPIST: And, you could maintain control of yourself for all that time.

CLIENT: I'd be very uncomfortable, but sure.

Finally, the nature of the concerns embodied in the recursive-anxiety process suggests that affected individuals would be vulnerable to characteristics associated with higher levels of anxiety. In contrast, there is a lower probability that these qualities would be associated with clients presenting with relatively uncomplicated anxiety-based complaints. Therefore, symptoms of high levels of anxiety such as panic, depersonalization, feelings of unreality, unusual physical sensations, and the effects of hyperventilation should direct the clinician to the possibility of a recursive-anxiety component, although these symptoms do not guarantee the existence of such a process. The comments in this section were meant to suggest the nature of the assessment process rather than to provide a complete delineation of an assessment procedure.

In sum, at present the clinical interview remains the most effective method for identifying the existence of a recursive element of an anxiety disorder or of an anxiety-based complaint. Relevant questions should be formulated to reveal individuals' views of issues that would be significant in the event of the possible presence of recursive anxiety. Pertinent topics on which to focus include: What qualitative changes does the client think will occur, both in the physiological experience of the individual and in behavior observable to others, as his or her level of anxiety increases? Does the client think that loss of control is a possibility, and, if so, what would the qualities of this process be? Does the client think that people can tell that he or she is becoming anxious, and, if so, what will be his or her associated thoughts? When experiencing anxiety, does the client focus on a specific aspect of sympathetic activity, and, if so, what is the meaning of this reaction for him or her? No matter how the disastrous consequence is described, is there significant concern about the possibility of negative social evaluation by observers? Are some observers more discomforting than others? What would be the nature of this negative evaluation? What would be some important aspects of the consequences of negative evaluation? Information regarding these and related issues can assist in developing a clear picture of the character of the recursive complication, should it exist.

Paradoxical Intention

Although techniques considered to be paradoxical have been used in a behavioral context for some time (e.g., Dunlap, 1928), the first person to employ a paradoxical method in a systematic fashion with anxiety-based difficulties was Viktor Frankl (1939, 1947). He labeled the procedure "paradoxical intention," using the term "paradoxical" in its medical sense (i.e., referring to a drug or procedure that produces a reaction in a circumscribed group of people that is opposite to that which commonly occurs in the broader population). The "intention" or wish that he encouraged his patients to embrace was the very thing that stimulated what he termed anticipatory anxiety. That is, certain individuals approach a situation that demands behavior associated with activity of the sympathetic nervous system (e.g., sexual responding) with apprehension regarding the success of the performance. It is this anticipatory anxiety that serves to impair the desired performance and that, in turn, generates additional anxiety.

The resulting anxiety ensures the self-fulfilling nature of the apprehension by obstructing attainment of the goal. Thus, in the case of insomnia accompanied by a recursive-anxiety element, the person with a history of sleep difficulty, fearing the inability to fall asleep, will try to control the process and will thereby generate high levels of anxiety that are incompatible with sleep. In this situation, the paradoxical intention instruction is simple: suggest to the individual that he or she get into bed with the intention of *remaining awake* for the entire night.

The efficacy of paradoxical intention is based on the fundamental principle that clients intend the very behavior that they had been avoiding. In this way, the self-maintaining circular process is broken, since endeavoring to perform the undesirable behavior is incompatible with—and eventually neutralizes—anticipatory anxiety. Frankl (1985) suggests that a wish and a fear regarding the same behavioral goal are incompatible. When the person is able to embrace the desire to remain awake, the fear of not falling asleep dissipates, permitting the onset of sleep.

Although Frankl's definition of paradox and his explanation of its efficacy in therapy are important in understanding its role in the treatment of anxiety disorders, alternative views that hold potential value for this area of behavioral problems have been suggested (e.g., Seltzer, 1986). For example, I have proposed (Ascher, 1989) that the emotional-processing literature (Lang, 1977; Rachman, 1980; Foa & Kozak, 1986) can provide direction for enhancing the efficacy of paradoxical intention with anxiety disorders.

For the present discussion, paradoxical intention is considered to be a behavioral procedure with recursive anxiety forming its primary focus of treatment. The common definition of paradox is quite useful in supporting this conception (i.e., information that contradicts received opinion). Specifically, the contravention here is through a suggestion, by the therapist, of behavioral restraint with respect to a particular goal. The therapist encourages the client to maintain, with great vigor, the problem behavior at its presenting level or, if possible, at a level that is even more discomforting. As mentioned in Chapter 1 of this volume, it has been hypothesized that the paradox in this approach is the inability of the client to execute the therapist's directive. If the client genuinely attempts to achieve the goal of becoming more symptomatic (e.g., increasing anxiety), he or she will not be successful but will instead experience the converse (e.g., increased calmness) (Bateson, Jackson, Haley, & Weakland, 1957; Watzlawick, Beavin, & Jackson, 1967).

Administration

Paradoxical intention requires two things of the anxious client: to relinquish control over anxiety and to will the fearful results that he or she attributes to anxiety. Because these are fairly arduous undertakings, a vital part of the procedure involves extensive explanation of the dynamics of the presenting complaint and of the manner in which a cognitive-behavioral treatment program organized around paradoxical intention may be of assistance. The material that follows was taken from the case of a 31-year-old married male executive who complained about anxiety and perspiration. Once again, social phobia played a major role. During the third session, I related his experiences to my understanding of recursive anxiety.

THERAPIST: It is understandable that a person in your position would experience greater anxiety under certain circumstances and with specific people relative to other circumstances and other people. However, I believe that you go one step further, and this leads to difficulty. Those who supervise and evaluate you expect that you will be anxious when there is pressure. Both they and you, as well as your peers, would be able to accurately assess the relative amount of anxiety that a person in your position would experience under varying conditions. They expect you to function, but they understand that you will be anxious. You, however, do not accept this. You expect perfection from yourself either in isolation of your supervisors or because you feel that they expect perfection, and perfection means no anxiety—perfect calmness. A problem lies in the fact that you are not perfectly calm but attempt to perpetrate a fraud, so to speak, by acting as if you are perfectly calm, completely free of anxiety, when this is not the case. Of course, the more significant the event, the more important will it be that you maintain the fraud and the more difficult it will be to do this, because the anxiety will be increasingly great . . .

The client recognized that he viewed his superiors as requiring perfection from him and was not quite ready to believe that this was not realistic.

THERAPIST: Look at the additional stress that you undergo relative to those on your level. They are anxious in specific situations but are able to function since the focus of their attention remains on their work. What you do that is different, and that exacerbates reasonable levels of anxiety, is that you focus on the anxiety. You are not primarily there for the same purpose as are your colleagues—to work. You are there engaged in reducing anxiety. You provide it with special meaning that others do not. Everyone knows that there is a stressful situation, supervisor and supervisee; low levels of anxiety are a reasonable part of the situation, even moderate levels under certain circumstances. You remove anxiety from its natural context and emphasize an idiosyncratic meaning for it. You have decided that you should not experience anxiety at work, and that you should, at all costs, never display discomfort should it exist. This is because you feel that if others thought that you were anxious they would assume that you were not "executive material," that you were not capable of moving up because you could not handle the "heat." So, rather than focusing on your performance and putting all of your energy and intellect into this, you are engaged in the task of reducing anxiety and appearing to be calm. In this way you reduce the quality of your performance, which probably serves to increase anxiety.

CLIENT: How do you know that they don't expect me to be calm? That they don't see me anxious and think that I won't make it?

THERAPIST: Several things suggest that I am correct. First, has anyone ever mentioned to you that they noticed that you were anxious or perspiring?

CLIENT: No. Well, once or twice someone mentioned that it was warm. But nothing about anxiety.

THERAPIST: And have any of the officers indicated that they demanded superhuman behavior from you, such as robot-like calmness in stressful situations?

CLIENT: Not that I can recall.

THERAPIST: Another reason that I feel that my position is correct is one I mentioned a while ago. I assume that most of these supervisors are successful, at least in part, because they understand and are sensitive to the behavior of others. That you should be anxious under certain situations would not come as a surprise to them. They would expect you to perform adequately, but they would not expect you to be anxiety-free. Does this make sense?

CLIENT: I suppose so.

THERAPIST: And finally, even though you are anxious, and even if it were true that these individuals would be critical of you if they were aware of it—and I emphasize that they would not—they would not notice it. Very often, even though we may feel anxious, others do not notice it. The next time you must give a presentation and you feel anxious, ask a friend if he noticed. Ordinarily he will not.

CLIENT: You're right there. I have given presentations and have been very anxious, and no one has said anything about it after, even when I asked indirectly.

THERAPIST: This is because the levels of anxiety that you have reached at work are not sufficiently high to generate outward signs. More important, people are fairly self-absorbed. They are not interested in you, they are concerned about themselves and their performance and what others are thinking of them, even the top executives. People are involved in their own thoughts. Subtle changes in your behavior or appearance will be ignored by them. If you were to flush or to perspire, this would go unnoticed. . . . A further point is that even if they were to notice slight perspiration—a very low-probability event, I emphasize—they would not necessarily attribute it to anxiety. You have said that your evaluations are generally excellent. Your supervisors would have little reason to assume that you are particularly anxious. They might therefore attribute the perspiration to a variety of other causes including the temperature in the room. We all know that some people are more sensitive to temperature than are others. . . . Now you have explained your experiences to yourself as you have previously related to me. And, while this explanation fits the data, it is only one of many possible explanations. I am suggesting that it is troublesome for you and that there are alternatives that you might consider. Does this make sense so far with respect to your experiences?

CLIENT: Yes, but where do we go from here?

THERAPIST: Well, let's just continue with this line of reasoning for a while. Imagine that you are scheduled to present a report at the Friday conference in several weeks. Many of the corporation's top officers would be in attendance, and many of the junior people would be reporting on their activities. This could be somewhat stressful, true?

CLIENT: Very true.

THERAPIST: Some time before the meeting you might not be very anxious, but as the meaning drew near, your anxiety would increase. Just before entering the room in which the meeting is to be held you will be quite anxious, and you may notice that you are perspiring a bit. Now you remember the explanation of the activity of the sympathetic nervous system. Well, perspiration is a normal component of this process, and the reaction is a normal response to a situation that you believe to be dangerous. Not dangerous in the sense of being life-threatening but in the sense, certainly, of threatening your way of life. Now as you notice more cues that have previously been associated with danger—that is, as the meeting progresses—you will experience greater anxiety. But there is another factor. As you become more anxious, your perspiration becomes more noticeable to you, but not necessarily to others, as I have said. So, you detect some perspiration, and you begin to think about it. You are certain that others notice it and that they are aware of its basis in anxiety. Then, it is only natural that they should be critical of you and all of your previous work. You begin to fantasize that you receive notice that your services are no longer required by the corporation. I don't know how far you actually get with this soap opera each time, but there is certainly more to it: you must move to another corporation and take a reduction in salary; this causes a long period of stress in your family for a variety of reasons; deteriorating mental health on your part; possible divorce; alcoholism; then, in the final scene, we see you on a vent at 15th and Walnut.

CLIENT: That's funny—but I have thought about similar possibilities.

THERAPIST: I know, I did not exactly make this whole thing up or I would be able to write dramas for Hollywood. So here you are, about to enter the meeting, and you notice a bit of perspiration. You have some of these thoughts. In addition to external cues associated with increasing anxiety, these thoughts are quite discomforting. So, your anxiety increases. What happens when your anxiety increases?

CLIENT: More perspiration?

THERAPIST: Possibly. Certainly you *think* that there is more perspiration. In any case, real or imagined, the increase in perspiration results in an increase in anxiety that serves to increase perspiration. So you can see that the process has a self-maintaining quality. Or, more properly, according to your information, a pernicious spiral. You experience increments of anxiety leading to what you think will be a loss of control and the embarrassing behavior [i.e., leaving the meeting in a disruptive manner with associated grave social and professional consequences]. This fear of losing control at high levels of anxiety is at the base of the problem since you think that you can prevent such an occurrence by maintaining control over anxiety.

CLIENT: I think you have the picture, especially the losing control. This is the most frightening part of it, as you say.

Before I described the treatment program, I provided the client with information that was aimed at increasing his understanding of his complaint. This was accomplished, in part, by incorporating his experience into a cohesive system that also happened to be congruent with the use of paradoxical intention. Unexplainable or unpredictable behavior tends to be discomforting; an explanation of the client's troubling behavior that seems reasonable to him or to her relieves this source of anxiety. If the therapist's account is compelling, it may also substitute for the client's preexisting hypotheses—especially those that generate maladaptive avoidance behavior. For example, some individuals develop the idea that the sudden relief of extreme anxiety that they sometimes experience while they are still in the dangerous situation represents a "lucky escape." This is not adaptive, since it assumes that there is something from which escape is necessary. It is important that the client become aware of alternate explanations that fit the facts and are more compatible with the idea of therapeutic change.

The introductory explanation therefore includes both the client's understanding of the circumstances and the proposed more adaptive hypotheses. Thus, this client's assumption that observers expect him to experience no anxiety even in highly stressful situations is contrasted with the more reasonable possibility that they assume that he is anxious but will nevertheless be able to perform effectively. This position was supported by a variety of points, each of which again related to the client's experiences. In a similar fashion, his focus on the control of anxiety rather than on the efficiency of his performance was emphasized and compared with the approach followed by his peers who, although they experience anxiety, view it as a normal and acceptable response to the situation.

In addition to generally increasing comfort through explanation, the introduction prepares the client for *in vivo* paradoxical intention by attempting to neutralize anxiety associated with loss of control and with the disastrous consequence. Accomplishing this goal is of major importance, since these concerns maintain the avoidance behavior that forms the presenting complaint and will, if unchecked, impede therapeutic progress. Furthermore, in order to execute the paradoxical intention, the client must be willing to risk the possibility of loss of control and a social catastrophe. The more realistic these events seem, the less willing he or she will be to employ the paradoxical suggestions.

Modification of these fears can be undertaken in a number of ways. A variety of cognitive and cognitive-behavioral procedures can be effectively employed in this regard. In addition, humor is an important device in reducing what Frankl refers to as the client's "serious concern" regarding anxiety and its repercussions. In the present case, the client was informed that: observers either understood or were ignorant of his anxiety; others with similar levels of anxiety coped with it more adaptively; he had no direct control over his anxiety, and, in fact, attempts to control served only to exacerbate it; he had never suffered loss of control or a disastrous social consequence even though he had endured high levels of anxiety.

CLIENT: What do you mean by "following the rules"?

THERAPIST: Well, a rule is a principle, a relationship, say, between an antecedent event and some behavior. For example, you think that your perspiration results in negative interpretation about you by observers. Therefore, when you notice perspiration, you must do something to reduce it and control your anxiety. You respond to this rule by using certain strategies that have largely been ineffective or, worse, have actually exacerbated the problem. These rules are based on certain assumptions that I believe to be unreasonable. The most important of these is that high levels of anxiety will lead to loss of control and to a disastrous consequence. Let me tell you why I do not agree with this. First, have you ever been in a meeting from which you could not escape even though you became increasingly anxious?

CLIENT: Yes, several times.

THERAPIST: And have you ever lost control or behaved in an embarrassing fashion?

CLIENT: No, never. But, I have been very anxious.

THERAPIST: I'm sure. But, like this most recent occasion, you eventually calm down. You continue to go through this because you do not accept your experience. You think, each time that this happens, that you have had a lucky escape. The next time, you think, some catastrophe really will occur. Actually, each occurrence provides you with the total picture. There is no more. There never has been and there never will be a social disaster. I think that you agree with this when we speak together and when you are *not* particularly anxious. Is that true?

CLIENT: Yes. I can agree with what you're saying now, and there are times when I feel very confident that I don't believe anything will happen. But when I get anxious, and especially at work, at a meeting, I am afraid of what could happen.

THERAPIST: That's part of the difficulty. When you are relatively comfortable, you realize the absurdity of the relationship. But when you are anxious, your intellect seems to be overcome, and you allow yourself to become mired in your fantasy. So, what you must do is to demonstrate to yourself that this relationship between anxiety and loss of control is fictitious even when you are extremely anxious. Once you have accomplished this, the need for avoidance will be arrested, and it will have the effect of modulating your anxiety experiences. But these benefits will not be easily earned. The bond that you formed long ago between anxiety and avoidance is now quite strong. It will be difficult to break it. . . . Therefore, I am not certain that your determination is sufficient to embark on such a rigorous undertaking.

CLIENT: I'm interested in any suggestions that you might have. Nothing could be worse than spending the rest of my life with this constant fear and anxiety.

THERAPIST: The scenario that I mentioned last week forms a good point of departure for a description of the procedure that I will suggest. You recall that I thought that you approached a difficult meeting with some trepidation, and for you, this means that you will begin to focus on perspiration. With the realization that you are perspiring comes anxiety and, naturally, more perspiration. What results is a self-maintaining circular process. Supporting this process is your concern that your superiors notice that you are anxious and attribute negative meaning to it, along with your fear that at high levels of anxiety you will lose control and do something that will cause you to lose your position in the firm. In order to prevent this hypothesized tragedy, you engage in behavior that you are convinced helps you to maintain control over this anxiety. As I have indicated, however, you cannot control anxiety directly, and attempts to do this serve only to aggravate the situation. Therefore, what I will suggest is that when you are in a circumstance similar to the one which I have previously described, you relinquish control.

CLIENT: I don't understand. How do I relinquish control if, as you say, I don't have any in the first place?

THERAPIST: Well, that's an interesting point. I am suggesting that you do not exert direct control over anxiety, but you act as though you do. And it is this behavior that I ask you to discontinue. As I indicated earlier, it is ironic that your attempts to reduce anxiety actually serve directly to exacerbate it instead. The implication that anxiety represents a significant detriment to your life forms the basis of your need to remain calm.

CLIENT: I think I understand what you are saying, but I'm not sure I understand what you are exactly asking me to do.

THERAPIST: Fine. What I would like you to do each time you attend one of your meetings is to permit anxiety to run its course without attempting to influence it. When you notice, just prior to a meeting, that you are becoming a bit anxious, allow yourself to experience the anxiety. Let yourself perspire. In other words, allow to happen what is happening. In fact, what I would like you to do is to try to magnify the feelings and changes that occur when you become anxious.

CLIENT: Aren't they pretty bad already?

THERAPIST: Yes, they are pretty bad, but they are not harmful to you physically. And you are behaving as though anxiety were the most terrible experience that one could have. As long as you accept this idea you will have to deal with continuous high levels of anxiety. When you can affect the attitude that anxiety is aversive but not dangerous or harmful in any way, then you will begin to notice some modulation. It is more productive to view anxiety as a class of discomforting, annoying experiences, like headaches. You would not avoid a meeting because you had a headache. You would probably not attribute any particular meaning to that headache, although you could. You would go to the meeting and function to the best of your ability in spite of the headache. This is the attitude that would be helpful to you to maintain with respect to anxiety. Suppose that anxiety were some phenomenon with which you could hold a discourse. What I would like you to say to it is, "Look here, I am not afraid of you. You can't hurt me. Do your worst, I will still be here when you are exhausted." The idea is that if you fear the results of anxiety it will taunt you, like a bully. But if you stand up to it, it will eventually desist. It may test you in an effort to discern whether you are bluffing, and it will know if you are. If it determines that you actually are bluffing, it will persist until it defeats you. And it wins when you do anything to avoid or control it. If, on the other hand, it establishes that you are not bluffing, that you are actually standing up to it, it will disengage, and you will experience the ebb of anxiety and developing tranquility.

CLIENT: I'm not sure I know how to go about doing this. How can I make anxiety worse, if I were foolish enough to try?

THERAPIST: Well, that's an interesting choice of phrases. I assume that what you mean by that is that most people, faced with your problem, would not follow this strategy on their own; and I agree. For example, you have been plagued by anxiety for some time, and you have never used this approach. You have, instead, done things that make sense under the circumstances. You have tried to confront anxiety in an effort to keep it under control and remain calm. But this type of direct confrontation has not worked. So I am suggesting a method that is different from that which most people would choose. It's like trying to solve one of those puzzles designed for amusement. There is an obvious strategy that is part of the problem because it is so compelling. The correct solution, however, is something that is much less conspicuous and therefore chosen by fewer people. In any case, you ask how to implement this uncommon solution. Let's use the typical executive meeting as an example. You would begin with anticipatory anxiety at its lowest differentiable level. This would be the cue for you to focus on the anxiety and amplify the experience. You do this by noticing each of the physiological changes that are taking place and concentrating on the one that seems most salient at the time. Suppose it is your heart rate. Try to increase the number of beats per minute or the strength of each beat. Perhaps the most salient aspect of your sympathetic activity is perspiration. In that case, try to increase the flow of perspiration. Whatever is most prominent is the process that you should work to intensify. As the meeting progresses, anxiety will increase, and the experience of discomfort will vary. The most pronounced system at one point will relinquish center stage to another symptom at another point. You will follow this changing order of salience, shifting your effort to intensify as required. The idea is that rather than attempting to maintain control in a direct fashion, you maintain control by relinquishing control and "willing" anxiety to do its worst.

CLIENT: If I could do this, how long would I have to keep going? How long would it take before the anxiety stopped?

THERAPIST: It is exactly that kind of concern that will doom you to eternal avoidance. You must court anxiety at these meetings. You must look forward to it as an interesting experience. You must intend anxiety; hope for it and be happy when it arrives. If you indicate to yourself that you will employ the procedure for the purpose of ridding yourself of anxiety and will discontinue it as soon as possible, then you will fail. This is what I referred to before as "bluffing." You are pretending that anxiety does not bother you, that you are not afraid of it, that you are relinquishing control. But these are merely pretenses. And, you can't fool yourself—or your anxiety. The only way to employ this procedure effectively is to actually intend the anxiety. In essence what I am saying is that I am not suggesting that you employ a technique for reducing anxiety but that you adopt the attitude that anxiety will not harm you—only its avoidance will reduce your effectiveness in life.

CLIENT: But isn't my purpose to get rid of anxiety?

THERAPIST: Certainly, but in order to get rid of it you must first be willing to demonstrate to yourself that you can abide it for as long as necessary. You must show yourself that it is no longer a threat. That it is not dangerous either physically, psychologically, or socially. Once you have accomplished this, anxiety will no longer represent a significant concern at work.

CLIENT: I have to have it to get rid of it.

THERAPIST: Right. Just as a large corporation has to establish that they don't need money before a bank will give them a large loan, you have to demonstrate that you can bear anxiety before you can experience permanent relief.

Emphasis in this fourth session was on the explanation and administration of paradoxical intention. Using, as a basis, the description of the hypothesized dynamics associated with an executive meeting, the components of paradoxical intention were introduced in a manner that highlighted their congruence with the client's concerns. Each of his major points was disputed in a manner that would eventually allow him to risk implementing the paradoxical suggestion and would converge on paradoxical intention as the best solution.

The central theme at this juncture was the client's ineffective attempt to directly control anxiety and the consequences of this behavior—namely the exacerbation of discomfort and maintenance of the recursive process. An alternate proposal involving the management of fear in an indirect fashion (i.e., the relinquishing of attempts to directly control the process) was emphasized. This is a difficult concept for clients to grasp, since it represents an antipode with respect to their understanding of, and strategies for coping with, anxiety. That is, most tactics aimed at managing fear are based on some form of direct confrontation designed to overpower and eradicate discomfort even at its highest levels.

Certain physiological processes that happen to be influenced by autonomic nervous system activity cannot be initiated, maintained, or terminated directly. Rather, they require a certain indifference on the part of the individual to operate in a satisfactory fashion. Again, efforts to initiate or to control such a system result in deterioration of the process through the generation and maintenance of recursive anxiety. As Watzlawick suggests (Watzlawick, Weakland, & Fisch, 1974), the treatment becomes the problem: the client is highly motivated to "do something." The essence of the procedure, then, becomes convincing the client to discontinue efforts at "doing something." He or she is to accept the situation as it is and even to wish for exacerbation of the *undesirable* emotional experience. The previous dialogue was intended to concretize this concept for the reader by illustrating the way in which this kind of idea can be introduced.

The next portion of the program is concerned with assisting the client to engage in the paradoxical-intention procedure in difficult situations. Again, this assistance generally takes the form of ancillary behavioral and cognitive-behavioral techniques and demonstrations. With regard to the latter, useful instances typically are presented during the initial phase of the program and can occur spontaneously or in a planned fashion. For example, the therapist may notice that the client is becoming anxious, perhaps in response to some element of the therapist's instructions for the *in vivo* application of paradoxical intention. This discomfort can be employed to illustrate the proposed use of paradoxical intention. In the following example, a 27-year-old agoraphobic woman—a homemaker and the mother of two children—exhibited indications of anxiety during a discussion of the use of the paradoxical procedure in situations that were difficult for her to approach. The following conversation occurred during the fourth session, following a protracted explanation of paradoxical intention.

THERAPIST: How are you feeling at this point?

CLIENT: I'm anxious and becoming more anxious the more you discuss these frightening places.

THERAPIST: How anxious are you in terms of SUDs [subjective units of discomfort]?

CLIENT: About 60.

THERAPIST: Fine. Now I want you to observe your physical experience of anxiety. See how this experience changes and shifts as you become more anxious. (*The client sits quietly for several minutes.*) Describe your experience to me if you can.

CLIENT: I feel warmth in my face, and my skin almost feels as though it's moist with sweat although it isn't. It's kind of clammy. Also my heart is beating faster, and I am having a little trouble breathing. My breathing is irregular.

THERAPIST: Good. Just continue to observe the physical experience of anxiety. Keep focusing on the physical experience. In particular, seek the most prominent component of your physical response of anxiety and stay with that. Try to make this aspect even more conspicuous. As prominence shifts from one physiological process to another, follow along with the shift, increasing the salience of each new system as it comes to your attention. (*The client sits quietly for approximately 5 minutes and appears to be calming.*) What is your level of anxiety now?

CLIENT: About 10; I feel much better.

THERAPIST: Good. You see, this is the first experience that you have had with the procedure in an actual anxiety-provoking situation, and you did very well with it. It is all a matter of understanding the procedure with respect to your concerns, and I think you are developing an understanding. Practice it as often as possible in fear-provoking situations.

Although the course of such demonstrations typically runs as smoothly as this illustration suggests, there are cases in which complications are encountered. The appearance of these obstacles in the office can be quite enlightening, since they provide the therapist with a controlled opportunity to instruct the client in dealing with the high-probability maladaptive strategies for managing anxiety. The illustration that follows was extracted from the case of another woman complaining of agoraphobia. This client was 34 years old, had two children, and maintained a part-time position as a bookkeeper for a small firm. An element of her presenting complaint included the concern that when she was engaged in conversation with one other person she felt as though she were trapped. She believed that she was the center of that person's attention and had to adhere to a rigid self-imposed code of deportment—that she was not permitted any behavioral variability. Thus, the circumstances of therapy itself represented an *in vivo* situation. As in the previous case, the client exhibited indications of discomfort during a discussion of the *in vivo* application of the paradoxical procedure.

THERAPIST: You appear to be a bit uncomfortable. Is that the case?

CLIENT: Yes, I feel very anxious.

THERAPIST: What is your SUDs rating?

CLIENT: 70.

THERAPIST: Tell me what you are feeling with respect to your anxiety.

CLIENT: I'm going to be standing in line at the supermarket, and I'm going to be very anxious. Then eventually . . .

THERAPIST: No, I do not want you to tell me what you are thinking, particularly not the horror stories that you can produce. I want you to tell me what you are feeling. What is your physical experience of anxiety? As we discussed, I want you to become a passive observer of your physiological experience as it comes into your awareness and changes along with the changing level of anxiety. Now tell me what it feels like to be anxious.

CLIENT: (*After a pause*) My heart is beating very fast, and I am feeling lightheaded. I think I'm going to faint.

THERAPIST: Fine. Can you attend to your physical experience once again and notice if there is anything else that you might report?

CLIENT: (*After a short pause*) No, nothing.

THERAPIST: What is your SUDs rating now?

CLIENT: 70 to 75.

THERAPIST: O.K. Now return the focus of your attention to the physical experience of your anxiety. If you notice that you are thinking of disastrous consequences, bring your attention back to the physical experience. Maintain your focus on the most salient aspect of the physical process, as we have discussed, and try to increase the prominence of this aspect, whatever it may be. Shift your efforts as one system becomes less pronounced and another grows in prominence. I want to give you one important note of caution, however. As I mentioned, the feeling of being lightheaded is probably caused by hyperventilation, which is a component of your anxiety experience. This is the only process that I would not like you to augment. Therefore, I want to again suggest that when you feel anxious you should use this as a cue to keep your mouth closed. This simple act will prevent the effects of hyperventilation. (*The client sits quietly for about 5 minutes, but the level of her anxiety does not appear to be diminishing.*) How do you feel? What is your SUDs level?

CLIENT: Still anxious, about 75.

THERAPIST: O.K., fine. Continue to observe yourself, and increase the prominence of the salient aspects of your physical experience. (*Approximately 5 minutes pass, and she remains quite anxious.*) What is your SUDs level now?

CLIENT: Around 80. I feel very anxious.

THERAPIST: Now I suspect that you are not observing your physical experience of anxiety but instead are concerned about what you might do if you become sufficiently anxious and what I might think of you in that case. Is that at all correct?

CLIENT: Well, yes, I feel like I'm going to faint.

THERAPIST: Just keep your mouth closed. You are not breathing sufficiently rapidly to create a problem, but you might be focusing on some minimal aspects of lightheadedness. As you notice yourself thinking about losing control and my response to this, return to your physical experience; stay with your physical experience. Push everything else out of your focus of attention. (*During the next 15 minutes, I made sporadic comments that coached her in applying the paradoxical intention strategy for managing anxiety.*) How do you feel now?

CLIENT: Better, around 45.

THERAPIST: Fine. Continue to focus on the salient aspect of the physical experience of your anxiety and increase its prominence. Keep your mouth closed. If you notice yourself thinking of anxiety-associated thoughts, shift to your physical experience. (*Approximately 5 minutes pass, and the client appears to be considerably calmer.*) How are you feeling?

CLIENT: Much better.

THERAPIST: Your SUDs level?

CLIENT: Less than 10.

THERAPIST: Good. Let me just review what happened. You began to think about losing control of your anxiety in my presence and the possible thoughts that I might have about this. Such patterns have been associated with anxiety in the past and serve to exacerbate existing anxiety in the present. Now we cannot control what thoughts come into our awareness, but we can, to some extent, determine what we do with such thoughts. You take these thoughts of disasters and embellish them. They come to you as fragments, and you use these to create the extensive soap opera that we have described. On the other hand, it would be more adaptive if you could shift your attention to something else; do not try to get these thoughts out of your awareness. You cannot do this directly, but shift your attention to something equally pronounced. In this case, it is the physical experience of your anxiety. By actively engaging in the manipulation of the components of this reaction, you can limit the effect of your maladaptive cognitions. So, in the last hour you approached anxiety both in the way you have done in the past and in this new way. By using this new strategy effectively, as you did, you were able to manage high levels of anxiety as you have not been able to do in the past.

In both of the above examples, it is assumed that the demonstrations reinforced clients' confidence in the paradoxical procedure. In the latter case the illustration was quite effective, since a great deal is learned when a high-probability maladaptive response is corrected under circumstances similar to those under which the behavior naturally occurs. Of course, in situations in which the client becomes anxious—perhaps even panicky—within the session or if accompanied by the therapist to *in vivo* sites, it is vital that the therapist remain calm. This implies to the client that the therapist (an "expert") judges the circumstances to be without danger and under the control of the client. The anxiety that he or she experiences as part of this situation may begin to be reinterpreted. This will especially be the case as the client learns to manage anxiety with the paradoxical procedure. If the therapist were to become agitated along with the client, this would have the detrimental effect of reinforcing, for the client, the idea that there actually *is* something to fear in situations in which he or she has previously experienced anxiety.

On the fifth session, the 31-year-old male executive discussed earlier reported attempting to use the paradoxical procedure in a social situation unrelated to his professional responsibilities. I had suggested to him that social activities independent of his corporation would be less difficult and therefore would be helpful in providing initial practice.

THERAPIST: I'm glad that you produced an opportunity to use the strategy. Tell me about your experience.

CLIENT: Well I tried it at a party that my wife and I were invited to last Saturday night, but I got anxious.

THERAPIST: Those are the highlights; let me have the details.

CLIENT: I went prepared to do as you had suggested.

THERAPIST: Were you able to practice imaginally during the week?

CLIENT: Yes, a little.

THERAPIST: Good, go on.

CLIENT: I wasn't very anxious when we got there. I sat down after a while and tried to imagine that people were getting more and more distant.

THERAPIST: Did you keep your mouth closed?

CLIENT: Yes. But I started to get anxious, so I continued to see the people get more distant, and my vision became foggy.

THERAPIST: Then what happened?

CLIENT: I got real anxious and got a drink. After that things got much better.

THERAPIST: Did you then continue with the experiment?

CLIENT: No, I thought I would just leave well enough alone.

THERAPIST: So, what do you think?

CLIENT: I'm not sure. Maybe it wasn't a good test.

THERAPIST: As I have told you, you are capable of successfully handling the most difficult situations at the present time. Success depends much less on the nature of the circumstances and much more on your thoughts about your ability to handle yourself and your definition of the specific event. But let me give you my interpretation of why things did not work out as well as you anticipated. First, I believe that you entered the party with the hope that you would not experience anxiety, and that you would be able to control any anxiety that arose with the new procedure. I assume that this is true based on my experiences with others but also as implied in some of the things that you said. Am I correct?

CLIENT: Yes. I couldn't help hoping for peace even though I knew I wasn't supposed to.

THERAPIST: You cannot prevent yourself from doing or thinking something that you cannot prevent yourself from doing or thinking. This is part of the process. You will come to a point at which anxiety will hold no special significance for you. You will be able to enter a social situation and not care about, or think about, the possibility of being anxious. At this point it will be helpful if you could hope to *have* anxiety in these situations and be prepared to deal with it. Another thing you implied was that you entered with the hope that the new strategy would work but with the idea that it might not. In the latter case you were prepared to fall back to your conventional procedures. For me, the clue in what you said was that you would "try" to use it. As I have said previously, you cannot try something. You can either do it or not do it, but you cannot try to do it. As it turns out, you did not do it. What you did do was to enter the party with the plan of maintaining control at any cost. If the new procedure worked, fine! If it didn't, you would try one of your tested methods of maintaining control. In this case it was having a drink. When you actually decide to use the procedure in some social situation, then you must commit yourself to its use no matter what happens. You see, every situation has associated with it a repertoire of responses. Some responses have occurred before and have a high probability of occurring in that situation. Other responses have a much lower probability of occurring. However, solutions to problems that might occur in the situation will come from this group of responses. The party that you attended represents a moderately difficult social situation for you. You have some high-probability responses like distracting yourself when anxious or, specific to the party, taking a drink. A much lower-probability response is using the new strategy. Now, when you entered the situation you intended to use the procedure and were able to because anxiety was not very high. As time went on, however, anxiety increased, as it always does under these circumstances, and you reverted to a response that had a higher associative strength. You took a drink, and you also distracted yourself with compelling thoughts of failure, like, "this isn't working, nothing ever has, and nothing ever will." Does this seem to describe your experience?

CLIENT: Yes. But what can I do about it if, as you say, I can't help doing what I do?

THERAPIST: It is most important that you have patience with yourself. You have chosen a very difficult task, and it will take time. Your maladaptive response to anxiety has taken a long time to learn; it will take some time to learn an alternative, more adaptive response. Perhaps you are trying too hard. What you must do is stop trying, stop attempting to maintain control, just become a passive observer of your anxiety and allow it to run its course. This can partly account for the difficulty that you had after you entered the party. Were you actually experiencing people becoming more distant?

CLIENT: No, but this is one of the most frightening things that happens when I do get very anxious.

THERAPIST: What you must do is to allow anxiety to run its natural course, and you must follow along. You should not initiate anything. If you did not experience people becoming progressively distant, then you should not have produced that sensation. What actually did you experience initially when you became anxious at the party?

CLIENT: I felt the tightness in my chest that I have mentioned.

THERAPIST: Then that is what you should have focused on. Just observe your chest tightening. Perhaps you can enhance the feeling of chest tightening. But I am more interested in your being a passive observer of the passing anxiety scene. Then, of course, you experienced the same old distracting thoughts of failure: The soap opera, "Our Guy Monday." If you think of anxiety-provoking thoughts, then there is a good chance that you will be anxious. Now, as I have said before, you cannot help thinking about what comes into your awareness. But you *can* avoid elaborating on these thoughts. And, the "soap opera" is an elaboration. It is these thoughts that maintain the experience of anxiety, and it is anxiety that maintains these thoughts. Think of this possibility: Do you ever awaken in the morning feeling very good for no apparent reason?

CLIENT: Sure.

THERAPIST: Now, if you wanted to maintain that good feeling, what would you do?

CLIENT: I would think of pleasant things.

THERAPIST: Right. That's the way to hold on to a good feeling. I wonder what would happen if you tried to maintain it by observing the physical sensations that composed it and trying to enhance these components. In fact, the feeling would disappear. An individual cannot maintain an emotion by concentrating on it. This is material that is neutral to the emotion. The content of cognitions must be congruent with the task of maintaining the emotion; if it is neutral, the emotion will dissipate. Imagine that you see a very attractive woman walking in front of you. Suppose you become aroused. Now if she should go into a store and you continue on, how would you maintain that feeling of sexual arousal? If you observed the physical feelings of arousal, the genital sensations, for example, the feeling would disappear. This is because thoughts of your sensations are neutral to the emotion and will not serve to support it. Only if you continue to think of the woman, perhaps in a sexually explicit way, can you continue to experience sexual arousal. Anxiety, which is an emotion, conforms to the same dynamics. If you think of an anxiety-provoking soap opera, you will be able to experience increasing levels of anxiety. On the other hand, if your attention is focused on something that is anxiety-neutral, then you will not be able to support the emotional experience, and it will dissipate.

Low self-esteem and low self-confidence are two important components of the social anxiety complex. Since I am suggesting that recursive anxiety is a variant of social phobia, it is not surprising that these two concepts are significant in the understanding and treatment of this phenomenon. Although the scope of the present chapter precludes a complete evaluation of the role of these factors in the recursive-anxiety process, because of the influence that self-esteem can exert on the therapeutic program, some suggestions on addressing this component in the clinical setting seem appropriate at this point. For the purpose of the present discussion, it will be assumed that self-esteem is determined by the nature of the individual's self-statements; thus, predominantly negative self-statements result in low self-esteem.

Of the variety of themes around which negative self-statements are organized, several that are commonly exhibited by individuals exhibiting a recursive component to their anxiety-based complaint are particularly detrimental to therapeutic progress. Two considerations are of some consequence here. First, many individuals reporting recursive concerns have a history of failures in formal and informal treatment contexts. This, of course, may be because therapeutic focus falls exclusively on the anxiety disorder, and the recursive component is largely ignored. Second, paradoxical intention is a counterintuitive technique. As such, it has a low probability of being spontaneously chosen by the individual as an anxiety-management strategy.

The individual with low self-esteem is generally pessimistic and unwilling to take chances. He or she expects failure. Therefore, therapists should be alert to clients expressing concerns that nothing has been effective in the past and that they do not expect that anything will be fruitful in the future. The ironic corollary is that although they are discounting all previous efforts, they are unwilling to attempt anything that deviates from their earlier treatment conceptions. A cognitive-behavioral approach that assists clients in gaining awareness and control over such negative themes represents an important adjunct to a paradoxical-intention program and prepares clients for *in vivo* implementation of the paradoxical procedure.

During the initial stages of the program, clients are hesitantly exploring the technique, alternately attempting to use it, in the most timorous fashion, and fearing to use it—choosing to escape from or avoid the anxiety instead. A good analogy to this approach/avoidance behavior is that of a young child at the beach who may be attracted to but frightened by the ocean. Thus, he or she may, in turns, run close to the water when the waves recede and run to the safety of parents when the waves return. This intermittent use of the procedure may be related to negative self-statements that seem invariably to follow initial successful *in vivo* experiences. This doubt in the face of adapative change represents a resurgence of the impeding self-statements previously mentioned and suggests the need for a cognitive-behavior therapeutic complement throughout the initial phase of the paradoxical-intention program.

Again, the attempt to protect oneself from the possibility of loss of control and of the consequent negative social evaluation may serve to maintain the recursive process. The paradoxical intention that breaks this circle is difficult for clients to undertake if they attribute great risk to the performance of the required behavior (e.g., allowing themselves to be anxious while attending a meeting of great importance). Low self-esteem contributes to enhancing, in clients' perception, the relative importance of others in comparison to themselves. This increases the significance of potential negative evaluation. Conversely, augmenting clients' self-esteem brings the role of others and of their influence on clients' lives into a more realistic focus. Therefore, the risk of fulfilling the requirements of the paradoxical intention is greatly reduced.

Paradoxical Intention and Exposure

Paradoxical intention is being proposed as a conventional behavioral treatment of choice for the amelioration of a specific anxiety complex. Consequently, information relating to general mechanisms of therapeutic change in the area of anxiety disorders would be of assistance in the formulation and administration of the procedure. For example, Lang (1977), Rachman (1980), and Foa and Kozak (1986) have attributed an important role in the reduction of anxiety to emotional processing. They suggest that effective procedures are those that provide optimal conditions for the client to experience the emotional responses that occur in association with the actual anxiety-provoking stimuli. Lang (1977) indicates that the focus of clients' attention should include both the stimulus aspect of the anxiety situation and the response component—that is, the cognitive and physiological experiences of the person when he or she is confronting the feared circumstances. To the extent that data continue to support this hypothesized relationship of emotional processing with therapeutic efficacy in the treatment of anxiety disorders, then it is worth noting such findings as those of Lang, Kozak, Miller, Levin, and McLean (1980) and of Lang, Levin, Miller, and Kozak (1983), indicating that subjects who were instructed to attend to response elements of the anxiety condition evinced greater physiological response than did those subjects who focused on the stimulus component.

As a result of its flexibility, paradoxical intention incorporates the characteristics necessary to promote emotional processing in clients. When it is presented as a conventional behavioral procedure, the client is involved in concentrating attention on the physiological experience of anxiety. For example, in agreement with the work of Foa and Kozak (1986), clients are specifically instructed to foster enthusiastically the physiological activity associated with the feared stimulus and are cautioned not to be distracted from this task by cognitions relating to the hypothesized disastrous consequence. However, since thoughts of the feared social catastrophe represent a significant element of the actual discomforting situations, requirements of emotional processing dictate that such images be included in the paradoxical-intention procedure. This is accomplished by encouraging the client to will or to intend catastrophic behavior that can serve to supplement the instructions to observe anxiety-provoking stimuli and the resultant physiological responses. Thus, to the extent that the role hypothesized for emotional processing in the treatment of anxiety disorders is supported by subsequent data, the effectiveness of paradoxical intention, when employed with anxiety-based complaints, can be enhanced by utilizing the implications of emotional processing as a guide in clinical application.

Client and Therapist Characteristics

Although there is little research to support the differential importance of specific client and therapist characteristics in the administration of an effective paradoxical-intention treatment program, clinical experience provides some leads and suggestions. For example, Frankl has associated humor with paradoxical intention from its inception. Behaviorally, this relationship seems to hold sufficient promise to warrant exploration, although most studies of the efficacy of the technique have not included humor among the variables studied.

Humor can serve a variety of functions when integrated with paradoxical intention. A most obvious role is that of a counterconditioner to modulate the effects of anxiety. This can be effective at any point in the administration of the procedure but would seem to be of particular value in association with aspects of the disastrous social consequence. Its role here would be that of reducing the potency of the emotional response to imagery of the hypothesized situation. For example, the therapist narrates the client's soap opera—including numerous humorous embellishments and a comically absurd conclusion. The client is encouraged both to imagine the story and to customize it by adding whatever amusing flourishes he or she wishes. Modification by the client enhances his or her ability to associate humor with the anxiety-provoking imagery as well as with aspects of the difficult social circumstances. In addition, any use of humor by the therapist can imply that, in the opinion of a caring expert, the situation is not nearly as serious as the client believes, and optimism concerning positive change is warranted.

For whatever reason, to the extent that humor may enhance the effectiveness of paradoxical intention, a prerequisite of its administration by the therapist and of its productive use by the client is that they each possess a sense of humor that they are willing to employ in conjunction with the therapeutic program (although data from a clinical analogue study conducted by Newton & Dowd, 1989, dispute this relationship to some extent). A more general effect is suggested by individuals such as Allport (1950) who proposes that clients experience significant improvement by virtue of their being able to view their problems with humorous indifference. The therapist, too, must be sufficiently comfortable in the therapeutic setting to be able to employ humor with clients who bring with them problems of a "life-threatening" nature. In addition, the therapist must have some facility and considerable experience with humor. If he or she does not, then this class of behavior should be avoided, since it can appear to be mechanical and artificial and could serve to impede progress by damaging the relationship between client and therapist. In addition, it should be noted that outcome studies do not indicate that failure to employ humor necessarily precludes effective administration of paradoxical intention (Ascher, 1989), since few investigations have specifically dealt with this question.

In utilizing paradox and humor, the therapist should be aware of the risk that he or she is taking in possibly appearing to be insensitive and uncaring. This is less of a problem when paradoxical intention is employed as a conventional treatment of choice, as compared with its more traditional method of application (e.g., Dowd & Milne, 1986), but it still remains a concern. In an effort to avoid damaging the therapeutic relationship, the therapist should remain within limits that he or she judges to be appropriate, associating paradox and humor in a circumspect fashion with issues specifically relevant to the presenting complaint.

Another speculation concerns the counterintuitive nature of paradoxical intention. One would expect that a therapists' ability to effectively administer the procedure and the clients' capacity for understanding and applying the concept in a variety of *in vivo* situations would be enhanced by what might be referred to as flexibility of thinking and tolerance for adventure and exploration within the therapeutic context.

Recursive anxiety is based on a relationship that the client believes exists between high levels of anxiety and the complex of consequences that include loss of control, embarrassing behavior, and negative social evaluation. This relationship typically develops during a specific period of elevated anxiety. The total situation may serve as the traumatic event on which the later avoidance behavior is based. Application of the hypothesis of emotional-state-dependent learning would predict that each time the individual experienced a high degree of anxiety, the authenticity of the hypothesized relationship would be unquestioned (e.g., Bower, 1981). On the other hand, during periods of calm, the unrealistic nature of the posited association would become evident. In fact, most clients exhibiting recursive anxiety report this cognitive-emotional association. That is, in safe situations, they are confident that the disaster cannot occur, whereas in anxiety-provoking circumstances, they consider inappropriate behavior (which they hypothesize is contingent on their losing control) to be highly probable. It is during periods of relative tranquility that clients are amenable to the procedures discussed in this chapter. However, if the client tenaciously maintains his or her belief in the relationship between anxiety and disaster even during states of low discomfort, then it becomes significantly more difficult to employ paradoxical intention, since the client will not willingly risk experiencing the feared circumstances.

Paradoxical Intention and Responsibility

One final speculation concerns a possible consequence of the use of paradoxical intention. Most people enter psychotherapy with the belief that the significant aspects of their lives, particularly those associated with the presenting complaint, are caused by external factors that are beyond their control. There are a number of problems with this position as it affects the therapeutic process, and although a detailed examination of these difficulties falls outside the scope of the present discussion, several relevant possibilities should be considered.

Believing oneself to be at the effect of, rather than the cause of, one's social and physical circumstances can contribute to reduced self-esteem and self-efficacy as well as to a variety of neurotic modes of adjustment. Yalom (1980) has speculated about the latter in detail. Therapeutic progress is influenced by a clients' willingness and ability to reevaluate his or her relationship with significant life components and to amend difficulties that seem to impede satisfactory adjustment. Obviously, if such elements are assumed to be beyond one's control, then change is impossible, and clients remain in the impasses with which they began. In response to this maladaptive attitude, many therapeutic approaches, based partially on Sartre's conception of individuals as the "authors" of the totality of their existence and Heidegger's view of "authenticity," encourage clients to accept personal responsibility in the creation of their lives.

With proper guidance, paradoxical intention can provide an important example for clients of the influence that they can exert on the tenor of their existence. Often people seeking the assistance of a therapist describe what they perceive to be a problem of immense proportions with respect to their well-being in society. Some anxiety-based complaints even possess an ostensible life-threatening character (e.g., cardiac arrest, inability to swallow with the possibility of choking, loss of consciousness while operating a motor vehicle). All of life's dissatisfactions are focused on such onerous concerns with the associated attitude that they represent difficulties whose solutions are well beyond their capabilities and that these problems make further progress impossible.

For example, a 31-year-old unmarried male physician sought help for his distress related to blushing in social situations. After describing the problem, he detailed its broad significance in his life:

THERAPIST: You say that this is a terrible problem. Generally people who are concerned about blushing consider it to be mildly embarrassing at worst. Why has it become so dreadful for you?

CLIENT: It has been with me all my life. I have always been embarrassed by it, and I am tired of it.

THERAPIST: Yes, but why are you embarrassed by this? Why is it so terrible? Do you think that it is offensive to others, for example?

CLIENT: (*Long pause*) No, not necessarily.

THERAPIST: Well then, why does it offend you? Would you be offended if someone with whom you were speaking were to blush?

CLIENT: No . . . I would wonder about it.

THERAPIST: I see. What would you think?

CLIENT: It would depend. I might think the person was nervous. In a girl it's all right. It can be nice.

THERAPIST: Why?

CLIENT: Because it may mean she likes you. But in a guy it's embarrassing.

THERAPIST: What accounts for the difference?

CLIENT: It just is. . . . It means you're weak. . . . You're nervous. . . . You don't know how to handle yourself with women. It's a "turn-off" for them. People have a negative view of you.

THERAPIST: And, at work you say you also blush. How is this a problem? After all, you are not interested in establishing dating relationships.

CLIENT: Maybe with nurses or other professionals. . . . It just may indicate a lack of sureness, knowing that I can take charge and handle any situation. I think patients and colleagues feel that I'm not sure of myself when I blush, that I'm sort of weak, that I don't know what I'm doing.

The client paints a dreary picture of life under the pervasive influence of uncontrollable blushing, primarily because of the meaning that he attributes to it and the role that it plays as the source of all of his difficulties. As is typical in such cases, he then went on in an effort to demonstrate that he had tried everything to reduce his blushing, but to no avail. In the client's view, the situation was hopeless, and there was nothing that could be done about it.

From the perspective of responsibility, the client was attempting to evade his obligation to himself by renouncing control over his behavior. To the extent that the therapist, implicitly or explicitly, agreed to accept this position, then he could possibly reinforce the client's conviction of being unable to deal with the presenting complaint and, by inference, because of its significance, of being incapable of handling his life in general. Using paradoxical intention enables the therapist to provide guidance without the unproductive connotations of giving "help."

By instructing the client to court the dreaded experience, the therapist suggested that he was confident in the capabilities of the client to withstand any consequent disaster; the experience could be controlled by the client; when he was able to actively "intend" the fearful experience, he would find that rather than producing a catastrophe, anxiety would first diminish, then dissipate and be followed by a period of calm. The accumulation of such experiences, accompanied by the therapist's explanations, can serve to emphasize that if this client is capable of controlling this most difficult problem, then he can master any situation and that his previous life circumstances are of his own creation. The client's acknowledgment of his personal influence in significant life situations that were previously perceived to be immutable can then result in a wide variety of positive effects that have broad implications for an increasingly rewarding adjustment. As Seltzer (1986) concluded after an exhaustive review of the use of paradox within the major schools of psychotherapy:

> Although rationales for paradoxical strategies frequently stress their utility in helping clients to reestablish feelings of self-control, *all* therapies can be perceived as endeavoring to assist clients in comprehending the voluntariness—and controllability—of behaviors that have come to appear nonvolitional. (p. 164)

To the extent that clients enter the psychotherapy situation with a sense of helplessness, then it can be said that the role of the therapist is to invest clients with the realization that they are in control of their lives and that they have the responsibility to undertake this management. If the therapist's behavior can be viewed by clients to be "helpful" or in some way appear to take responsibility from them, then the therapist is corroborating clients' beliefs that they need the help of other people in order to do well. This would seem to function as an impediment to the self-sufficiency objective of therapy.

The therapist must therefore be careful that his or her actions not be thus misinterpreted. For example, certain clients employ behavior to which individuals in their environment react in a manner that serves to maintain the clients' problem adjustment. If the therapist, by his or her behavior, promotes a similar relationship in therapy, then a corresponding outcome may be expected. It is thus incumbent on therapists to behave in ways that will support and enhance clients' self-sufficiency in accomplishing their goals. Answering anxiety-based questions, making decisions, and giving advice are among the "helpful" therapist behaviors that may not be appropriate for therapists interested in the development of client responsibility.

As previously noted in this section, paradoxical intention can be especially useful in these circumstances, since its premises are congruent with the concept of individual responsibility. Thus, it can be administered in a manner that provides the client with sole attribution for any behavioral improvement. Even the perception of the paradox itself is assumed by some to be the responsibility of the client (Dell, 1981). In this regard, Dell (1986) hypothesizes that the system that maintains the concept of "therapeutic paradox" also serves to compromise clients' responsibility. He suggests that when we examine and successfully confront this system of beliefs, what presently seems paradoxical will constitute a component of a comprehensive theory of human behavior and effective therapeutic methods. (These latter, I assume, will be more effective, in part, because they will be more congruent with the client's sense of self-sufficiency.)

A traditional question concerning the administration of therapeutic paradox is: should the paradox be explained to the client? Haley (1973) suggests not. Using the double-bind hypothesis to clarify the operation of paradoxical procedures, he proposes that these techniques are effective because they appropriately harness the client's struggle for control in therapy. In a sense, the therapist employs an artifice by redirecting the client's resistance to serve the therapeutic goal. If the client becomes aware of the nature of the procedure or of the therapist's motives in administering it, then the strategy will fail to have its intended effect.

On the other hand, it would seem more beneficial, in light of current discussion of responsibility, if the client were provided with all of the information available to the therapist. There are explanatory hypotheses that are congruent with a veridical approach (e.g., Ascher, 1980; Newton, 1968; Watzlawick et al., 1974). Furthermore, most experimental studies of therapeutic paradox use a procedure that incorporates detailed presentation of the rationale of paradoxical intention to the subject. This does not seem to detract from its effectiveness. In fact, in a specific test of this question (Ascher & Turner, 1980), a group of clients complaining of insomnia received a candid explanation and exhibited significantly greater improvement when compared with members of a similar group exposed to a logical, but somewhat deceptive, interpretation.

Ethical Considerations

The caveats that are typically appended to papers devoted to the application of techniques of therapeutic paradox when employed to enhance client cooperation do not seem relevant here. This is because paradoxical intention is presented as a conventional behavioral procedure that is proposed as a treatment of choice for certain complaints. That is, using the classification system developed by Rohrbaugh, Tennen, and coworkers (e.g., Rohrbaugh, Tennen, Press, & White, 1981), behavior therapists have employed paradoxical intention as a "compliance-based" strategy for the amelioration of anxiety as opposed to a "defiance-based" device. Therefore, cautionary statements referring to the use of powerful communication phenomena that could be used to satisfy the evil aims of an unscrupulous therapist as easily as the adaptive therapeutic goals of the client would seem to be irrelevant under these circumstances. Rather, more realistic concerns relate to such factors as manner of presentation and suitability of behavioral targets. With respect to the latter, for example, preliminary data from several studies (Ascher, 1984, 1985; Ascher & Schotte, 1987) as well as clinical experience suggest that a program consisting of paradoxical intention and ancillary procedures may be the treatment of choice for recursive anxiety. Further, it is advised that when recursive anxiety is exhibited, a treatment program that is devoid of paradoxical intention or a similar technique will possibly result in a protracted course of therapy yielding a relatively unsatisfactory outcome. However, this information also indicates that in the absence of a recursive-anxiety element, paradoxical intention may produce results that are inferior to the improvement possible with a different behavioral program.

Therefore, as is the case with any behavioral technique, paradoxical intention is not presented as a panacea that can be generally applied to a wide variety of behaviors in isolation of important contextual factors. Rather, the most salient caveat that can be associated with paradoxical intention as a conventional behavioral treatment of choice is that it be administered subsequent to a properly conducted behavioral analysis. Only then can the clinician be certain that he or she has conditions that are appropriate for effective administration with clients and presenting problems that have a high probability of promoting clinical success with this procedure.

References

Allport, G. W. (1950). *The individual and his religion: A psychological interpretation.* New York: Macmillan.

American Psychiatric Association. (1987). *Diagnostic and statistical manual of mental disorders* (3rd ed.—rev.). Washington, D.C.: American Psychiatric Association.

Ascher, L. M. (1980). Paradoxical intention. In A. J. Goldstein & E. B. Foa (Eds.), *Handbook of behavioral interventions: A clinical guide.* New York: Wiley.

Ascher, L. M. (1984, November). *Paradoxical intention and the recursive aspect of social anxiety.* Paper presented at the Association for Advancement of Behavior Therapy, Philadelphia.

Ascher, L. M. (1985). Die paradoxe intention aus der Sicht des Verhaltenstherapeuten. In A. Laengle (Ed.), *Wege Zum Sinn: Logotherapie als orientierungshilfe.* Munich: Piper.

Ascher, L. M. (1989). Paradoxical intention: Its clarification and emergence as a conventional behavioral procedure. *the Behavior Therapist, 12,* 23–28.

Ascher, L. M., Bowers, M. R., & Schotte, D. E. (1985). A review of data from controlled case studies and experiments evaluating the clinical efficacy of paradoxical intention. In G. R. Weeks (Ed.), *Promoting change through paradoxical therapy.* Homewood, IL: Dow Jones-Irwin.

Ascher, L. M., & Schotte, D. E. (1987). *Paradoxical intention and recursive anxiety.* Unpublished manuscript, Department of Psychiatry, Temple University Health Sciences Center, Philadelphia.

Ascher, L. M., & Turner, R. M. (1980). A comparison of two methods for the administration of paradoxical intention. *Behaviour Research and Therapy, 18,* 121–126.

Bateson, G., Jackson, D. D., Haley, J., & Weakland, J. H. (1956). Toward a theory of schizophrenia. *Behavioral Science, 1,* 251–264.

Bower, G. H. (1981). Mood and memory. *American Psychologist, 36,* 129–148.

Chambless, D. L., Caputo, C., Gallagher, R., & Bright, P. (1984). Assessment of fear in agoraphobia: The body sensations questionnaire and the agoraphobic cognitions questionnaire. *Journal of Consulting and Clinical Psychology, 52,* 1090–1097.

Chambless, D. L., & Gracely, E. J. (1989). Fear of fear and the anxiety disorders. *Cognitive Therapy and Research, 13,* 9–20.

Dell, P. F. (1981). Paradox redux. *Journal of Marital and Family Therapy, 7,* 127–134.

Dell, P. F. (1986). Why do we still call them "paradoxes"? *Family Process, 25,* 223–234.

Dowd, T., & Milne, D. R. (1986). Paradoxical interventions in counseling psychology. *The Counseling Psychologist, 14,* 237–282.

Dunlap, K. (1928). A revision of the fundamental law of habit formation. *Science, 67,* 360–362.

Evans, I. M. (1972). A conditioning model of a common fear pattern—fear of fear. *Psychotherapy: Theory, Research, and Practice, 9,* 238–241.

Foa, E. B., & Kozak, M. J. (1986). Emotional processing of fear: Exposure to corrective information. *Psychological Bulletin, 99,* 20–35.

Frankl, V. E. (1939). Zur memischen Bejahung und Vermeinung. *Internationale Zeitschrift fuer Psychoanalyse, 43,* 26–31.

Frankl, V. E. (1947). *Die Psychotherapie in der Praxis.* Vienna: Deuticke.

Frankl, V. E. (1955). *The doctor and the soul: From psychotherapy to logotherapy.* New York: Knopf.

Frankl, V. E. (1975). Paradoxical intention and dereflection. *Psychotherapy: Theory, Research and Practice, 12,* 226–237.

Frankl, V. E. (1985). Logos, paradox, and the search for meaning. In M. J. Mahoney & A. Freeman (Eds.), *Cognition and psychotherapy.* New York: Plenum.

Goldstein, A. J., & Chambless, D. L. (1978). A reanalysis of agoraphobia. *Behavior Therapy, 9,* 47–59.
Haley, J. (1973). *Uncommon therapy: The psychiatric techniques of Milton H. Erickson, M.D.* New York: Norton.
Lang, P. J. (1977). Imagery in therapy: An informative processing analysis of fear. *Behavior Therapy, 8,* 862–886.
Lang, P. J., Kozak, M. J., Miller, G. A., Levin, D. N., & McLean, A. (1980). Emotional imagery: Conceptual structure and pattern of somatic–visceral response. *Psychophysiology, 17,* 179–192.
Lang, P. J. Levin, D. N., Miller, G. A., & Kozak, M. J. (1983). Fear behavior, fear imagery, and the psychophysiology of emotion: The problem of affective response integration. *Journal of Abnormal Psychology, 92,* 276–306.
Masters, W. H., & Johnson, V. E. (1970). *Human sexual inadequacy.* Boston: Little, Brown.
Newton, J. R. (1968). Considerations for the psychotherapeutic technique of symptom scheduling. *Psychotherapy: Theory, Research and Practice, 5,* 95–103.
Newton, G. M., & Dowd, E. T. (1989). *Effect of client sense of humor and paradoxical interventions on test anxiety.* Unpublished manuscript, Kent State University.
Omer, H. (1981). Paradoxical treatments: A unified concept. *Psychotherapy: Theory, Research, and Practice, 18,* 320–324.
Rachman, S. (1980). Emotional processing. *Behaviour Research and Therapy, 18,* 51–60.
Reiss, S. (1987). Theoretical perspectives on fear of anxiety. *Clinical Psychology Review, 7,* 585–596.
Reiss, S., Peterson, R. A., Gursky, D. M., & McNally, R. J. (1986). Anxiety sensitivity, anxiety frequency, and the prediction of fearfulness. *Behaviour Research and Therapy, 24,* 1–8.
Rohrbaugh, M., Tennen, H., Press, S., & White, L. (1981). Compliance, defiance, and therapeutic paradox; Guidelines for strategic use of paradox interventions. *American Journal of Orthopsychiatry, 51,* 454–467.
Seltzer, L. F. (1986). *Paradoxical strategies in psychotherapy: A comprehensive overview and guidebook.* New York: Wiley.
Watzlawick, P., Beavin, J. H., & Jackson, D. D. (1967). *Pragmatics of human communication.* New York: Norton.
Watzlawick, P., Weakland, J., & Fisch, R. (1974). *Change: Principles of problem formulation and problem resolution.* New York: Norton.
Webster's new collegiate dictionary. (1977). Springfield, MA: G. & C. Merriam Co.
Weekes, C. (1976). *Simple, effective treatment for agoraphobia.* New York: Hawthorn.
Weeks, G. R., & L'Abate, L. A. (1982). *Paradoxical psychotherapy: Theory and practice with individuals, couples, and families.* New York: Brunner/Mazel.
Yalom, I. D. (1980). *Existential psychotherapy.* New York: Basic Books.

Chapter 5

Eating Disorders

June Chiodo

The "multifaceted" nature of eating disorders has been addressed in numerous writings (Bruch, 1985; Garfinkel & Garner, 1982; Kaye & Gwirtsman, 1985). The development and maintenance of clinical symptomatology involve the intricate interaction among biological, psychological, and environmental factors. The most salient psychological feature may be the patient's beliefs, attitudes, and assumptions about her[1] body weight; the unyielding belief that "it is absolutely essential that I be thin" (Garner & Bemis, 1985, p. 108).

The undue importance that patients place on their body shape and weight may be the core psychopathological feature (Fairburn, 1985, 1987). Much of eating-disordered behavior such as frequent weighing and repeated dietary restriction can be accounted for by this specific psychopathology. Alteration of the dysfunctional beliefs and attitudes concerning weight, therefore, is considered essential for long-term behavioral change (Fairburn, 1985; Garner & Bemis, 1985).

Paradoxical intention may be of therapeutic value in helping to facilitate behavioral and cognitive change. Unlike other clinical syndromes and problems for which efficacy has been studied empirically (e.g., agoraphobia, insomnia, psychogenic urinary retention), the use of paradox with eating-disordered patients involves either anecdotal reports or uncontrolled case studies. However, at this stage of knowledge, descriptive reports can serve to stimulate clinical thinking and to promote the formulation of testable hypotheses that allow for critical evaluation of paradoxical intention for eating disorders. Based on this premise, this

[1]For ease in reading, the feminine pronoun is used throughout this chapter; however, it is acknowledged that males are affected by the disorder, although to a lesser extent.

chapter offers suggestions to stimulate clinical and scientific thinking regarding the utility of paradoxical strategies for this patient population.

Diagnostic Criteria

The diagnostic criteria for anorexia nervosa are outlined in the *Diagnostic and Statistical Manual of Mental Disorders* (3rd ed.—revised) (DSM-III-R; American Psychiatric Association, 1987). To warrant a clinical diagnosis, the patient must refuse to maintain her weight above a minimum that is deemed appropriate for age and height and that allows for normal biological hormonal functioning; the absence of three menstrual cycles indicates hormonal dysregulation. Despite the low weight and emaciated appearance, the patient expresses an intense fear of gaining weight or becoming fat. Her perception of body weight, size, or shape is disturbed.

There are two subtypes of anorexic patients: restrictive and bulimic. Restrictive anorexics achieve their marked weight loss by abstaining from any significant intake of food. Bulimic anorexics, on the other hand, engage in episodic bouts of binge eating but maintain their low weight by extensive purging, exercising, or some other compensatory behavior (Casper, Eckert, Halmi, Goldberg, & Davis, 1980; Garfinkel, Moldofsky, & Garner, 1980).

The DSM-III-R (American Psychiatric Association, 1987) clinical diagnosis for the syndrome of bulimia nervosa requires the presence of three core features: binge-eating episodes perceived to be outside of the individual's voluntary control that occur at least twice a week for a minimum of 3 months; drastic weight-control methods including self-induced vomiting, ingestion of laxatives or diuretics, strict dieting, fasting, and/or vigorous exercise; and a persistent overconcern regarding shape and weight.

A number of studies demonstrate that females are affected by eating disorders to a much larger extent than are males (Bemis, 1978; Halmi, 1974). Some researchers suspect that anorexia nervosa may be more common in males than the current statistics would suggest (Hay & Leonard, 1979) and that the difference may be reflected, in part, to the reluctance among males to seek help or to admit to a stereotypically female disorder (Herzog, Norman, Gordon, & Pepose, 1984).

Some athletes, and in particular, those identified as "obligatory runners," were hypothesized to resemble eating-disordered patients. That is, some researchers have suggested that obligatory runners who show extreme weight loss, preoccupation with diet, and concern with body fat composition resemble anorexics on personality and behavioral measures (Yates, Leehey, & Shisslak, 1983). Others (Blumenthal, O'Toole, & Chang, 1984), however, have shown that such athletes do not manifest the characteristic psychopathology that is associated with eating disorders. Unlike eating disorders wherein the loss of weight and preoccupation with diet and fat composition are primary concerns, these are considered to be secondary to the athlete's primary concern of performance and physical endurance.

Conceptual Overview

Social Stigmatization of Obesity

Unlike the cultural norm in the early 1800s where "every thin woman wants to grow plump" (Brillat-Savarin, 1825/1970, p. 272), our society harbors strong feelings of prejudice against obese persons (Wadden & Stunkard, 1985). Obese individuals are discriminated against in the workplace (Allon, 1982), in academic settings (Canning & Mayer, 1966), and by health care professionals (Maddox & Liederman, 1969). Children as young as 6 years have learned to attribute negative characteristics such as lazy, sloppy, dirty, stupid, ugly, forgetful, and undesirable behaviors such as lying and cheating to obese children (Richardson, Hastorf, Goodman, & Dornbusch, 1961; Staffieri, 1967). They prefer to maintain greater personal distance from overweight than from average or thin children (Lerner, 1973).

During adolescence, negative attitudes toward obesity are intensified. Few adolescent females believe that they are thin enough, and a large number are dieting (Halmi, Goldberg, & Cunningham, 1977; Nielsen, 1979). In fact, approximately 79% of females have dieted by the age of 18 (Nylander, 1971).

During the process of socialization, some obese people may internalize the social stigma toward body fat and, consequently, become full of self-disparagement and self-hatred to the point where they believe that they merit discriminatory treatment (Cahnman, 1968; Rodin & Slochower, 1974).

The Fear of Fatness and Dysfunctional Styles of Reasoning

The social acceptance of prejudicial attitudes and discriminatory behavior toward the obese has kindled a "fear of fat" or "fear of becoming obese." Much has been written about the contribution of sociocultural values of thinness to a rising prevalence of eating disorders (Bruch, 1973, 1978; Garner & Garfinkel, 1978, 1980; Ryle, 1939; Selvini Palazzoli, 1978). Society's values are filtered through family systems. Patients are likely to come from families where weight control represents a general sense of well-being, self-control, and "rightness" (Kalucy, Crisp, & Harding, 1977).

The rigidity, extremeness, and personal meaning that patients attach to a belief system that equates thinness with happiness, success, attractiveness, and a sense of self-control accounts for their disturbed behavior (Fairburn, 1985). The rigid belief system brings order to the patient's chaotic environment. The belief system generates rules that allow the patient a means to process her experiences, integrate information, and evaluate her performance and self-worth (Garner & Bemis, 1982; Fairburn, 1981; Fairburn, Cooper, & Cooper, 1986). Based largely on Beck's theory and treatment for depression (Beck, Rush, Shaw, & Emery, 1979), a number of dysfunctional styles of reasoning have been identified: dichotomous reasoning, superstitious thinking, personalization, magnification, selective abstraction, and overgeneralization (for full descriptions, see Garner & Bemis, 1982; Garner, Garfinkel, & Bemis, 1982).

Cognitive Self-Reinforcement of Dieting

Patients initiate dieting when they begin to feel a loss of control, being overwhelmed, or experience feelings of stress and failure that then affect self-esteem. To the exclusion of other problem-solving behaviors that would be effective coping strategies in these situations, dieting becomes an adaptive way to alleviate such mood states. It is "a potent cognitive self-reinforcement" (Garner & Bemis, 1985, p. 109) for it restores the patient's feelings of self-control, self-efficacy, competence, and self-esteem or self-worth (Bruch, 1973; Garfinkel & Garner, 1982; Johnson, Connors, & Tobin, 1987; Slade, 1982; Vandereycken & Meerman, 1984).

Dieting, Binge Eating, and Purging Behavior

A minority of patients are able to sustain chronic dietary restriction to the point where they experience marked weight loss and warrant a clinical diagnosis of (restrictive) anorexia nervosa (Fairburn & Cooper, 1984). The majority of patients, however, are unable to adhere to rigid dietary rules, and restriction gives way to episodic binge eating (Agras & Kirkley, 1986).

Dietary restriction itself may account for the occurrence of binge-eating episodes (Polivy & Herman, 1985). On a cognitive level, the nature of dichotomous thinking among eating-disordered patients is to view even a small ingestion of "forbidden food" as an infraction of her total dietary control. Since this momentary lapse is perceived as catastrophic and evidence of weakness, she loses all control around food (Fairburn & Cooper, 1984; Garfinkel & Garner, 1982). On a physiological level, the person's vulnerability to disinhibition of dietary restraint may be exacerbated if she shows basal or acute hyperinsulinemia and exaggerated cephalic responding to the sight or thought of food (for review, see Rodin, 1985). Further, severe dietary restriction may deplete the level of the neurotransmitter serotonin in the brain (Fernstrom & Wurtman, 1971) and signal carbohydrate-specific food cravings (Wurtman et al., 1981).

Negative mood states, most notably anxiety and depression, also may disinhibit dietary restraint and trigger binge-eating episodes (Abraham & Beumont, 1982; Cooper & Bowskill, 1986; Davis, Freeman, & Solyom, 1985; Johnson & Larson, 1982; Johnson et al., 1987). As patients learn that purging alleviates feelings of guilt and an anxiety about weight gain, they may find it increasingly more difficult to resist the urge to binge (Chiodo & Latimer, 1983; J. Rosen & Leitenberg, 1982).

Interpersonal Difficulties

Difficulties in interpersonal relationships are widely recognized among these patients (Bruch, 1973; Crisp, 1967; Garfinkel & Garner, 1982; Slade, 1982). Social adjustment is markedly impaired (Johnson & Berndt, 1983; Leon, Carroll, Chernyk, & Finn, 1985; Norman & Herzog, 1984). Social skills deficits, anxiety, social isolation, and nonassertiveness may be characteristic predisposing factors (Chiodo, 1987; Fremouw & Heyneman, 1985; Loro, 1984). The family environment may foster patterns that make it difficult for the patient to develop a stable identity, autonomous functioning, and a sense of self-efficacy (Strober & Humphrey, 1987).

Biological Factors

An individual's biology may increase her vulnerability to eating disorders, although it may be difficult to identify and separate predisposing biological mechanisms from those that perpetuate the disorder. Five systems are believed to be pathogenetic: hypothalamic–pituitary axis, central nervous system amines, central nervous system peptides, carbohydrate metabolism, and gastrointestinal hormones (for reviews, see Garfinkel & Kaplan, 1985; Kaplan & Woodside, 1987).

An Overview of Treatment

The classic study of Ansel Keys and colleagues (Keys, Brozek, Henschel, Mickelsen, & Taylor, 1950) was instrumental in identifying cognitive, mood, and behavioral changes that are directly related to the physiological process of starvation. A number of these starvation-related behaviors are evident in anorexia nervosa: greater preoccupation with food, including collecting recipes and reading cookbooks; hoarding food; unusual mixing of food combinations; increased gum chewing and nail-biting; greater coffee and tea consumption; sleep disturbances; food-related dreams; and decreased social and sexual activities and interest (Casper & Davis, 1977; Crisp & Stonehill, 1971; Garfinkel & Garner, 1982).

The lifetime mortality rate for anorexics is approximately 20% greater than that of a control population (Theander, 1983). Patients die from suicide, starvation, and perhaps the secondary effects of starvation. It is necessary, therefore, to address the starvation-related symptomatology by reversing the weight loss and restoring the patient's weight. The goal weight should be set above her menstrual threshold to insure a certain, but necessary, percentage of body fat for the onset and continuation of menses (Frisch & McArthur, 1974). This goal weight should be nonnegotiable, for failure to do so would only perpetuate the illness and render psychotherapy ineffective (Garner & Bemis, 1985).

For nonemaciated eating-disordered patients, the immediate therapeutic goals are to normalize eating patterns, eliminate unhealthy weight-control behaviors, and improve overall social and interpersonal functioning. The patient's overvalued belief system concerning body shape and weight must be altered. Long-term goals are designed for the patient to respond to a changing, stressful environment without relapse and without reengagement of her dysfunctional style of reasoning.

Treatment programs for eating-disordered patients are generally multidisciplinary. Depending on the availability of inpatient management, programs involve a working alliance among some combination of specialists including psychologists, internists, pediatricians, psychiatrists, nutritionists, nurses, art therapists, and occupational therapists (Andersen, 1985; Brownell & Foreyt, 1986; Garner & Garfinkel, 1985). A number of clinical decisions need to be made such as the necessity and therapeutic value of inpatient hospitalization, use of medications, involvement of other family members, and psychotherapy. The multidisciplinary approach enables treatment recommendations to be based on a thorough evaluation of the patient's biological, familial, psychosocial, and psychological functioning.

Paradoxical Techniques in the Treatment of Eating Disorders: Review of the Literature

Paradox is discussed as a treatment intervention primarily for anorexia nervosa. It has been employed to facilitate eating behavior, lower resistance to treatment, and decrease unusual eating or food habits that persist despite the patient's weight gain. As part of a multidisciplinary treatment approach, paradox has been suggested as a means to enable patients to gain control over binge-eating behavior. This discussion now turns to a review of the handful of published reports of the use of paradoxical techniques as applied to the treatment of eating disorders.

Anorexia Nervosa

Refusal to Eat

As a strategic family therapist, Selvini Palazzoli (1978) approaches the patient and her family looking to uncover the hidden "family game" that maintains maladaptive behavioral patterns. She views the anorexic symptomatology as the family's pursuit to preserve unity and stability. By using positive connotation or reframing, Selvini Palazzoli restores balance to the roles of family members. The anorexic is seen not as a "sick patient," but as a co-equal who "is so sensitive and generous that she cannot help sacrificing herself for her family, much as the others cannot help sacrificing themselves" (p. 235). The anorexic symptom is reframed as a behavior that is beneficial to family functioning. The therapist is then free to administer the paradox of symptom prescription. The therapist instructs the patient to maintain dietary restriction, at least for a while, and asks family members to continue their usual behavioral patterns. The rationale of this approach is that the therapist hypothesizes that the patient will rebel, and when she does, will abandon the symptom of food restriction.

Although Selvini Palazzoli (1978) observed dramatic improvements among some patients, occasionally even during the first therapy session, she cautions that the sudden change may not address important family dynamics. To alter well-ingrained familial patterns, additional treatment interventions are necessary.

Resistance to Therapy

Hsu and Lieberman (1982) examined the therapeutic effectiveness of symptom prescription among eight chronic anorexics. All patients (six female and two male) ranged in age from 21 to 34 years and had been symptomatic for at least 5 years without any remission for any length of time greater than 4 months. They had all been hospitalized previously, undergone refeeding procedures, received intensive individual psychotherapy; some had participated in family therapy, and one patient had had a stereotaxic leucotomy. All patients expressed a fear of fatness despite weights that ranged from 25% to 75% below matched population means. To maintain the marked weight loss, patients restricted food intake, purged, and exercised excessively.

Patients were instructed that it "was better for them to keep their anorexia nervosa because previous attempts to treat them had resulted only in temporary remissions of the illness" (p. 651). During therapy sessions (at least six, 1-hour sessions at weekly intervals), patients explored beneficial reasons for maintaining the illness and were encouraged to voice their agreement or disagreement with the therapeutic instructions. Therapists administered the paradox in the presence of family members or friends.

The authors provide two brief case vignettes to describe the therapeutic intervention and progress in more detail. The rationale for the paradox was explained to one patient on the grounds that "attempts to make her gain weight seemed to make her even more unhappy . . . thinness had won her admiration . . . [and binge eating, purging, and amphetamine abuse] was the price she had to pay for wanting to be different" (p. 651). Although a 3-year follow up indicated that the patient had maintained a satisfactory weight, became married, secured steady employment, and participated in social activities, she continued to ingest up to 10 laxatives daily and to overeat when bored.

All patients were relatively stable at a 2- to 4-year follow-up. None were under psychiatric care. Only one patient continued to maintain a weight that was 71% below average; one patient's weight had fluctuated between 86 pounds and 97 pounds during the previous 9 months, and the remaining patients had achieved a weight within 76% to 91% of population mean.

Hsu and Lieberman (1982) emphasize the extreme care that must be taken when employing paradoxical intention with anorexic patients. Given the psychopathology of anorexics who could adversely construe a paradox as abandonment, confrontation, or condemnation, the technique "should be used with caution, even in apparently appropriate patients" (p. 651).

Aberrant Eating, Food, or Weight-Related Behaviors

Even when anorexics achieve a satisfactory weight, some may develop or maintain ritualistic eating or weight-related behaviors (Hall, Slim, Hawker, & Salmond, 1984; Hsu, Crisp, & Harding, 1979). For example, the patient described in the case vignette presented by Hsu and Lieberman (1982) continued to take laxatives daily despite good overall social functioning.

L. Rosen (1980) attempted to address directly the ritualized and secretive eating and food behaviors. Patients were 12 young females who ranged in age from 11 to 21 years and who met diagnostic criteria for anorexia nervosa. The goal of the initial phase of treatment was to restore their weight, and this was accomplished by an operant conditioning paradigm that made social reinforcers contingent on weight gain. Four of the 12 patients required hospitalization because of medical complications (e.g., syncopal episodes, hypoproteinemia with edema, or cardiovascular complications). Within 4 to 10 weeks, all patients had achieved a satisfactory weight gain.

The second phase of treatment targeted the secretive and ritualized eating behaviors. These patterns included the patients' hoarding or hiding food, refusing to eat with others, eating only when alone, refraining from eating forbidden foods, and "claiming" part of the refrigerator and food storage areas. Patients and family members were provided the rationale that in order "to fully confront the meaning and import of their behavior, [patients were] restricted to their self-imposed maladaptive eating styles" (p. 102). Patients were allowed to eat only those foods that they had hoarded or hidden, and all eating had to be done in private. The rationale was supplemented with the message that the procedures should not be regarded as punitive, but rather as an opportunity for patients to acquire a more adaptive eating style. Patients and family members were encouraged to contact the therapist at any time should questions or problems arise.

Two confounding stipulations were enforced. First, before the patient was allowed to engage in any normal eating patterns with family members, she had to "convince the therapist and family that this was so" (p. 102). Second, hospitalization was made contingent on the patient's failure to maintain both her weight and normal eating patterns.

Rosen reports that within three days all patients had resumed normal eating patterns. It is difficult, however, to determine the efficacy of the paradox alone, whether behavior would have changed spontaneously, or whether the procedures would impact on the habitual, ritualistic behaviors among older, more chronic patients.

Bulimia Nervosa

Paradox may play an ancillary role in a treatment package that is designed to relax dietary restraint, alter dysfunctional reasoning styles, and reduce the frequency of binge-eating episodes. Andersen (1985) advocates that a paradoxical instruction of asking patients to plan an extra meal when they feel stressed may enable them to gain a sense of control. By planning to eat ahead of time, patients may begin to confront their dichotomous style of thinking and learn that one bite of food, especially taken when feeling distressed, does not necessarily trigger a binge episode. As they ease their rigid dietary restraint and become more comfortable with eating, patients may learn not to fear the urge to binge as intensely as they currently do.

A rationale that Andersen (1985) finds helpful for some patients is telling them that "If the other techniques we've talked about and tried out don't work, let's plan on a binge—but a smaller one, eaten more slowly, and enjoyed as much as possible" (p. 123). This rationale may be helpful in two ways. First, patients may perceive eating under these conditions as a "relapse." However, by prescribing the event, the therapist is using the technique of restraining. This technique appears to be effective with entrenched and resistant habits (Dowd & Swoboda, 1984). Second, by prescribing the symptom of binge eating, patients are exposed to their fear of eating particular amounts or types of food and, more importantly, to the disastrous consequences that they believe might occur. As Wolpe (1958, 1973) has shown, repeated exposure to the feared stimulus may help to extinguish the anxiety components.

Therapeutic Paradox in Clinical Practice

The few published reports described in the previous section form the basis of the clinical literature of paradoxical intention with eating-disordered patients. The obvious conclusion is the proverbial "more research is needed" statement. Having acknowledged this, we now examine how a behavior therapist might incorporate therapeutic paradox in his or her clinical practice.

The overall treatment goal is that the patient develop a healthy lifestyle, including satisfactory interpersonal and vocational functioning. As steppingstones to achieve this goal, more immediate and specific treatment goals recognize the need to normalize eating patterns by relaxing dietary restraint and binge-eating episodes, to eliminate unhealthy weight-control behaviors, to improve overall social and interpersonal functioning, and, most importantly, to maintain such changes during periods of stress or change.

Therapeutic paradox may be used to help facilitate the immediate goals of treatment in two ways. First, it may be incorporated as an ancillary strategy, most often as a means to help decrease the patient's "resistance" to some aspect of the therapeutic process. For example, a patient may demonstrate noncompliance to a prescribed treatment protocol even though she has expressed a genuine desire for change. Another example of resistance may arise in some situations because the patient feels coerced into seeking treatment, often at the urging of well-meaning and concerned friends and family. Second, therapeutic paradox may be incorporated as a treatment intervention to help alter the frequency or occurrence of some undesired or target behavior, such as rigid dieting or binge eating. For example, a paradoxical instruction to increase dieting behavior may actually help the patient to relax her rigid dietary control.

The defining feature of the use of therapeutic paradox is that the patient is instructed in a manner that appears to be in direct opposition from what should be done. In this sense, we agree with Ascher's (1989) definition that describes paradox as "contradicting received opinion" (p. 23). Although the patient receives instructions that appear to be contradictory to treatment goals, such instructions are in agreement with the therapist's behavioral analysis of *how* to help the patient achieve improvements. The remainder of this chapter illustrates both uses of therapeutic paradox with eating-disordered patients.

The Therapeutic Relationship

A strong therapeutic relationship is essential for behavioral change (Bellack & Hersen, 1985). One of the characteristic features of anorexic patients is the genuine conviction with which they deny their illness. The fear of gaining weight may even lead them to hide behind a veil of deceit (Andersen, 1985). The decision to seek treatment is usually initiated by family members whose feelings of desperation intensify as they realize the impotency of their efforts (Garfinkel & Garner, 1982).

On presentation for treatment, the patient may express great resistance, feelings of ambivalence, and a basic mistrust of herself and others (Garner & Bemis, 1985). Openness, trust, and a genuine desire for change, however, may be evident among patients who have had the disorder for a relatively brief period of time or among chronic patients who are finally willing to give up the struggle (Garner & Bemis, 1985).

Whereas bulimics, in contrast, generally seek professional help on their own accord, at times they may be forced into making an initial appointment by well-meaning friends and family. In these cases, the patient may expect to receive additional pressure from the therapist. She may believe that the therapist is working in collaboration with others to force her to change. The following illustration is taken from a transcript of a case treated by the author in which a college junior was coerced into making an intake appointment by her three roommates who "wanted to help" when their suspicions of her binging and purging behaviors were confirmed. Her roommates had accompanied her to the session and were seated in the waiting room.

PATIENT: You know, I'm only here because my roommates brought me. I know what they're doing, and I know what they want.

THERAPIST: Tell me what it is that you think they want.

PATIENT: They want me to stop using the bathroom to throw up. They think that just by telling me to stop, I can. Hey, I'd like to stop. I'd just like to stop eating. Believe me, I've tried. It just doesn't work.

THERAPIST: How have you tried before to change?

PATIENT: I went to a couple of Support Group meetings. I went to the Counseling Center. I've read a lot. Every time I try, I can't keep it up. If I don't watch my weight, I'll get fat. My family's got weight problems. There's just got to be a pill that can make me stop. Now, they think that by bringing me here, I'm going to stop tomorrow.

THERAPIST: Have you explained to your roommates how much you've tried to change?

PATIENT: Are you kidding? They're so perfect. Once they make up their minds to do something, that's it. They do it. I wish I could be like them. I wish I could really control my eating. Sometimes I can't stop. If I told them, they wouldn't believe it.

As the session continued, it became clear that the patient was angry with her roommates for forcing her to make the appointment. She was afraid that any attempts to change would lead to further failure and decreased self-esteem, particularly as she now feels that her roommates vigilantly watch her and would judge her every move. A "Beck-style" analysis might conclude that her perfectionist tendencies contributed to a dichotomous style of thinking.

It was hypothesized that any direct attempt to enact change or even undertake an assessment would exacerbate the patient's fear and dissuade her from scheduling a second session.

THERAPIST: You know that our program has three parts. During the first part we try to conduct a thorough assessment. This means that you'll be seen by our physician, our nutritionist, and then a long session with me where I'll want to ask you lots of questions about your eating habits. Only then can we talk about what treatment would be best for you.

PATIENT: Look, you're probably good at what you do, but it's not going to work. Don't you see? I've tried before.

THERAPIST: You know, you're right. You really can't expect to change. In fact, no matter who you see or what program you begin, you can't expect to see any change for some time. Maybe 1 month, but probably 2, or maybe even 3 months.

PATIENT: And who can wait that long? I know my roommates can't.

THERAPIST: Sometimes it's best not to even try to change too much. Even if you notice some small change, you don't really know what caused it.

PATIENT: Yeah. Then I won't know how to keep it up.

THERAPIST: Exactly. So, maybe the best idea in your situation would be not to even try making any changes for a while. Go ahead and binge eat. Then, every time that you do, we'll be able to talk about it and try to understand why.

PATIENT: Right. Sure thing. And what are my roommates going to say about that?

THERAPIST: They'll need to know that every time you binge eat, you'll be closer to understanding why it happens.

PATIENT: You think they're going to believe that?

THERAPIST: Why don't we talk to them together? I'll explain that we can't do anything until we understand what's behind your eating. In order to find out, I have to insist that you keep your eating habits just the way they are. And, if they're going to help you, they have to keep doing just what they were doing before asking you to get help. No one is to change. If we're going to see any permanent change, we have to wait about 3 months. Maybe before that, though, you and I might want to meet again with them. How does that sound?

PATIENT: Well, maybe it's worth a try.

Three paradoxes were used. First, the patient and her roommates were instructed to maintain their behavioral patterns in order to enhance therapeutic outcome. By prescribing the symptom, the patient was relieved of close scrutiny by her roommates' vigilance. The roommates were provided guidelines on how to "help" the patient. Second, positive connotations or reframing was utilized as a means to interpret and evaluate the occurrence of the patient's binge-eating episode. An episode was to be viewed as an opportunity to learn and to understand better the patient's reasons for eating. The third paradox was a restraining strategy, whereby the patient was forbidden to change. By being forbidden to change, patients sometimes insist that they do (Weeks & L'Abate, 1982). The ultimate benefit of the paradoxical instructions was that a therapeutic relationship was formed with the patient. The therapist and patient were united as a team that joined forces in working with the roommates.

Decreasing Attempts at Rigid Dietary Restraint

Despite an intellectual understanding of the relationship between dietary restriction and binge eating, patients generally cannot relax dieting standards. They fear to trust the advice that "the best defense against binge eating is to eat" (Johnson et al., 1987). A number of behavioral interventions such as cognitive restructuring, self-monitoring, and stimulus control (meal planning, portion control, timing and spacing of meals) are helpful to break the diet–binge cycle (cf. Garner, Rockert, Olmsted, Johnson, & Coscina, 1985).

Nearly 23% (Gormally, Black, Daston, & Rardin, 1982) to 29% (Loro & Orleans, 1981) of obese persons who seek treatment report bouts of episodic binge eating. Among obese binge eaters, 68% report frequent attempts at strict dieting (Marcus, Wing, & Hopkins, 1988). They share cognitive, affective, and behavioral characteristics with normal-weight bulimics and are more likely to drop out of treatment.

The patient, a 24-year-old single female, initially contacted a weight-management program to help in losing weight. Prior to contacting the program, she had reduced by strict dieting from a high weight of 284 pounds to her current weight of 253 pounds. She had a bachelor's degree in biochemistry and stated that she had researched the use of the protein-sparing modified fast (Genuth, Castro, & Vertes, 1974) and believed that she could benefit greatly from participation in a medically supervised fast with weekly cognitive-behavioral group meetings.

She was admitted to the weight-reduction program but within 3 weeks had voluntarily terminated the fast. At that time, she scheduled an individual appointment to discuss her distress at her inability to adhere to the fast. She perceived herself to be a "total failure." Despite her background in biology and extensive discussion of the role of dieting and binge eating in weight management, she resisted any therapeutic attempts to relax her rigid dieting standards.

PATIENT: I wish my mind would "click" again. When I lost those 30 pounds, I had no trouble not eating. I didn't think about it. I don't know how to get back that feeling. It's all that I need to lose the rest of this weight.

THERAPIST: It seems as if you're looking for some motivation, inspiration, or maybe even magic. When you find it, you'll be O.K.

PATIENT: I know it sounds a little crazy. But nothing else seems to work for me. I've tried Weight Watchers®, grapefruits, and starch blockers. My mother always had me dieting. She even took me to the doctor to get pills . . . and I was only 12 years old at the time. I know that the only way to lose weight is to stop putting the food in my mouth.

THERAPIST: Do you remember in group last week when we talked about how your body's metabolism slows down during periods of food deprivation? We talked about the benefits of dividing your total caloric intake into three or four meals per day. We talked about the benefits of a meal plan that is high in complex carbohydrates and low in fat. We talked about regular aerobic exercise.

THERAPIST: I remember. I remember very well. But those approaches don't work for me.

The remainder of the session was spent in discussion of the patient's options for further professional help, and she decided to pursue individual therapy. When she returned the following week, she seemed determined to extract a promise from the therapist that the content of the sessions would focus on strategies for successful dieting. She resisted therapeutic efforts to shift the dialogue from dieting to other areas.

THERAPIST: You may be right. You certainly know your body better than any of us here could ever hope for. Maybe by doing all that you can to commit yourself to a strict diet for a set period of time, your mind might just "click."

PATIENT: That's what I've been hoping would happen.

THERAPIST: O.K., then. Let's try to devise an ultimate diet and diet strategies for you.

PATIENT: Great.

THERAPIST: For a moment, though, let's put off discussing what exactly you'll eat. We can play around with some ideas ourselves, or maybe you should see a nutritionist. Maybe even two nutritionists so that you could compare what they say and then fashion your own plan.

PATIENT: O.K.

THERAPIST: Let's talk diet strategies now. Tell me how you propose to start.

PATIENT: Well, I do best when I don't eat breakfast. Really. I can take something to work for lunch and then eat only a small dinner.

THERAPIST: Now there you go tempting yourself with some food at lunchtime. Why don't you tell yourself every morning that you won't eat lunch that day?

PATIENT: O.K.

THERAPIST: You should also practice some self-talk in the morning. Maybe for a few minutes each morning, you should repeat statements to yourself that you cannot have even one bite of some foods.

PATIENT: Especially any of the foods that someone in work might bring from home.

THERAPIST: Especially. But is that enough?

PATIENT: Well, maybe I could do more.

THERAPIST: You're the one who knows your body. Maybe you should.

PATIENT: O.K. What about writing everything down that I eat?

THERAPIST: Write down all that you eat. Do you think you should write more down?

PATIENT: I should write down the calories.

THERAPIST: Can you do more?

PATIENT: I could add where I eat the foods.

THERAPIST: Is that enough? Remember, the better you plan strategies to stick to your diet, the better off you'll be in the long run to lose weight, right?

As the patient suggested additional dieting strategies, she was asked to think of even more. This pattern continued for a few more rounds until she began to exhaust herself of ideas.

THERAPIST: O.K. What else can you do?

PATIENT: Well . . . I'm not sure. I think I have a lot here.

THERAPIST: Why don't you read them back, and then we'll see if we can't think of any more that would help you.

PATIENT: (*Reads back the list.*)

THERAPIST: That sounds like a good start. I'll bet that we could think of a few more.

PATIENT: (*Pauses for a few moments.*) Are you serious?

THERAPIST: What do you mean?

PATIENT: Serious about me doing all of these.

THERAPIST: Well, you convinced me earlier that the harder you try to diet, the better chance you will have of "clicking," or sticking to a diet and then, finally, losing weight in the long run. That's the goal I thought we were trying to accomplish.

PATIENT: You want me to do all of these?

THERAPIST: *You* want to do all of those.

The patient began to slowly reread the list. As the items were read, she continued closely to watch the therapist's face. The rate of reading slowed even more approximately midway through the list. By this time, the therapist nodded her head in an affirmative fashion after each item. As the patient continued to observe, the therapist gradually smiled and increased the smile as the items continued. Finally, near the end of the rather long list, the patient also began to smile and eventually started to laugh, at which point the therapist joined in.

PATIENT: All right . . . I guess it sounds pretty silly, huh?

THERAPIST: What's that?

PATIENT: Here I am, I really want to get strict with my dieting. And, you know, there's no end in sight to what I could do if I really wanted to diet. I could drive myself crazy. Is that what you're trying to do?

THERAPIST: Up to this point, all that you have wanted to talk about was how to really diet because you really wanted to lose weight. But, as you can see, you can let yourself get carried away with rigid dieting rules. And, in the process, you will keep yourself in a position where all you can do is fail.

PATIENT: So what can we do about it?

THERAPIST: For starters, why don't you carry this list with you. And every time you begin to think about how much you need to set diet rules, you remember how you eventually had to laugh at yourself because you can get carried away with the rules. Now, if you're going to get serious about your weight, we have to start with understanding you. We have to understand how you think, when and why you eat besides being physically hungry, of course. Are you ready to do all of that?

This extraction from the second therapy session illustrates two aspects of the use of paradox. The first aspect is the extent to which the therapist shares the rationale of paradox with the patient (Ascher & Pollard, 1983). In this case, the rationale was implied to the patient. In such instances, the patient understands the use of the purpose of paradox by the context in which it is administered (Ascher & Pollard, 1983).

Humor also helped to direct the patient's behavior away from an oppositional antitherapeutic position to one that enlisted her cooperation as an active participant in behavioral assessment. As Weeks and L'Abate (1982) explain, when patients "can laugh at the symptom, see it as absurd, or gain some distance from it, then the symptom has acquired a different emotional meaning. Humor itself is paradoxical" (p. 229). This explanation echoes Frankl's (1967) view that the use of humor in paradoxical intention helps to change the patient's attitude toward her neurosis.

Of course, not all therapists can use humor as a component of paradox. Ascher and Pollard (1983) advise that "If a therapist chooses to use humor, it should be a natural part of his or her own therapeutic style and should not be mechanically interjected" (p. 146).

Illustrative Case

The previous two case excerpts illustrate selected aspects of the use of paradox with eating-disordered patients. Paradox typically serves in an ancillary or adjunct function to the larger treatment program. The following case is presented to illustrate a comprehensive approach to the treatment of bulimia and how paradox was used at several points during therapy to facilitate cognitive and behavioral change.

The patient was referred to an Eating Disorders Clinic at a primary teaching hospital by a fellow member of the campus's Eating Disorders Support Group. The fall semester had begun, and the patient was a senior. One of the goals she had set for herself when she started college was that she would have control over her binge-eating problem by the time she graduated. Somehow she had expected that the eating problem "would just go away" during college, but it never had. As the new semester began, she decided to seek professional help.

As part of the full evaluation, the patient was seen by an internist, clinical psychologist, and nutritionist. Resuls of the physical examination and lab studies (EKG, blood chemistries, urinalysis) were within normal limits, and treatment recommendations included individual therapy, nutritional counseling, and continued participation in the support group.

The history and assessment revealed that the patient was the younger of two children. Her sister was 2 years older, and the patient always perceived herself to be inferior by comparison. The patient believed that their mother favored her sister because she was more outgoing, more athletically inclined, attractive, and liked to wear nice clothes. The patient was extremely shy and did not socialize with any friends of her own. Rather, her sister had allowed her to tag along, and the patient had spent a considerable amount of time on the golf range either alone or with her father. The patient's father, however, died suddenly of a heart attack when she was 12 years old. She recalled feeling abandoned at this time and responded by increasing the amount of time she spent alone driving golf balls. She also recalled that she must have overeaten quite a bit because shortly thereafter her mother began to remark on her weight and how tightly her clothes were fitting.

The mother seemed to have been quite distressed at the patient's weight gain. She had tried to encourage her to lose weight by numerous strategies, including starting a three-way "competition" among sisters and mother. But whereas the sister and mother lost weight, the patient gained.

The patient remained socially isolated and spent her time studying and playing golf. She graduated from high school with good grades and moved away from home to a college within 250 miles with the approval of her mother.

Her social isolation continued at college; in fact, she believes that her social discomfort and anxiety increased. Skills deficits were evident during assessment. She had poor verbal and nonverbal skills, spoke very softly, found expressing her thoughts and emotions difficult, and often was at a loss for words.

Her sense of inferiority and poor self-esteem increased. During telephone conversations with her mother and home visits, she learned of her sister's accomplishments.

The frequency of binge eating and vomiting increased to where cycles occurred once per day, usually beginning in the early evening when she returned home. Feelings of disappointment, frustration, anger, failure, and stress precipitated a greater sense of "feeling fat." She resolved to try to "lose weight" to help maintain self-discipline and control.

The patient remained cooperative throughout the first 3 weeks of treatment. She met for 1-hour sessions, twice a week. She complied with requests for self-monitoring. With the aid of nutritional counseling, she learned to choose average portions from the four basic food groups. Stimulus-control strategies facilitated adherence to the meal plan. She accepted the rationale of cognitive restructuring and eagerly identified examples of errors of reasoning.

The following excerpt is taken from the start of the fourth week of therapy.

PATIENT: I almost didn't come today.

THERAPIST: Tell me why.

PATIENT: Last night was terrible. I did it again. I couldn't stop my eating.

THERAPIST: Do you remember when we first started to work I said that there would be ups and downs?

PATIENT: Yeah. But I haven't thrown up since then. I've been doing well. Now I'm starting over again.

THERAPIST: Wait a minute. As a matter of fact, you're ahead of me. You see, we were getting ready to start the part of the program that helps you to bounce back after a binge episode. Part of your ability to bounce back can really only be accomplished by the cognitive and behavioral skills that we talk about in our therapy session after you have had a binge episode. I was going to ask you to plan a minibinge. Now, you've had a binge episode yesterday, right?

PATIENT: Right.

THERAPIST: Now we're ready to move on and look at some skills that help you to bounce back. You've jumped the gun by a few days, but that must mean that you are eager to make progress. What do you think?

PATIENT: Yeah.

This excerpt shows how two paradoxes can be used. First, the patient's relapse was reframed from the negative perspective of failure to the positive view that it provided an opportunity to learn essential cognitive and behavioral skills. Recategorizing the behavior from one conceptual class to another makes it difficult for the patient to dwell on the negative or failure aspects (Watzlawick, Weakland, & Fisch, 1974). The second paradox involved utilization strategies (Goldfried & Davison, 1976). This strategy involves accepting attitudes and behavior change as therapeutic progress. In essence, it is difficult for the patient to fail because whatever inter-session behavior change occurs is evidence of change and progress.

Satisfactory progress continued for 2 more weeks, and the frequency of sessions was reduced to once per week. The focus of the sessions was improving social and communication skills. Role playing, behavioral rehearsal, shaping, and immediate feedback strategies were employed. Homework assignments required the patient to expose herself to situations that aroused a small amount of anxiety in order to provide opportunities for her to practice (e.g., asking a salesperson in a hobby shop for information).

Although significant improvements in communication skills were noted, the patient reported difficulties in maintaining her exercise regimen.

PATIENT: I haven't exercised at all for the past 10 days.

THERAPIST: Why do you think that is?

PATIENT: I just don't have the time.

THERAPIST: We're talking about 30 to 40 minutes, four times a week.

PATIENT: It's a lot to do. I know I should, but I can't.

During the next few minutes, the patient resisted any attempts to problem-solve the situation. In fact, rather than pursuing an interaction that was increasing in opposition, a restraining strategy was tried.

THERAPIST: O.K., the exercise plan may be asking you to do a lot . . . especially with your schedule, your term paper, the exam. Asking yourself to try to fit exercise in might be asking yourself to do too much.

PATIENT: I'm sorry.

THERAPIST: There's nothing to be sorry about, is there? Four times a week is too much. Can you cut back to three times?

PATIENT: Well . . .

THERAPIST: All right, three may be too many. Let's just say two.

PATIENT: Uh . . .

THERAPIST: It's probably time to back off from exercise. Don't even try to do anything. In fact, you should really cut back on riding your bike and golfing. You might be trying to do too much. At least for the next couple of weeks, if you get the urge to do anything, including bike riding and golfing, don't do it. Give your body a rest.

The patient seemed surprised by these instructions, and within a period of 10 days, she was excited to report that she had gotten over her difficulty in exercising during the week.

The next several sessions focused on increasing the patient's skill at identifying, monitoring, and expressing mood states. A checklist of adjectives of various mood states was given to her. She used the list to help identify and articulate her internal states. Homework assignments required her to use the list during trips to such places as the mall and library as an aid and practice in identifying the mood states of other people. Much discussion centered on how to "read" people. Some sessions were conducted outside of the clinic rooms (e.g., student center, cafeteria) during which time the therapist and patient discussed and compared their observations of other people.

These sessions proved particularly helpful. Overall progress remained satisfactory until a significant relapse occurred. Extensive probing suggested that the trigger for this episode was the patient's anxiety surrounding an upcoming visit from her mother. She expressed a number of fears about her mother's visit, particularly since she had confided to her mother the history of her eating problem. One fear was that the patient believed that her mother would watch her every mouthful and try to "help" by giving her advice on her eating patterns. At this point, the patient was accustomed to eating a substantial breakfast. Her mother had always scorned breakfast as "unnecessary calories."

Various options regarding how to handle this situation were proposed and discussed. The patient wanted to use a symptom prescription and reframing strategies. She would explain to her mother any and all food that she ate was only what we had prescribed and that any overeating was a learning opportunity for her to practice her newly acquired skills.

The patient continued in therapy for the next 7 months and continued to make progress. Binge eating had subsided. She decreased her social isolation by becoming involved with a group of students who took short bike trips on the weekends. She graduated from college and remained in the area for the summer. She secured an out-of-state job and was eagerly anticipating her move and new opportunities. She continues to keep in touch by letter and is doing well.

One of the interesting outcomes of paradox in this case is that the patient learned to use the strategy herself. By suggesting and applying it on her mother, she found a new way to interpret and evaluate her own behavior.

Summary

The review of the clinical literature on the use of therapeutic paradox with eating-disordered patients reveals a limited empirical or scientific base. The purpose of this chapter is to describe ways in which paradox has been used to enhance therapeutic outcome. It may be used as an ancillary strategy in order to facilitate the cooperation of the patient or it may be incorporated as a treatment component designed to alter the frequency of a target behavior. As with any intervention, however, its use is guided by the therapist's behavioral analysis of the individual patient. Future research can help to clarify factors that enhance and/or preclude its application in the clinical setting.

Acknowledgment

Appreciation is expressed to Charles Mansueto, Ph.D., who provided critical comments on an earlier draft of this chapter.

References

Abraham, S. F., & Beumont, P. J. V. (1982). How patients describe bulimia or binge eating. *Psychological Medicine, 12,* 625–635.

Agras, W. S., & Kirkley, B. G. (1986). Bulimia: Theories of etiology. In K. D. Brownell & J. P. Foreyt (Eds.), *Handbook of eating disorders* (pp. 367–378). New York: Basic Books.

Allon, N. (1982). The stigma of overweight in everyday life. In B. Wolman (Ed.), *Psychological aspects of obesity: A handbook* (pp. 130–174). New York: Van Nostrand Reinhold.

American Psychiatric Association. (1987). *Diagnostic and statistical manual of mental disorders* (3rd ed.—rev.). Washington, D.C.: American Psychiatric Association.

Andersen, A. E. (1985). *Practical comprehensive treatment of anorexia nervosa and bulimia.* Baltimore, MD: Johns Hopkins University Press.

Ascher, L. M. (1989). Paradoxical intention: Its clarification and emergence as a conventional behavioral procedure. *the Behavior Therapist, 12,* 23–28.

Ascher, L. M., & Pollard, C. A. (1983). Paradoxical intention. In J. Larcinan (Ed.), *The therapeutic efficacy of the major psychotherapeutic techniques* (pp. 139–149). Springfield, IL: Charles C. Thomas.

Beck, A. T., Rush, A. J., Shaw, B. F., & Emery, G. (1979). *Cognitive therapy of depression.* New York: The Guilford Press.

Bellack, A. S., & Hersen, M. (1985). General considerations. In M. Hersen & A. S. Bellack (Eds.), *Handbook of clinical behavior therapy with adults* (pp. 3–22). New York: Plenum Press.

Bemis, K. (1978). Current approaches to the etiology and treatment of anorexia nervosa. *Psychological Buleltin, 85,* 593–617.

Blumenthal, J. A., O'Toole, L. C., & Chang, J. L. (1984). Is running an analogue of anorexia nervosa? An empirical study of obligatory running analogue of anorexia nervosa. *Journal of the American Medical Association, 252,* 520–523.

Brillat-Savarin, J. (1970). *The philosopher in the kitchen* (A. Drayton, Trans.). Baltimore, MD: Penguin Books. (Original work published 1825)

Brownell, K. D., & Foreyt, J. P. (Eds.). (1986). *Handbook of eating disorders.* New York: Basic Books.

Bruch, H. (1973). *Eating disorders.* New York: Basic Books

Bruch, H. (1978). *The golden cage.* Cambridge, MA: Harvard University Press.

Bruch, H. (1985). Four decades of eating disorders. In D. M. Garner & P. E. Garfinkel (Eds.), *Handbook of psychotherapy for anorexia nervosa and bulimia* (pp. 7–18). New York: The Guilford Press.

Cahnman, W. J. (1968). The stigma of obesity. *Sociological Quarterly, 9,* 283–299.

Canning, H., & Mayer, J. (1966). Obesity—its possible effects on college admissions. *New England Journal of Medicine, 275,* 1172–1174.

Casper, R. C., & Davis, J. M. (1977). On the course of anorexia nervosa. *American Journal of Psychiatry, 134,* 974–978.

Casper, R. C., Eckert, E. D., Halmi, K. A., Goldberg, S. C., & Davis, J. M. (1980). Bulimia: Its incidence and clinical importance in patients with anorexia nervosa. *Archives of General Psychiatry, 37,* 1030–1034.

Chiodo, J. (1987). Bulimia: An individual behavioral analysis. *Journal of Behavior Therapy and Experimental Psychiatry, 18,* 41–49.

Chiodo, J., & Latimer, P. R. (1983). Vomiting as a learned weight-control technique in bulimia. *Journal of Behavior Therapy and Experimental Psychiatry, 14,* 131–135.

Cooper, P. J., & Bowskill, R. (1986). Dysphoric mood and overeating. *British Journal of Clinical Psychology, 25,* 155–156.

Crisp, A. H. (1967). The possible significance of some behavioral correlates of weight and carbohydrate intake. *Journal of Psychosomatic Research, 11,* 117–121.

Crisp, A. H., & Stonehill, E. (1971). Aspects of the relationship between psychiatric status, sleep, nocturnal motility and nutrition. *Journal of Psychosomatic Research, 15,* 501–509.

Davis, R., Freeman, J. J., & Solyom, L. (1985). Mood and food: An analysis of bulimic episodes. *Journal of Psychiatric Research, 19,* 331–335.

Dowd, E. T., & Swoboda, J. S. (1984). Paradoxical interventions in behavior therapy. *Journal of Behavior Therapy and Experimental Psychiatry, 15,* 229–234.

Fairburn, C. G. (1981). A cognitive behavioral approach to the treatment of bulimia. *Psychological Medicine, 11,* 707–711.

Fairburn, C. G. (1985). Cognitive-behavioral treatment for bulimia. In D. M. Garner & P. E. Garfinkel (Eds.), *Handbook of psychotherapy for anorexia nervosa and bulimia* (pp. 160–192). New York: The Guilford Press.

Fairburn, C. G. (1987). The definition of bulimia nervosa: Guidelines for clinicians and research workers. *Annals of Behavioral Medicine, 4,* 3–7.

Fairburn, C. G., & Cooper, P. J. (1984). The clinical features of bulimia nervosa. *British Journal of Psychiatry, 284,* 1153–1155.

Fairburn, C. G., Cooper, Z., & Cooper, P. J. (1986). The clinical features and maintenance of bulimia nervosa. In K. D. Brownell & J. P. Foreyt (Eds.), *Handbook of eating disorders* (pp. 389–404. New York: Basic Books.

Fernstrom, J. D., & Wurtman, R. J. (1971). Brain serotonin content: Increase following ingestion of carbohydrate diet. *Science, 174,* 1023–1025.

Frankl, V. (1967). *Psychotherapy and existentialism: Selected papers on logotherapy.* New York: Simon and Schuster.

Fremouw, W. J., & Heyneman, N. E. (1985). Cognitive styles and bulimia. *the Behavior Therapist, 6,* 143–144.

Frisch, R. E., & McArthur, J. W. (1974). Menstrual cycles: Fatness as a determinant of minimum weight necessary for their maintenance or onset. *Science, 185,* 949-951.

Garfinkel, P. E., & Garner, D. M. (1982). *Anorexia nervosa—a multidimensional perspective.* New York: Brunner/Mazel

Garfinkel, P. E., & Kaplan, A. S. (1985). Starvation based perpetuating mechanisms in anorexia nervosa and bulimia. *International Journal of Eating Disorders, 4,* 651–665.

Garfinkel, P. E., Moldofsky, H., & Garner, D. M. (1980). The heterogeneity of anorexia nervosa. *Archives of General Psychiatry, 37,* 1036–1040.

Garner, D. M., & Bemis, K. M. (1982). A cognitive-behavioral approach to anorexia nervosa. *Cognitive Therapy and Research, 6,* 123–150.

Garner, D. M., & Bemis, K. M. (1985). Cognitive therapy for anorexia nervosa. In D. M. Garner & P. E. Garfinkel (Eds.), *Handbook of psychotherapy for anorexia nervosa and bulimia* (pp. 107–146). New York: The Guilford Press.

Garner, D. M., & Garfinkel, P. E. (1978). Socio-cultural factors in the development of anorexia nervosa. *Lancet, 2,* 674.

Garner, D. M., & Garfinkel, P. E. (1980). Sociocultural factors in the development of anorexia nervosa. *Psychological Medicine, 10,* 647–656.

Garner, D. M., & Garfinkel, P. E. (Eds.). (1985). *Handbook of psychotherapy for anorexia nervosa and bulimia.* New York: The Guilford Press.

Garner, D. M., Garfinkel, P. E., & Bemis, K. (1982). A multidimensional psychotherapy for anorexia nervosa. *International Journal of Eating Disorders, 1,* 3–46.

Garner, D. M., Rockert, W., Olmsted, M. P., Johnson, C., & Coscina, D. V. (1985). Psychoeducational principles in the treatment of bulimia and anorexia nervosa. In D. M. Garner & P. E. Garfinkel (Eds.), *Handbook of psychotherapy for anorexia nervosa and bulimia* (pp. 513–572). New York: The Guilford Press.

Genuth, S. M., Castro, J., & Vertes, V. (1974). Weight reduction in obesity by outpatient semi-starvation. *Journal of the American Medical Association, 230,* 987–991.

Goldfried, M. R., & Davison, G. C. (1976). *Clinical behavior therapy.* New York: Holt, Rinehart, & Winston.

Gormally, J., Black, S., Daston, S., & Rardin, D. (1982). The assessment of binge eating severity among obese persons. *Addictive Behaviors, 7,* 47–55.

Hall, A., Slim, E., Hawker, F., & Salmond, C. (1984). Anorexia nervosa: Long-term outcome in 50 female patients. *British Journal of Psychiatry, 145,* 407–413.

Halmi, K. A. (1974). Anorexia nervosa: Demographic and clinical features in 94 cases. *Psychosomatic Medicine, 36,* 18–25.

Halmi, K. A., Goldberg, S. C., & Cunningham, S. (1977). Perceptual distortion of body image in adolescent girls: Distortion of body image in adolescence. *Psychological Medicine, 7,* 253–257.

Hay, G., & Leonard, J. C. (1979). Anorexia nervosa in males. *Lancet, 2,* 574–575.

Herzog, D. B., Norman, D. K., Gordon, C., & Pepose, M. (1984). Sexual conflict and eating disorders in 27 males. *American Journal of Psychiatry, 141,* 989-990.

Hsu, L. K. G., Crisp, A. H., & Harding, B. (1979). Outcome of anorexia nervosa. *Lancet, 1,* 61–65.

Hsu, L. K. G., & Lieberman, S. (1982). Paradoxical intention in the treatment of chronic anorexia nervosa. *American Journal of Psychiatry, 139(5),* 650–653.

Johnson, C., & Berndt, D. J. (1983). Preliminary investigation of bulimia and life adjustment. *American Journal of Psychiatry, 140,* 6.

Johnson, C., Connors, M. E., & Tobin, D. L. (1987). Symptom management of bulimia. *Journal of Consulting and Clinical Psychology, 55,* 668–676.

Johnson, C., & Larson, R. (1982). Bulimia: An analysis of moods and behavior. *Psychosomatic Medicine, 44,* 341–351.

Kalucy, R. S., Crisp, A. H., & Harding, B. (1977). A study of 56 families with anorexia nervosa. *British Journal of Medical Psychology, 50,* 381–395.

Kaplan, A. S., & Woodside, D. B. (1987). Biological aspects of anorexia nervosa and bulimia nervosa. *Journal of Consulting and Clinical Psychology, 55,* 645–653.

Kaye, W. J., & Gwirtsman, H. E. (Eds.). (1985). *A comprehensive approach to the treatment of normal weight bulimia.* Washington, DC: American Psychiatric Press.

Keys, A., Brozek, J., Henschel, A., Mickelsen, O., & Taylor, H. L. (1950). *The biology of human starvation* (Vol. 1). Minneapolis: University of Minnesota Press.

Leon, G. R., Carroll, K., Chernyk, B., & Finn, S. (1985). Binge eating and associated habit patterns within college student and identified bulimic population. *International Journal of Eating Disorders, 4,* 43–57.

Lerner, R. M. (1973). The development of personal space schemata toward body build. *Journal of Psychology, 84,* 229–235.

Loro, A. D., Jr. (1984). Binge eating: A cognitive-behavioral treatment approach. In R. C. Hawkins, W. J. Fremouw, & P. F. Clement (Eds.), *The binge-purge syndrome: Diagnosis, treatment, and research* (pp. 183–210). New York: Springer Publishing.

Loro, A. D., Jr., & Orleans, C. S. (1981). Binge eating in obesity: Preliminary findings and guidelines for behavioral analysis and treatment. *Addictive Behaviors, 6,* 155–166.

Maddox, G. L., & Lieberman, V. (1969). Overweight as a social disability with medical implications. *Journal of Medical Education, 44,* 214–220.

Marcus, M. D., Wing, R. R., & Hopkins, J. (1988). Obese binge eaters: Affect, cognitions, and response to behavioral weight control. *Journal of Consulting and Clinical Psychology, 56,* 433–439.

Nielsen, A. C. (1979). *Who is dieting and why?* Chicago: Author.

Norman, D. K., & Herzog, D. B. (1984). Persistent social maladjustment in bulimia: A one-year follow-up. *American Journal of Psychiatry, 141,* 444–446.

Nylander, I. (1971). The feeling of being fat and dieting in a school population. *Acta Sociomedica Scandinavica, 1,* 17–26.

Polivy, J., & Herman, C. P. (1985). Dieting and bingeing. *American Psychologist, 40,* 193–201.

Richardson, S. A., Hastorf, A. H., Goodman, N., & Dornbusch, S. M. (1961). Cultural uniformity in reaction to physical disabilities. *American Sociological Review, 26,* 241–247.

Rodin, J. (1985). Insulin levels, hunger, and food intake: An example of feedback loops in weight regulation. *Health Psychology, 4,* 1-24.

Rodin, J., & Slochower, J. (1974). Fat chance for a favor: Obese-normal differences in compliance and incidental learning. *Journal of Personality and Social Psychology, 29,* 557-565.

Rosen, J. C., & Leitenberg, H. (1982). Bulimia nervosa: Treatment with exposure and response prevention. *Behavior Therapy, 8,* 385-392.

Rosen, L. W. (1980). Modification of secretive or ritualized eating behavior in anorexia nervosa. *Journal of Behavior Therapy and Experimental Psychiatry, 11,* 101-104.

Ryle, J. A. (1939). Discussion on anorexia nervosa. *Proceedings of the Royal Society of Medicine, 32,* 735-739.

Selvini Palazzoli, M. (1978). *Self-starvation* (A. Pomerans, Trans.). New York: Jason Aronson. (Original work published 1974)

Slade, P. (1982). Towards a functional analysis of anorexia nervosa and bulimia nervosa. *British Journal of Clinical Psychology, 21,* 53-61.

Staffieri, J. R. (1967). A study of social stereotype of body image in children. *Journal of Personality and Social Psychology, 7,* 101-104.

Strober, M., & Humphrey, L. L. (1987). Familial contributions to the etiology and course of anorexia nervosa and bulimia. *Journal of Consulting and Clinical Psychology, 55,* 654-659.

Theander, S. (1983). Research on outcome and prognosis of anorexia nervosa and some results from a Swedish long-term study. *International Journal of Eating Disorders, 2,* 167-174.

Vandereycken, W., & Meermann, R. (1984). *Anorexia nervosa—a clinician's guide to treatment.* New York: Walter de Gruyter.

Wadden, T. A., & Stunkard, A. J. (1985). Social and psychological consequences of obesity. *Annals of Internal Medicine, 103,* 1062-1067.

Watzlawick, P., Weakland, J., & Fisch, R. (1974). *Change: Principles of problem formation and problem resolution.* New York: W. W. Norton.

Weeks, G. R., & L'Abate, L. (1982). *Paradoxical psychotherapy: Theory and practice with individuals, couples, and families.* New York: Brunner/Mazel.

Wolpe, J. (1958). *Psychotherapy by reciprocal inhibition.* Stanford: Stanford University Press.

Wolpe, J. (1973). *The practice of behavior therapy* (2nd ed.). New York: Pergamon Press.

Wurtmann, J. J., Wurtman, R. J., Growdon, J. H., Henry, P., Lipscomb, A., & Zeisel, S. H. (1981). Carbohydrate craving in obese people: Suppression by treatments affecting serotoninergic transmission. *International Journal of Eating Disorders, 1,* 1-15.

Yates, A., Leehey, K., & Shisslak, C. M. (1983). Running—an analogue of anorexia? *New England Journal of Medicine, 308,* 251-255.

Chapter 6

Employing Therapeutic Paradox in the Treatment of Depression

James C. Coyne

Over the past few decades, evidence has accumulated that narrowly insight-oriented therapies may be insufficient as treatment for depression (McLean & Hakstian, 1979). However, it appears that cognitive (Rush, Beck, Kovacs, & Hollon, 1977; Murphy, Simons, Wetzel, & Lustman, 1984), behavioral (McLean & Hakstian, 1979), and interpersonal (Elkin, Shea, Watkins, & Colloins, 1986) therapies may be as effective as antidepressant medication for outpatient depressed persons. The theoretical rationales for these approaches differ, yet they share some common features. All are relatively brief and highly structured, they are goal-oriented, and they focus on initiating constructive changes in behavior as an alternative to the depressed person's dwelling on negative feelings or the attainment of insight.

Strategic therapy for depression (Coyne, 1984, 1986a, 1988a) shares these features but has some additional emphases. First, it acknowledges some of the key ironies and paradoxes of depression, and it counters them with what are often paradoxical interventions. Second, strategic therapy highlights how persons who are significant in the lives of depressed persons may usefully be involved in therapy. Without necessarily implicating them as the source of the depressed person's problems, they may be enlisted as part of their solution. However depression has come about, its resolution frequently involves the renegotiation of close relationships. This may proceed more smoothly and more efficiently if significant others are directly involved. Finally, the modal depressed outpatient is a woman who is married and who complains of marital difficulties. More than other approaches, strategic therapy comes to terms with the association between marital problems and depression, but in doing so, it also acknowledges what are likely to be important differences in the agenda of depressed persons and their spouses.

Overview

Strategic therapy is a pragmatic, goal-oriented, short-term approach that focuses on how the miscarried coping efforts of depressed persons and key persons in their lives are perpetuating their problems and how these efforts can be redirected. In a sense, these coping efforts, rather than depression *per se*, become the target of change. The assumption is that with a redirection of these efforts and appropriate application of the resources that were misapplied or unrecognized an episode of depression will prove self-limiting or otherwise be resolved.

Discussions of depression often start with too much imagination about what depressed persons are like and too little consideration of how their problems and complaints may be linked to their situations. Indeed, one inaccurate stereotype, exemplified by the learned helplessness model of depression (Abramson, Seligman, & Teasdale, 1978), involves a conception of depressed persons as uniformly passive, resigned, lacking in hostility, and unresponsive to positive aspects of their exchanges with their environments. This has little relationship to what most depressed persons are like, and it is a misleading basis for intervention.

Depression typically involves a struggle, either to change one's situation, overcome feeling depressed, or maintain some semblance of a normal life in the face of being depressed. Rather than being resigned, depressed persons are often characterized by a stubborn refusal to accept the status quo (Coyne, Aldwin, & Lazarus, 1981). Yet, they cope in a way that fails to alleviate their situation and may even aggravate it. In stressful encounters with others, depressed persons are characterized by confrontative strategies, ineffective support-seeking, wishful thinking, and efforts at escape and avoidance (Coyne et al., 1981; Folkman & Lazarus, 1986). Despite the psychodynamic conception of depressed persons as those who turn their anger inward, overt hostility and anger are key features of their close relationships with others (Kahn, Coyne, & Margolin, 1985). Depressed persons may complain that they are helpless, but may feel this way only because they are trying—struggling with their problems in a way that convinces them that these problems are intractable. Paradoxically, depressed persons may remain miserable because they are trying so hard not to be. Depressed persons are responsive to success experiences (Beck, 1967), perhaps too much so, in that they are then set up for disappointments in the face of a situation or relationship that responds inconsistently to their efforts.

Depressed persons are highly anxious. In the studies validating the Hopkins Symptom Checklist, they were more anxious than were the patients having diagnosed anxious disorders (Derogotis, Lipman, Rickels, Uhlenhulth, & Covi, 1974). Efforts to manage that anxiety, not to appear inept, and to avoid criticism and failure can be an important part of the depressed individual's miscarried coping efforts. Depressed persons are frequently avoidant and indecisive, and they can find ample evidence that they are irresponsible and incompetent. Yet, such an unsuccessful style of coping is often maintained by high standards and a definition of the task at hand that makes any accomplishment seem insufficient and any effort seem futile. If they could be a bit more accepting of their situation without giving up, and if they could be induced to set out to do less, they might accomplish more. Yet, it is the failure of the existing coping strategies of such individuals to have the desired outcome that may lead them to raise their standards and redouble their efforts.

Persons in a depressive episode can be difficult and overly sensitive interpersonally. They may complain incessantly, and interactions with them can be complicated by implicit demands, indirect communication, sensitivity to rejection, and irritability punctuated by outright hostility. Yet, the depressed person's distress, dependency, inhibition, and difficulties dealing with hostility do not occur in a vacuum. These problems may be maintained by involvement in relationships that are distressing, insecure, and not conducive to having expectations renegotiated or to overt disagreement or to the direct expression of negative affect. Thus, Leff and Vaughn (1985) found that depressed persons, particularly women, tended to be fearful of loss and rejection and desirous of continual comfort and support. However, Leff and Vaughn were able to contextualize this observation and identify reasons why depressed persons might persist in such fears and perceptions. Namely, "few depressed patients described as chronically insecure or lacking in self-confidence were living with supportive or sympathetic spouses. . . . [W]hen this was the case, the patients were well at followup" (p. 95).

It has been suggested that the behavior of depressed persons can be aversive, powerful in its ability to induce negative moods in others, and yet that it is also guilt-inducing and inhibiting (Coyne, 1976). For their part, others may fall into a strategy of trying to reduce the aversiveness of depressed persons by providing the support that is seemingly being sought, even while leaking impatience, hostility, and rejection. The subtle and overt hostility and rejection that depressed persons receive elicits further expression of distress, strengthening the pattern. Troublesome in themselves, such interactions can be expected to interfere with everyone's ability to maintain a life together, solve problems, or renegotiate their relationships. Further, therapists are not immune to participating in this counterproductive pattern. Like other persons in depressed persons' lives, therapists may become overinvolved in miscarried efforts to assist them to feel better, increasing depressed persons' sense of responsibility and failure, with the therapists ultimately personalizing the depressed persons' problems and blaming and rejecting the clients (Coyne, Wortman, & Lehman, 1988).

There is an established empirical association between depression and concurrent marital problems: having marital problems may increase the probability that one is clinically depressed by 24-fold (Weissman, 1987)! How this association comes about will vary from case to case. In strategic therapy, the working hypotheses are simply that marital interactions may be relevant to the persistence and resolution of a depressive episode and that the behavior of depressed persons and the responses of their spouses are likely to become interwoven and concatenated over time. Tracking the precise nature of this patterning in a given case is one of the key assessment tasks facing the strategic therapist. As I have noted, there is less interest in the reasons why someone is depressed than in how depression may be perpetuated by the miscarried coping or attempted solutions of the depressed person and the spouse. Therapy is focused on interdicting or modifying these efforts and thereby remedying the circumstances maintaining the patient's distress.

Depression frequently arises in the context of life transitions, and it may be that the depressed person, the partner, or both have been unable or unwilling to make an adaptation to these changes that is mutually satisfying. It may be that distressing circumstances have required one or both of them to rely more heavily on the marriage. In the process of this, what had previously been a bearable, but basically unfulfilling or unsatisfying, relationship may now become intolerable. Alternatively, one person becoming depressed for any reason impinges on a close relationship and may burden the partner in important ways (Coyne et al., 1987). Depressed persons may make demands or depend on their marriage and spouses differently than in the past, and spouses may feel that their needs are not met, resist the coping efforts of depressed persons, or otherwise react negatively.

Depressed persons and their spouses generally agree on difficulty discussing problems as a primary complaint about their marriage, although depressed persons tend to localize problems in the relationship, whereas their spouses localize the problems in the defects of the depressed person (Coyne, 1988b; Leff & Vaughn, 1985). In problem-solving interactions, depressed persons and their spouses are similar in being high in expression of negative affect, withdrawal, and avoidance, and low in constructive problem-solving behaviors (Kahn et al., 1985). Such a pattern can be self-perpetuating: the pain and seeming futility of efforts to confront problems lead to avoidance and the accumulation of unresolved issues, which in turn overwhelm the couple when they must deal with specific issues. This can be a stumbling block to a therapist's efforts to instigate change. However, some important therapeutic resources can be salvaged if the therapist can identify the positive commitments and miscarried initiatives behind some of the destructiveness that has occurred and utilize them in ways that lead to different outcomes.

Even when depressed persons are not experiencing marital problems, the recovery process generally necessitates a renegotiation of the marital relationship. Couples who have seemed previously to be functioning well may differ in their ability to cope with this. Recovering depressed persons often become less inhibited and more independent, assertive, and demanding, and this may prove to be a source of friction and conflict. Sometimes the reaction of spouses may make it difficult for depressed persons to pace the resumption of previous role responsibilities, or the depressed persons' experimentation with new ways of handling disagreement and hostility may make it difficult for spouses to remain supportive.

Discussions of marital interaction in depression are incomplete without an acknowledgment that wives are more likely to be depressed than husbands and that women are more vulnerable to the quality of the marital relationship and a lack of intimacy than are men. A variety of sociocultural and economic factors make it more difficult for women to renegotiate their marital relationships in times of stress of dissatisfaction. In conducting marital therapy for depression, the therapist is often inadvertently assisting a woman to continue by other means an attempt at renegotiation of her relationship that has somehow become thwarted or stalemated. In such a context, it is important that the therapist not adopt a critical, blaming stance with respect to either partner. Rather, the key to facilitating the husband's participation frequently lies in recognizing that his principal motive for considering changes in the relationship that he would otherwise not deem necessary or useful may be the hope of reducing the difficulties of living with a depressed wife.

Overview of Therapy

The therapy session is viewed as a staging area for small, but strategic changes in how depressed persons tackle their problems and how they interact with key persons, particularly the spouse. Sessions tend to be low-key, and the therapist's major activities are to elicit detailed descriptions of interactions in problematic situations, set goals, prepare the key persons for extratherapy tasks, assign the tasks, and to follow up. Therapy is explicitly time-limited, with either a preset number of sessions or a contracting for subsequent sessions based on the demonstration of progress. Thus, the therapist may contract with a depressed person to work on a particular problem, and if progress can be seen in six sessions, a new goal will be set, and an additional six sessions offered to pursue it.

Goals are typically small, but strategic changes in behavior that are intended to instigate change of a more general nature. Achievement of them is often operationalized in terms of the occurrence of specific observable events that would indicate that there is indeed progress, even if not resolution of key problems. Therapeutic sessions are seen mainly as an opportunity to prepare the persons involved for making these changes in their everyday life, rather as than the primary place in which change takes place.

Extensive use is made of extratherapy task assignments, often of a paradoxical nature and often utilizing *reframing* (Coyne, 1985; Watzlawick, Weakland, & Fisch, 1974). In reframing, the therapist works to grasp the language with which a person describes a problem, actively acknowledges an acceptance of this perspective to him or her, and then extends or turns it in a direction that allows new behavior to be initiated. The theme of many reframings of behavior with depressed persons is to develop positive connotations of what might otherwise be the basis of depressed persons' self-derogations and to utilize these connotations as the basis for constructive action. Thus, in response to a depressed woman who berates herself for her irritability with her husband, a therapist might suggest that she is irritable because she is so invested in being nice that her husband has been lulled into ignoring her needs and wishes, and the situation that has developed would make anyone irritable, if not outraged.

One characteristic feature of strategic therapy for depression is that it tends to involve significant others directly in the process of therapy, even when relationship issues are not explicitly defined as part of the presenting problem. It is assumed that the therapist is rarely in a position to ignore how significant others may be reacting to the depressed person, attempting to preserve their own well-being, or otherwise coping with their predicament. Yet, even when therapy is explicitly marital or family in focus, sessions tend to be split among key persons, rather than conjoint, and confrontations and enactment of problematic interactions in the session tend to be avoided. For instance, the typical marital session tends to involve 20 to 25 minutes with each spouse, and a briefer wrap-up meeting at the end of which the therapist makes summary comments and provides extratherapy tasks. The multiple reasons for this structure have been presented in greater detail elsewhere (Coyne, 1986b). Basically, it is assumed that depressed persons and their spouses may have quite different ideas about the locus of problems and the responsibility for change and that this format allows therapy to proceed without requiring resolution of these differences as a precondition. Working with the partners separately, but coordinating these efforts, the therapist can avoid depending on their feeling reconciliatory or altruistic and, instead, focus on what is personally distressing to each of them, as well as on what would constitute a reasonable goal and acceptable signs of progress for them.

At least one psychotherapy project found that efforts to induce depressed persons and their spouses to share their feelings toward each other can prove counterproductive and even destructive (E. Waring, personal communication, 1984). In conjoint sessions, a couple that has a depressed person will often lapse into its characteristic pattern of outbursts and accusations or, alternatively, inhibition and withdrawal, and this interferes with the therapist's ability to obtain a picture of what happens outside of therapy. Furthermore, there is a concern that conflict enacted in the session may reflect the artificiality of the setting, and, in particular, the presence of the therapist as a possible ally, referee, or commentator. Such exchanges may not be representative of what occurs outside of therapy and may leave the couple less prepared to undertake any initiative for change. There is evidence that depressed persons are less dysfunctional in the absence of significant others (Hinchcliffe, Hopper, & Roberts, 1978), and there is the possibility that both depressed persons and their spouses will be less defensive, clearer, and to the point in the information that they provide, as well as more compromising and accepting of responsibility for change, if their partners are not present during the interview.

Strategies and Tactics

Before discussing specific interventions, some caveats are in order. First, working with depressed persons and their relationships can be difficult and often frustrating. Appreciating how the well-meant efforts of depressed persons and significant others as well as therapists can paradoxically become miscarried should make therapy more respectful, humane, and effective. Yet it is unlikely to make it easy, only less difficult. Second, therapists sometimes look to writings on strategic therapy for provocative and counterintuitive interventions without paying attention to how much the appropriateness of such interventions depends on careful information gathering, negotiation of goals, shaping of clients' expectations and willingness to accept intervention, and timing (Coyne, 1986b). There are enough recurring themes in work with depressed persons to organize a discussion of strategic therapy around them, but there is also a tremendous heterogeneity to depressed persons, their relationships, and the problems and opportunities that their situations present. A therapeutic stalemate is less likely to be resolved with the application of some elusive omnibus paradoxical intervention for depression than by the therapist's sharing of the dilemma with the clients, listening, negotiating, and collaborating so as to develop a more promising perspective.

In meeting with depressed persons and their significant others, the therapist seeks to gather the particulars of what is most upsetting to them, why it is upsetting, and what they are doing to cope with or resolve their situation. With this information, the therapist attempts to identify small changes that would indicate significant progress was being made if they occurred and to secure agreement that therapy should focus on the attainment of these changes. One principle in the selection of goals and interventions is that they should be attuned to what would leave key persons feeling *empowered* (Coyne, 1987): that they are facing manageable difficulties, that the immediate coping tasks facing them afford some opportunity to observe progress, and that they are challenged, rather than threatened with the prospect of another failure. A second principle is that goals and interventions should be *ecological,* in that they are attuned to what changes are likely to be viable in particular situations, what opportunities and constraints on change exist, and how key persons are likely to react.

The strategic therapist thus construes the problem-solving efforts of depressed persons and the key persons in their lives in interactional terms, sensitive to how in key sequences these efforts and the pertinent perceptions of each other may be mutually maintaining. Yet for the purposes of intervention, the therapist may think linearly, in terms of how the actions of particular persons can be isolated and targeted for change. It is therefore useful to distinguish among interventions targeting (1) the depressed person, (2) significant others (in this chapter I will focus on the spouse), and (3) relationships, although recognizing that such distinctions are provisional and somewhat arbitrary.

Work with Depressed Persons

Perhaps the most basic rule in working with depressed persons is not to dispute their right and privilege to be depressed but, rather, to acknowledge that they have good reason to be depressed or else they would not be. Strategic therapists are thus careful not to replicate what have likely been futile efforts by depressed persons and those around them to make them feel better by arguing them out of their depression.

A second rule is that strategic therapists avoid framing the goals or stakes in the coping tasks facing depressed persons in terms of dichotomous, all-or-nothing, successes or failures. Too often, depressed persons have maintained their inhibition or abulia and their overwhelming sense of incompetence and failure with an expectation that if they are to make any progress at all, it must be in terms of a decisive resolution of their situation. As a result, any sign of change may be rejected as insufficient, and the whole enterprise of coping more effectively may be seen as too threatening to undertake.

Strategic therapists are therefore studiously cautious, restrained, and even restraining in proposing that depressed persons undertake particular initiatives. For example, a housewife has expressed distress about her lack of outside employment, but she reveals that she ruminates about this without doing anything constructive. The therapist might suggest that she go to the store three times a week, purchase a newspaper, and read the sports page and the classified advertisements for used cars, but not the employment section that falls between them. Another depressed woman who has expressed interest in exercising but has done nothing about it is asked to drive to the parking lot of the community gym and park without getting out each time she is on the way to the grocery store.

In each instance, the depressed person is asked to take a small step that invites another. Further, it is preferable that there be some absurdity in *not* taking the next step. If the depressed person protests that she wants to do more, the therapist may caution that she may not be ready, and that unless she is absolutely overwhelmed by the urge to do more, she should try to stay within the limits of the goal for the next session as it has been discussed. If the depressed person subsequently reports she has done more, the therapist might dismiss this with "No one is perfect" and caution her to go slowly. If the depressed person has failed to undertake even the small initiative that was discussed, it is important that the therapist remain nonjudgmental. The therapist should generally acknowledge that such an initiative was badly framed or timed and that it is good that they now both know that change is difficult. The therapist might then propose a more modest step, discuss a different focus, or raise the issue that it might be untimely to rock the boat with efforts to change.

Sometimes therapists will avoid constructing initiatives or therapeutic tasks in terms of success and failure by framing them as *assessments,* preliminary to any effort to bring about change. Thus, a therapist agreed with a rather introverted woman that she was quiet; the therapist asked her to spend one half-hour a day at work expressing this as shyness and one half-hour expressing it as being mysterious. In each instance, she was to record the thoughts that might distinguish between the two states and notice how others reacted differently. When the task was completed each day, she should then be free to be herself and note whatever thoughts and reactions occurred that distinguished this from the other two states.

Alternatively, the same woman might be asked to discover which small social initiatives made her palms sweat and which only made her mildly uncomfortable. The rationale that would be provided is that the therapist does not want to exceed her tolerance for distress, and so it would be useful to get as much information as possible.

Therapists may also avoid constructing tasks in terms of success and failure by framing them as *practice*. The depressed person is asked to engage in certain behaviors so that these will become more refined or accessible for later use when the timing is more appropriate without regard to whether they now produce results. A woman might thus be encouraged to ask her husband for assistance in household tasks for the practice of it, knowing that he is not yet likely to be responsive. Another lonely, depressed person might be asked to ask co-workers to go to lunch, but only in situations in which it is particularly unlikely that they could accept. Aside from providing practice under conditions of reduced evaluation apprehension, such a task makes it more likely that co-workers will take the initiative and ask the depressed person to lunch under more appropriate circumstances.

As I have noted, a common problem for depressed persons, and depressed women in particular, is involvement in a problematic close relationship that is not conducive to assertiveness. In many instances, the futility of past efforts to change this and the likelihood of another failure experience discourages even the imagination of change. The *in vivo* thought experiment is an intervention tailored to such situations. The depressed person is asked to be prepared to pick out a target interaction as it is occurring and to be particularly acquiescent and more unassertive than is characteristic. However, in that situation, the depressed person should also imagine bold acts of assertion or even defiance or aggression. For instance, when her cooking is criticized by her husband, a woman might imagine deliberately reducing a roast to a smoking ashen mess, waving it at her husband, and saying, "I guess we are going to eat out tonight, asshole." After completing this exercise, she should atone for such bad thoughts by being even more agreeable and pleasant. The key features of such assignments are that they are absurd and safely in imagination, and yet they make explicit depressed persons' existing decisions to avoid confrontation, even to their detriment. Usually, such assignments are followed quickly by spontaneous assertive actions. Further, in the wake of such assignments, straightforward efforts to be more assertive become more palatable.

The therapist must decide how to deal with observable signs of progress as they occur. In many instances, they invite another assignment, building in stepwise fashion upon what has already occurred. If that can be done without undue risk of failure, then that is the preferable course of action. However, therapists should be sensitive about the sometimes paradoxical drawbacks and pitfalls of improvement. It is important that small changes not become burdensome, in that they might carry with them the demand that such progress be maintained with new more, threatening initiatives, or that they invalidate the depressed person's distress or continued dissatisfaction with the status quo. The therapist often does well to adopt an attitude of restraint, perhaps urging the depressed person to go slowly or suggesting that "every silver lining has a wisp of dark cloud attached to it." The therapist might even connote positively the persistence of depression. He or she might say that "depression is a sacrifice for your marriage, a way of insuring that you won't leave it and of protecting your husband from confronting his own inadequacies. You have been willing to be depressed for this long, and so could you suffer it for another 3 weeks?"

Alternatively, "depression is an understandable reason someone cannot get much done. In your case, it keeps in check your own overwhelming sense of responsibility. If you were to find yourself suddenly without your depression, you'd face the depressing prospect of believing that you had to get more done than anyone could possibly get done. I'm sure you would not be so demanding of someone else. . . . The problem is that depressions sometimes leave when we could use them the most. Could you take care not to get ahead of yourself? You don't need to malinger or fake being depressed, but could you be careful not exaggerate or burden yourself with any improvement that might improve?"

Work with Spouses

It is important that therapists approach them with an open mind, but spouses will frequently be critical of depressed partners and sensitive to any suggestion that they are to blame for the depression. Two studies have found that the majority of the spouses of depressed persons were critical of them and that such criticism was a strong predictor of relapse (Hooly, Orley, & Teasdale, 1986; Leff & Vaughn, 1985).

Just as it is important to acknowledge to depressed persons that it is understandable that they are depressed, so too, the therapist should work to grasp and acknowledge whatever frustrations, sacrifices, and disappointments may color the spouses' reactions to depressed persons and the prospect of participating in therapy. The therapist should recognize how, in attempting to cope with the depressed partner, the spouse may have stifled complaints, faced what is seen as unjustified hostility and criticism, and made numerous unappreciated concessions. The therapist should look for opportunities to connote these efforts positively, in terms of spouses' absorption in efforts to help the depressed partner and how difficult it is to remain supportive in such circumstances. When possible, the therapist should link the occurrence of miscarried helping efforts to the positive intentions from which they spring. The basic theme is that people would not get trapped into such destructive interactions if they were not so committed to making a difference. The therapist should be careful to respect statements by spouses that they see nothing wrong with the marriage except their partner's depression. It may be helpful not to label what is taking place as marital therapy. Often it is advantageous to frame therapy to the spouse as focusing on how she or he is dealing with the difficulties that the depressed partner presents. When that is done, it is then useful to identify principal sources of problems or distress for spouses and their attempted solutions.

Sometimes the contribution of spouses to the predicament of depressed persons is that they have remained aloof, indifferent, or unavailable. If so, the key is to increase their involvement in specific supportive efforts, even while helping them to avoid personalizing the depressed person's distress. Frequently, husbands of depressed women have adopted an overly instrumental view of how to cope with their wives' depressive complaints: unable to identify any specific action that would answer the complaints, they seek to avoid or even supress discussion. It may be helpful to raise the issue that there are sex differences in what are considered helpful responses and to frame simply listening as an effective instrumental response. This can serve as the groundwork for later couple-focused interventions.

Usually, however, the issue is one of the spouses being overinvolved in efforts to get the depressed person to feel better and act less dysfunctionally. There may have been a progression from initial efforts to be comforting and supportive to advice and disputation of the depressed person's negative views, and then to coercion and characterological criticism (Coyne et al., 1988). In the process, any sense of what is beneficial to either the spouse or the depressed person may be lost. In such situations, the therapist may pursue a course of *strategic disengagement.* As an experiment, the spouse is encouraged to limit efforts to be helpful to small gestures that do not allow an immediate acknowledgment. For instance, the spouse might leave a note or small present or do a chore in the morning, knowing that the depressed person will not see this until later. Generally speaking, it is easier for spouses to remain humane and supportive when their responsibilities are limited and defined in terms of discrete small tasks, and when they are not anticipating immediate results for what they do. The assumption is that much of the harshness that is inflicted on depressed persons comes from others assuming more responsibility for their well-being than they can effectively discharge. Helping becomes miscarried or deteriorates when someone cares too much or tries too hard to obtain an outcome that is not immediately within their control.

Often spouses have been too absorbed in struggles with their depressed partner to look after their own needs. They are likely to be angry about having made this sacrifice, and it may seem all the more imperative for them to get the depressed person to feel better. At least some of their negative affect and unhelpful demands on their partner may be reduced if the therapist legitimizes their needs and wants, particularly as expressed in activities that do not involve the depressed partner. The therapist might even suggest that for the benefit of the depressed person, they do something special for themselves on a schedule, whether or not they feel such efforts are needed. Depending on the circumstances, the therapist may begin with such assignments or reserve them to take advantage of when the spouse is particularly frustrated, utilizing them as part of a broader strategy of committing the spouse to backing off.

Work with the Couple

Interventions that target the couple as a unit build on what has transpired with the individual partners, and they are generally delivered at the end of the session. Before asking that the two work together as a couple, the therapist is careful to acknowledge the problems in the relationship and to warn that many of the things that they attempt to do for each other will either backfire, go unrecognized, or be misunderstood. Only later will they be able to appreciate the helpfulness of what each is about to do now. Rather than pushing for change, the strategic therapist generally suggests proceeding slowly and cautiously. An effort is made to frame the immediate future as a time of change, one aspect of which is that they may need to tolerate what they would not want to be an enduring feature of the relationship.

With couples in which both partners are inhibited in their communication, the current period may be framed as a time for indelicacy, with a greater need to be direct and to encourage each other to be direct by not attempting to read the other's mind or fathom how he or she really feels. They may be specifically asked to make at least three unreasonable requests of each other before the next session in order to give the partner an opportunity to say emphatically "No!" without feeling guilty. As a start, one spouse should be picked to ask the other to go out and get a particular kind of ice cream or cookies when the other is already undressed to go to bed that night.

With more overtly conflictual couples, the therapists may adopt the strategy of having them stage recurring arguments with more of a sense of theater or play. According to Bateson (1955), play is a transformation of serious activity characterized by exaggeration, stylization, disruption of key sequences or limits on how engrossed participants become. For instance, in a couple in which the husband had taken to reacting harshly to any pessimistic or negative statement from his wife, the therapist first reviewed with the husband how women might be different in that they benefited from simply having an opportunity to vent, and how men might make it difficult for them by taking responsibility to refute or resolve their complaints. It was further suggested that hearing oneself speak was different than silently thinking the same idea and that maybe his wife needed to hear her own complaints without being distracted by his well-meant, but unneeded efforts. The couple was then asked to stage situations in which she complained, but he resisted his urge to intervene. Taking it a step further, she was asked to complain in a way that invited his advice, and both should see if he was able to maintain a stance of simply attentively listening. Such assignments sometimes have immediate benefits. The husband feels less responsible and so is free to listen, whereas the wife is more confident of being able to speak and be heard, and may even become less pessimistic or despondent—particularly when his intolerance was a factor in her hopelessness.

The Raisins of Wrath

The following example illustrates how a simple task assignment was delivered to a depressed woman, and a report from the next session reveals what then unfolded in her everyday life. The example highlights both how the effects of interventions reverberate in patients' lives and close relationships and also how recovery from depression often involves a renegotiation of relationships. In the follow-up session, a number of couple-oriented interventions are delivered.

The patient, a 34-year-old married woman, had just returned from another hospitalization for depression. Over the first three sessions, she had been given a series of assignments aimed at structuring her resumption of activities so as to give her some immediate sense of accomplishment, along with admonitions to "take it slow." She also had been reading *Feeling Good* (Burns, 1980).

Between the second and fourth sessions, she showed considerable improvement in mood, but she became preoccupied with her 8-year-old son's school performance. The son was a C student, but Rhonda was convinced that if he had only been given more attention, he would be getting A's. She expressed considerable guilt over this, and her unrealistic commitment to remedy the situation immediately was leaving her with a sense of failure and jeopardizing the progress that had been made. At the end of the fourth session, the therapist encouraged her to make a "slough-off list" for the next 2 weeks.

THERAPIST: I would like to suggest a list that Dave Burns didn't think of in his book. And that is, that you make a "slough-off list." A "slough-off list" is a list of things that you could have done or would have been of benefit if they had been done, but you didn't get to them. It's unfortunate, but that's just what a "slough-off list" is about.

RHONDA: Do you make the list after the week's over or before the week's over and then not do what is on it?

THERAPIST: Well . . . try to do the best you can and anticipate some things that would be nice to get done, that would be of some clear benefit to other people if they were done, but you just do not get to them . . .

RHONDA: Because you just don't want to do them?

THERAPIST: No, because you, Rhonda, are apparently not like some other people who, when they feel they need some time off, take it, even if that means leaving some things undone. You are damn responsible. In the past, you had an enormous barrier to doing too much, even though sometimes you tried anyway. That was being very depressed. You have to rediscover some of the constraints and excuses that everybody has, but that you haven't had to use. They are dusty, they've been up on the shelf for you because you had been too depressed and that was a reason not to jump in over your head. In fact, sometimes people who don't know how to set limits wear themselves out and get depressed. So the main accomplishment for now would be to be able to tell in 2 weeks what you let slide. That's hard, harder than it sounds.

The following report was received the next session:

RHONDA: I felt many times during the week that I was right on a tightrope. I could go either one way or the other. I was real close to just falling off the deep end. But I managed to keep it together. Ralph and I had a big long talk one night, and I told him, "If I had been working with Allen these last 2 years the way I worked with him in kindergarten, he wouldn't be in the mess he's in right now." But, then Ralph finally convinced me that in those 2 years I couldn't even take care of myself, let alone do this. So I kind of got rid of that guilt, but then by Sunday night . . .

THERAPIST: I think Ralph feels guilty.

RHONDA: About not working with Allen? He told me that night that if anyone should feel guilty, he should. Because since I was so sick, I couldn't even take care of myself.

THERAPIST: How could you trade off for a while? Ever watch the wrestling matches on TV? You know, the tag teams where the other person goes in when one gets tired? How could we get a tag team going? I know you would be tugging on the rope, wanting to get back into the ring.

RHONDA: That's sort of what Ralph says too. But you know something, he's too easy with Allen. . . . If he can't get the problem, he won't help him think it through; he just gives him the answer and that doesn't help. He's got to learn to think it through.

THERAPIST: I'm torn about this, because I certainly can see your helpfulness and your willingness to make a sacrifice to help Allen, but this seems to be a big sacrifice. The other thing that I'm curious about is what you'd be doing if you weren't having to deal with this whole thing. It takes a lot of emotional energy.

RHONDA: (*Groans.*) Oooh, oooh, . . . I know.

THERAPIST: I bet this just keeps you from doing a lot of other things. What's had to be put aside?

RHONDA: I didn't. . . . Well, remember this was supposed to be our slough-off 2 weeks? Hugh . . . I mean I sloughed-off cooking. We had canned soup, we had (*ha ha*), we had frozen fish sticks, hot dogs, and hamburgers. And there was 1 hour one day, when I thought, "Shit, I'm going to sit here and do not a Goddamn thing," so I sat there and for an hour didn't do anything. I just smoked a few cigarettes and drank diet soda; that's all I did.

THERAPIST: Aha, sounds relaxing. Was it a satisfying hour?

RHONDA: Yeah, it was. . . . But the rest of the time when I would try to relax, my brain is just going, going, going . . . I was so bothered by my not having done more all these years. But, that was towards the beginning of it, when it wasn't as bad. As the week went on, it got worse. I felt like all this responsibility. . . . By Sunday night, I was so tired of reading *Feeling Good* and trying to figure it out. I was so tired of this shit going through my head. I just said, "Screw it, if I get depressed, I don't care." . . . And you know what happened? It was like 1,000 pounds was lifted off my back, and I thought I was going to get depressed, but a few minutes later, I realized that was the first time in a week that I finally felt relieved, when I just said, "Screw it. Whatever happens, happens."

THERAPIST: Bravo!

RHONDA: And I felt real good for the next 4 or 5 days, I worked with Allen. We did real good. Then, Thanksgiving came. My mother . . .

did I ever tell you how my mother and I got along? We didn't. She's real bossy, and tells you what to do. But lately she's been leaving me alone. Except, the day we last came here, she had brought these raisins over, a whole laundry basket of them. You have to stem them and wash them. She had done a little of it but left most of it for me to do. And during the 2 weeks she kept asking me, "Have you cleaned the raisins, have you cleaned the raisins?" And I thought, "No, that's one of the things I'm going to slough off these 2 weeks . . . I'm not going to clean those Goddamn raisins!"

THERAPIST: Good, good.

RHONDA: So, Thanksgiving night she was talking to my sister, and I was watching TV, and I heard her telling my sister, "Rhonda's had these raisins for 2 weeks and hasn't even cleaned them." And it just pissed me off. And I turned around, and I told her, "I've had enough on my mind for 2 weeks with Allen. I'm supposed to be 'sloughing-off' for these 2 weeks. I don't give a shit about those Goddamn raisins." It just pissed me off, and my sister said, "All right, all right. Just cool it." And then I thought maybe I shouldn't have gotten upset.

THERAPIST: I wish I'd been there to congratulate you.

RHONDA: It pissed me off . . . she knows what I've gone through in the last 4 years . . . and she knows that I've finally been feeling better. Why get on my back about some Goddamn lousy raisins? They're not going to rot, even if they sat there 2 years.

THERAPIST: I don't have much to say except "congratulations."

Session Wrap Up and New Assignment

THERAPIST: Well, you are certainly way out ahead of me, but if I let you set the pace, you certainly encourage me to push forward. Let me try some ideas I have about what might be done in the next 2 weeks. It's a bit challenging, and you could always back off and coast a bit. It's up to you. The holiday season makes me think. Sometimes, gifts come wrapped in funny paper, and we don't always appreciate what is involved until we get them fully unwrapped. For instance, in an odd way I think that your Mom gave you a present. I tend to think that if your Mom hadn't provoked you with the raisins, we would have had to invent something. She gave you the opportunity to assert yourself and you arose to the occasion. Do you know what we're talking about, about the raisins, Ralph?

RALPH: Yeah, yeah, I agree about what she did.

RHONDA: I almost apologized for not being more grateful.

THERAPIST: Well, no one is perfect, and there *was* something to be grateful about, but different than it first looked.

The therapist went on to describe how sometimes people do not take a stand because they are uncertain whether they have a right to do so. The beauty of the provocation with the raisins was that Rhonda's rights were clear, and she availed herself of an excellent opportunity to redefine her relationship with her mother. It was proposed that the couple might similarly exchange such gifts by each provoking the other at least once and thereby giving the other an ambiguous chance to speak up. Jokingly, the therapist suggested that if everything else failed, they could go and get more raisins. Because this task would be difficult, they might consider making it easier by being nice at other times.

Secondly, the therapist proposed it was time for a tag team:

THERAPIST: Ralph, would you let Rhonda tag you so you pick up the challenge of Allen? It's kind of like the tag team that we talked about. But, Ralph, I'm calling on you to do something else, and this is where the sacrifice comes in. What I would like is, whether or not you're running into difficulties, for you to complain a lot about them in a way that invites Rhonda to jump in and bail you out. It is Rhonda's job to hold herself in reserve, and your's to tempt her to jump in.

RALPH: Can you give me an example of that.

THERAPIST: Sure, suppose Allen had a workbook he has brought home. You might go and help him with it or review what he has done and then put the workbook back in its place so it looks like it hadn't been moved. By various ways try to make it look like less is going on than is going on, and less is being accomplished with your efforts, that you're less optimistic than you are. This is tricky.

RHONDA: So I'm not supposed to tell him what to work on with Allen? It is all his responsibility; I have nothing to do with it.

THERAPIST: That's right, nothing but resist taking over, at least until the next session.

RHONDA: Oh, I could find lots of things to do. I have been thinking that if I only had more time to myself, I'd start painting again. I haven't done that in a few years. That would be a big step.

THERAPIST: That sounds interesting, but it is up to you. Do what you need to do not to jump back in the ring. Ralph make it difficult for her to resist.

Who Is the Recipient of Intervention?

I have discussed various strategies and tactics of intervention as if therapists sit back and decide how they are going to influence the depressed person, the spouse, or the couple. However, taken to its fullest implications, the interactional perspective denies that the therapists are that removed, and instead it provides a way of considering how therapists and couples make up systems of a higher order.

There is something compelling about the distress of depressed persons. It registers quickly in the nonverbal behavior and even pupillary response of persons with whom they interact (see Coyne, in press, for a review). It is further frustrating for therapists to commit themselves to be of help and yet have to witness depressed persons seemingly remaining in great distress and not be able to take the minimal initiative that might make a difference for them. I have tried to spell out why it may be more difficult than it seems for depressed persons do take such a step. The interventions that have been presented may make it less difficult for therapists to tolerate this. In admonishing depressed persons to take it slowly or to be careful of the dangers of improvement, therapists are making a communicative act that will influence how they, as well as depressed persons, will subsequently act. They are taking an explicit position that will hopefully restrain them from pushing depressed persons to do more than they feel ready to do. More generally, the minimalism and structure provided by the interventions can be seen as a way of organizing the nature of therapist involvement. Facing dilemmas paralleling those of the spouses of depressed persons, therapists may find it less difficult to remain accepting and supportive when their responsibilities are limited and defined in terms of small, discrete tasks and when they are not demanding immediate results for what they do.

References

Abramson, L. Y., Seligman, M. E. P., & Teasdale, J. D. (1978). Learned helplessness in humans: Critique and reformulation. *Journal of Abnormal Psychology, 87,* 49–74.

Bateson, G. (1955). A theory of play and fantasy. *A.P.A. Psychiatric Research Reports, 2,* 177–193.

Beck, A. T. (1967). *Depression: Clinical, experimental, and theoretical aspects.* New York: Harper & Row.

Burns, D. D. (1980). *Feeling good.* New York: Signet.

Coyne, J. C. (1976). Toward an interactional description of depression. *Psychiatry, 39,* 28–40.

Coyne, J. C. (1984). Strategic therapy with married depressed persons: Agenda, themes, and interventions. *Journal of Marital and Family Therapy, 10,* 53–62.

Coyne, J. C. (1985). Toward a theory of frames and reframing: The social nature of frames. *Journal of Marital and Family Therapy, 11,* 337–344.

Coyne, J. C. (1986a). Strategic marital therapy for depression. In N. S. Jacobson & A. S. Gurman (Eds.), *Clinical handbook of marital therapy.* New York: The Guilford Press.

Coyne, J. C. (1986b). The significance of the interview in strategic therapy. *Journal of Strategic and Systemic Therapies, 5,* 63–70.

Coyne, J. C. (1987). The concept of empowerment in strategic therapy. *Psychotherapy, 24,* 539–545.

Coyne, J. C. (1988a). Strategic therapy. In J. F. Clarkin, G. Haas, I. D. Glick (Eds.), *Affective disorders and the family.* New York: The Guilford Press.

Coyne, J. C. (1988b). *Depression, marriage, and the family: Implications for intervention.* Invited address at the Annual Convention of the American Psychological Association, Atlanta.

Coyne, J. C. (in press). Interpersonal processes in depression. In G. I. Keitner (Ed.), *Depression and families.* Washington, DC: American Psychiatric Press.

Coyne, J. C., Aldwin, C., & Lazarus, R. S. (1981). Depression and coping in stressful episodes. *Journal of Abnormal Psychology, 90,* 439–447.

Coyne, J. C., Kessler, R. C., Tal, M., Turnbull, J., Wortman, C., & Greden, J. (1987). Living with a depressed person: Burden and psychological distress. *Journal of Consulting and Clinical Psychology, 55,* 347–352.

Coyne, J. C., Wortman, C., & Lehman, D. (1988). The other side of support: Emotional overinvolvement and miscarried helping. In B. Gottlieb (Ed.), *Social support: Formats, processes, and effects.* New York: Sage.

Derogotis, L. R., Lipman, R. S., Rickels, K., Uhlenhulth, E. H., & Covi, L. (1974). The Hopkins Symptom Checklist (HSCL): A measure of primary symptom dimensions. In P. Pichot (Ed.), *Psychological measurements in psychopharmacology. Modern problems in pharmacopsychiatry,* 7. Basel: Karger.

Elkin, I., Shea, T., Watkins, J., & Colloins, J. (1986). *Comparative treatment findings: Presentation of the National Institute of Mental Health Treatment of Depression Collaborative Research Program.* Paper presented at the annual meeting of the American Psychiatric Association, Washington, DC.

Folkman, S., & Lazarus, R. S. (1986). Stress processes and depressive symptomatology. *Journal of Abnormal Psychology, 95,* 107–113.

Hinchcliffe, M., Hopper, D., & Roberts, F. J. (1978). *The melancholy marriage.* New York: Wiley.

Hooley, J. M., Orley, J., & Teasdale, J. D. (1986). Levels of expressed emotion and relapse in depressed patients. *British Journal of Psychiatry, 148,* 642–647.

Kahn, J., Coyne, J. C., & Margolin, G. (1985). Depression and marital conflict: The social construction of despair. *Journal of Social and Personal Relationships, 2,* 447–462.

Leff, J., & Vaughn, C. (1985). *Expressed emotion in families: Its significance for mental illness.* New York: The Guilford Press.

McLean, P. D., & Hakstian, A. R. (1979). Clinical depression: Comparative efficacy of outpatient treatment. *Journal of Consulting and Clinical Psychology, 47,* 818–836.

Murphy, G. E., Simons, A. D., Wetzel, R. D., & Lustman, P. J. (1984). Cognitive therapy and pharmacotherapy, singly and together in the treatment of depression. *Archives of General Psychiatry, 41,* 33–41.

Rush, A. J., Beck, A. T., Kovacs, M., & Hollon, S. (1977). Comparative efficacy of cognitive therapy and pharmacotherapy in the treatment of depressed outpatients. *Cognitive Therapy and Research, 1*, 17–37.

Watzlawick, P., Weakland, J., & Fisch, R. (1974). *Change: Principles of problem formation and problem resolution.* New York: Norton.

Weissman, M. M. (1987). Psychiatric epidemiology: Rates and risks for major depression. *American Journal of Public Health, 77*, 445–451.

Chapter 7

Comprehensive Distancing, Paradox, and the Treatment of Emotional Avoidance

Steven C. Hayes
Susan M. Melancon

For most clients, the world of private events (including thoughts, feelings, memories, beliefs, evaluations, and so forth) seemingly contains the "problems" that bring them to the therapist's office. For example, the client may report that he is *depressed,* or *irritable,* or *anxious*; that she is *thinking* about leaving her husband, or *worried* about her career, or unable to *keep her mind* on her work; an overweight person *wants* to eat too much; a smoker *craves* a cigarette; and so on.

These kinds of troublesome emotions and thoughts usually are accompanied by the belief that they need to be changed or eliminated in order for the "problem" to be solved. For example, an anxious person needs to relax; an obsessive needs to think differently; a drug addict needs to get over the craving. Even in those cases where there are clearly identifiable external events that can be labeled "The Problem," the client typically focuses on his or her internal responses to the problem in the therapeutic hour. For example, a client may have a serious physical illness, but it is his "depression" about the illness that the clinician will attempt to change.

Clients come to therapy when the problem is one they feel unable to resolve on their own, and they need help implementing a sensible solution. Although the *technique* or *method* of a solution may be unclear to a client, its *goal* or *purpose* is often quite clear. Therapists are daily asked to support the belief that the changing of private events is an essential part of solving clients' problems.

The ability to change "maladaptive" inner experiences is considered widely by clients and therapists alike to be one of the best indicants of whether or not therapy has been successful. The culture of psychotherapy has embraced the notion that changing the way people think and feel about themselves and the world around them will lead to more successful living. The potency of this notion is illustrated, for instance, by modern psychological diagnostic categories. DSM-III-R (American Psychiatric Association, 1987) describes clusters of mood disorders, anxiety disorders, and cognitive disorders, such as schizophrenic or delusional syndromes. In all cases, it is assumed that there are "disordered" patterns of thoughts and emotions that, if corrected, will restore the individual to psychological health. Most of the modern cognitive, existential, and humanistic therapies, either through insight or abreaction or cognitive reframing, seek to change private events on the road to psychological health. The very names of many specific techniques reflect this perspective: anxiety management, cognitive restructuring, and so on.

Emotional Avoidance

The present chapter takes a contrary position. We argue that a single common denominator, namely, emotional avoidance, underlies many of the diagnostic classifications, client expectations, and therapeutic interventions in clinical psychology. Emotional avoidance, we argue, is often the real "problem" our clients are dealing with, and clinical psychology is a major supporter of the difficulty.

An "emotional avoidance" perspective has gained some clinical acceptance, but primarily in work with anxiety disorders (Barlow & Beck, 1984; Frankl, 1975; Goldstein & Chambless, 1978). For example, the agoraphobic who fears being in a crowded mall after having a panic attack while shopping may initially only avoid the mall in which the attack occurred. However, it is not really the mall that the client fears, but the physical, emotional, and cognitive phenomena associated with the panic that she experienced there. For that reason, she may stop going to all malls, in an attempt to avoid triggering another panic event. In time, her avoidance may generalize to other crowded stores, or to crowded freeways, or to being in a vehicle during busy traffic or to being alone in an elevator. The one common denominator in all of these dreaded situations is a possibility that anxiety will show up, and escape from the anxiety would be difficult or impossible. In this example, it is not too difficult to interpret the client's main therapeutic dilemma as a "fear of fear"; that is, the attempt to avoid the private events associated with anxiety (thoughts, emotions, physiological responses) is itself part of the problem.

A less obvious example, however, is the case of a client who comes to therapy and is diagnosed with major depression. His symptoms might include reports of a depressed or irritable mood, loss of interest or pleasure in daily activities, loss of energy, feelings of worthlessness or excessive guilt, and suicidal ideation. Such a client typically will be treated using techniques geared to alter these depressive complaints. Thus, his feelings of worthlessness or guilt may be challenged by the therapist as "irrational beliefs." The client may negotiate and sign a therapeutic contract to engage in pleasurable activities with the explicit or implicit promise that these activities will lead to increased energy, self-esteem, and emotional satisfaction. Drugs may be given to "alleviate depressed mood." The therapist may interpret the client's depression as a reenactment of a childhood response to some traumatic loss, or as a form of interpersonal aggression against others, or even a type of reinforcing self-indulgence. Such interpretations seek to increase the client's insight into his emotional patterns, with the hope that this "insight" will change the pattern.

We would argue, however, that the above client's real problem is not his feelings of guilt, depressed mood, or suicidal thoughts, but his unwillingness to feel depressed feelings as they are (not as what they *say* they are). The problem is his unwillingness to think guilty thoughts (again, as they are, not as they say they are). Suicide is the ultimate attempt to avoid feeling "bad," but many other classic depressive behaviors can also be viewed as attempts to avoid experiencing unpleasant thoughts and emotions. For example, in order to keep from feeling the emotional pain that accompanies rejection by a loved one, the depressive may avoid forming intimate relationships, or avoid confronting problems in existing ones. The unsatisfying relationships that result may occasion self-accusatory or punishing statements in the client, which *themselves* become something to be avoided, because it is impossible for the client to live with himself if he is really as cowardly or wretched as he is thinking and feeling himself to be.

Unfortunately, as with anxiety disorders, the depressive's attempts to escape from what he is feeling and thinking create a type of anticipatory cycle of depression that is self-sustaining. Trying so hard not to be depressed is itself depressing. Attempts to avoid guilty thoughts or depressive feelings reinforce the notion that they are "bad" and something to be depressed about, thus, something to be avoided, and so on. This is not to say that clients never experience any "secondary gain" from depressive symptoms. Rather, we would argue that even the client who seemingly embraces and nurtures depression is probably doing so in order to avoid some *other* painful inner experience. For example, a chronically depressed housewife may find that her depression keeps her husband and children home at night. For her, then, what is being avoided may not be depression; rather, depression may be the means by which this client avoids the pain of loneliness, fear of rejection, or insecurity over her abilities to function in the social arena. Nevertheless, emotional avoidance remains the most salient therapeutic concern.

The above arguments about the role of emotional avoidance in psychopathology can, in fact, be made for many diagnostic groups. For example, insomniacs attempt to avoid sleeplessness and the worries that sleeplessness occasions. This avoidance itself is a prime contributor to their staying awake. Sexual arousal and orgasmic dysfunctions are often found to be linked with the client's attempts to avoid sexual impotence and the feelings that impotence will precipitate. The obsessive or compulsive client develops elaborate ways to avoid the thoughts and feelings that something disastrous will happen if a given ritual isn't performed. The alcoholic drinks to avoid feeling a craving for alcohol.

Although the potential for psychological disturbance inherent in avoidance of unpleasant private experiences has long been recognized (Rachman, 1980), the breadth and depth of the sources of this avoidance seem greatly underappreciated. It is our position that emotional avoidance is predictable and virtually inevitable within the prevalent social-verbal community which (1) supports the belief that private events (thoughts, feelings, memories, behavioral predispositions, etc.) are legitimate causes of behavior, (2) labels certain private events as "bad," (3) comes to accept literally the "badness" of these events, and (4) fails to distinguish the behaving organism from the behavior of the organism. As participants in this social-verbal system, we have all been, in a sense, "set-up" to develop life-adjustment problems. Our clients are just persons for whom the unhealthy effects of emotional avoidance are more obvious.

We see the goals of therapy to be largely those of emotional exposure and behavioral commitment. We assist the client in making contact with the contingencies of his or her environment, experiencing fully whatever are the emotional consequences of that contact, and then doing what needs to be done. Emotional exposure goes beyond bringing the client into contact with a specific feared stimulus. Rather, the client is asked to be willing to experience, fully and unconditionally, *whatever* thoughts, feelings, evaluations, behavioral predispositions, and so on, they happen to be experiencing at any given point in time.

A key element in our approach is our encouragement of the client to challenge the literal and causal features of language, since much of our day-to-day language supports and maintains emotional avoidance. Within the context of this challenge, it is then possible to work therapeutically with the intra- and interpersonal dynamics of the client's problem in a particularly powerful way. Many of the techniques we use to break down literal, causal language are paradoxical in nature. However, in order to explain adequately the paradoxical quality of our treatment approach, which we call *comprehensive distancing*, it is necessary first to describe some of the philosophical assumptions on which the approach is built. We will then describe some of the specific goals and techniques of our therapeutic work. Finally, we will discuss its paradoxical nature.

Philosophical Assumptions

The assumptions of this work can be described in four words: contextualism, monism, functionalism, and antimentalism. The first of these, contextualism, means that human actions must be understood in and with the context in which they occur (Hayes, Hayes, & Reese, 1988). Such a context is made up of the functional relationships that exist between an act and those events in time and space that precede and follow it. These "contexts" are both historical and situational. The history of exposure to cultural, somatic, evolutionary, and reinforcement contingencies (Hayes, 1988) structures the functional characteristics of the immediate situation. *All* acts are viewed in this way, including private events such as thoughts, feelings, or behavioral predispositions. "Behavior" does not refer to a subset of the contextualized actions of whole organisms—it is the entire set.

The relationships between thoughts and feelings on the one hand and overt behaviors on the other are thus interpreted as behavior-behavior relations. These relationships too, can be examined and understood in contextual terms (Hayes & Brownstein, 1986). We must understand the contextual arrangements giving rise to each behavior *and* the relationship between them. This view is inherently antimentalistic and monistic because thoughts and feelings are not then viewed as causal agents controlling other behaviors, but as contextualized acts, related to other acts by additional contextual arrangements. Because contextualism is holistic, all units of analysis (all instances of breaking an event into pieces) are taken to be constructions, not discoveries. There is no "one true analysis." Rather, many analyses may be true in the sense that they advance progress toward a given goal. We assume no causes in an ontological sense—that is, there are no assumptions that the world consists of parts that cause other parts. Rather, when we say "A causes B," we are constructing a functional relationship that allows *us* to describe and interact with the world more efficiently.

The goal of scientific analysis is fairly clear in clinical work: to make a difference in clients' lives. Thus, the clinician's task is to identify those constructions that lead to effective action with regard to changing clients' lives in a healthy way. This goal, in turn, affects the kinds of analyses that are deemed useful. In particular, all analyses are considered to be incomplete unless the environmental context leading to the phenomenon is specified. To change clients, we must change something in their world. We cannot change an act directly—we can at best alter the context of that act. Constructions about the causal role of one behavior over another are inherently useless or incomplete when measured against this criterion. For this reason, all causal constructions in comprehensive distancing are limited to the relationship between manipulable contextual conditions and relevant acts and not between thoughts and behavior, feelings and behavior, and so on.

A contextual approach to private events and their role in overt action differs fundamentally from more mainstream approaches. A traditional "hard-core" behavioral perspective argues for a change in overt behavior, which may then change undesirable thoughts and feelings. Cognitive-behavior therapy, and most other forms of psychotherapy, argues for a change in undesirable thoughts or feelings, which may then enable a change in overt behavior. Thus, one group argues that the arrow points to the left, the other that it points to the right. A contextual approach argues that the destructive relationship between given thoughts and feelings and given overt behaviors is the result of a social-verbal context. The arrow can point in any direction as is determined by the relevant context. Thus, a third treatment path opens up: to modify that social-verbal context. Such is the goal of our treatment approach.

Comprehensive Distancing

Comprehensive distancing is a behaviorally based therapeutic strategy in which a variety of techniques can be usefully applied (Hayes, 1987). The approach has five main goals that we can present here to correspond roughly to the order in which they appear in actual therapy. These goals are (1) establishment of a state of "creative hopelessness" in the client; (2) identification of *control* as the client's primary therapeutic problem; (3) assisting the client in distinguishing him- or herself as a person who is distinct from the problem behavior; (4) encouraging the client to let go of the struggle with control; and (5) making a commitment to action (see Hayes, 1987, for a more detailed discussion of each component). Each of these goals will be discussed and the role of paradox in achieving the goal described. Although the above are presented as being client goals, therapists who are engaged in this kind of work will find themselves repeatedly challenged to grapple with the same goals in their own life and work.

Creative Hopelessness

In the first stage of comprehensive distancing, an attempt is made to establish a state of "creative hopelessness" in the client. The client typically comes into therapy with a set of identified problems, and most often, a set of logical solutions to the problems. The therapist is then asked to assist the client in implementing these solutions (e.g., anxious clients wish to be calm). This identified set of problems and solutions arises from a set of practices established and maintained by the community of verbal organisms of which we all are a part. As we have described above, in our view of the client's "solutions" are almost always actually part of the source of their problems. Creative hopelessness is our name for the condition in which the client's "solutions" begin to be seen as problems themselves, or at least, as impossible to implement. When all "solutions" are no longer solutions, the client feels hopeless, but it is a creative hopelessness because out of this context fundamentally new approaches are possible.

Comprehensive distancing is a paradoxical strategy, but it is paradoxical in a somewhat atypical way. In order to make sense of this use of paradox we will require a rather extended discussion of the social-verbal contexts that lead to the client's set of problems and solutions. This digression is warranted because the notions of "hopelessness" and "the-solution-is-part-of-the-problem" are found in other paradoxical interventions, most of which are better known than our own. However, our therapeutic use of these paradoxical notions is in some ways different from how they are generally used and understood. For us, "hopeless" and "the solution as the problem" underline certain problematic social-verbal contexts. We will return to our discussion of the goals of comprehensive distancing after first clarifying what we mean by "social-verbal contexts," and the clinical significance we assign to them.

The most characteristic contexts in which client problems are embedded are literality, reason-giving, and the need for control. The first of these, literality, sets the stage for the others. Throughout the client's lifetime, words are used as if they mean or *are* the things to which they *refer*. Thus, a word and the situation that it refers to can easily be confused. For example, "I'm sick" literally means that the situation of sickness has arrived. The even more direct fact, that the situation of *saying* "I'm sick" has arrived, is virtually buried in the avalanche of literal meaning.

This is the problem explicated almost 100 years ago by the German mathematician Frege, who emphasized the necessity for differentiating clearly "between the cases in which I am speaking about the sign *itself* and those in which I am speaking about *its meaning*" (Watzlawick,

Weakland, & Fisch, 1974, p. 8). Everyday language makes this distinction difficult to recognize. But if the referent is taken to be present when a word is present, actions appropriate to the referent are likely to be activated by the word. For example, the thought "I'm sick" may result in a child asking to stay home from school, regardless of the actual state of her health. If the mother is convinced by the child's words that she feels poorly, she will most likely be allowed to stay home. A behavior-behavior relationship between saying things (e.g., thinking "I'm sick") and overt action is thereby established by the "context of literality" created and supported by the verbal community at large. For example, that same child may be likely to stop working after thinking, "I don't want to do this" or to stop cleaning her room because she thinks, "I'm too tired."

The Source of the Context of Literality

We conceptualize these relationships by an appeal to "stimulus equivalence" and other such relational classes. There have been notable developments recently in the basic behavior analytic area that are almost completely unknown to behavior therapists. Stimulus equivalence is an important example.

Consider a situation in which a human is taught that some arbitrary stimulus goes with several others. For example, suppose that we show a young child a picture of several imaginary animals. We tell the child to pick out the "wheezu," and say "correct" only when she points to an imaginary animal shaped like a balloon. We do this again, but this time the child can select from several names, not pictures. We say "correct" only when "wheezu" is selected. We can say that we teach the child that A goes with B, and A goes with C, where A refers to the spoken name, B to the picture, and C to the written name. If we now ask the child to select the picture that goes with the written word "wheezu" (i.e., to match B and C), she will do this quite readily (Sidman & Tailby, 1982), even though the choice of B in the presence of C has never been explicitly reinforced. Similarly, the child will probably say "wheezu" in response to the picture or the word (i.e., will select A given either B or C). This phenomenon is called "stimulus equivalence" and seems to represent a fundamentally different kind of stimulus control. Note that the equivalence class is arbitrary. There is nothing about the stimulus events themselves that leads them to go together. Rather they go together by social convention. These conventions are what we mean by "the context of literality."

If stimulus equivalence is a preliminary model of verbal stimulation, one would expect to see it emerge readily in humans, but not so readily or perhaps not at all in nonhumans. This turns out to be the case. Stimulus equivalence has been shown with a wide variety of human subjects using a wide variety of stimulus materials (Dixon, 1977; Dixon & Spradlin, 1976; Gast, VanBiervlet, & Spradlin, 1979; Hayes, Tilley, & Hayes, 1988; Mackay & Sidman, 1984; Sidman, 1971; Sidman, Cresson, & Willson-Morris, 1974; Sidman & Tailby, 1982; Spradlin, Cotter, & Baxley, 1973; Spradlin & Dixon, 1976; VanBiervlet, 1977; Wulfert & Hayes, 1988). Even children as young as 2 years old will display such performances without explicit experimental training (Devany, Hayes, & Nelson, 1986). Stimulus equivalence has not been shown with nonhuman organisms, however. Although conditional relationships have been demonstrated in a large variety of animals, including dolphins (Herman & Thompson, 1982), rats (Lashley, 1938), and monkeys (Nissen, 1951), these do not result in stimulus equivalence. To date, not a single unequivocal demonstration of stimulus equivalence in nonhumans has been shown (D'Amato, Salmon, Loukas, & Tomie, 1985; Kendall, 1983; Sidman et al., 1982; Lipkens, Kop, & Matthijs, 1988; for McIntire, Cleary, & Thompson, 1987, and Vaughan, 1988, see Hayes, 1989). Furthermore, children without spontaneous productive use of signs or speech also do not show equivalence (Devany et al., 1986).

The implication of stimulus equivalence for an analysis of clinical phenomenon is that patients have a history with any given situation that they can indirectly bring to bear in new situations. For example, suppose a child has established an equivalence class between the written word "dog," the spoken word "dog," and dogs. Suppose further that the child loves to play with dogs and will approach dogs if one is seen. With these elements in place, if the child sees you looking behind a door while saying, "Oh, a dog," the child may go behind the door *without ever having responded to such a rule in the past and securing reinforcement.* Such effects have already been documented in the equivalence literature (Hayes, Devany, Kohlenberg, Brownstein, & Shelby, in press; Wulfert & Hayes, 1988).

We have extensive training histories in the verbal community for maintaining a rough equivalence between words and events. We are encouraged to engage in formal verbal analyses of situations and then to respond to these analyses. The verbal community is constantly tightening the equivalence between our talk and the world. Verbal stimuli are purely arbitrary stimuli, and there are few impediments to fairly tight equivalence classes emerging.

Consequently, when we think something, it is not always obvious that it is even a thought. In a sense, the equivalence class is so tight that it is hard to see that it *is* a class. Thus, one member of the class is treated as if it is the same as another member of the same class. For example, a person may think, "this is awful." The person may then act as if he or she is in an awful situation, not in a situation in which he or she has had the thought "this is awful."

As an end result, certain words (particularly those with emotional or pejorative meanings) become connected to powerful and predictable behavior patterns. The client comes to see his or her constructions of reality to be the substance of reality. For example, "anxiety" almost ceases to be a mere word, so completely has it become part of a set of physiological, emotional, and cognitive events. The word "anxiety" takes on a literal meaning, and the very reading or thinking of the word can bring into the client's immediate experience the entire spectrum of negatively perceived events with which it is related. It becomes almost impossible to see that the literality of words emerges within a particular social-verbal context and is not directly equivalent to the events the words represent (i.e., to the other members of a given equivalence class).

Reason-Giving and Control

In the context of literality, verbal reason-giving acquires considerable potency. If words *are* what they describe, then verbal reasons assume the same power to control behavior that appears to be inherent in the external events they describe. It is generally accepted by the social-verbal community that certain events can explain other events. For example, the agoraphobic tells her husband that she did not go to the grocery store today because she was too anxious. This explanation for her avoidance behavior is likely to generate sympathy and support from the community at large, since many people can identify with the experience of avoiding a situation where they might become afraid. Not only do reasons create social permission for behavior, they also constrain behavior. If I cannot go to a meeting "because I don't feel well," then I must not be found going to the store during that period either. Thus, within the social-verbal community a particular behavior-behavior relationship is established that appears to be of a causal nature: when I have a reason, I must behave consistently with it. If I am severely anxious, it makes me avoid what is feared, and this avoidance in turn makes the anxiety go away. A behavior-behavior relationship is established.

In other words, the client's thought "I am afraid" literally seems to cause her avoidance, and the avoidance seems to cause the reduction in fear. Given the general acceptability of this position, it is only natural that the agoraphobic's husband will begin to do the family shopping. His behavior thus reinforces the notion that "anxiety" is a good explanation for (and cause of) his wife's failure to go to the store. Functionally speaking, the thoughts and emotions associated with anxiety have in fact come to control both the agoraphobic's and her husband's behavior, but only because a context exists that sustains the relationship.

In the above examples, we see how the belief that thoughts and feelings control behavior is supported by the social-verbal community at large. Given the "logical" contexts of literality, reason-giving, and control, we come to believe that situations can only change after something that is "causing" the situation changes. In the case of the aforementioned agoraphobic, both she and her husband may implicitly agree that before she can resume the family shopping, her anxiety will have to be eliminated, or at least brought to a manageable level. By the time she comes to therapy, the agoraphobic client almost inevitably believes that she must learn to control her anxiety before her life can improve.

The Problem and the Solution

This is the client's "solution." In our view, it is instead one aspect of the problem. To the extent that the agoraphobic insists on continuing to apply the "solution," her situation is indeed "hopeless." The contexts of literality, reason-giving, and control in which clients find themselves are so pervasive that they have a difficult time stepping outside of them. The contexts are ubiquitous but unseen.

Communication theorists have described two types of change that are possible in a given situation: "One that occurs within a given system which itself remains unchanged, and one whose occurrence changes the system itself" (Watzlawick et al., 1974, p. 10); these are "first-order" and "second-order" change, respectively. First-order change is based on common sense principles, on the rationale of "more of the same." Second-order change, on the other hand, completely recontextualizes the problem and solution, creating a sense of surprise and the unexpected. From this view, the solutions typically identified by a client are of the first-order category. Their ineffectiveness lies in their inability to examine the problem from outside the system in which it exists. Often second-order change is needed for a client to get "unstuck" and move ahead.

Comprehensive distancing can be described as a means of establishing a therapeutic context in which second-order change is facilitated. We seek to do so by undermining the three contexts of literality, reason-giving, and control. Since each is not only part of the client's perspective, but also part of the social-verbal community's perspective (including the therapist's), they are very difficult to challenge. In fact, the only way possible to do so is by behaving in ways that are not "logical," not "reasonable," and thus outside the verbal contexts the therapist is seeking to suspend.

In this first part of therapy, the client is told that the "solution" he or she is proposing is part of the problem, and that the therapist cannot possibly provide a technique to eliminate, control, or reduce the distressing emotions or reactions the client is experiencing. The situation *is* "hopeless," because even if the therapist could do what the client is asking, it would not yield the desired result.

This declaration of clients' problems as "hopeless" is similar to the "hard restraining" techniques used in other paradoxical therapies (Rohrbaugh, Tennen, Press, & White, 1981; Weeks & L'Abate, 1982). However, whereas traditionally this is a "last resort" intervention (even for paradoxical therapists who are themselves often a last resort after other therapies have failed), "creative hopelessness" declares early in therapy that the client is helpless and hopeless to change, *within the context from which he or she currently is operating*. Clients are told they are not to blame for this hopelessness, but that they are responsible, that is, able-to-respond. The many and varied ways the client has already tried to change, which have failed, are explored with the therapist. Since the things clients have already attempted and abandoned typically are logical, common-sense solutions, it becomes clear that some second-order change, some solution beyond ordinary verbal logic, is needed. However, the client does not yet have experience in the kind of problem-solving that is needed to bring about truly radical change. Using metaphor, the therapist describes the "hopeless" dilemma in terms that identify the social-verbal system in which the client was trained, not the client personally, as the real problem.

Confusion is maintained deliberately to prevent clients from intellectualizing and compartmentalizing their dilemma into the same solutions and common-sense insights that have failed in the past (Erickson, Rossi, & Rossi, 1976). For example, the client is told that if he or she seems to be understanding what the therapist is saying, then indeed, he or she is *not* understanding it, since within the logical verbal context from which they are operating, the therapist's real meaning cannot possibly be understood.

Such use of paradoxical confusion can serve to challenge the firmly entrenched contexts of literality, reason-giving, and control:

> After the initial shock, confusion triggers off an immediate search for meaning or order to reduce the anxiety inherent in any uncertain situation. The result is an unusual increase in attention, coupled with a readiness to assume causal connections even where such connections may appear to be quite nonsensical. While the search can be continued to include such small details or such remote possibilities that it leads to further confusion, it can equally well lead to fresh and creative ways of conceptualizing reality. (Watzlawick, 1976, pp. 27–28)

By creating confusion through the use of seemingly nonsensical statements, the therapist creates a new verbal context in which the client is likely to invest the first understandable piece of information he or she is given with a high degree of significance or validity. When the therapist later presents an alternative context from which to view the client's problems, it then is more likely to be considered as a viable option. Metaphor is used extensively to impress on the client that the therapist is *not* presenting a new and different belief system to be embraced literally. Rather, the new context is itself a metaphor for living, that is, simply a different construction from which to view the world.

Control

The second goal of comprehensive distancing is to focus on the issues of emotional and cognitive control. As mentioned earlier, by the time the client comes to therapy, he or she has been well trained to view many of his problems as a result of failure to control thoughts and feelings in his or her own life (e.g., temper, anxiety, depression). This viewpoint has been supported by the social-verbal community at large, and recently, by many psychological theories that have had wide exposure among non-professional readers. For example, clients can pick up any magazine in the doctor's office and learn techniques to replace anxiety with relaxation, depressive thoughts with happy ones, a poor self-image with positive thinking, and so on.

The attempted implementation of internal control is the client's primary vehicle for emotional avoidance. In our work, we view such attempts to control private events (thoughts, feelings, opinions, etc.) as themselves causes of many major life difficulties. Clients are told that the rule "If you don't want it, get rid of it" is ineffective in the world of private experience, despite its obvious reasonableness and cultural advantages in the physical world around them. Rather, in the world inside the skin, the rule can more accurately be stated, "If you aren't willing to have it, you've got it." Trying to get rid of anxiety will inevitably lead to thoughts about anxiety, thus producing the very thing the client is seeking to eliminate; trying not be depressed is depressing.

The ineffectiveness of "If you don't want it, get rid of it" has been described elsewhere by referring to the principle of "more of the same" (Watzlawick et al., 1974). The same old solutions may not help solve new problems, particularly when dealing with the world of inner experience. In the external world, it is often the case that the best solution to a given problem is the reestablishment of some previously accepted or desired norm. For example, a light is turned on at night to reestablish a condition of being able to see. If that light is inadequate, turning on a brighter light, or a greater quantity of dim ones, will eventually do the job. The final solution comes from applying more of the original one. However, in many social or interpersonal dilemmas, "more of the same" does not produce the desired result. Rather, the very solution being so stringently applied tends to exacerbate the problem.

Comprehensive distancing expresses the "more of the same" dilemma through literal paradox and metaphor in hopes of loosening up clients' emotional and verbal control. The statement "If you aren't willing to have it, you've got it" is impossible for the client to make use of literally. For example, the agoraphobic is told that if she expresses a willingness to have anxiety, but only because such willingness will ultimately serve to eliminate anxiety, then she really is *unwilling*, and, as a consequence, anxiety is certain to continue. Once again, confusion is created deliberately in order to weaken the existing contexts of literality and control. The agoraphobic's application of "more of the same" (ways to avoid anxiety) is short-circuited and a therapeutic double-bind effectively established.

This phase of therapy is characterized by a type of *symptom prescription* or "paradoxical intention" that has been widely used in other strategic or paradoxical therapies (Cade, 1984; Frankl, 1960; Mozdzierz, Macchitelli, & Lisiecki, 1967; Seltzer, 1986; Watzlawick, Beavin, & Jackson, 1967). As traditionally used, symptom prescription: (1) gives the client permission to have what he or she already has (the symptom); (2) overexposes the client to the symptom, with the unspoken hope that the symptom will lose its functional significance and thus be abandoned; and (3) creates a paradoxical double-bind by implying that the only way the client will change is by remaining unchanged. Clients are told, often in a humorous tone with a serious undervein, to practice symptoms that appear out of their control (by exaggerating them, scheduling them, and so on). In this way, the client gains control over a previously "uncontrollable" behavior, the anxiety cycle maintaining the symptom is broken, and the symptom often disappears. Symptom prescription thus is a means to a particular end, namely, that of leading the client ultimately to be symptom-free.

In comprehensive distancing, symptom prescription also serves to give clients permission to be exactly where they are, and it creates a therapeutic double-bind. However, the long-term goal in our work is not symptom reduction. In fact, we tell clients, in all earnestness, that we are *not* trying to make their symptoms go away. Symptom "prescription" as it is used here exposes the client to the feared symptom, and this exposure leads to the symptom losing its functional significance. Whether the symptom disappears in the process is irrelevant to our work. We want to help clients' lives expand, symptom-free or not. To illustrate, we have treated an obsessive-compulsive with this approach who was paralyzed with the fear that, while driving, she had run over a pedestrian. She would literally spend hours driving around a parking lot looking to see if she had run over someone, and after each circle around the lot, she would have to return to check once again. After termination of therapy, the client reported that her frequency of thoughts that she had run someone over had declined only slightly. But the impact of the thoughts had plummeted. She was willing to have the thought *and* not go back to check and see. The previous relationship between her obsessive thoughts and behavior was changed, without the symptom itself having changed in frequency. The thoughts still occurred but without initiating a destructive chain motivated by an attempt to "reassure" herself and thereby eliminate the thought.

Who Am I?

The third goal identified in comprehensive distancing is that of helping the client to distinguish between the person he or she calls "I," and the problem behaviors that the client wants eliminated. Such a distinction is more or less explicit in many forms of traditional psychotherapy, particularly humanistic and existential traditions that stress the teleological "becoming" or self-actualization of the client.

The distinction is also not alien to the philosophy and treatment of paradoxical therapies. For example, reactance theory, on which much paradoxical theory is based, refers to emotions, attitudes, and beliefs as "free behaviors" that humans believe they choose to emit (Brehm & Brehm, 1981).

The distinction between that part of oneself that the client calls "I" and the things (thoughts, emotions, overt behaviors) that he or she is struggling with is not in itself inherently paradoxical. It is, however, a difficult distinction for most of us to make. Language itself obscures the difference, for at least two reasons. First, the awareness established by language is often not reflective. A person can be aware of events, but it is difficult to be aware of awareness (for a behavioral discussion of this difficulty see Hayes, 1984). Awareness is context, not content. As soon as one observes the context of observation, from what context is *this* observation made? Second, a variety of verbal conventions confuse the distinction between a behaving oganism and the behavior *of* an organism. For example, we often do not say, "I *feel* angry" but rather, "I *am* angry."

At this stage of therapy, we frequently do experiential exercises designed to help the client become more aware of awareness. We also adopt the somewhat awkward convention of framing statements in such a way as to make clear the distinction between the self and the behavior being emitted. For example, we instruct clients to say, "I'm having the thought that I can't go to the mall" (as opposed to simply stating, "I can't go to the mall"), or "I'm having the evaluation that I'm a bad person." This simple technique (which gestalt therapists have used to get clients to "own" their thoughts and feelings) very powerfully brings home to the client the distinction we are trying to make between the person they are and the things in their life.

Letting Go of the Struggle

The notion of one giving up the struggle with one's symptoms appears paradoxical to clients, because it is against every instinct within them that initially led them into therapy. The activity of downhill skiing illustrates our point: when a person is on a steep slope, skiing downhill for the first time, the natural inclination is to lean back on the skis in order to slow down and keep in control of speed and steering. However, any experienced skier knows that, in fact, the opposite is true—the only way to gain maximum control over your speed and course is to lean *forward* into the slope. When we encourage clients to give up the struggle with control, we are *not* asking them to "grin and bear it," or "tough out" their symptoms until these are able to be endured. Rather, we are asking the clients to lean into the symptoms; we encourage them not only to stop struggling, but seemingly to embrace the very things that they most dread.

A client can only begin to do this if he or she has successfully negotiated the earlier stages of therapy. The only way it is possible for clients to cease struggling with depression, anxiety, self-deprecation, obsessions, and so on, is if they can begin to view these phenomena from a different context that has been established in the therapeutic setting. In this context, the client can recognize emotions or thoughts or bodily sensations *for what they are* (i.e., emotions, thoughts, bodily sensations), not for what they seem to be.

For example, the thought "I am a bad person" is not the same as actually being a bad person. We ask the client to give up the struggle with the thought, *as a thought—not* to resign himself to being a bad person. The feeling the agoraphobic has during a panic attack that she is going to go crazy is not the same as the actual experience of becoming psychotic. We ask the client to experience the *fear* of craziness, not actually to experience slipping into psychosis. Only if clients have glimpsed the reality that they are much more than the thoughts, feelings, etc., that are part of their lives is this possible.

This notion of relinquishing control to gain control is more commonly accepted in Eastern philosophical traditions than in the Western world where logic is so linear in its derivations. For example, Morita therapy, which is based on ancient Zen teachings, states:

> Once you are friendly with your symptoms and accept them as reality, you find yourself cured—able to function—whether or not you still have them. . . . One of the main aims of the treatment is to persuade the patient not to eradicate his symptoms by force of will. (Mozdzierz et al., 1976)

Other therapeutic approaches have used the notion as well. For example, Adler's use of paradoxical strategies included stressing that the *therapist* must give up the struggle with the client, that is, the therapist must avoid opposing the patient (Mozdzierz et al., 1976). In so doing, the competitive element in therapy is removed, and the likelihood that the client will enter into a cooperative relationship with the therapist is enhanced.

In traditional paradoxical interventions, humor is one of the most powerful means used to assist clients in gaining some detachment or sense of "distance" from their symptoms (Fay, 1978; Frankl, 1960; Mozdzierz et al., 1976; Omer, 1981). This is true in our work as well. For example, when talking about anxiety we might unexpectedly revert into a cartoon-like voice and throw in asides (e.g., "Me? Go into that mall? Forget it!"). Properly timed, a lifted eyebrow or impish grin reminds the client that we are all in this social-verbal stew together, working to distinguish ourselves from the "stuff" in our lives. Humor is never used in our work to punish or to mock. It always is intended to give clients a less ponderous perspective on their problems and to strengthen the common bond of the therapeutic relationship.

Finally, in our work, it is stressed that "giving up the struggle" is a process, not a final destination or state that the client will ever fully achieve. No matter how big an infinitely expanding balloon becomes, there is always more "big" to get. Similarly, no sooner does the client (or therapist) cease fighting a particular emotion or thought, than a new, more difficult struggle emerges. From our perspective, this is the quality of life: the ability to face change and move forward where more change is waiting.

Commitment

The fifth goal of comprehensive distancing is making a commitment to action. At this stage of therapy, the client has been led to view reasons as mere verbal behavior, not literal causes. The client has been encouraged to distinguish between the "I" and one's behavior. Within this therapeutic context, the client who makes a commitment has no acceptable excuses for a failure to follow through. This stage of treatment is also not punitive; there is no attempt to "punish" the recalcitrant client or trick him or her into keeping his or her commitments. Rather, a verbal environment has been created in therapy that allows no logical escape. The client is response-*able*; not to blame, but able to act and change.

Thus, the goal of therapy at this point is to practice the successful making and keeping of commitments. The commitments clients come to set for themselves often bear little resemblance to the presenting complaints that initially brought them into therapy. The size or labeled "importance" of each commitment is considered irrelevant to the process, so long as it is growth-enhancing rather than growth-inhibiting. Therapy at this point resembles more traditional approaches, albeit within the unique social-verbal system that has been established. In particular, interpersonal issues can be explored, since the client no longer has the old familiar excuses of unpleasant thoughts, feelings, and evaluations on which to blame maladaptive relationships. Overt literal paradox is a less salient feature of therapy at this point, although it will be utilized as needed until the end of treatment.

The Paradoxical Quality of Comprehensive Distancing

The term paradox is derived from the Latin *paradoxum,* with "para" meaning "contrary to," and "doxy" translating as "opinion"; it is, in other words, something contrary to received opinion or expectation. It is a word used loosely throughout the psychotherapy literature, referring to all sorts of contradictory, startling, or unexpected interventions on the part of the therapist, and in fact, it has been noted that "paradox [is] used implicitly in all forms of effective psychotherapy" (Mozdzierz et al., 1976). Many authors (Dell, 1981; Rorhbaugh et al., 1981; Watzlawick et al., 1974; Weeks & L'Abate, 1982; Kercher & Smith, 1985a, 1985b) have remarked on how difficult it is to describe the theory and logic underlying unorthodox and paradoxical therapeutic interventions: "There is, as yet, no unified theoretical framework for describing and understanding paradoxical psychotherapy" (Cade, 1984, p. 513).

Paradoxical interventions have been explained in terms of cognitive dissonance or dialectical theories, which stress the importance of struggle, contradiction or dichotomy, and crisis in bringing about dynamic life change (Kercher & Smith, 1985b; Weeks & L'Abate, 1982). Other authors have explained paradoxical interventions using a psychoanalytic drive-reduction approach (Marshall, 1976). A third view is derived from

Brehm's (1966) theory of psychological reactance. Here, the therapist attempts to "join forces" with the client's resistance through such techniques as reframing, confusion, and prescribing the very symptom the client seeks to eliminate (Kercher & Smith, 1985a, 1985b; Raskin & Klein, 1976; Seltzer, 1986; Tennen, Rohrbaugh, Press, & White, 1981).

The best developed descriptions of paradoxical and strategic interventions, however, are found in the writings of the systems and communication theorists (Bateson, Jackson, Haley, & Weakland, 1963; Fisch, Weakland, & Segal, 1982; Selvini Palazzoli, Boscolo, Cecchin, & Prata, 1978; Watzlawick et al., 1967, 1974). These writings focus on the interpersonal context in which symptoms develop and are maintained. This context may be based in the relationship between client and therapist, or (more commonly) in the client's relationships with family, work environment, and so on. Paradoxical interventions use surprise and the unexpected in an attempt to restructure maladaptive communication patterns and thus to break down self-perpetuating cycles of interactions in which the client's symptom serves a function.

Discussion of the various theories of paradox is relevant because paradoxical interventions are found in so many schools of psychotherapy and with so many different rationales to explain its effectiveness:

> The question at hand is whether these [various rationales] have only superficial similarities, consisting at bottom of quite different change producing agents, or whether it is better to subsume them all under one broad explanatory principle which then may serve as a bridge between the various paradigms. (Omer, 1981, p. 320)

It has been suggested that the common element in all therapeutic uses of paradox is decontextualization of the symptomatic behavior (Omer, 1981). In other words, paradox leads the client to experience the symptom in a different context where it loses its original function and meaning and, consequently, disappears.

In comprehensive distancing, the therapist is often talking and behaving "funny," that is, in ways that leave the client befuddled. However, the paradoxical quality of our work primarily utilizes *literal paradox*, rather than *social paradox*. That is, statements are made during therapy that, if taken literally, can no longer be accepted at all. The "sense" of these statements is seen only when the client gives up trying to make sense of them. What is paradoxical in comprehensive distancing is our attack on the "orthodoxy" of literal meaning, since this attack necessarily relies on the same literal meaning it undermines in order to be understood at all. We are interested in the social relationships between the client and therapist, family, or other significant persons in the environment, but we only focus on these relationships after a therapeutic context built on literal paradox has been established.

Thus, comprehensive distancing alters not only the inter- or intrapersonal context of the symptom, but the context of language itself. This alteration facilitates the client's efforts to face squarely thoughts and emotions that have been previously avoided. Verbal language is acknowledged by other paradoxical theorists as the mechanism by which individual and societal values and beliefs are maintained (Teismann, 1979; Tennen et al., 1981). However, our use of paradox to undermine literal meaning and believability of language (and consequently the power it leads to reason-giving and control) seems to be clinically much more powerful. Paradox is not the driving force *per se* behind this approach to therapy; instead, the driving force behind the therapy (i.e., the attack on literal meaning and a shift to the experiential) is itself inherently paradoxical. We seek to disconnect the clients' symptoms from daily functioning without asking them to give up the symptoms entirely or at all.

In this unique context, the role of paradoxical intervention is radically altered. For example, in a traditional paradoxical intervention, the therapist may request a person with insomnia to stay awake all night. If the client complies, the client has formed an alliance with the therapist. If the client disobeys, the symptom is being successfully treated. This is the type of therapeutic "deception" of which (justly or unjustly) many paradoxical interventions have been accused (Cade, 1984; L'Abate & Weeks, 1978; Mozdzierz et al., 1976; Rosenbaum, 1982; Weeks & L'Abate, 1982).

In comprehensive distancing, "obedience" is not a therapeutic issue because there is nothing to obey. We make no effort to put clients into the position where they "win" by disobeying the therapist. When we make statements to the client such as "don't believe a word we say," we are making a literally paradoxical injunction to which the client cannot logically respond. Our goal is not break down resistance so the client *will* believe our words; rather, we *mean* what we say—but we mean it so radically that even *this* statement is not to be believed. Comprehensive distancing puts all the "cards" on the table; it is only the nature of the cards themselves that is paradoxical.

Traditionally, therapeutic paradox is often used as a "last resort," after other interventions have failed to bring about behavioral change (Bergman, 1982; Greenberg, 1973; Seltzer, 1986; Whitaker, 1975). In particular, "hard restraining" techniques, that is, telling the client that his or her problem is hopeless and he or she would be advised just to try to make the best out of life in spite of it, are used only when success with other therapeutic approaches seem unlikely. When paradox *is* used early, it is usually because the therapist has enough history to know the client is "reactant" and likely to resist more supportive efforts to elicit change.

In comprehensive distancing, we *begin* therapy with paradox and metaphor and continue to use it consistently throughout the duration of treatment. Since comprehensive distancing uses literal, not social paradox, there is never a sense of "one-upmanship" on the therapist's part. The therapist and client are united in a common struggle to undermine the maladaptive confines of the verbal system in which both are operating. The challenge is a difficult one, since it must be accomplished using the very verbal system that is being placed under scrutiny.

A Therapeutic Sample

In order to illustrate some of the paradoxical principles of comprehensive distancing, we present here some brief excerpts from actual therapy sessions conducted with a client we will call Ted. (Readers who have not done so are encouraged to read Hayes, 1987, for examples of other typical metaphors and therapist interventions used in comprehensive distancing.) Ted was a 43-year-old married white male with two children. He had two other children from a previous marriage whom he had not contacted in many years. Ted was referred to us for treatment of chronic depression; his score on the Beck Depression Inventory (BDI) when he began therapy was 32, and he was taking an antidepressant prescription. His speech was full of self-deprecating remarks and expressions of hopelessness, and he was often near tears. His body posture was rigid and inflexible.

Ted also suffered from such severe social anxieties that he had difficulty speaking his name aloud when going to vote, answering the telephone, or talking to his next-door neighbor over the back fence. More importantly (to Ted), he was unable to participate actively in business meetings or to confront co-workers when his job required it. He felt unable to enjoy most social functions and would go to great lengths to avoid them.

Ted admitted that he was an angry man who was frustrated that several years of previous therapy had made little impact on the quality of his life. His primary way of expressing this anger was through procrastination: he was continually neglecting things that needed to be done, whether it was putting away his laundry, paying his taxes, or registering his automobile. Going to work in the morning was a daily struggle for Ted, and he was fearful that one day he would no longer be able to force himself to do so. To assist in motivating himself, Ted consumed large quantitites of an amphetamine derivative, a habit that he hid from his wife.

Ted was highly reactant and could be counted on to do the opposite of whatever he was asked to do, especially if the request came from an authority figure. Throughout treatment, attempts to elicit his participation in homework assignments were unsuccessful. When we began comprehensive distancing with Ted, we asked that he commit to 10 sessions, after which it would be clear whether or not this therapeutic approach was going to be helpful or not. Ultimately, Ted remained in therapy for a little over 1 year. By the time he terminated, he had reestablished regular contact with his two children from his previous marriage, had accepted a new job where he was a supervisor with many responsibilities, and had discontinued all amphetamine use. His BDI scores had dropped to below 10, and his relationship with his wife had improved.

The following is an excerpt from session 3 with Ted. The client has been saying that things the past week had been going "real bad." In particular, he had been having problems getting to work on time. Once he got there he would sit in his car, drinking cola, waiting until the last minute before the supervisor would arrive. For Ted, this behavior was typical of problems he had struggled with for much of his life. In it, the therapist is using the client's confusion to address the problems inherent in emotional control. (Bracketed material contains explanatory comments not in the transcripts.)

THERAPIST: I was asking you about this issue of control, about how the rule seems to work differently, that in the world outside the skin, it seems to be, "If you don't want it, figure out how to get rid of it and then get rid of it." In the world inside the skin, it seems that doesn't work, in fact, it's actually harmful. There, it's more like, if you're not willing to have it, then you've got it. [This material was covered in an earlier session.]

CLIENT: Basically what I've thought about this past week is just what you've said. There's really not a whole lot more to say about it, is there?

THERAPIST: Well, did you notice yourself this week relating to your emotions and thoughts and memories and so forth, from the position of "This is bad and I have to get rid of it," or "This is good and I have to make sure it happens," relating to it as if it were dirt on the carpet or peeling paint on the walls, as if it were the *things* in your life that you've learned to deal with?

CLIENT: I'm having trouble keeping my mind together here. Just a second here, let me get myself together . . .

THERAPIST: No, wait a minute. Tell me about *that*. Because this will be a concrete example. When you have that feeling that things are confusing, what do you do with it?

CLIENT: I just try to catch flashes that pop back into my mind and build on it until I can figure out what is going on. Eventually I get it put back together.

THERAPIST: O.K. But would it be fair to say this, that when you get confused, you try to get rid of the confusion?

CLIENT: Oh, yeah. Absolutely.

THERAPIST: O.K. Except, can you see that struggling to get rid of the confusion might itself create a fair amount of confusion? I mean, you eventually get through it, and it looks to you like you got through it because you were struggling with the confusion, but doesn't that seem a little fishy to you, because the confusion hangs around. You've been confused for how long?

CLIENT: Forever I think. Yeah, forever.

THERAPIST: So if this move really works, why are you still confused? I mean it clearly doesn't solve your confusion, right?

CLIENT: It just handles the immediate situation I'm in.

THERAPIST: So it *seems*. Actually, I'm not sure it does even that. Let's take a situation. Can you deliberately get yourself confused?

CLIENT: Probably not.

THERAPIST: Well, let's try. Let's really try. Let's get yourself good and confused.

CLIENT: I can't, I don't know if I can make myself do that. My mind is blanking; it's not letting me do it.

THERAPIST: O.K., now go with that. Try to get really confused. You really want to be just totally unclear about what you're trying to do. Really just lost. Really just try to lose yourself. Just gone.

CLIENT: I don't think that ever happens to me. It only happens when I'm listening to somebody.

THERAPIST: Yes. Now follow the wisdom of that. The meaning of what you just did. Suppose you were confused at a moment, and at that very moment, you did not fight the confusion, but really saw, clearly, that you were confused?

CLIENT: Kind of admitted it, sort of?

THERAPIST: Yep. Can you see that, if you did that, at that moment you're no longer confused, because it's absolutely clear, it's actually *clear that you're confused*!

CLIENT: Right. That would clear up at least that confusion about being confused.

THERAPIST: In fact, at that moment, you wouldn't *be* confused. You would be clear about a thing that you're calling confusion, but you would not be a state of confusion, you would be in a state of clarity about something . . .

Two weeks later (session 5), Ted was talking about an event that had happened to him during the past week that had been particularly embarrassing. For the first time, Ted had been able to experience his embarrassment without struggling with it. Much to his surprise, the embarrassment had not led to the depression and self-deprecation that normally would have followed such an episode. In excerpts from the following session, we see how symptom prescription and metaphor continue to be used to address the problem underlying emotional control.

THERAPIST: As we go along, one of the things we're going to want to do in here, and also out there, is find places where your buttons get pushed, and going into those places instead of staying away from them.

CLIENT: And feeling the emotion, finding out I *can* feel them?

THERAPIST: Yes. And shifting the arena in which that emotion is occurring. So when embarrassment shows up, that's good stuff. It gives you a chance, right then and there, to make a change that makes a difference. A metaphor that might help a little bit is this. It would be like if we had a bus. And you're the driver. And on this bus you've got a bunch of passengers. The passengers are thoughts and feelings and memories and all that kind of stuff. Now some of them are scary, dressed up in black leather jackets with switchblades and knives. What tends to happen is that you're driving along and the passengers start threatening you, telling you what you have to do, where you have to go.

CLIENT: O.K.

THERAPIST: Telling you that you've got to turn left, you've got to turn right. The threat that they have over you is that, if you don't, they're going to come up from the back of the bus. It's like you make deals with these passengers. And the deal is, "You sit at the back of the bus and scrunch down so that I can't see you very often, and I'll do what you say." So let's say you get tired of that and say, I don't like this, I'm going to throw this passenger off the bus. If I just get this SOB off the bus, I can drive it wherever I want to. So you stop. And you go back to deal with the passenger at the back. Except you notice the very first thing you had to do?

CLIENT: Stop.

THERAPIST: Right. Stop. So now, you're not driving anywhere, you're just dealing with this passenger. And plus, they're real strong. They don't intend to leave. So you wrestle with them; it doesn't seem very successful.

CLIENT: I've made efforts to get rid of certain parts of myself. Like New Year's resolutions. "I'm going to do it," period. I used to think I did it a little bit, but not anymore.

THERAPIST: Yes. Probably the reason is that you made enough of a deal that they sat down so that you couldn't see them.

CLIENT: Probably so. I guess so, since they're never permanent. And they're worse when they come back.

THERAPIST: Yes. And I'll tell you why that is. If the reason why you didn't see them was that you made a deal with them to sit down, the problem with that is now you'll pretty much do what they say in exchange for them getting out of your life. If you're good enough at it, you can almost pretend as though they're not on the bus at all. They won't show up. But when they *do* show up, it's with the added power of the deals that you've made with them in the past. They're much more powerful now.

CLIENT: Every time they win, I give up more every time.

THERAPIST: If you're good enough at it, you can even almost pretend that you're going where *you* want to go with the bus.

CLIENT: At some point, I know I'm not ever going to get there. And it's getting worse as I get older. Just lately, the last few years, I'm getting the feeling that I know I'm never going to get there. But there's nowhere else to go.

THERAPIST: Let's look at this. Because what I'm trying to do with this metaphor is get back to the original question I asked which is, What would you be like if you stopped riding yourself, stopped coming from the place where you have to be driven and trying to beat yourself into submission? What would you be like if you gave up the struggle? [This material had been covered earlier in the session.] This thing of making yourself do it, is like sending on passenger back to fight with the other passengers. It might appear to work except the problem is, *you're still not in charge of what's going on here.* And the trick about the whole thing, the power the passenger has over you is 100% based on this: "If you don't do what I say, I'm coming up and I'm making you look at me." That's it. Now it's true that when they come up, they *look* as if they can do more. They've got knives and chains and whips and it looks like you're going to be destroyed.

CLIENT: I don't quite understand, grasp that.

THERAPIST: The tradeoff or secret deal that gets made is based on this: if you do what they say, they won't come up and make you look at them. They're not going to come up and stand next to you. That's too scary.

CLIENT: I can't imagine being afraid to look at them.

THERAPIST: Well, let's look at this. What about things like this?: "I don't like telling other people what I feel." [This was one of the things the client said he hated to do.] In the terms of this metaphor, isn't that a passenger saying, "Turn left?" Suppose down the road there's a sign that says, "Telling People What You Feel—Turn Right." So you're driving along and say to yourself, Well, I hardly ever go over there. I have a sense that that's the road for me to take. . . . What's going to happen?

CLIENT: I'd go left. I'd go the opposite way.

THERAPIST: Sure. And at the moment, what's happening? *You* may see that this would work for me to do, but something else, someone else doesn't. It could be a thought-passenger who says, "Oh, but that would be embarrassing." Or a feeling-passenger. Right? So you make a deal with it. You say, O.K., I don't like feeling *that.* But what's "that"? It's the passenger, the feeling you would feel if you were more self-disclosing.

CLIENT: But there's always something a person holds back.

THERAPIST: Yes, but you've laid out before that sense that for *you* to be self-disclosing is really creepy. You don't like it. It doesn't feel good. Right?

CLIENT: Right.

THERAPIST: That feeling is the passenger I'm talking about, and you made a deal with him. The deal is, "I won't turn right, and you won't show up."

CLIENT: Oh, that's the deal, yes. That's what I do.

THERAPIST: But he's on the bus, right? It's not like, I won't turn right and he'll be out of my life. Because if you try to turn right he'll be right there. Are you with me?

CLIENT: Oh, yes, I'm with you 100%. I do have a really hard time telling people, not telling them how I feel, but just letting my feelings out as I'm feeling them. It always turns into a clinical telling-them-how-I-feel sort of thing. It's not a real feeling. My voice is monotone. I'm very aware of how I come across to people. I hear myself on a recorder, and I know I sound very nondescriptive emotionally, and it doesn't ever seem to change. I'd like to change it up here, but I can't. But it doesn't seem that scary right now to me.

THERAPIST: Yes. Can you see that, in the bus metaphor, the driver has control of the bus? Except he trades off that control in secret deals he makes with the passengers. Now, if those passengers were real, physical things that could make you do things, it would sort of make sense that the passengers could wrest control from you whether you liked it or not and make you turn left or right. Like if you were a real bus driver and someone came up and stuck a gun at your head. However, what I want you to notice is that, although the passengers *claim* they can do that, they've never been able to, without your cooperation. You've *never* had the experience—check this out, tell me if I'm wrong—you've never had the experience of a feeling coming and without your cooperation, wresting control of your life away from you so that you no longer have anything to do with what's going on, and you now go driving off, careening down some mountain ravine.

CLIENT: I can't imagine them ever really having control.

THERAPIST: Right. But they give you a good show. They say, turn left or I'll stick you with this knife, so you turn left. At the moment that the hoodlum shows up, scowling at you—when Mr. Embarrassment shows up, or Mr. Social Insecurity shows up, or Mr. You're-Really-Deep-Down-A-Bad-Person shows up (you've got lots of passengers)—at the moment they show up, they look like they're real.

CLIENT: I've never given into the feelings. I've always fought them.

THERAPIST: Right. Fighting them is the secret deal, the keeping them in the back of the bus. The problem is that if you fight a feeling, and have to keep it in the back of the bus, it has complete power over you because when it shows up, it can make you do anything. Now, what would happen if you gave up completely on your concern over where the passengers sit?

CLIENT: I'd go wherever I please, it wouldn't make any difference at all.

THERAPIST: Right. Unless they really are concrete and they really can stick a knife in you. Now, that's possible. But I can tell you, you've never experienced that, and I've never met anyone who has.

CLIENT: That's a pretty funny scene, to picture looking back and seeing them and yet being able to go where I want to go. That would be quite nice. It would be really hilarious.

THERAPIST: It is kind of hilarious. They're welcome to come along for the ride!

CLIENT: The idea of that really tickles me, doing what you want to do. I've always seen myself as driving an empty bus. That's the picture I've had for myself. But I guess I've known for a long time that's never going to happen.

In the next session, Ted opened the conversation by saying that the previous week had been "horrible," that he just "couldn't make any sense of it" (what he had been talking about last session). The therapist continues to use the bus metaphor to discuss the problems of emotional control.

THERAPIST: You're here now, living your life. The issue is: to what degree can I make room for the passengers on the bus and keep my hands on the steering wheel? What does the driver have to do to get his hands on the steering wheel and be in charge? Can you make a deal with your passengers and still be in control of where the bus goes?

CLIENT: Sure.

THERAPIST: How so? What's the deal going to be?

CLIENT: It would have to be different—if you made a deal—from where you were going to go originally.

THERAPIST: Let's say Mr. Anxiety shows up. The deal will have to be that they get some control, right? In exchange for what? What do they give you in return?

CLIENT: They just shut up.

THERAPIST: Right, they slump down a little bit, they don't show up so much, at least not so obviously. They show up in the form of where the bus is going, but they don't show up so much by coming up and leaning on you. For example: "Don't go to the party, Ted. . . ." "Why not? I kind of like parties!" "I'll show up. . . ." (That's Mr. Anxiety talking to you.) So you tell your wife, "Uh, I'm not really feeling good tonight, I have some papers to look over," or something. And it's true, when you do that, he doesn't show up so much, but who's in charge?

CLIENT: Well, he's got all the control there.

THERAPIST: So would it be fair to say that, in your own experience, it seems to be that giving away control over what's there to be done occurs out of an unwillingness to experience the stuff that will show up when you do anything else?

CLIENT: Well, with anxiety, yes; that's pretty clear there. But I can't seem to think of any other items. . . . Does that seem to run with all of them?

THERAPIST: Check it out.

CLIENT: Well, I guess it is true with all those other cases. Otherwise you could do whatever you wanted.

THERAPIST: So let's put it this way. Willingness to experience stuff is the issue. It's the only issue. There isn't any other issue.

CLIENT: Then they wouldn't have any control over you. It wouldn't matter if you experienced them or not.

THERAPIST: Right. The whole thing that we're doing in here is discriminating *where you can have control, and where you can't,* and the deal is this: you can get in control of your life, hands on the steering wheel, by giving up the attempt to get in control of the passengers. Conversely, if you want to get in control of the passengers, you lose control of your life. That's the choice.

CLIENT: That sounds awful simple. Is it really that simple?

THERAPIST: Well, look at your own experience. You tell me whether or not that fits. When you've tried to control the passengers, staying away from anxiety, making sure depression and confusion don't show up, are you more or less in control of your life?

CLIENT: In my *real* life, I'm less in control. I mean, I'm in control here-and-now all the time, but not in control the way that I want to be in control.

THERAPIST: Right. And which is more important to you, if you really just had to choose? Would you rather have control over how your life's working, or moment-to-moment control over what you're feeling, thinking, etc.?

CLIENT: Oh, the life, for sure. There's no doubt about it.

THERAPIST: So let's ask the key question: out of the place from which there is a distinction between you and "that" ("that" meaning the feeling that comes forward when you're doing some behavior), are you willing to feel that, think that, experience that, *and* do what works for you in the situation?

CLIENT: Yeah, I'm willing to do that. I never knew that's what it took. Of course I will.

THERAPIST: So for example, talking to people. Out of the place from which there is a distinction between you, the person, and the feelings that will come when you talk to people, are you willing to experience all those feelings, fully and without defense, and, do what works for you in this situation, which may be talking to them? Will you put on the front of the bus—as a sign, a destination—"I'm Goin' To Go Talk To That Person," *and* keep your hands on the steering wheel, *and* invite all the passengers up? You can get right up close to people! You can *really* feel uncomfortable! And then you won't like it, and you can *really* not like it! Now, be real clear, I'm not trying to trivialize the experience—the experience is exactly what it is. I'm not saying, oh, that's just anxiety. It's exactly what it is.

CLIENT: Yeh, I'm willing to do that. . . .

The above transcriptions can perhaps capture some of the flavor of comprehensive distancing. The samples included here are from early sessions with Ted, and so the ratio of therapist-to-client talk is higher than in later sessions. It is also difficult to communicate in transcripts the continual vein of humor and empathy that pervade our treatment. Nevertheless, they demonstrate the emphasis on metaphorical talk and willingness to experience that are characteristic of comprehensive distancing even in later sessions. In Ted's case, the major life changes described above did not occur until approximately 10 months into therapy. At that point, Ted simply began coming into sessions unexpectedly announcing that he had contacted his children, or stopping taking pills, or changed jobs. The changes often had little to do with material that had been discussed the previous week in session, and they were presented by Ted in a very matter-of-fact way. What there was to be done in his life, what "worked" for him, seemed to become perfectly clear, and Ted's inner experiences no longer were obstacles to his moving ahead.

Contraindications and Caveats for Comprehensive Distancing

There have been descriptions of many types of clients, particularly types of families, for whom paradoxical therapies are contraindicated (Cade, 1984; Fisher, Anderson, & Jones, 1981; Mozdzierz et al., 1976). These include: clients who are impulsive or suffering from acute grief reactions (particularly those prone towards suicidal or homicidal ideation); families in which the family structure is chaotic or excessively immature and in need of therapeutic structure; clients who are considered to be sociopathic or paranoid; or clients who are showing therapeutic improvement and commitment with other, more supportive, forms of intervention.

We have not found that the above client types are unsuited for work with comprehensive distancing. In particular, clients who are capable of profiting from an alternative form of therapy are not ruled out. Since we consider the problems of most clients ("compliant" and "resistant" alike) to come largely from emotional avoidance, and see emotional avoidance a a universal phenomenon in verbal organisms, we believe our approach may apply to many clients, so long as they are ready for fundamental change.

Similarly, clients who are suffering from acute grief or suicidal ideation are not excluded. Suicide is the ultimate attempt to avoid the suffering of life. Most therapists would agree that what grieving and suicidal persons need is the capacity to experience the pain of their loss and then to move through it into fuller living. Comprehensive distancing provides a means by which people can find a core of existence that is distinct from their emotional pain, and it is from out of that core that clients can recover from catastrophic grief. In fact, with some acute reactions, this approach is exceptionally parsimonious, since it does not require the person's suffering or depression to be gone before they can move on to richer living.

The question of whether persons with paranoid or sociopathic tendencies will profit from the approach is more difficult to answer. In fact, some clients tell us in therapy that they fear they will *become* sociopathic if they are not as tied as they are to social-verbal rules as a means of controlling their behavior. In our experience, this has not happened. Rather, clients who begin to take responsibility for their behavior without verbal excuses or blame to control them may be confronted, for the first time in their life, with the challenge of considering what they want their life "to stand for," and what direction they will choose to take. We interpret the fear of sociopathy to be a reflection of the ways in which the social-verbal community coerces compliance with an unhealthy system.

As far as the paranoid individual goes, we enter therapy with a forthright and genuinely honest approach, albeit one that may be confusing and unpredictable. To the extent that confusion and unpredictability may alienate the paranoid client, the approach may be (at least temporarily) ineffective. However, the absence of deception or manipulative trickery in our use of paradox increases the possibility that even the paranoid client could begin to live more fully despite the continuing suspicious thoughts and fears regarding his environment.

We do not intend to imply that all clients have profited from a comprehensive distancing approach (for a review of the data on therapeutic outcome, see Hayes, 1987). In particular, the approach is unlikely to work if the client is not ready for a fundamental reworking of basic life assumptions. It is not for the faint at heart, or for idle dabblers. For example, one of us (SCH) had a client who could not urinate in a public restroom. The client was a millionaire. He was, with the exception of this one problem, seemingly entirely self-satisfied. He said that he expected that such a "minor problem" should be very easy to "get rid of" in a few weeks (even though the problem had been chronic for many years) and viewed the failure to do so to be a problem with the therapist. In our opinion, the client had far more basic problems. His shallow relationships and bravado reflected a deep insecurity; it was not by accident that even the most basic biological function was a cause for social concern and inhibition. After several other procedures were used, a brief attempt with comprehensive distancing was made to see if it would help open up the client to the more general emotional difficulties it was felt he had. The client rejected this approach because he felt no need to work on such basic issues as the role of emotion in his life. In his firmly held view, his problem was urination in public, pure and simple.

We have, on the other hand, observed that certain therapist characteristics make one practitioner better suited to this kind of work than another. Clinicians who can bring a sense of humor to therapy, and who are able to think quickly on their feet, do well in comprehensive distancing. It helps if the therapist is able to express himself or herself metaphorically, particularly using material that has personal significance to the client. We have also found that therapists must be willing to see themselves as part of the same social-verbal system with which the clients are grappling. Clinicans who see themselves in an "expert" role, or who are committed to the use of linear, verbal reasoning, or who prefer to work in highly structured settings are unlikely to engage effectively in this approach. We feel that the therapists who are most effective are those who are actively applying the same principles to their own lives that they are asking the client to embrace.

When beginning therapy, we ask clients to make a 10- to 12-week commitment. At that point, we tell them, it will be clear to client and therapist alike whether or not the approach is leading the client in a direction that is growth-enhancing and life-expanding. After the initial period, some clients terminate, but most continue, working on whatever life issues are important to them within the new social-verbal context that has been established in therapy. Once a client completes treatment, he or she is typically invited to participate in a monthly support group. The group meets not to provide psychotherapy so much as to provide an alternative social-verbal community in which more effective verbal practices can be maintained. Such support is important, since it is easy to slip back into the literality, reason-giving, emotional avoidance and control that is supported by the client's everyday social-verbal community. In our experience, however, even those clients who do not enter the group rarely lose permanently the new perspective they have gained in therapy.

We have had less success in finding objective measures by which to measure clients' "progress" in our work. By definition, "success" in this form of therapy is the client demonstrating willingness to experience whatever thoughts and emotions show up in daily living *and* doing what is there to be done. Many clients show significant clinical improvement on standardized personality assessment instruments (e.g., the MMPI or the STAI) but others who do not sometimes still show major behavioral changes. Most of the major clinical measures assess the presence or absence of emotions and thoughts—not the effectiveness of living *per se.* This is a difficulty, because we do not seek to remove "bad" emotions from the person's life, nor to insert "good" emotions. That may happen, but it is not our goal.

We collect pre- and posttherapy data, as well as daily diaries. We also develop "scenes" at the start of therapy of events the client considers emotionally charged and then weekly rate the client's emotional reaction to each scene and his or her willingness to experience that reaction in that context. We also use a "distancing questionnaire" to try and measure some of the underlying changes in perspective that we believe are important in bringing about client change in therapy. Such measures, however, are still in the developmental stage.

The theoretical basis of comprehensive distancing itself requires additional evaluation. Its operating assumptions and principles have been drawn from the basic behavior analytic literature on rule-governance and semantic classes (see Hayes, 1987). These principles seem to lead to surprising conclusions, such as that attempts to avoid anxiety instead create anxiety. Such extensions themselves can be tested. The literature on paradoxical interventions has not been driven, in the behavior therapy area, by systematic theory. In addition to the technical value of comprehensive distancing, it may offer a connection to basic behavioral analysis of use to behavior therapists interested in paradoxical interventions.

References

American Psychiatric Association. (1987). *Diagnostic and statistical manual of mental disorders* (3rd ed.—rev.). Washington, DC: American Psychiatric Association.

Barlow, D. H., & Beck, J. G. (1984). The psychosocial treatment of anxiety disorders: Current status, future directions. In J. B. W. Williams & R. L. Spitzer (Eds.), *Psychotherapy research: Where are we and where should we go?* (pp. 29-66). New York: The Guilford Press.

Bateson, G., Jackson, D. D., Haley, J., & Weakland, J. H. (1963). A note on the double-bind—1962. *Family Process, 2,* 154-161.

Bergman, J. S. (1982). Paradoxical interventions with people who insist on acting crazy. *American Journal of Psychotherapy, 36,* 214-222.

Brehm, J. W. (1966). *A theory of psychological reactance.* New York: Academic Press.

Brehm, J. W., & Brehm, S. S. (1981). *Psychological reactance.* New York: Wiley.

Cade, B. (1984). Paradoxical techniques in therapy. *Journal of Child Psychology and Psychiatry, 25,* 509-516.

D'Amato, M. R., Salmon, D. P., Loukas, E., & Tomie, A. (1985). Symmetry and transitivity of conditional relations in monkeys (*Cebus apella*) and pigeons (*Columba livia*). *Journal of the Experimental Analysis of Behavior, 44,* 35-47.

Dell, P. F. (1981). Some irreverent thoughts on paradox. *Family Process, 20,* 37-51.

Devany, J. M., Hayes, S. C., & Nelson, R. O. (1986). Equivalence class formation in language-able and language-disabled children. *Journal of the Experimental Analysis of Behavior, 46,* 243-252.

Dixon, L. S. (1977). The nature of control by spoken words over visual stimulus selection. *Journal of the Experimental Analysis of Behavior, 27,* 433-442.

Dixon, M. H., & Spradlin, J. E. (1976). Establishing stimulus equivalences among retarded adolescents. *Journal of Experimental Child Psychology, 21,* 144-164.

Erickson, M. H., Rossi, E. L., & Rossi, S. I. (1976). *Hypnotic realities.* New York: Irvington.

Fay, A. (1978). *Making things better by making them worse.* New York: Hawthorn.

Fisch, R., Weakland, J. H., & Segal, L. (1982). *The tactics of change: Doing therapy briefly.* San Francisco: Jossey-Bass.

Fisher, L., Anderson, A., & Jones, J. (1981). Types of paradoxical intervention and indications/contraindications for use in clinical practice. *Family Process, 20,* 25-35.

Frankl, V. E. (1960). Paradoxical intention: A logotherapeutic technique. *American Journal of Psychotherapy, 14,* 520-535.

Frankl, V. E. (1975). Paradoxical intention and deflection. *Psychotherapy: Theory, Research, and Practice, 12,* 226-237.

Gast, D., VanBiervlet, A., & Spradlin, J. E. (1979). Teaching number-word equivalences: A study of transfer. *American Journal of Mental Deficiency, 83,* 524-527.

Goldstein, A. J., & Chambless, D. L. (1978). A reanalysis of agoraphobia. *Behavior Therapy, 9,* 47-59.

Greenberg, R. P. (1973). Anti-expectation techniques in psychotherapy: The power of negative thinking. *Psychotherapy: Theory, Research, and Practice, 10,* 145-148.

Hayes, S. C. (1984). Making sense of spirituality. *Behaviorism, 12,* 99-110.

Hayes, S. C. (1987). A contextual approach to therapeutic change. In N. S. Jacobson (Ed.), *Psychotherapists in clinical practice: Cognitive and behavioral perspectives* (pp. 327-387). New York: The Guilford Press.

Hayes, S. C. (1988). Contextualism and the next wave of behavioral psychology. *Behavior Analysis, 23,* 7-22.

Hayes, S. C. (1989). Nonhumans have not yet shown stimulus equivalence. *Journal of the Experimental Analysis of Behavior, 51,* 385-392.

Hayes, S. C., & Brownstein, A. J. (1986). Mentalism, behavior-behavior relations, and a behavior analytic view of the purposes of science. *The Behavior Analyst, 9,* 175-190.

Hayes, S. C., Devany, J. M., Kohlenberg, B., Brownstein, A. J., & Shelby, J. (in press). Stimulus equivalence and the symbolic control of behavior. *Mexican Journal of Behavior Analysis.*

Hayes, S. C., Hayes, L. J., & Reese, H. W. (1988). Finding the philosophical core: A review of S. C. Pepper's "World hypotheses: A study in evidence." *Journal of the Experimental Analysis of Behavior, 50,* 97-111.

Hayes, L. J., Tilley, K. L., & Hayes, S. C. (1988). Extending equivalence class membership to gustatory stimuli. *The Psychological Record, 38,* 473-482.

Herman, L. M., & Thompson, R. K. (1982). Symbolic, identity and probe-delayed matching of sounds in the bottle-nosed dolphin. *Animal Learning and Behavior, 10,* 22-34.

Kendall, S. B. (1983). Tests for mediated transfer in pigeons. *The Psychological Record, 33,* 245-256.

Kercher, G., & Smith, D. (1985a). *Paradoxical psychotherapy: Theory and practice with individuals, couples and families.* New York: Brunner/Mazel.

Kercher, G., & Smith, D. (1985b). Reframing paradoxical psychotherapy. *Psychotherapy, 22,* 786-792.

L'Abate, L., & Weeks, G. (1978). A bibliography of paradoxical methods in psychotherapy of family systems. *Family Process, 17,* 95-98.

Lashley, K. S. (1938). Conditional reactions in the rat. *Journal of Psychology, 6,* 311-324.

Lipkens, R., Kop, P. F. M., & Matthijs, W. (1988). A test of symmetry and transitivity in the conditional discrimination performances of pigeons. *Journal of the Experimental Analysis of Behavior, 49,* 395-409.

Mackay, H. A., & Sidman, M. (1984). Teaching new behaviors via equivalence relations. In P. Brooks, R. Sperber, & C. McCauley (Eds.), *Learning and cognition in the mentally retarded* (pp. 493-513). Hillsdale, NJ: Lawrence Erlbaum.

Marshall, R. J. (1976). "Joining techniques" in the treatment of resistant children and adolescents. *American Journal of Psychotherapy, 30,* 73-84.

McIntire, K. D., Cleary, J., & Thompson, T. (1987). Conditional relations by monkeys: Reflexivity, symmetry, and transitivity. *Journal of the Experimental Analysis of Behavior, 47,* 279-285.

Mozdzierz, G. J., Macchitelli, F. J., & Lisiecki, J. (1976). The paradox in psychotherapy: An Adlerian perspective. *Journal of Individual Psychology, 32,* 169-184.

Nissen, H. (1951). Analysis of complex conditional reaction in the chimpanzee. *Journal of Comparative and Physiological Psychology,* 7, 449-516.

Omer, H. (1981). Paradoxical treatments: A unified concept. *Psychotherapy: Theory, Research, and Practice, 18,* 320-324.

Rachman, S. J. (1980). Emotional processing. *Behaviour Research and Therapy, 18,* 51-60.

Raskin, D. E., & Klein, Z. E. (1976). Losing a symptom through keeping it. *Archives of General Psychiatry, 33,* 548-555.

Rohrbaugh, M., Tennen, H., Press, S., & White, L. (1981). Compliance, defiance, and therapeutic paradox: Guidelines for strategic use of paradoxical interventions. *American Journal of Orthopsychiatry, 51,* 454-467.

Rosenbaum, R. L. (1982). Paradox as epistemological jump. *Family Process, 21,* 85-90.

Seltzer, L. F. (1986). *Paradoxical strategies in psychotherapy: A comprehensive overview and guidebook.* New York: Wiley.

Selvini Palazzoli, M., Boscolo, L., Cecchin, G., & Prata, G. (1978). *Paradox and counterparadox: A new model in the therapy of the family in schizophrenic transaction* (E. V. Burt, Trans.). New York: Jason Aronson.

Sidman, M. (1971). Reading and auditory-visual equivalences. *Journal of Speech and Hearing Research, 14,* 5–13.

Sidman, M., Cresson, O., & Willson-Morris, M. (1974). Acquisition of matching-to-sample via mediated transfer. *Journal of the Experimental Analysis of Behavior, 22,* 261–273.

Sidman, M., Rauzin, R., Lazar, R., Cunningham, S., Tailby, W., & Carrigan, P. (1982). A search for symmetry in the conditional discriminations of rhesus monkeys, baboons and children. *Journal of the Experimental Analysis of Behavior, 37,* 23–44.

Sidman, M., & Tailby, W. (1982). Conditional discrimination versus matching to sample: An expansion of the testing paradigm. *Journal of the Experimental Analysis of Behavior, 37,* 5–22.

Spradlin, J. E., Cotter, V. W., & Baxley, N. (1973). Establishing a conditional discrimination without direct training: A study of transfer with retarded adolescents. *American Journal of Mental Deficiency, 77,* 556–566.

Spradlin, J. E., & Dixon, M. (1976). Establishing a conditional discrimination without direct training: Stimulus classes and labels. *American Journal of Mental Deficiency, 80,* 555–561.

Teismann, M. (1979). Jealousy: Systematic, problem-solving therapy with couples. *Family Process, 18,* 151–160.

Tennen, H., Rohrbaugh, M., Press, S., & White, L. (1981). Reactance theory and therapeutic paradox: A compliance-defiance model. *Psychotherapy: Theory, Research, and Practice, 18,* 14–22.

VanBiervlet, A. (1977). Establishing words and objects as functionally equivalent through manual sign training. *American Journal of Mental Deficiency, 82,* 178–186.

Vaughn, W. (1988). Formation of equivalence sets in pigeons. *Journal of Experimental Psychology: Animal Behavior Processes, 14,* 36–42.

Watzlawick, P. (1976). *How real is real?* New York: Random House.

Watzlawick, P., Beavin, J. H., & Jackson, D. D. (1967). *Pragmatics of human communication.* New York: W. W. Norton.

Watzlawick, P., Weakland, J., & Fisch, R. (1974). *Change: Principles of problem formation and problem resolution.* New York: W. W. Norton.

Weeks, G. R., & L'Abate, L. (1982). *Paradoxical psychotherapy: Theory and practice with individuals, couples, and families.* New York: Brunner/Mazel.

Whitaker, C. A. (1975). Psychotherapy of the absurd: With a special emphasis on the psychotherapy of aggression. *Family Process, 14,* 1–16.

Wulfert, E., & Hayes, S. C. (1988). Transfer of conditional sequencing through conditional equivalence classes. *Journal of the Experimental Analysis of Behavior, 50,* 125–144.

Chapter 8

Use of Inherent Paradox in Postmodern Sexual-Marital Therapy

David Morris Schnarch

The use of paradox for the treatment of sexual-marital difficulties is not new. Victor Frankl (1967), one of the earliest proponents of paradoxical psychotherapy, used *paradoxical intent* to reduce anticipatory anxiety as early as 1939 (cited by Weeks & L'Abate, 1982). In 1946, Frankl reported the treatment of erectile difficulty by prohibition of intercourse (Weeks, 1986). In this proscription, the patient was instructed to avoid the sexual behavior he was seeking help in mastering.

In his review of the literature, Stanton (1981) found that paradoxical intervention had been successfully used in the treatment of premature ejaculation and other sexual problems. Stampfl and Levis (1967) used *implosion* techniques, flooding individuals with sexual performance anxieties and fears of rejection to produce extinction of anxiety and avoidance behaviors. Milton Erickson used *relabeling* (cited by Haley, 1973) in a case of erectile dysfunction. Erickson relabeled wedding-night impotency as a "compliment," in which he suggested that the groom was so overwhelmed by the bride's beauty that he felt "incompetent."

Paradox and Modern Sex Therapy

Behavior therapy has been demonstrated to be efficacious with a wide range of adjustment problems, including physical symptomatology. It was the application of behavioral techniques to the treatment of sexual dysfunction and the resulting quantum leap in efficacy that supplanted psychoanalysis as the approach of choice and highlighted many erroneous beliefs about the nature of sexual dysfunction.

Modern sex therapy, evolving out of the work of Masters and Johnson in the early 1970s, was primarily conceptualized in a cognitive-behavioral learning theory model (Masters & Johnson, 1970; Lobitz & LoPiccolo, 1972). Modern sex therapy has provided a more specific arsenal of behavioral techniques, addressing the moment-to-moment physical exchanges that occur during patients' sexual encounters.

However, experience has shown that this is not without its own pitfalls. Compliance with behavioral proscriptions and prescriptions in sex therapy has always been a problem. Kaplan, Levay, LoPiccolo and other clinicians attempted to address the problem of resistance and noncompliance with the sensate focus exercises originally developed by Masters and Johnson. This is not a critique of behavior therapy *per se* but, rather, a more sophisticated appreciation of the snares and quandaries in any particular therapeutic approach that emerges with time and experience in a particular application.

Like Frankl, Masters and Johnson used the ban on intercourse as a performance anxiety reduction technique. Others have noted that the ban on intercourse sometimes functions as a defiance-based injunction for individuals who have been resistant to having sex with their partner. However, deliberate use of the *ban* for this reason in Masters and Johnson's work is overrated, since the metacommunication of their approach is that the ban on intercourse is suggested to facilitate progress, and compliance with therapist authority is crucial.

"Restriction of progress" (defiance-based paradox) approaches to sex therapy are more common to marital therapists who only address the sexual difficulty as a symptom of the system. Such therapists either anticipate that spontaneous symptom resolution will occur when the system is reorganized, without using modern sensate focus activities, or shift to a more rational, logical approach once the resistance has subsided. Defiance-based paradoxical approaches tend to be short-lived in modern sex therapy and do not provide continuity in approach given the inevitable shift to nonparadoxical compliance-based prescriptions in the middle phase of treatment.

The content of sex therapy prescriptions and proscriptions, as well as the inherent focus on sexuality, lends itself to problems of resistance and patient noncompliance. Couples are often hesitant to discuss the details of their bedroom behavior and even more resistant to allowing someone else to tell them what they should and should not do. Revealing the details of the couple's sexual rituals to an "outsider," and, moreover, doing so in a matter-of-fact way, is an unusual experience for most people. Issues of shame, feelings of sexual inadequacy, competition between the therapist and the same-gender patient in the couple, and fears of sexual attraction between the opposite-gender patient and the therapist may often lurk just below the surface.

Common proscriptions involving abstinence from intercourse or genital touch, the prescription of sequential rather than simultaneous touch, focus on pleasure rather than performance, and shifts in traditional giver and receiver roles, are usually illogical from the vantage point of most patients. These modifications also disrupt existing power and status hierarchies as well as dependency and autonomy issues within the couple.

Behavioral suggestions of modern sex therapy lend themselves to being rejected purely on a cognitive, rational basis. Is it really logical that a woman who is unable to have orgasm during intercourse should avoid having intercourse as a way of eventually reaching that goal? Is it really considerate for a man who is failing in his attempts to maintain his erection during intercourse, to stop trying to please his wife in this manner, which both regard as the only "normal" way? In so doing, won't he feel more insecure, more inadequate, and more selfish than he already does? From the patient's perspective, the most basic interventions of modern sex therapy appear to be inherently paradoxical.

The "Modern" View of Sex as a Natural Function

What has complicated the situation is the legacy of the rational, cognitive-behavioral approach to modern sex therapy from the seminal work of Masters and Johnson. Masters and Johnson advanced the viewpoint that patients should relax and let their bodies function as they are designed to do, proposing that sex is a natural function.

There is no doubt that this naturalized view of sexuality has an intuitive appeal to the humanistic values of this era and represents a vast improvement over the view of sexuality as sinful or dirty that characterized the rise of Christianity. However, the erroneous assumptions and attributions about the nature of human sexuality inherent in this relatively new view of sexuality are only starting to surface in the minds of health professionals treating sexuality problems (Simon, 1987).

Although there has been much societal benefit in the "naturalization" of sexuality, the notion that sex is a naturally occurring, healthy function is a strategically unreasoned position for sex and marital therapy and the treatment of sexual dysfunctions. The naturalized view is basically a unidimensional intervention aimed primarily at the reduction of performance anxiety and fear of failure that naively assumes people function primarily on a rational, conscious level. The naturalized paradigm of sex therapy ignores the wealth of experience from the fields of individual (psychodynamic/analytic) and marriage and family therapy, which suggests that unconscious and systemic issues are major determinants of individual behavior and the meaning attributed to that behavior.

The modern "naturalized" framework of sexuality creates an unfortunate paradigm in which it is perfectly logical for the patient to ask: "If sex is a natural function, why should I have to do these strange behaviors you are suggesting for me? Other people don't need to do them to function normally." Seemingly logical anxiety-reduction activities can, paradoxically, have an anxiety-increasing impact on both the individual and the dyad. What at first glance would appear to reduce a patient's performance anxiety and encourage him or her to relax and let go, actually confirms the patient's growing feeling of being "different" and inadequate compared to other people. Moreover, the naturalized view of sexual functioning reinforces patients' common belief that they should not be having their difficulty to begin with.

Since prescribed and proscribed changes in sexual behavior often generate anxiety and resistance to change, it is important to modulate the overall level of these reactions and also to provide a paradigm in which their occurrence can be used for optimal therapeutic impact. Sex therapy "pleasuring activities" depart from familiar sexual individual repertoires, violate role expectations in the relationship, and stimulate fears of failure. There exists an alternative "nonrational" paradigm that works at least as well, and often better, than a "naturalized model" in addressing these inherent pitfalls in sex therapy.

A Paradigm Shift to a "Postmodern" Approach

In contrast to the logical, rational, "normalized" view of sexual functioning, a nonrational paradoxical style of sex therapy is presented in this chapter.

This paradigm shift is based on a premise that even the most ardent proponents of "sex comes natural" usually will accept. That is: Although reproductive sex is a natural function, intimate sex is not. Intimacy during sexuality is an acquired skill and a developed taste.

By the redefining of the goal of sexuality as intimacy (a nonnatural function), rather than "pleasure" (a natural function), performance anxiety and fears of failure are inherently reduced because the expectation of immediate success is diminished. Moreover, this framework provides an explanation for the couple's prior lack of success in the bedroom, reducing their feelings of inadequacy regarding their spontaneous efforts.

Whereas I have found this to be a far superior paradigm in my own clinical practice, other practitioners may wish simply to consider this as an alternative to the "naturalized" paradigm in a broader therapeutic repertoire.

In the initial application of this model, the patients are encouraged to review each and every solution they have attempted prior to seeing the therapist. During this review, the therapist compliments the couple on the logicality of their attempts. The therapist "benefits from the couple's experience," vowing not to suggest anything that the couple has already tried and failed with. After pointing out that the couple has tried everything that makes sense, (and possibly a few things that didn't), the therapist concludes that the solution the couple has been seeking does not exist within that scope. The therapist also suggests that anything that might really work will not make sense, since the couple has already done everything that makes sense.

Although the therapist may not know what will ultimately be suggested (or want to appear that way for the time being), the couple can rest assured on the basis of logic that an effective course of treatment will seem illogical to them. However, the need for an "illogical" treatment will now be logical to the couple. The final step is to propose that the couple might want to pray that the therapist *can* find something to suggest that will make no sense, for without this, there is likely to be no new solution.

Secondary Utility of an "Unnatural" Model of Sexual Intimacy

The review of the couple's prior unsuccessful attempts and the therapist's vow to find something "illogical" offer a number of subtle but important secondary impacts in treatment. First, it is common for the review to reveal behaviors that the couple has previously found successful in improving their interaction which they spontaneously decline to do. This often clarifies that the problem is imbedded in individual and marital issues rather than sexual ignorance. Moreover, it reveals the range and flexibility of the couple's sexual repertoire.

Second, the review of prior failures exacerbates patients' ambivalence about the current homeostasis and taps what is perhaps the most powerful intrinsic motivator of change: the patients' fear that things will remain the same.

Third, it frees the therapist from the anticipation of patients' negative reaction to suggested proscriptions and prescriptions. When patients are dubious, reluctant, or "confused" by the therapist's suggestions, this can be interpreted as a positive sign, since what doesn't make sense to the patient offers hope for new options. This approach also allows the introduction of shared humor into the therapy hour. When patients readily accept the therapist's suggestions as reasonable and state their intention to implement them, the therapist can feign dismay, suggesting that if it makes sense, it probably won't work, but that the couple might just want to give it a try until the therapist can conjure up something that is more illogical.

Finally, the "unnaturalized" approach is particularly effective with couples who are embroiled in conflict and who attempt to push the therapist into the role of the *mediator*. Once this paradigm is established, it can be broadened out to intervene with chronic fighting.

The therapist can point out that during the time prior to treatment in which either partner was sure he was "correct" in his "logical" assessment of the difficulties, no significant improvement occurred. Thus, they might not want the therapist to agree with either one of them, because an effective solution probably lies outside what either partner is pushing for as the solution.

In cases where one partner *does* believe that his or her solution is "the truth," the therapist can take the position of "encouraging" the patient to trust him- or herself and not the therapist. The therapist points out that the couple implicitly believe that the problem is that the partner is either deaf or stupid, since the speaker's solution is to offer the same message repeatedly and louder. (The couple's laughter usually changes the mood of locked combat at this point.) The therapist then encourages the individual to increase the efforts to convince the "stupid" partner of the wisdom of his or her own solution, if he or she truly believes this is the case. However, the therapist offers this solution to both partners in the interest of neutrality. Usually, the offer to escalate the combat is declined by both partners, who suggest they are looking for new alternatives.

Inherent versus Constructed Paradoxical Interventions in Sex Therapy

The reader will note the paradigmatic shift and the resultant reorganization of the vectors for change in the above example. And although the approach is wonderfully paradoxical, no actual prescription or double-bind was constructed for the patients. Moreover, the paradigm shift develops out of an inherently logical premise, creating a demand from the patients for something illogical. To understand this approach, it is necessary to consider *types* of paradox.

Watzlawick, Beavin, and Jackson (1967) distinguish three types of paradox:

1. *Antimony*: paradoxical statements that are logical contradictions, mainly of interest to logicians, mathematicians, and theoreticians.

2. *Semantic antimony or paradoxical definition*: statements stemming from hidden inconsistencies in language structure, such as Epimenides's famous "All Cretans are liars" paradox. In this chapter, paradoxical definition will be referred to as *inherent paradox*, reflecting the therapist's process of focusing attention on preexisting paradoxes transparently embedded in the couple's reality. *Inherent paradox* is expanded beyond linguistic anomalies to include hidden inconsistencies in cultural sexual beliefs, practices, and values as well as unresolved interlocking individual conflicts of the partners in the relationship. Such conflicts and inconsistencies are often expressed in the simultaneous parallel meanings encoded in the couple's vocabulary of verbal and physical exchanges.

3. *Pragmatic paradox*: often known as "double-bind" (Bateson, Jackson, Haley, & Weakland, 1956), and therapeutic double-bind (Watzlawick et al., 1967), this form of paradox comprises the foundation of most "paradoxical" psychotherapies. In this chapter, it will be referred to as *constructed paradox*, reflecting the therapist's process of constructing therapeutic paradoxical binds that patients are induced to enter.

Constructed Paradox

Paradoxical double-binds and therapeutic counterparadoxes are more than simple contradictory injunctions that leave the recipient no choice. One requirement for the paradox to be effective is that the recipient not be able to communicate with others about the paradoxical injunction itself. This is usually the rule in relationships that forbid discussion of the pathogenic double-bind, and it is continued in treatment. Therapists generally refuse to discuss the "contradictory" paradoxical nature of suggestions and injunctions given to patients.

Another requirement of constructed paradox is that the recipient not be allowed to move to a higher level of abstraction or functioning in order to avoid the bind. That is, the therapist refuses to discuss the metacommunication involved in the paradoxical injunctions or to discuss the injunctions as reflecting a therapeutic style known as paradox.

Constructed paradoxical interventions have often been seen as a way of dealing with patient resistance. In fact, one guideline often used in the application of paradoxical intervention is that straightforward, rational approaches are preferred, as long as the patient or the relationship system is operating in a logical, rational manner. When the patient or the system appears to function in an irrational manner, the therapist shifts to constructed paradoxical interventions.

Constructed paradox is readily appealing to therapists who come from a general therapy approach involving construction of activities for patients to fulfill. Constructed paradoxical prescriptions often take on the quality of "blockbuster" interventions delivered with great ceremony to the patient at the conclusion of a session. Emphasis is placed on the therapist's skill in its delivery, with a premium being placed on showmanship and benevolent cunningness.

Moreover, the proclivity for many therapists to see sex therapy as a behavior-modification approach involving prescribed activities also makes the use of constructed paradox an appealing form of intervention in sex therapy. The tendency for therapists to view patient noncompliance with initially prescribed activities as *resistance to treatment* and defiance of the therapist makes utilization of other constructed prescriptions quite inviting.

Inherent Paradox

Although they dismissed the corresponding categories from clinical consideration, Weeks and L'Abate (1982) pointed out that the solution to avoiding *inherent paradoxes* is to promote a quantum jump in the complexity of the solution, going to a higher level of functioning. They offer as an example Bertrand Russell's theory of logical types, in which to establish the concept of a *class* of objects, one must move to a higher level of abstraction than a collection of the objects that comprise the class.

Resolution of problems in marital and sexual functioning stemming from inherent paradox requires shifting to a higher level of functioning. In the case where the paradox results from embedded cultural values and beliefs, it requires establishing a viewpoint outside of the culture from which the implicit cultural information can be viewed and examined. When it results from interlocking unresolved individual dynamics, the solution requires an increment in emotional development for one or both individuals. From this vantage point, the individual can recognize that the current impasse reflects his or her own expectations and projections rather than the simple validity of the perception of the partner. Without this increment in *differentiation of self* (Kerr & Bowen, 1988), the individual is trapped by a culture, a language, and typical personality development that are inextricably intertwined, reciprocally validating, and mutually perpetuating of inherent paradox.

In contrast to the view in constructed paradox of paradox as pathology and counterparadox as curative technique, inherent paradox is considered to be a fundamental characteristic of complex systems. Whereas constructed paradox is generally employed only after the patient has demonstrated resistance to change, inherent paradox is utilized throughout the course of sexual-marital therapy. This provides a consistent treatment framework that prepares individuals for the reality that marriage, intimacy, and sexuality embody paradoxical elements at the most profound levels. Friedman (1988) astutely noted that the opposite of a shallow truth is generally false, but the opposite of a deep truth is generally true as well. Campbell (1982) has pointed out that as systems (such as marriages and families) increase in complexity and sophistication, the system shifts from predictability to probability. Need for certainty and intolerance of paradox obviate the possibility of spontaneous resolution of sexual and marital difficulties and inhibit the emergence of complex systems.

John von Neumann (1949/1966) suggests that living organisms, organizations, and even machines have "complexity barriers." When systems of high complexity exceed the complexity barrier, new principles of organization and operation (metastructures) emerge, allowing development of ever increasingly complex adaptations. The mark of a complex relationship is the occurrence of paradox. Below the complexity barrier, synthesis decays, and simpler systems emerge (stuck families and couples). In this view, the goal of sexual-marital therapy is not merely the resolution of sexual dysfunctions but also the facilitation of complex functioning within the relationship. In contrast to the view of paradox as pathology, sexual-marital therapy can utilize inherent paradox as a vehicle for developing tolerance and appreciation for complex functioning and the additional paradoxes that are likely to emerge. Campbell (1982) noted: "It is the changing pattern of gene activity, rather than changes in structural genes themselves, that led away from biological simplicity and toward the higher forms of life" (p. 133).

In this form of paradoxical treatment, the therapist encourages the patients to discuss inherent paradoxes in their situation, violating one of the main rules of constructed paradox. Where inherent paradox results from underlying interlocking unresolved individual issues of personal development and unconscious conflict, it provides a vehicle for the examination and resolution of arrested individual development.

Examples of Constructed Paradoxical "Interventions"

One example of constructed paradox might involve a therapist purportedly "putting off treatment" of sexual difficulties and suggesting that the couple "merely touch each other" while they are waiting for treatment to begin. Or the couple is instructed not to have intercourse and to maintain this ban long enough that sexual desire or frustration exceeds the fear of failure or the relationship difficulties. Or a man who is frustrated that he cannot bring his wife to orgasm, and who resents any instruction from her regarding his technique, is instructed to go home and *make* her reach orgasm and not take no for an answer.

Example of Use of Inherent Paradox

In contrast, use of inherent paradox might involve pointing out to a husband angered by his wife's lack of sexual desire that the more he demands sex, the less he is wanted, although he may eventually pressure his wife into having it. Likewise, the therapist can point out to the wife that she is conditioning him to initiate sex far more frequently than he actually wants it, because he knows that she will respond when her guilt gets high enough.

Each partner now realizes that escalating their entrenched positions only further exacerbates their individual and mutual dilemma: the couple is caught in the grips of two simultaneously interlocking double-binds. The paradoxical situations are the result of culturally transmitted sexual expectations and gender roles, and the inevitable double-binds of sexually incongruous power hierarchies and unresolved personal issues. As such, the solution is not amenable to "negotiation": unresolved individual conflicts are not negotiable. There is little need for the therapist to construct any additional paradox. At this point, the therapist merely needs to offer an illogical solution for the ones the couple has brought with them into treatment.

In the common viewpoint of *constructed* double-bind, the source of the "bind" is a single agent (e.g., a parent, or both parents acting as a single, contradictory locus of control). This is characteristic, whether it is an individual family member issuing paradoxical injunctions to other family members or a therapist developing counterparadoxes to neutralize or amplify the existing binds.

In contrast, *inherent paradox* does not result from a single source. In some cases it arises from a message by each partner that is reciprocally binding the other. The "source" of the paradox is in the interaction of individual unresolved issues expressed through daily patterns of interaction and the particular partner selected. Through the selection of a different partner or significant resolution of either individual's underlying personal conflicts, the same messages and the meanings and behaviors elicited might be sufficiently variable to preclude a reciprocal bind.

Gordon (1988) has noted a number of inherent paradoxes in contemporary society:

If you comfort (give to) me, you are more powerful than I am.
I will not accept your comfort.
If I comfort you, you are comforted.
I resent you for being comfortable when I never can be. (p. 26)

If you don't love me, stay with me, I will die.
Therefore, I must cling to you no matter what the price.
The more I cling, the more you feel smothered and distance.
The more you distance, the more I cling. (p. 27)

Case Example: Dr. and Mrs. Jones

Dr. and Mrs. Jones, both age 49, requested treatment for their sexual and marital difficulty. They have been married for 25 years and have two sons, ages 18 and 20.

At the outset of the initial interview, the couple related that Dr. Jones was threatening divorce over his wife's lack of interest in sex. After mentioning that her husband blamed all of their marital problems on her "frigidity," Mrs. Jones defensively reported that she was not "frigid" and that she had been orgasmic until their marital conflicts became increasingly severe in the last 18 months. She reported that Dr. Jones also has difficulty with rapid ejaculation, which he refused to discuss with her and blamed on their infrequent sexual contact.

At a momentary pause in the middle of the interview, the couple had the following interchange:

MRS. JONES: He really didn't want to come today. He feels like coming to treatment is like admitting that there is something wrong with him. He could only come here by insisting that he is perfect and that the problem is me.

Dr. Jones looked defensive about his defensiveness, confirming the accuracy of his wife's statement but also making him less amenable to treatment.

DR. JONES: Well, I think that we should be able to take care of this. But I have also studied psychiatry during my medical school training, and I am enlightened enough to know that sometimes you have to go to a doctor to get something fixed even if it is an emotional problem. After all, that is my business too.

THERAPIST: I have seen a lot of couples, and it is fairly common for people to feel like coming to see a therapist, particularly about sexual and marital problems, is a *de facto* declaration of sexual incompe-

> tency and inadequacy. The funny thing about it is, I have never seen a truly inadequate man or woman in all the years I have been in practice. The truly inadequate ones don't come in here. To come to see me, people have to have some basic faith in themselves, that they can do better. The really inadequate people just hide in shame, and just showing up here often makes people feel better after they get over the initial anxiety.

During the session, Dr. Jones claimed that he didn't care what anybody thought of him, he would say and do whatever he wanted (a counterdependent declaration, spoken as autonomy and independence). Yet his style demonstrated his dependency on his wife. In the session, he could not say one sentence and complete it if his wife gave any nonverbal indication of disagreement. He immediately turned to her to ask her to verbalize her disagreement and then argue with it. He could not even continue to look at the therapist to whom he was talking and continue with "his side" of recent events at home.

At one point, the therapist volunteered his surprise that Dr. Jones did not simply take the opportunity to continue telling his side of the story without stopping, an opportunity he would seemingly desire and demand. While then doing so, Dr. Jones repeatedly looked at his wife after every statement. The wife continued to make her typical minor signs of disagreement, which continued to infuriate him. As he talked, Dr. Jones's head swiveled rapidly with each statement, from the therapist to his wife and then back again.

After several minutes, the therapist interrupted the husband, complaining that the therapist was becoming "increasingly confused." In response to the doctor's question about the nature of the therapist's confusion, the therapist stated that he wanted the doctor to inform him which of two messages the therapist was to listen to. On the one hand, the therapist pointed out, the doctor's verbal behavior suggested he was very independent, if not indifferent, to his wife's opinions and that he repeatedly demeaned the value of his wife's ability to think clearly. On the other hand, the doctor's nonverbal behavior suggested that he was extremely attentive to her and accorded her opinions the greatest respect: his anger was actually a reflection of his valuing (but not tolerating) her opinions and his need for her concurrence. His head swiveling suggested he was anything but indifferent to his wife.

In pointing this pattern out to the husband, the therapist offered the initial interpretation that perhaps the couple was having difficulty resolving their difficulties because they did not appreciate the whimsical, paradoxical nature of their relationship. The therapist suggested that although it might appear that Dr. Jones was indifferent, he was highly emotionally dependent on his wife. Mrs. Jones merely smiled knowingly to herself, while her husband nervously and angrily turned to her and said "You don't believe that, do you?" The therapist suggested that the doctor had actually just confirmed the interpretation he was also disagreeing with.

Note that the therapist never actually offered a defiance-based paradoxical suggestion for the husband to ignore his wife and talk and look at the therapist. Had this been done, it might have threatened the therapist's alliance with Mrs. Jones and removed the opportunity to interpret the husband's spontaneous behavior pattern. Instead, the therapist had only to utilize what was already occurring without taking a personal position in the dynamic, and to function as an uncommitted observer rather than as a "player."

DR. JONES: I am not sure that I totally agree with you.

THERAPIST: I couldn't agree with you more, and everything you just said is absolutely true.

DR. JONES: What is that?

THERAPIST: You are not sure yet. I encourage you not to agree with me. It is probably totally true that it is not totally true. It is a half truth, like so many things in life and in your relationship. If you maintain your own good judgment, you will end up making up your own mind about the merit and meaning of this observation. Besides, if you are dependent on what your wife thinks of you, we won't get anywhere if I encourage you to become dependent on what I think also. But, it is interesting that somehow you manage to make a statement that something might not be totally true and make it sound like it is totally false. If I didn't listen very carefully, I might think that you were disagreeing with what I said, which you never literally did. Perhaps there might be *something* of value in the idea that you give your wife's opinions credit and that her opinion of you is crucially important to you.

At this point, Dr. Jones voiced a seemingly simple statement that illustrated his view of autonomy as indifference and masculine impregnability, his attempt to hoist the therapist on his own petard, and a common confusion of dependency with closeness and communication.

DR. JONES: Well, If I was not emotionally dependent on her, then what would I do, never listen to her opinions? This is what she is already complaining about, and you seem to be telling me that I should be more like that.

THERAPIST: That is an interesting view of the potential negative effects that greater autonomy might create in your relationship. You seem to think that the sign of an emotionally independent man would be that he would be more indifferent and insensitive to his wife's opinions about him and listen to her even less. On the contrary, a man who is really independent would be able to truly listen to his wife's opinions even more. And not because he believed they lacked any merit at all or listened for their flaws and inaccuracies. But rather, he would listen to them to glean what partial truths she might have to offer him. He would be able to tolerate listening to opinions and facts that expressed alternative viewpoints and half-truths about reality without hearing them as contradictions to his own. (*tone and volume dropping*) He would be able to recognize that he and his wife exist in separate realities, not because they can't communicate or aren't compatible, but, rather, that they are inextricably separate people. He would be able to be closer and more intimate with his wife, not less, because he was willing and able to maintain himself as a separate person. Not in defiance of his wife, but because his feelings of self-worth and identity were not at issue. The inevitable surfacing of alternative viewpoints highlighted that he and his wife were two separate people and would never become one.

As the therapist's tone dropped, he emphasized the issues of aloneness and feelings of deprivation the man was obviously feeling. In the last few minutes, Dr. Jones was flooding with obvious feelings of sadness. The therapist offered the following observation:

THERAPIST: I have another half-truth to offer. Sometimes couples fight because it is both their way of being as close as they can tolerate and as a way of not being closer, although it looks like they are fighting *because* they are not closer.

DR. JONES: I can't stand the fighting. When I come home, I want harmony. I grew up with constant fighting in my home and with my aunts and uncles. I can't stand the constant need to be on guard. I didn't have any warmth or closeness when I was growing up, and I swore that my own family would not be that way.

THERAPIST: It is hard to have really intense intimacy and sex, because it requires two very separate people who can stand on their own two feet and tolerate the aloneness of being separate. Because the intense sex provides both an intense awareness of closeness, but the closeness is highlighted by the awareness that the two people are actually separate and not fused. Only when both people accept that they will never know each other "totally" can they appreciate the full extent to which two people can become intimate and knowledgeable about what is going on inside their partner.

DR. JONES: You mean we have to get more separate so that we can be closer? (*with humor in his voice*)

THERAPIST: I couldn't agree with you more.

DR. JONES: I am not saying that I agree with that.

THERAPIST: I agree with that too. By the way, any notion why the lack of certainty about something seems to mean to you that it is certain it can't be counted on?

DR. JONES: Uhh, you mean like in my family, you could never count on anything if it didn't already happen. Something like that?

THERAPIST: Yeah, somethin' like that. And you are uncertain whether or not you and Mrs. Jones will be able to resolve the sexual and marital difficulties between you and have better sex than you have ever had?

DR. JONES: Correct. If I were certain that things couldn't get any better, then I wouldn't be here.

THERAPIST: Well, then look at the bright side. In the past, uncertainty meant that you were probably not going to get what you want. Now, uncertainty holds the possibility that you will. You just have to be able to tolerate the ambiguity while you both are creating new possibilities. If you need certainty at this point, the only way you can get it is by insisting on failure. If you want an opportunity at the best sex and relationship you ever had, you better wish for ambiguity. Ironic isn't it. You grow up not liking uncertainty, and now you have to hope for it. At least it tells you that maybe your marriage doesn't have to be like the home you grew up in.

At this point, several changes had occurred in the session. The alliance with Dr. Jones was much stronger and more collaborative, and he was less defiant. This was accomplished, in part, by the reframing of strength as flexibility. Mrs. Jones had observed the therapist deal with her husband in a way no one ever had. She also observed her husband to be more sensitive and needy, and less defiant and overpowering. Mrs. Jones intuitively knew this side of her husband, although it produced explosions in the relationship when her behavior reflected this awareness. Although never directly interpreted, the husband's reaction formation to insecurity, hunger for affiliation, and childhood deprivation surfaced to explain his pressure on her to perform sexually and to avoid confrontations.

There was greater congruence between the superficial content of the session and the underlying dynamics of the relationship. The power hierarchy had been rebalanced, with less focus on the wife as the identified patient.

There was now much greater tolerance for ambiguity, less need for immediate results, and reduction in performance pressure on the wife to gratify her husband's insecurity by "adequate functioning."

In contrast to the husband's potential defiance of any prescription by the therapist to change their style of lovemaking, which Dr. Jones would have taken as an implicit indictment of his prior competency as a partner, the therapist was now able to couch modifications in sexual technique as "the creation of ambiguity and the opportunity for new gratifications."

After several sessions devoted to the "problem of the day," Dr. and Mrs. Jones reported their relationship becoming increasingly stable and less volatile. Mrs. Jones suggested that perhaps the improvement was related to the therapist, which Dr. Jones took issue with. The therapist agreed with Dr. Jones, suggesting that any change that occurred was probably the result of something that the couple had done. Since it was not evident to them what had changed, the therapist made several observations: first, the therapist was happy for them that they were more comfortable with each other; second, change did not have to be as painful, difficult, or as deliberate as they may have anticipated; third, although they might not understand yet what had spoiled their relationship and, moreover, what it took to improve it, they could now use the relationship itself, in its ebb and flow, as a way of learning about it.

Dr. Jones began to complain that "all this is well and good, but I don't see how it is helping us with our sex problems, which is what we came here for." The therapist suggested that Dr. Jones's comment was timely, because the couple seemed to be approaching the point that exchanging physical gratification might be congruent with a more positive emotional connection between them.

The therapist invited the couple to describe the manner in which they "made love," to which the couple responded with some discomfort and nervous laughter as they looked at each other and invited the other to talk first. Eventually Mrs. Jones described that it was invariably done late at night, in the dark. Her statement suggested that the lack of light was her husband's preference, and his discomfort appeared to corroborate this. Further exploration revealed a typical pattern for couples with difficulty with ejaculatory control: "foreplay" consisted entirely of Dr. Jones briefly kissing and fondling his wife, rapidly shifting to touching her genitals enough to permit a rapid shift to vaginal penetration without pain. He refused to allow his wife to touch his penis for fear of ejaculating prior to penetration. After approximately 10 seconds of penetration, he would ejaculate. Thereupon, Dr. Jones usually became upset and angry with himself and with his wife, alternately apologizing to her and blaming her: this would not happen if they tried more frequently. He would then withdraw into sullen silence. Mrs. Jones would often make some attempt to console him, but lately she just withdrew to the bathroom to wash up. The couple seemed somewhat embarrassed about having revealed the "secret" details of their sexual encounters.

THERAPIST: What you are describing is a very typical problem that many couples have. You are also describing a very common sexual style that both creates this type of problem and also results from it. Although you might think what I am about to say is odd, you have also thought similarly about many of the things I have said so far. You might want to feel relieved that you have arrived at a common problem in the common way. If you are willing to change the way you use physical contact between you, at least for a brief period of time, you can probably turn this around.

MRS. JONES: He won't make any changes, I have made several suggestions, and he insists on doing it his own way.

DR. JONES: Why should I have to change?

THERAPIST: I can't think of a reason why you have to change. It's your penis, and it's your relationship. You are not a man who will tolerate anyone telling him what to do, and perhaps that is as it should be. At least this way, you know that, success or failure, the responsibility is your own.

DR. JONES: Why should I change? I am doing things the way that things are supposed to be done. The problem is her.

THERAPIST: I am surprised that you would really want to believe that. You seem to be a man who is used to being in control. When you suggest that your wife is the total problem, she also has total control of the solution. If this has been your attitude, no wonder you have been feeling frustrated and helpless to make changes.

DR. JONES: What? What can we do?

THERAPIST: I can think of two possible approaches. One is to continue to believe that no change should be made in the way that the two of you make love and, moreover, that the main problem is low frequency. When you see it that way, it makes sense to try to solve the situation by pressuring your wife to have sex more frequently. And if that is what you really believe, then you also have the notion that no progress has been made because you have not pushed her hard enough. In that case, I have no choice but to encourage you to push her harder and become more demanding of more frequent sex.

DR. JONES: You want me to be more demanding?

THERAPIST: I don't want you to do anything. I am simply trying to help you follow your own good judgment. If I am not going to be duplicitous and mean what I say when I encourage you to trust yourself rather than trusting me, I will *have* to offer to help you figure out more ways to pressure her and push her. On the other hand, since I have also encouraged your wife to trust herself, and she does not believe that simply increasing the frequency of sexual contact is the solution, I will also have to teach her how to maintain herself in the face of that pressure, so that we can have two strong, independent people. And as I hear myself say this, it doesn't sound like such a bad idea in any event. I have no difficulty supporting either of you in your own view of your difficulty.

DR. JONES: Well, what if we were willing to change our sex?

THERAPIST: Well, there may be a therapeutic benefit in not changing, at least for right now.

DR. JONES: And what is that?

THERAPIST: Well if you change too quickly, you will not be able to find out what has been causing many of your difficulties. If you continue to do things exactly as you have done them, at least for a while, you will be able to get some insight into some personal difficulties that are transparent at the moment.

MRS. JONES: (*picking at her husband*) He won't even agree to turning the lights on.

THERAPIST: Well, that makes perfect sense to me. I can't think of why either one of you would want to put the lights on, although it might really help. If you put the lights on, your partner might see you!

MRS. JONES: What is wrong with that?

THERAPIST: Nothing is wrong with it. It just sounds like more intimacy than either of you can tolerate.

DR. JONES: It is more romantic that way.

THERAPIST: I am not disagreeing that you feel that way about it. In fact, it is useful to note that it is the way it seems to you. Because it allows us to begin to use your sexual behavior in a new way: to learn about the two of you in ways that are not available in your words. In the dark, you can't really see who your partner is. You both want to feel that your partner is interested specifically in you and not just having sex with anyone. And yet you won't let them see who it is they are having sex with. You may believe that love is blind, but you are also insisting that it be that way. If it is more romantic that way for you, and I am not suggesting that it is not, then I wonder if what you are indirectly showing us is that you don't think your wife would really love you if she really could see you and know you, physically and emotionally. And I wonder if you are also suggesting that it is easier for you to expose the more romantic and tender side of you when you are somewhat hidden and so is her response to you.

DR. JONES: I never thought about it in quite that way. I always hear about everyone else wanting to do it in the dark, too. (*to wife*) Well, are *you* so comfortable with the idea of the lights on?

MRS. JONES: I always thought you wanted the lights off because you didn't like my body. I am not as young as I used to be.

THERAPIST: No one is as young as they used to be, but that is not the real issue. The more relevant question is whether or not you are more lovable and sexual than you used to be. Whether or not your husband has some discomfort with your body, it sounds like you *both* are somewhat ill at ease with being intimate during sex. (*Long pause of silence in the session, followed by Dr. and Mrs. Jones nervously laughing with each other.*) Well, maybe you two aren't the only ones with fears of really being loved and loving, and maybe you aren't the only ones with this type of sexual difficulty. On the other hand, I can't imagine that you go through other aspects of your life priding yourself on being just like everyone else, questing for being "average."

MRS. JONES: Are you suggesting that we stop and turn the lights on? Donald will never go for that. He keeps insisting that we have to be more "spontaneous" when we have sex.

THERAPIST: That's interesting. Another way you folks are perfectly "normal." Lots of people keep stressing spontaneity because they are looking to feel something special and don't know what it really is. There is nothing special about spontaneous sex, but it isn't as good as most people anticipate. Let me ask: what would you both prefer, having intercourse on the ride down from my office on the 5th floor of this building till you reached the guard downstairs or taking a suite at the Regency, chilling a bottle of champagne, finding your partner in silk lounging clothes, and spending the whole morning with delicious fantasies of what comes next?

DR. JONES: I'd settle for the ride down the elevator; the Regency never happens.

THERAPIST: As long as you are willing to settle for a ride down the elevator, why should it? If you are willing to settle for spontaneous sex, why should you get anything else.

DR. JONES: Now it sounds like spontaneous sex is not the best sex.

THERAPIST: I think I'd best let you judge from your own experience, if you are willing to do some experimenting with both. But if you think sex should be a spontaneous event, perhaps you would oblige us with an erection now? (*mutual laughter*) (*changing the subject*) What is your theory about why you are ejaculating so rapidly?

DR. JONES: I get so sexually aroused, I can't hold back.

THERAPIST: You mean her vagina is so stimulating you can't tolerate it?

DR. JONES: Yeah. And also the feeling of being close to her.

THERAPIST: Now I am confused. (*long pause*)

MRS. JONES: What are you confused about?

THERAPIST: Well I hear what your husband is saying, and perhaps now that I am confused, I understand why you both can't figure out what the sexual difficulty has been.

DR. JONES: What do you mean?

THERAPIST: How long would you say goes by between the time you insert your penis in your wife's vagina and the time you ejaculate?

DR. JONES: About 10 seconds.

THERAPIST: And how long could you last if your wife just stroked your penis with her hand, without attempting penetration.

DR. JONES: We never do that, I want to come inside her.

THERAPIST: Well, if you did, what would you estimate.

DR. JONES: Maybe a minute.

THERAPIST: A minute? Can your wife stimulate your penis with her hand well?

MRS. JONES: He use to complain that it felt too good, and he made me stop.

DR. JONES: I didn't want to ejaculate before I was inside her.

THERAPIST: And how long does it take you to bring yourself to orgasm when you are by yourself?

DR. JONES: I don't masturbate; I haven't done that since I got married.

THERAPIST: Well, take an estimate; would you bring your self to orgasm in 10 seconds?

DR. JONES: No, it was more like 3 to 4 minutes, but that was a long time ago.

THERAPIST: I understand. But what I am confused about is the pattern of what you are telling me. How do you make sense out of the fact that you can last 3 to 4 minutes when you are stimulating yourself, one minute when your wife stimulates you manually, and 10 seconds of intercourse with almost no prior stimulation to your penis?

DR. JONES: I can't take too much of the good stuff. Her vagina feels the best.

THERAPIST: Well, I have to accept what you are saying as your subjective experience of it, but it is getting more and more interesting. What if I told you that on a pure physiological level, masturbatory orgasms are more intense than coital orgasm, in part because you can pump in exactly the stimulation you like. Moreover, your wife can probably move her hand better than she can move her vagina.

DR. JONES: I am not sure.

THERAPIST: Well, If I put a hundred dollar bill on the table here and told her she could have it if she could pick it up, which part of her anatomy would you tell her to use. (*lots of laughter, and tension reduction in the session*) What is curious about that is that you have better ejaculatory control to the forms of stimulation that might actually provide greater intensity of tactile stimulation, and less control in the one situation that offers the least. This is exactly the opposite of your theory that you ejaculate quickly during intercourse because it is "the good stuff."

DR. JONES: I guess I don't know why.

THERAPIST: Well, maybe it is some other "stuff" that is making you ejaculate quickly?

DR. JONES: Well, maybe its best because I feel the closest to her when we have intercourse.

THERAPIST: How do you mean?

DR. JONES: I start thinking about making love to her, and making her feel good; we get close, and I get so excited and aroused that I just come.

THERAPIST: My past experience with couples who have difficulties like yours is that they arrive at the same theory as you have but actually are doing the exact opposite. Very quickly they stop thinking about making love and become preoccupied with the anticipation of *not* being able to make love. Rather than thinking about making your wife feel good, men in your situation start thinking about *not* being able to please their partners. As the time approaches for penetration, both partners begin to worry in silence.

DR. JONES: Yes, I guess I do that. I never looked at it that way. (*smiling*)

THERAPIST: It is not a normal way to look at it. It is exactly backwards from the way that couples try to make themselves see what is happening. I see you have some appreciation of the paradox in all this. So . . . it doesn't sound like what is making you come more quickly during intercourse is the intimacy of the moment. Let me ask you another question. How do you try to delay your ejaculation during intercourse?

DR. JONES: (*embarrassed*) I try to think about something else. I know that I am supposed to be thinking about her, but if I do, I come.

THERAPIST: I am impressed at your ability to see you are caught on the horns of a dilemma. On the other hand, you have hit upon the most common technique men use to delay their ejaculations: stimulus reduction. It doesn't work effectively in the long run and can eventually cause difficulty with erection, so I don't recommend you continue it. But let me just point out that it cannot be that you are ejaculating more quickly during intercourse than during manual stimulation because it is more intimate, because you are actually trying to tune your partner out during intercourse. You are actually not very intimate when you are focused on failure either. So if you are ejaculating quickly during intercourse, it isn't out of sheer density of sexual stimulation, and it isn't out of being the most intimate form of sexual expression.

MRS. JONES: Then what is it?

THERAPIST: I am not sure yet, but if you are willing to continue using your sexual behavior in the way that we have just used it, I am pretty sure that you will be able to figure out what the reason is and take care of it in the process.

At this point, the couple requested suggestions about how to go about this "new approach." Dr. Jones was more amenable to making some changes for a variety of reasons that were embedded in the interchanges of the session. The therapist engaged the couple in a mutual exploration of their sexual behaviors and perceptions in a problem-solving context, piquing their curiosity and exploring the paradoxes of their sexual experiences as "normal" pitfalls. In addressing the paradoxes of their report, the therapist demonstrated humor, acceptance, and reorganized their experiences in new ways that permitted them to use their own thinking and resources. The therapist did not focus on technique as an end in itself but, rather, used it to highlight aspects that have been invisible to the couple and offered meaning where there had not been even an inkling of a need for attention. The therapist demonstrated how the details of their sexual encounters would be used in nonblaming, helpful ways before any change in behavior was required. In so doing, the therapist demonstrated the utility in looking at the couple's spontaneous behavior, rather than focusing on getting the couple to do prescribed behaviors as the key.

During this session there was a subtle paradigm shift that allowed the couple to permit a tentative modification of sexual interaction without triggering the personal issues about adequacy and blame that previously had precluded spontaneous change. At this point the therapist was able to recommend that the couple temporarily agree to dispense with intercourse because it was "not useful," in lieu of other, more effective, forms of stimulation. However, it still required the therapist to avoid engagement by Dr. Jones in a familiar power struggle.

DR. JONES: Are you telling us to give up on intercourse altogether.

THERAPIST: I am not suggesting that you give up anything in any way, nor am I telling you to do it. I am merely remembering that you have been willing to throw away more intense forms of stimulation in lieu of less dense, less intimate, and briefer forms like intercourse. I am suggesting that you might want to do some things that will take care of some immediate problems that I am concerned about. You both seem to be suffering from feeling emotional withdrawal from each other, including during sex. I suggest that you do something that may allow you to be more intimate during lovemaking and, in fact, allow the two of you to put some lovemaking in the lovemaking. I also suggest that there is no real gift in you (*to Dr. Jones*) being willing to diminish the intensity of your experience in an effort to please your wife. It only seems to accomplish the opposite. I suggest that if you are willing to provide more intense pleasurable stimulation for each other, you may enjoy it more, as well as enjoy it longer. That is your pattern, isn't it. You do last longer to more intense forms of stimulation?

DR. JONES: I want to be able to do it like a man is supposed to do it.

THERAPIST: Well, then you have already succeeded. If you are willing to kill yourself, or at least your sexual pleasure, trying to measure up to your expectation of what a real man is, and you are still feeling inadequate, then I guess you have already made it to being a "real man." On the other hand, you are telling me that you like to feel that you are your *own* man. In that case, you need to do in your own bedroom what you think you ought to be doing and not what you think someone else wants you to do, including what you think I want you to do. If you think it is in your best interest to have intercourse, I encourage you to do so. I am sure that you are a reasonable man, and you will do what you think is in your own best interest.

DR. JONES: How will not having intercourse ever help me to have intercourse? (*smiling*)

THERAPIST: Dr. Jones, it looks like you are appreciating the paradox of living and loving. Look at the bright side: having intercourse hasn't helped you to have intercourse. If it doesn't make sense, maybe there is new opportunity. Doing what makes sense hasn't gotten you anywhere. Besides, the more we talk in ways that don't make sense, the more it seems to make sense to you. That makes sense, right?

DR. JONES: (*laughing*) I don't know why I am laughing, I could never repeat back what you just said, but I understood it and it makes sense.

MRS. JONES: (*also laughing*) Are you suggesting that we simply don't have intercourse?

THERAPIST: No, I am suggesting that if you really love each other and want to use your touch to express it, that you go home and do exactly that.

DR. JONES: Like how.

THERAPIST: Well if you want to feel that the sex is personal, why not do it in a personal way: use some 3-inch-thick candles to light the bedroom, so you can see your partner seeing you.

DR. JONES: Why 3-inch-thick candles?

THERAPIST: Because if you use narrow dinner taper candles, you have to think about the wax melting on the nightstand. It is a distraction from focusing on what is going on between the two of you, and there is already enough of that going on when either of you is thinking about failing. On the other hand, real intimacy is hard to tolerate, so if you need to worry about failing for a while, please feel free to do so.

DR. JONES: I know I will still worry about coming too quick.

THERAPIST: That will be fine. If you are not going to be having intercourse, there is less external reason for you to do so. However, if you continue to be worried about failing, that is just fine. If it continues, it will be more of a clear reflection of things going on inside you, and we can use it very productively to find out what has always killed sex and intimacy for you. So actually, you can't loose either way. Either you will be able to focus more on the interaction between you, or you will find out what has always been in the way. Feel free to worry about ejaculating too quickly if that is what you seem to want to do, only this time also pay close attention to your thoughts and feelings at that moment, so we can use them.

DR. JONES: Is this going to make her want to have sex more often with me?

THERAPIST: I can't guarantee anything. If you haven't been successful in making your wife have sex, and you are actually at home with her, then I know that I never will be able to *make* her have sex. On the other hand, I doubt that anyone has to make her have it. It sounds like your wife's lack of desire for the sex that the two of you have been having is a testimony to her good judgment. The sex has not been focused on pleasure but rather on avoiding failure. It sounds like the sex has been rather dismal for you both. *You* have been willing to settle for rather dull sex as long as you get it frequently. If you think your wife has any good judgment, perhaps you can trust that when the sex gets worth wanting she will want it. On the other hand, your struggles with yourself to get comfortable focusing on pleasure and tolerating the increased closeness will also be very helpful for your wife.

DR. JONES: In what way?

THERAPIST: Well, I gather that she is not used to the idea that anyone would really want to be with her, just for her.

MRS. JONES: (*suddenly in tears*) I never think anyone could love me just for me, even my children. My parents were only interested in me not embarrassing them and doing good in school. They only paid attention when I was not measuring up to their standards. (*Husband is suddenly very attentive, and uncomfortable and recognizing the similarity of his own behavior with the report of her parents.*)

THERAPIST: Well, then, if your husband could make some headway with giving up focusing on whether his penis shot off and could look you in the eye while he touched you rather than preparing you to be penetrated, it might be very helpful in producing exactly the type of internal conflict you might need. As long as he continues to focus on ejaculation and intercourse, you might not like it, but it fits the style of interaction that makes sense to you. If he can light a candle, perhaps even get it himself, it will not make much sense to you in terms of "why would anyone want to make me feel good for me?" But his progress would set the stage for your own. If you want to avoid the answer, keep the lights off and have intercourse. I guess this stuff works pretty good. You haven't even had to go home and do anything and already you both are starting to use your sexuality in a new way for both your developments. Although you have different sexual symptoms, you have relatively similar issues underlying them. Both of you find it hard to accept that anyone could love you, want to please you, or find you pleasing if you are not trying to perform for them. (*to Dr. Jones*) I guess as long as you focus on whether or not you are going to fail, you don't have to deal with the nasty questions about whether the people you really love will love you if you stop performing and trying to measure up.

DR. JONES: I guess my family wasn't much different. You could never satisfy my mother. And the only time the family talked, it was about a fight and someone being blamed. I never saw my parents exchange one shred of affection or a kind word. They just argued if my father made enough money and if my mother spent too much.

THERAPIST: And what impact did that have on you?

DR. JONES: I just tried to give her what she wanted and stay out of her attention. But you could never succeed, because she always found something wrong.

THERAPIST: Well, since both of you have been really doing your part in this endeavor, I should also do mine. Now that I see where we are, I can suggest another modification that might not make sense to you, but it might make things more difficult for you because it will probably address these issues.

MRS. JONES: Will it help us get over our problems?

THERAPIST: It will either help you get over them or make it clearer what they are about.

MRS. JONES: What do you think will help?

THERAPIST: Do you normally touch each other at the same time?

MRS. JONES: Unless he is just touching my vagina getting me ready for intercourse, yes we do. Why?

THERAPIST: Well, you might want to try taking turns touching each other, so that there is a clear giver and clear receiver at any given time. After one of you has a chance to receive, you could switch so that you each got some exposure in the opposite roles.

MRS. JONES: Why would this help us?

THERAPIST: Well, it might help embody more clearly the very issues both of you seem to be struggling with: "Why would anybody really want me, to please me, just for me?" Simultaneous touch is just a convenient way to bypass this thorny question. It might also make it easier for each of you, as the receiver, to focus on the pleasurable sensations in your own body. Which will either make you feel much better or much guiltier and unworthy. And under the circumstances, I can't decide which would be better for both of you. I know it might not make sense, but I have this weird thought that having a good enough time so that you each felt unworthy might be a good thing for you.

DR. JONES: It makes sense to me!

THERAPIST: I am sorry to hear that, maybe we are on the wrong track. (*all three are laughing*)

DR. JONES: I don't agree at all with what you just said.

THERAPIST: Once again, I agree with you completely. (*much laughter again*)

Case Material of Subsequent Course of Treatment

The couple returned to report that they had set aside time to "touch" twice in the intervening week. They reported a marked reduction in estrangement and hostility between them both in and out of the bedroom. There was a notable softening in their eye contact during the session, and they had the look of a couple with a new, fragile sense of hope, which neither partner was eager to rupture.

They reported lighting candles for their physical contact, and he proudly reported that the encounter was actually more like "lovemaking" than when they had been having intercourse. He reported continued but markedly reduced fears of ejaculating when receiving genital stimulation from his wife. The wife was surprised and gratified by the encounter, complimenting her husband on his tenderness with her. To her surprise, she found it "nerve-wracking" to receive her husband's touch, although she seemed secure that he would not try to push her to have intercourse. The therapist encouraged Dr. Jones and his wife for making progress in reducing their fears of failure on the level of the immediate situation and on the longer-term issues.

The subsequent sessions consisted of increasing the amount of stimulation both partners could provide for each other and monitoring attempts on either part to avoid, reduce, or mitigate the resulting exchange of emotional and physical gratification. Such efforts were interpreted in a positive light of resolving the concerns about self-acceptance, bonding, and fears of loss in the context of the marital relationship, and the family-of-origin object-relations issues. Within the subsequent three sessions (during which time they maintained a ban on intercourse), the couple reported having their most prolonged erotic interactions ever, which further reduced the focus on intercourse. Dr. Jones became able to tolerate 5 minutes of intense manual and oral stimulation by his wife, and she in turn became increasingly responsive during the sessions as well as more aggressive in initiating.

The couple returned from one session to ask when they should resume intercourse, clearly stating that both would follow the therapist's suggestion. The therapist pointed out that Dr. Jones was already able to tolerate far more intense stimulation during their current sexual activity than he had ever been exposed to during coitus. The therapist opined that Dr. Jones could probably last longer during intercourse than he had in the past but questioned why they would want to return to a "less intense" form of stimulation?

The therapist suggested that if the couple wanted to see how intercourse had destroyed their sexual relationship in the past, all they had to do was return to their prior style of focusing exclusively on intercourse. On the other hand, if the couple wanted to use "simultaneous genital to genital" stimulation (involving vaginal containment of the penis), as an addition to their currently successful activities, they could learn to master it as they had mastered more difficult forms of stimulation. In the event they decided to add this form of stimulation, the couple was encouraged to make sure that it was neither the first nor the last form of stimulation to occur.

The subsequent week the couple returned to report that they had decided to remain with their current activities and not add "the new activity." Thereafter, Dr. and Mrs. Jones returned to say that at the conclusion to a very pleasurable and intense session of noncoital lovemaking, they had "simultaneous genital to genital stimulation" for approximately 4 minutes.

Debriefing from Case Example

In the above case, the therapist decided not to give detailed instructions in the initial prescriptions about the nature of the touch in terms of style and location. The inherent questions of "massage" versus more sensual caress, genital versus nongenital touch, and the handling of orgasmic release were not discussed with the couple for several reasons. First, issues of pacing of time and material precluded further discussion. There was tremendous emotional focus and alliance building in this session, and the decision was made to not dilute it with a concluding emphasis on technique. Second, the nature of the touching could be refined in subsequent sessions. Third, the couple's own spontaneous construction and execution of the touching could be used more productively from an interpretive basis than directing behavioral activities toward rapid symptom relief. In the absence of (or sometimes in spite of) detailed instructions, the style in which couples touch reflects their unstated and often unrecognized assumptions about themselves, their sexuality, and their relationship. In this manner, the therapist is able to use the prescription of touch both as a behavioral intervention and as a vehicle for eliciting unconscious aspects of both individuals. Fourth, a productive, collaborative alliance with the husband had been established with sufficient flexibility in his stance to modify his physical interaction with his wife. Further intervention might trigger his issues about autonomy, control, and status with the therapist. In subsequent sessions when the therapist had demonstrated the process of debriefing and established a stronger alliance, greater clarity and refinement of bedroom suggestions could be made.

Paradoxical interventions were made in session rather than as prescription for homework assignments. Although behavioral suggestions may have had some paradoxical flavor, they were not inherently designed as paradoxical interventions *per se*. The intent was to encourage activities that would address the sexual and marital issues undermining greater satisfaction. No major "paradoxical suggestions" were delivered at end of session to deal with their resistance. Instead, inherent paradox was used throughout the sessions so that by the time behavioral suggestions were given, the push for homeostasis has already reduced. The therapist's focus on the behavioral suggestions as a vehicle for resolution of family-of-origin issues rather than being merely sexual technique was also paradoxical from the patients' perspective.

The therapist's strategic stance, his affect during the banter, and the eventual alliance were paradoxical from the doctor's perspective. He was expecting that disagreement should lead to combat. Instead his disagreement led to further alliance, since the therapist did not become defensive, insecure, or invalidated by his disagreement. Confusion was redefined as positive experience. The tone and style are perhaps more similar to the unstructured hypnotic induction work of Milton Erickson (Erickson, Rossi, & Rossi, 1976).

The sessions embodied Frankl's emphasis on the use of humor, which allowed the patients to develop a more detached existential view of the problematic behavior and allowed them to shift from laughter to tears in very brief periods of time. The reader may also recognize some similarity between the therapist's dialogue and the "confusion technique" made popular by Minuchin and Fishman (1981). However, the purpose in the intervention described was not only to derail ("confuse") existing dysfunctional patterns but also to encourage acceptance of uncertainty and paradox as a fact of stable relationships.

A rereading of the dialogue will reveal that the therapist's statements were literally true and substantive rather than merely being doubletalk. Repeated statements from a therapist that are paradoxical merely in the sense of being self-contradictory may diminish the alliance with the patient. Patients sometimes respond to poorly implemented confusional techniques by deciding that it is the therapist who is confused. The exploration of inherent paradox, involving the presentation of statements that although seemingly contradictory, absurd, or opposed to common sense are compellingly true, avoids this pitfall.

The Subtle Approach to Paradox

Many therapists might not even identify this approach as "paradoxical." However, it does fulfill the quality of paradox in being in the mind of the beholder, contrary to and dependent on his or her expectations, and an intuitive and experiential phenomenon.

Obviously one of the major differences is that the therapist does not create or prescribe the paradox. Pathogenic double-bind systems usually develop imperceptibly over the course of time. The therapist's paradoxical intervention often consists of condensing time in a manner that individual or systemic defenses have not permitted to show connectivity and impact of events that are denied in the individual or collective consciousness.

In treatment, the therapist simply focuses on the naturally occurring paradoxes within which the patients have been existing even prior to treatment. This is a shift in the meaning of the phrase "the use of paradox in treatment." Many therapists implicitly perceive paradoxical intervention as a specific technique used on patients, such as symptom prescription. Paradoxical interventions are usually divided into compliance-based and defiance-based paradoxes (Rohrbaugh, Tennen, Press, & White, 1981; Tennen, Rohrbaugh, Press, & White, 1981).

The use of inherent paradox has the advantages of removing the pressure from the therapist to "construct" a paradoxical intervention and maneuver the patient in a particular direction. It reduces the adversarial, manipulative tenor often accompanying traditional paradoxical approaches because the focus is not around an impending or current defiance of therapist suggestions. Sometimes therapists are blinded by infatuation with their ability to reframe problems. Although reframing arguments as "positive" efforts to create needed boundaries is sometimes effective in reducing animosity about the fights, systemic therapists may overlook that a "reframe" may actually be *true* and that truth is often the best reframe.

Existing paradoxes in the relationship often reflect an incomplete definition of the problem, where each half of the couple uses his or her piece of the truth (usually a truth about the other partner) as a way of negating the truth about him- or herself. Interwoven half-truths are often the best paradox the therapist can use. For instance, a husband may accurately perceive that his wife is chronically dissatisfied with him and that this parallels her own family of origin in which her mother berated her father. The therapist can point out that whereas this may be true, the husband's repeated interpretation of this seems to suggest a denial of his own dynamics and their role in the current impasse. That is, the husband's perception of his wife does not negate that the husband feels both obligated and resentful of responsibility for his wife's gratification, that he is dependent on her statement of satisfaction as an evaluation of his own self-worth, and that this parallels his own family of origin.

Therapists who become enamored of the use of paradox as a demonstration of their own creativity or power often miss the elegance of naturally occurring paradox and the needed resolution of the individual and relationship difficulties. Spontaneous paradox often results from the defense mechanisms of splitting and isolation. Thus, interlocking paradoxical double-binds result from interlocking sets of unresolved individual issues in a relationship, defenses against the resolution of internal conflict on an individual level, and commonly internalized conflicting social values and standards. Inherent paradoxes also arise from the nature of human biological and emotional maturation, interwoven with the socialization and culture-defined roles and expectations that are imperceptibly inculcated in men and women.

Exploration of inherent paradox keeps the focus on the problems that originally brought the couple into treatment rather than a "manufactured" focus of the therapist's design. Since the paradox is already preexisting and "anchored" within the realities of the couple, use of inherent paradox neither requires nor encourages greater trust or dependence on the therapist. For these reasons, exploitation of inherent paradox often offers more leverage as a fulcrum for change than does constructed paradox.

Use of inherent paradox does not require a strong treatment alliance, rapport, or therapist credibility with highly resistant patients early in treatment. Inherent paradox can be used from the outset of treatment in sexual-marital therapy and does not even require patients to *do* anything. There is much less adversarial and manipulative potential between patients and the therapist, and it is exceedingly rare for the patients to suggest that the therapist is "trying to do something to them" or "trying to paradox the patients." Use of inherent paradox *does* require that the therapist challenge himself or herself to see beyond the embedded biases of his or her own society, family, marriage, and personal adjustment.

Utilization of inherent paradox is more in keeping with recent advances in the use of the interview as the therapeutic intervention rather than on behavioral homework prescriptions. It shifts the focus from the curative aspects of the activities at home to the subsequent session when these activities are debriefed. The questions the therapist asks are designed to elicit alternative views of the problem that can be supported by the patients' personal experience. For example, although many people believe that one's ability to "make love" diminishes with increasing age in later life, many couples will agree that the husband's ability to be tender, compassionate, and listen to his partner's instructions tends to increase with age.

In contrast to constructed paradox, the therapist utilizing inherent paradox never actually encourages the couple to do anything. Patients' realization of their implicit dilemma is usually sufficient motivation for change. The couple is approached in such a way that it is they who seek the therapist's help for their problem, rather than the therapist trying to get the couple to implement his or her suggestion. The therapist appears to be one step behind the couple rather than leading them. It is instructive to watch couples attempt to subtly shift the therapist's position to one consistent with constructed paradox because it is an easier position in which to deal with the therapist. "We didn't do what you told us to do" suggests that the conflict is between the therapist and the patients. However, maintenance of the therapeutic position of suggesting options in response to patient request, rather than actually prescribing activities, reinforces the patients' inextricable dilemma.

In the paradox versus counterparadox view common to constructed paradox, there is an implicit assumption that the initial paradox is the pathogen. Treatment involves the construction of an antigen counterparadox to negate the original paradox. At the conclusion of successful treatment, the original paradox is neutralized or nonexistent. In the exploration of inherent paradox, the pathogen is considered to be intolerance for paradox and complex probabilities. It is assumed that such paradoxes are inherent to complex living systems and that they will exist at the conclusion of successful treatment (and are likely to increase).

For example, consider a man who initiated sex "all the time" with his wife whom he believed was "sexually unresponsive" to his effort to increase their frequency of sexual contact. Using constructed paradox, the therapist might prescribe that the husband initiate sex daily whether he wanted sex or not "to insure getting the sex he needed and to help his wife get over her 'inhibitions.'" When the man eventually feels coerced and rebels against the schedule of initiation, his frequency of initiation might diminish.

In utilizing inherent paradox, the therapist might simply point out that the individual with the lower sexual desire always controls the frequency of sex and that the husband's efforts to increase his wife's sexual desire make him more powerless. Moreover, the husband's frequent invitations allow his wife to remain passive and have sex when she wants it without ever initiating. Although the husband is likely to perceive the therapist's implied solution as being the inhibition of his sexuality with his wife, the therapist can suggest that broadening the depth and intensity of his sexual intimacy, rather than merely the frequency, will often result in the changes he desires (although this may make no sense to the patient at the outset).

Other authors have suggested constructed paradoxes should link symptoms to other people in the system (Selvini Palazzoli, Boscolo, Cecchin, & Prata, 1978). There is a tendency for linear shifts in linkage, reframing the difficulty from an individual focus to an interactional focus. In the approach demonstrated here, there is a repeated shifting back and forth of reframing from individual focus to interpersonal focus and back to individual focus, reflecting the circularity of the processes involved. The current approach demonstrates positive connotation by positive therapeutic utilization rather than reframing symptoms from negative to positive connotation by the attribution of benevolent intent. Therapeutic utilization of the interlocking unresolved issues of the partner *produces* the positive experience of the symptom rather than encouraging naivete or redefinition of prior experience.

In many applications of paradoxical approaches with couples, the asymptomatic partner is put in charge of the identified patient's symptom or at least made responsible for getting the asymptomatic partner to allow the symptom to occur. This is antithetical to the approach illustrated in the preceding example. Both are encouraged to be in control of themselves, reinforcing autonomy and boundaries. One partner is never put in charge of the symptoms of the other. On the other hand, individuals in a relationship are encouraged that their own personal development will stimulate the growth of the partner.

One important goal of treatment is developing the capacity for independent emotional and sexual self-maintenance in addition to or in spite of the partner's behavior, rather than reinforcing the expectation of interlocking behavioral sequences. Demands for the partner to emit some desired behavior as the necessary precursor for one's own behavior are a debilitating interactional pattern common to couples with sexual and marital difficulty. It seems rather self-defeating for the treatment process indirectly to reinforce this dynamic by having one partner attempt to make the other emit a particular response in the arena of sexual–marital therapy.

The ability of an individual, and a relationship, to function based on the probability of the partner's behavior rather than on strictly enforced contingencies is often crucial to enhancing intimacy, sexuality, and the flexibility of the relationship. According to Campbell (1982):

> . . . to understand complex systems, such as a large computer or a living organism, we cannot use ordinary formal logic, which deals with events that definitely will happen or definitely will not happen. A probabilistic logic is needed, one that makes statements about how likely or unlikely it is that various events will happen. The reason for this is that computers and living organisms must function reliably as a whole, even though their component parts cannot be expected to perform perfectly all the time. The parts function correctly only with a certain probability, and this probability must be built into the logic of the system. The aim is to insure that even if single parts are very likely to malfunction, the chance of the entire system breaking down is reasonably small. (p. 105)

Constructed paradoxical intervention may be successful in resolving an immediate impasse without necessarily addressing the underlying issues that give rise to it. However, inherent paradox, which derives from these underlying unresolved conflicts, can actually be used to resolve them.

Most of All, Paradox Is Not a "Magic" Quick Fix

Resolution of inherent paradox involves a shift and escalation to a higher order of perspective (metaperspective). It requires a corresponding development of an *observing ego,* required to tolerate ambivalence and the simultaneous *validity of multiple realities.* Only by assuming a metalevel can the individual do so without conflict. On an intrapsychic level, this corresponds to the resolution of splitting, projection, and denial.

The metalevel is not just the ability to observe one's own processes simultaneously with the reality of the partner. It is also the ability to accept that one's own immediate reality and responses are determined in some measure by one's own unresolved issues and unconscious processes. It is the intolerance for inherent paradox, both in terms of content and degree, that each of us can see the side of ourselves that we refuse to see. It is for this reason that the use of paradox can be so valuable.

It may seem contradictory, if not paradoxical, that this chapter would discuss *truth* while also discussing relativity of perception. Simultaneous appreciation of constructionism, cybernetic epistomology (Keeney, 1983), and notions of a concrete external reality embody the clinician's paradox. Likewise, the concepts of behaviorism, systems theory, and psychoanalysis that appear in this discussion embody the meaning of paradox: the *apparent* inherent tension between seemingly true viewpoints. Eliminating this tension by restricting oneself to a single vantage point is as deadly to the development of a clinician as it is to the development of a relationship. Tolerating this tension spawns more elegant ways of understanding existence, as demonstrated in the work of Maturana (Maturana & Varela, 1988) and Campbell (1982):

> Above a certain level of complexity, there are intrinsic limits to a logical system, if that system is consistent. There will always be true statements which can neither be shown to be true nor proved to be false within the confines of the system, using the axioms and rules of the system. Moving outside the original system, enlarging it by adding new axioms or rules, might make the statement provable, but within this wider metasystem, there would be other statements that could not be proved without further expansions, and so on without end. Perfect completeness is never reached. (Campbell, 1982, p. 109)

In the constructed paradox approach, the end of therapy often contains a final "bind" designed to progressively reduce the possibility of reemergence of symptoms. In the use of inherent paradox, there is no additional prescriptive "bind" (nor were there any previously) beyond the inherent paradoxes of the system itself. The goal of using inherent paradox is freedom and autonomy from the binds of being "normal." This includes the resolution of unconscious conflicts, enhancement of individuation and differentiation, increased flexibility in the relationship, and emancipation from the "normal neurosis" inherent in cultural sexual prescriptions in western society (Putney & Putney, 1964).

If the couple has accepted the idea that sexuality, loving, relationships, and life itself are paradoxical in nature, there is increasingly little that the couple approaches as "contrary" to expectations. The couple develops a tolerance for ambiguity, and anticipation of uncertainty; what would previously be perceived as paradoxical is now perceived as the "joke of life." The couple identifies such events as "what I used to think as paradoxical" in an ego-syntonic rather than ego-alien manner.

Referring to the work of Ilya Prigogine (1977 Nobel Prize winner in chemistry), Campbell (1982) notes:

> The tendency to move forward toward a highly organized state, rather than backward toward a simpler state, is a property of open systems, those that exchange matter and energy with their surroundings. Open systems do not behave in the same way as closed systems, which for a long time were the chief objects of study in physical chemistry. Under certain circumstances, open systems reach a steady state in which they are far from equilibrium, or maximum entropy, and they maintain that

> state. They are highly "improbable," highly complex. What is more, such a steady state can be reached from different starting points, and in spite of disruptions a long the way. The state is what is called "equifinal." (p. 101)

The therapist who loves the paradoxes of life can join with the couple in the final stages of treatment as simply another adult sharing an appreciation of the wonderful contradictions of reality from our expectations and our childhood images. As the sense of "knowing wonderment" grows, the couple increasingly becomes their own sex therapists, increasingly able to modulate their sexual and other intimate behavior to cope with the ever-shifting circumstances and day-to-day fluctuations that characterize the mutuality (Wynne & Wynne, 1986) of a healthy relationship.

References

Bateson, G., Jackson, D., Haley, J., & Weakland, J. (1956). Toward a theory of schizophrenia. *Behavioral Science, 2,* 4.

Campbell, J. (1982). *Grammatical man.* New York: Simon & Schuster.

Erickson, M. H., Rossi, E. I., & Rossi, S. I. (1976). *Hypnotic realities.* New York: Irvington.

Frankl, V. E. (1967). *Psychotherapy and existentialism.* New York: Washington Square Press.

Friedman, E. (1988). *Denial and spirituality.* Paper presented at the AAMFT annual conference, New Orleans.

Gordon, L. H. (1988). *A laundry list of marital mishaps, marital knots and double binds.* Falls Church, VA: PAIRS Foundation.

Haley, J. (1973). *Uncommon therapy: The psychiatric techniques of Milton H. Erickson.* New York: Ballantine.

Keeney, B. P. (1983). *Aesthetics of change.* New York: The Guilford Press.

Kerr, M. E., & Bowen, M. (1988). *Family evaluation.* New York: W. W. Norton.

Lobitz, N.C., & LoPiccolo, J. (1972). New methods in the behavioral treatment of sexual dysfunction. *Journal of Behavior Therapy and Experimental Psychiatry, 3,* 265–271.

Masters, W. H., & Johnson, V. E. (1970). *Human sexual inadequacy.* Boston: Little, Brown.

Maturana, H. R., & Varela, F. J. (1988). *The tree of knowledge: The biological roots of human understanding.* Boston: New Science Library.

Minuchin, S., & Fishman, H. C. (1981). *Family therapy techniques.* Cambridge, MA: Harvard University Press.

Putney, S., & Putney, G. J. (1964). *The adjusted American.* New York: Perennial Library/ Harper & Row.

Rohrbaugh, M., Tennen, H., Press, S., & White, L. (1981). Compliance, defiance, and therapeutic paradox. *American Journal of Orthopsychiatry, 51,* 454–467.

Selvini Palazzoli, M., Boscolo, L., Cecchin, G., & Prata, G. (1978). *Paradox and counterparadox.* New York: Jason Aronson.

Simon, W. (1987). *Oral sex: A critical overview.* Paper presented at Western Regional Society for Scientific Study of Sex, Dallas.

Stampfl, T., & Levis, D. (1967). Essentials of implosive therapy: A learning theory-based psychodynamic behavior therapy. *Journal of Abnormal Psychology, 72,* 496–503.

Stanton, M. (1981). Strategic approaches to family therapy. In A. S. Gurman & D. P. Kniskern (Eds.), *Handbook of family therapy*. New York: Brunner/Mazel.

Tennen, H., Rohrbaugh, M., Press, S., & White, L. (1981). Reactance theory and therapeutic paradox: A compliance-defiance model. *Psychotherapy, 18,* 14–22.

von Neumann, J. (1966). Lecture at University of Illinois. In A. W. Burks (Ed.), *Theory of self-reproducing automata*. Urbana: University of Illinois Press. (Lecture presented 1949).

Watzlawick, P., Beavin, J., & Jackson, D. (1967). *Pragmatics of human communication*. New York: W. W. Norton.

Weeks, G. (1986). *Paradoxical intervention*. Paper presented at AAMFT annual conference. (Available as Audiotape 505, Creative Audio Co., Highland, IN)

Weeks, G. R., & L'Abate, L. (1982). *Paradoxical psychotherapy: Theory and practice with individuals, couples and families*. New York: Brunner/Mazel.

Wynne, L., & Wynne, A. R. (1986). The quest for intimacy. *Journal of Marital and Family Therapy, 12(4)*, 383–394.

Chapter 9

Dialectics and Behavior Therapy: A Metaparadoxical Approach to the Treatment of Borderline Personality Disorder

Edward N. Shearin
Marsha M. Linehan

The treatment of individuals with a diagnosis of borderline personality disorder (BPD) is something that many clinicians approach with trepidation and concern, and for good reason. The incidence of self-destructive behavior is generally high (Gunderson & Kolb, 1978; Gunderson, 1984), and although much of this behavior is without lethal intent, the percentage who eventually die is at least 5–10% (Frances, Fyer, & Clarkin, 1986). Long-term follow-up for this population has shown that the diagnosis is stable over a 15-year period (McGlashan, 1983) and that serious psychological and social morbidity comparable to schizophrenic individuals can be expected for at least 5 years following the initiation of treatment (Pope, Jonas, Hudson, Cohen, & Gunderson, 1983). Indeed, the long-term improvement described by McGlashan may have been a consequence of unusually extensive treatment including more than 3 years of hospitalization and intensive psychotherapy (Gunderson & Elliott, 1985). Based on these data, for a clinician to avoid taking on such a responsibility given the resources of the average clinic or private practice seems professionally understandable.

Yet, with the common prevalance of the diagnosis among more severely disordered populations (Widiger, Frances, Warner, & Bluhm, 1986), the low economic level of many clients, and the mixed effects of general psychiatric hospitalizations for such chronic disorders (Hargreaves & Shumway, 1987), there has been a clear need for a treatment which could be used by an experienced clinician to fill the gap between intensive, specialized hospitalization and longer-term community resources. That was the objective of Linehan and her associates in developing her treatment for parasuicidal individuals with borderline characteristics. In this chapter, our goals are to describe Linehan's therapy in detail as well as to relate it theoretically to paradoxical and other modes of treatment with which it shares some characteristics. The therapy we describe has been found in preliminary studies to be effective in reducing parasuicidal behavior compared to controls receiving customary therapies in the community (Linehan, 1987a).

Treatment Population

Historically, the meaning of the label "borderline" has varied significantly depending on the labeler (Stone, 1980). Furthermore, the use of terms such as "suicidal" or "attempted suicide" in the clinical literature has been a methodological nightmare (Linehan & Shearin, 1988). For these reasons, we will clarify the meanings of our diagnostic terms before using them to define the treatment population.

Among the different criteria that have been used in the definition of BPD, the most common set in current usage employs the five of eight symptoms defined by DSM-III-R (American Psychiatric Association, 1987). These are: (1) impulsivity or unpredictability in self-damaging areas; (2) a pattern of unstable and intense interpersonal relationships; (3) inappropriate, intense anger or lack of control of anger; (4) identity disturbance; (5) affective instability; (6) frantic efforts to avoid abandonment; (7) physically self-damaging acts; and (8) chronic feelings of emptiness or boredom. Another set frequently used by researchers is based on the Diagnostic Interview for Borderlines (DIB; Gunderson, Kolb, & Austin, 1981). The DIB investigates five areas of functioning: social adaptation, impulse patterns, affect, psychosis, and interpersonal relations. Our diagnosis of BPD is based on both sets of criteria. This intersection of the DSM-III-R and Gunderson criteria defines a population that is both more severe and concentrated more toward the affective disorder end of the spectrum than individuals meeting either the unmodified DSM-III-R criteria or Kernberg's (1984) structural criteria (see Stone, 1980, pp. 42–43, for the relationship of various criteria).

Much controversy has surrounded the labeling of nonfatal self-harm with disagreements generally over the degree of intent required (Linehan & Shearin, 1988). To deal with this problem, Kreitman (1977) introduced the term *parasuicide* as the label for nonfatal, intentional, self-injurious behavior. According to Dyer and Kreitman (1984), parasuicide is "a non-fatal act in which an individual deliberately causes self-injury or ingests a substance in excess of any prescribed or generally recognized therapeutic dosage." This term has the advantage of eliminating the difficulty and inaccuracy associated with inferences regarding the degree of suicidal intent, as well as avoiding the use of pejorative words such as "suicide gesture." Unfortunately, it also labels as parasuicide much drug use that occurs without either harm or intent of harm. For these reasons, our definition of the term parasuicide is: any intentional, acute, self-injurious act (i.e., dangling from a bridge does not count) resulting in actual tissue damage, illness, or risk of death; or any ingestion of drugs or other substances not prescribed or in excess of prescription with clear intent to cause bodily harm or death. Not included in this are the taking of nonprescribed drugs to get high, to get a normal night of sleep, or as self-medication. We will use the term parasuicide as defined here in place of phrases such as suicide attempt or suicide gesture. The term *suicidal* will not be used unless the more general class of behaviors including suicide ideation and/or fatal self-harm is under consideration.

The population for whom Linehan's treatment was developed were women meeting the above definition of BPD and additionally having at least two parasuicides as defined above. This group was a more severely disordered subset of the women who might generally be diagnosed with borderline personality disorder as defined by DSM-III-R. Although dialectical behavior therapy is probably relevant for men meeting the same criteria, its effectiveness has not been tested on them. Furthermore, it has not been evaluated with nonsuicidal women meeting criteria for BPD.

In keeping with the focus on women during treatment development, we have used only the feminine pronoun in the following sections when referring to individuals with BPD. This usage does not imply that the disorder is limited to women or that the statements made might not also apply to men with the disorder.

Theoretical Framework

Dialectical versus Paradoxical

Linehan and her associates' use of what are typically called paradoxical techniques is centered in a broader, dialectical view of psychotherapy. This approach began in the early 1980s with a series of therapy observation and discussions by her clinical research team focusing on behavior therapy performed by Linehan with parasuicidal clients. At that time, the aims were to identify the techniques that seemed frequently helpful and to apply them in a consistent manner in subsequent sessions. Paradoxical techniques were identified as being a major subset of the helpful operations (this was somewhat of a surprise since the aim had been to perform behavior therapy). These techniques were things such as matter-of-fact exaggerations of the implications of events, similar to Whitaker (1975, pp. 12–13), encouraging the acceptance of feelings and situations in the tradition of Zen Buddhism (e.g., Watts, 1961), and double-bind statements such as those of the Bateson project directed at pathological behavior (Watzlawick, 1978).

During the course of writing a treatment manual, however, the choice was made to label the overall view as dialectical rather than paradoxical for two reasons. First, there appeared to be a strong need for a therapy emphasizing synthesis to deal with the lack of generalization of competencies across all relevant situations (Linehan, 1987b) as well as with frequently described personality characteristics such as cognitive rigidity and dichotomous thinking. The focus of dialectics is synthesis, whereas paradoxical theories have had less to say on the topic. The second reason was the fear that inexperienced therapists might overgeneralize from the paradoxical label and prescribe suicidal behavior itself; this prescription was and is explicitly *not* done in the therapy. However serendipitous the original choice of a label was, the choice of a dialectical view subsequently guided the therapy development in a much broader fashion than would have been possible with just a paradoxical twist to techniques. Consequently, the treatment has evolved as an interaction between therapy process and dialectical theory to its form of the past few years (Linehan, 1987b, 1987c).

Although most clinicians do not commonly use the word "dialectics" in conceptualizing psychotherapy, the psychotherapeutic relationship between the opposites embodied in the term has been regularly pointed out since the early writings of Freud (Seltzer, 1986). The current dictionary meanings (*Webster's New Collegiate Dictionary*, 1979) closest to this use are: "The Hegelian process of change in which a concept or its realization passes over into and is preserved and fulfilled by its opposite," "Development through the stages of thesis, antithesis, and synthesis," "Any systematic reasoning, exposition, or argument that juxtaposes opposed or contradictory ideas and usually seeks to resolve their conflict," and "The dialectical tension or opposition between two interacting forces or elements." The word itself has a long history beginning with the Greek philosophers Zeno, Socrates, and Aristotle, who were concerned about ways of changing thinking and describing this in a holistic complex manner. In *Topics,* Aristotle separated formal, impersonal logic from the process of change by persuasion or dialectics which, unlike the process of formal analytical reasoning, is personal because of its effect on the mind of some person (Perelman, 1982, pp. 2–3). This distinction was ignored by Western thought in favor of linear analytical thinking until, with the Hegelian process defined above, dialectics came to include change via a thesis–antithesis–synthesis sequence. It is this latter meaning that has become useful in psychotherapy and has led to the observation that: "Paradox is dialectics as applied to psychotherapy" (Mozdzierz, Macchitelli, & Lisiecki, 1976, cited in Seltzer, 1986).

From the position of Linehan and associates, a dialectical view is far more encompassing than most definitions of paradox. For example, Seltzer's (1986) definition is:

> A paradoxical strategy refers to a therapist directive or attitude that is perceived by the client, at least initially, as contrary to therapeutic goals, but which is yet rationally understandable and specifically devised by the therapist to achieve these goals. (p. 10)

Seltzer goes on to add that such tactics are regularly associated with reactions of surprise, confusion, and/or disbelief and that such reactions help define a technique as paradoxical.

For Linehan, surprise or disbelief might be associated with an intervention, but the therapist's recognition of the opposites embodied in a statement is far more important, at least initially, than a full perception by the client. Paradox enters in her dialectical view more in the fashion of Goldberg (1980, pp. 295–296) who stated: "I assume that truth is paradoxical, that each article of wisdom contains within it its own contradictions, that *truths stand side by side*. . . . Contradictory truths do not necessarily cancel each other out or dominate each other, but stand side by side, inviting participation and experimentation." The therapist must understand the dialectic and use it to guide interventions in order to be effective, but the seeming contradictions need not be obvious to the client. On the other hand, interactions between therapist and supervisor are also guided by a dialectical view but with the distinction that both parties are generally aware of its use. A goal of therapy is for the client eventually to see both the parallel relationship of contradictory truths and the synthesis that emerges, but since many borderline individuals hold rigidly to a dichotomous, either/or style of thinking, such a change is generally not expected in the short term.

Basic Theory

The dialectical philosophy underlies both Linehan's approach to treatment and her theory of BPD. The next sections give a more complete definition of this dialectical approach and how it organizes what is both a diathesis-stress and development/learning model of BPD. The influence on treatment is described in the section on therapeutic process.

Dialectics

A dialectical approach has been related to socioeconomic history (Marx & Engels, 1970), the development of science (Kuhn, 1970), biological evolution (Levins & Lewontin, 1985), and analyses of sexual relations (Firestone, 1970). Wells (1972) has documented a shift toward dialectical analyses in almost every social and natural science during the last 150 years. Within psychology, dialectical viewpoints have included applications to feminist therapy (Adams & Durham, 1977) and thinking in adults (Basseches, 1984). Seltzer (1986, p. 75) pointed out that dialectical principles are the major underpinnings of gestalt therapy.

Most recently, Sperry (1988) has described the integration over the last few decades of the cognitive and behavioral approaches in psychology as dialectical cognitivism. He sees the cognitive-behavioral view as containing a dialectical tension between two sources of control, that from bottom up (the microdeterministic assumption of behaviorism, biology, and all natural sciences) and that from mental states down (the macro or emergent determinism of cognitive theory). In this dialectic, "Mental states, as emergent properties of brain activity, thus exert downward control over their constituent neuronal events—at the same time that they are being determined by them" (p. 609). He thinks the resulting flexibility of the cognitive-behavioral view lends itself to much broader applications than previous approaches that are primarily mentalistic or reductionistic.

A dialectical approach directly contradicts traditional Cartesian reductionism by stressing the fundamental interrelatedness and wholeness of reality. In the Cartesian world view, Levins and Lewontin (1985) note that parts exist separately as homogeneous entities apart from the whole they comprise, whereas this is not possible from a dialectical world view that sees the internal heterogeneity of elements at every level. Thus, knowing the parts of the whole depends on what facets of the whole are considered. Parts exist only as they relate to a particular whole and not in some *a priori* independent fashion. Thus, parts are also not reducible. Correspondingly, wholes are not static but rather composed of internal opposing forces (the thesis and antithesis described above) from whose synthesis a new set of opposing forces emerges. In sum, parts and whole constantly interact and recreate each other. This always-changing whole also affects and is affected by the external world of which it is a part. Thus, the basic principles of the dialectical world view include the *nonreducible* nature of reality and the *interconnectedness* of all things, both of which lead to a *wholeness* that is continually in the process of *change.*

An implication of this view is that techniques that appear to be paradoxical seem so because they are conceptualized as independent elements rather than interrelated parts of a whole. For example, encouraging acceptance of a client's meager employment possibilities may facilitate a discussion of pathways that can be opened by further education. At one level this is paradoxical; from a dialectical perspective, acceptance is a necessary part of change and no paradox exists. An acceptance of current limitations is a necessary foundation for further growth. Another level of analysis might say that this procedure worked because of a reduction in anticipatory anxiety associated with the proposed changes (Frankl, 1975). This may also be "correct" but as a guiding principle, it is more restricted in its use.

Another implication is that the behavioral tripartite systems view, which Linehan (1979, 1981) has used in describing behavior, must be modified somewhat from its initial description by Staats (1975). In this original view, behavioral responses are divided into three general subsystems: the overt motor, the physiological/emotional, and the cognitive/verbal systems. No one system is primary, and relationships among the three systems are dynamic such that change in any one will produce system-wide changes. From a dialectical view, addressing any one system apart from the others is not meaningful, and as noted by Sperry (1988), extremely limiting. An example of such single-mindedness would be the attempting of a cognitive intervention without careful consideration of concurrent emotional and behavioral states. Most experienced therapists would readily see this as a problem, so an observation of this type is hardly new; what is new is a succinct theory that incorporates it as a basic tenet. If this principle is extended to the environment, equal significance is accorded to both the person and social-environmental systems. The individual cannot be isolated from the environment, and conversely, the environment cannot be isolated from the individual (Linehan & Wasson, in press).

As a consequence of a broad viewpoint, a dialectical perspective also shares characteristics and goals with other approaches to therapy. The emphasis on interrelatedness is quite compatible with a systems approach as can be seen from the preceding paragraph. Shared also with a systems view is an incompatibility with assigning blame, which is particularly important given the pejorative misuse of the BPD diagnosis among mental health professionals (Reiser & Levenson, 1984). This emphasis also fits well with the focus of integration in feminist therapy, which, like dialectics, synthesizes opposites and stresses wholeness

(Miller, 1983). Many of the techniques and strategies are common between the two approaches (Linehan & Wagner, in press).

Behavioral Syndromes of BPD

The dialectical view with its emphasis on wholeness does not mean that one cannot proceed to talk about specific characteristics of individuals. It does require, however, that the discussion take place in a relational manner. Furthermore, since a dimensional approach is more compatible than a categorical one (Linehan & Wasson, in press), it is clearest to view BPD as a series of dimensions that are defined by their opposite poles. In this perspective, Linehan has organized the behavioral characteristics of adults meeting borderline criteria along three dialectical poles forming a biosocial plane. These are: (1) emotional vulnerability versus invalidation; (2) active passivity versus the apparently competent person; and (3) unrelenting crises versus inhibited grieving. If one conceptually divides each dimension at its midpoint, the characteristics above the midpoint, emotional vulnerability, active passivity, and unrelenting crises, are the ones that developmentally have been the most influenced by the biological substrate for emotional regulation. Correspondingly, the characteristics below the midpoint, invalidation, apparent competency, and inhibited grieving, have during development been influenced more by the social consequences of emotional expression. The empirical bases of these dimensions are given in Linehan (1987b).

Emotional Vulnerability versus Invalidation. The emotional vulnerability syndrome refers to the extreme difficulty that many BPD individuals have in regulating emotional responses. They are extremely sensitive to all stimuli, and to emotional stimuli in particular. With even low-level stimuli, BPD individuals respond intensely and have difficulty returning to their emotional baselines. They cope by a mixture of shutting down, avoiding, and blocking all emotional stimuli, internal or external, and intensely overreacting. This pattern generally includes dysfunctional escape behaviors such as substance abuse and parasuicide.

Recent temperament research (Derryberry & Rothbart, 1984; Strelau, Farley, & Gale, 1986; Thomas & Chess, 1986) implies that high autonomic and emotional reactivity may often be of constitutional origin. Borderline clients may have a low threshold for activation of the limbic structures, brain structures associated with emotional regulation, according to Cowdry and associates (cited in Turkington, 1986). Previous literature also describes the emotional experience of parasuicidal individuals as one of chronic, aversive affect including anger, hostility, irritability, depression, anxiety, and social discomfort (Linehan, 1981). The emotional vulnerability syndrome is consistent with these findings as well as the DSM-III-R criteria of excessive anger and affective instability.

The invalidation syndrome describes the penchant of those in the borderline individual's environment to disregard affective experiences, oversimplify the ease of solving significant problems, and to highly value positive thinking as an approach to all problems. Although all of these approaches have their merit, when overapplied to emotionally vulnerable individuals, the pattern can be similar to the high-expressed-emotion environment (high criticism and overinvolvement) found in families of both depressed and schizophrenic clients with high relapse rates (Leff & Vaughn, 1985). Additional behaviors beyond these two that are relevant for BPD individuals include abusive behaviors, and the failing to recognize the individual's emotional or physical state, such as in nonempathic parenting.

Inadequate training in emotion-regulation skills is the crucial developmental consequence of the invalidating environment. Vulnerable individuals in these environments learn neither to trust their own perceptions and feelings nor to label and control emotional reactions adequately. Instead, they may learn that extreme emotional outbursts are necessary to elicit a helpful response from others. The longer-term consequences are that the individual does not develop either emotional tolerance or stability. If frequent emotional issues are not accepted as either normal or resolvable, the development of maladaptive escape behaviors increases in likelihood. Additionally, if the individual's own sense of events is never "correct" nor experienced in a stable fashion, both an overdependence on others and a lack of self-identity are likely. These characteristics all lead to the interpersonal problems associated with the borderline diagnosis.

Active Passivity versus the Apparently Competent Person. Active passivity describes the inclination of many borderline individuals to approach problems in a passive and helpless manner rather than to employ a determined active approach. A concomitant of these behaviors in times of extreme distress is to demand active problem solving by others. Recent research suggests that this problem-solving style is closely related to the vulnerability-invalidation dimension described in the preceding section. Bialowas (cited in Strelau et al., 1986) found a positive relationship between high autonomic reactivity and dependency in social influence situations. Data of Eliasz (1985) indicates that a preference for passive self-regulation may be a characteristic of individuals with high autonomic reactivity. The interpersonal dependency of BPD clients may arise in part from their great difficulty in protecting themselves from high levels of negative affect and their subsequent hopelessness. At peak moments, an overreliance on others for problem solving leads to emotional clinging and demands for help. The intense emotional responses to the threatened or actual loss of significant others is consistent with this constellation.

The apparently competent person syndrome describes the illusory competence of many BPD individuals. This illusion arises because their actual competences are not generalized across all relevant situations. The illusion is furthered in some situations by an almost completely inhibited expression of negative affect. This smiling, competent facade is easily mistaken by others for reality, and can lead to the perception that the borderline client is feigning helplessness to get attention or to frustrate others. The competent appearance is sometimes enhanced by borderline individuals' adopting the beliefs of their environment, that they are also competent across related situations and over time. Subsequent failures are consequently accompanied by extreme guilt over their perceived lack of motivation. When these beliefs are rejected, they may instead experience extreme anger toward others for their expectations and lack of understanding. Parasuicide and suicide are likely to be some of the dysfunctional behaviors employed in an attempt to reduce the distress associated with either the guilt or anger.

Unrelenting Crises versus Inhibited Grieving. The unrelenting crises syndrome describes the effect of the borderline individual's high emotional reactivity combined with chronic stress. The individual is constantly reaching Selye's (1956) exhaustion stage of stress adaptation rather than having the chance to return to emotional baseline before the next stressor. The hypothesized developmental scenario begins with constitutional factors both amplifying the initial emotional response and inhibiting the rate of return to baseline after each stressor. This unresolved response then exacerbates the number and effect of subsequent stressors. Dysfunctional escape behaviors come into use because of an inability to tolerate or otherwise reduce stress levels, which in turn leads to additional stressors. The development of adequate coping skills needed to lower the stress is further inhibited by poor interpersonal skills and inadequate social support.

The inhibited grieving syndrome describes a pattern of repetitive, significant trauma and loss combined with failures to experience and integrate these events. These losses arise inevitably from the continual cycle of crises. They may have a concrete form such as the loss of a person through death or divorce, or the loss of a job or income. Just as importantly, however, losses may come in psychological events such as the loss of predictability or control, or the loss of acceptance from others. Bereavement overload, a concept of Kastenbaum (1969), is the consequence of this procession of crisis and loss. The inhibition of grieving seems understandable given the continual nature of the losses, the deficits in coping abilities, and high emotional reactivity. We frequently hear borderline clients say that if they ever start to cry, they are unable to stop. Nonetheless, this inhibition serves to exacerbate the effect of stressful events and continues a vicious cycle.

Other Dialectical, Paradoxical, or Behavioral Approaches to BPD

The first use of paradoxical techniques with borderline individuals was by psychoanalytic therapists in the 1950s (Seltzer, 1986). Marie Coleman Nelson and her colleagues of the Paradigmatic Behavior Studies Seminar in New York City considered what they called paradigmatic techniques to be helpful with clients, specifically borderline and juvenile individuals, whose defenses made them poor candidates for more classical kinds of interpretation (Coleman, 1956; Coleman & Nelson, 1957; Nelson, 1962). Although it is unclear how well their use of the term borderline compares to the criteria described previously, their research was highly advanced for their time in their willingness to audiotape and transcribe sessions for analysis of the therapy process. As she described it (Nelson, 1962):

> The term *paradigm* means essentially "a setting forth by example." Hence, *paradigmatic psychotherapy* means the systematic setting forth of examples by the analyst to enable the patient to understand the significant intrapsychic processes or interpersonal situations of his life, past and present. (p. 120)
>
> The method recognizes that borderline patients have not developed an integrated concept of self and that the ego is composed chiefly of partial introjects and multiple identifications. Hence, the paradigmatic psychotherapist views the patient as a group—an aggregate of selves—as well as an individual. Thus the therapist may elect to impersonate in his communication with the patient any one of these selves, in order to enable the patient to ventilate fantasies, experiences, and feelings associated with the particular imago. (p. 121)

She continued with the description of a variety of techniques designed to mirror one of these "selves" or a transference image, or to "duplicate" some misperceived experience that has been reported. These were certainly paradoxical, both in the sense of being unexpected by clients expecting classical interpretations, and in the Bateson sense of placing the client's psychopathology (resistance to interpretation in this case) in a double-bind. When this resistance had decreased to levels associated with traditional analysis, these paradigmatic techniques could be discarded in favor of classical interpretation. In keeping with the seeming atheoretical nature of the paradigmatic approach, she noted that nothing in the techniques precluded their use of those with theoretical persuasions other than Freudian psychoanalysis.

Another approach was described by Scanlon (1980) as part of gestalt therapy with borderline clients. He advocated gestalt dialogues at different times in therapy involving the client's symptoms and "strength and weakness." As noted before, the gestalt technique of "being more what one is" in order to grow is distinctly dialectical, and is paradoxical only in the sense that the dialectical view of change is paradoxical.

Seltzer (1986) has listed applications of paradox to the problems of self-mutilation and suicidal behavior commonly associated with the borderline disorder. For most of the parasuicidal behavior examples (Fay, 1978; Haley, 1973; Madanes, 1984; Whitaker, 1975), the paradoxical strategies were directed at dynamics that the intervening therapists thought were causing the parasuicidal behaviors rather than the behavior itself. In more recent studies involving parasuicidal behavior, the paradoxical techniques were directed at such targets as criminal behavior (Chase, Shea, & Dougherty, 1984) and depression (Main & West, 1987). In no case that we could find did a therapist prescribe behavior that was considered suicidal. Andolfi (1979), however, described a study involving a parasuicidal woman in which he reframed the presenting behavior (scratching her face with her nails) as a creative attempt to deal with her boring life. Although we question the misinterpretation possible with the use of a word like "creative," the reframing of parasuicidal behavior as an attempt to solve serious problems is quite consistent with Linehan's theory of parasuicide (Linehan, 1981; Linehan & Shearin, 1988).

Finally, Turner (1987) has also investigated the effects of behavior therapy on BPD. Since his approach contained no paradoxical elements, we mention it simply for completeness.

Therapeutic Process

Treatment Goals

Dialectical behavior therapy (DBT) as applied to BPD involves concurrent individual and group treatment. The five treatment foci in individual therapy are: (1) suicidal behaviors; (2) therapy-interfering behaviors; (3) escape behaviors that interfere with a reasonable life; (4) behavioral skill acquisition involving interpersonal effectiveness, emotion regulation, distress tolerance, and self-management; and finally, (5) any other goals that the client has. These targets are approached hierarchically and, if a higher priority behavior reappears, recursively. The group therapy uses a psychoeducational approach to address its treatment targets. Hierarchically these are: therapy-threatening behaviors (the most serious interfering behaviors of individual therapy); behavioral passivity; teaching the preceding list of behavior skills; and other therapy-interfering behaviors.

The reduction of high-risk suicidal behavior is the first individual DBT goal, since a client must be alive in order to work toward achieving other goals. Although many parasuicide methods are only infrequently lethal, the occurrence of cumulative, irreversible physical damage as well as both the potential for accidental death and the connection of parasuicide with subsequent suicide demand immediate attention. Furthermore, since parasuicidal behavior and clients' statements about suicide are the most stressful client behaviors for many therapists (Hellman, Morrison, & Abramowitz, 1986), reductions in these are essential both to the delivery of effective therapy (Roswell, 1988), and, in our view, the willingness of the therapist to continue seeing the client.

For these reasons, the first priority in the individual session following any parasuicide is to discuss the behavior and obtain detailed information about both preceding and following events. The aim is to replace the parasuicidal behavior with more adaptive problem solutions by applying the problem-solving strategies discussed later. In an effective intervention, the likelihood of four outcomes will be enhanced. The first is that the amount of parasuicidal behavior will decrease as the client applies other solutions to distressing events. Secondly, the therapist will communicate that she or he takes the behavior very seriously. Given the invalidating environment frequently associated with borderline clients, this is especially important. The next outcome is that a contingency for parasuicidal behavior is established; that is, clients decrease their opportunities to talk about other issues when they engage in parasuicidal behavior. Although some BPD individuals talk freely about their harmful behavior and could find therapist attention reinforcing, in the experience of Linehan and her associates, a therapeutic focus on both the events preceding parasuicide and alternative-coping strategies is universally disliked. Finally, the stress for the therapist caused by the parasuicidal behavior will be reduced. In the long run, this is clearly in the best interest of the client, since a poorer quality of therapy or a therapist who has become depleted of the emotional resources to continue such a stressful relationship will not be good for the client.

The focus on parasuicidal behavior is not made in the group treatment for two reasons. First, in groups with several individuals engaging in frequent parasuicide, there simply is not time to deal adequately with the events surrounding the behavior. Secondly, the explicit discussion that is necessary to analyze any parasuicide functionally is usually highly upsetting to other group members and may lead to a contagion effect. Clients who bring up parasuicidal behavior (in contrast to the precipitating events) are therefore encouraged to pursue the discussion with their individual therapist.

The second goal of individual DBT and the first of group DBT is the reduction of *both* client and therapist behaviors that interfere with therapy. For clients in individual therapy, these include things such as frequently missing sessions, an inability or refusal to work in therapy, continuous disruptive crises, excessive hospital commitment, psychotic episodes, dissatisfaction with therapy, lying, excessive demands on the therapist, and other behaviors that have a negative effect on the therapeutic relationship. In the group, this list is shortened to the behaviors that are immediately threatening to the therapy: nonattendance, highly disruptive behavior in group, and overt hostility to other group members. Other therapy-interfering behaviors of the client in the group are ignored for the moment. Negative therapist behaviors for both individual and group include: not returning telephone calls, being late to appointments, engaging in hostile or negative comments, and wanting to terminate therapy or reject the client. All these issues are treated nonjudgmentally as problems to be solved in treatment sessions or supervision so that both the therapist and client can continue working together. An effective focus on these problems not only clears the way for further therapy but also functions to empower and validate all parties as their viewpoints and needs in the relationship are considered. This explicit focus on both sides of the therapeutic relationship is consistent with both the traditional collaboration of behavioral approaches and the dialectical philosophy.

The third goal of individual DBT is the reduction of other escape behaviors that threaten the development of a better life for the client. These behaviors include substance abuse or addiction, antisocial or illegal behavior, and illness-producing behaviors. Substance abuse particularly has often been associated with the first two targets of therapy. All share the characteristic that they may afford temporary relief from the client's distress at the cost of severe long term consequences for the client's quality of life. A failure to prioritize treating such maladaptive escape behaviors and to clearly emphasize their destructiveness quickly undermines one of the stated overall aims of therapy, to build a life worth living.

Escape behaviors are not an explicit focus for group DBT because of the sensitive nature of many of the behaviors. The next and more general goal of the group after addressing the severe therapy-interfering behaviors is to reduce behavioral passivity. For any problem presented by a client, a two-fold response is made. First, the client's distress at this is validated. This often comes as a surprise to the client since many have had repeated experiences, as noted above in describing the invalidating environment, of being told that either they had no problem or that they should not let it bother them. Secondly, the client is asked how she might solve it, that is, how the skills that are being taught might be applied to it. The notion that the therapist expects the client to do something may come as much of a surprise as the validation; persistence of the therapist is necessary for even small changes in activity to emerge. The explicit tie to the behavioral skills is extremely important, since almost all clients will feel there is no solution. Furthermore, the focus on the process of active problem solving prevents the group from becoming bogged down with crises themselves. In this context, to the degree that a client is willing to discuss the antecedents to escape or parasuicidal behavior that would not be discussed directly, the group can be used to teach and develop alternative coping skills and strategies while promoting active responses.

The fourth goal of individual DBT and the third of group DBT centers on the behavioral skills for interpersonal effectiveness, emotional regulation, distress tolerance, and self-management. In the individual session, the aim is to integrate these skills into the client's daily life and increase the frequency of use. Numerous opportunities for this may present as the therapist deals with the higher priority goals, but if not, the therapist must facilitate progress in coping with problems in the preceding areas. From the stress-diathesis viewpoint (Linehan & Shearin, 1988), an increase in skill knowledge and performance is one major way of preventing a relapse and returning to the self-destructive or quality-of-life destructive behaviors. In the group session, the aim is to introduce the four areas of skills, demonstrate their relevance to typical problems, and facilitate their acquisition by both practice in the group and appropriate homework. As a consequence, most of the group time is focused on what clients attempted to do in coping with the week's problems and how new skills can be applied to current or likely problems.

The fourth and final goal of group DBT is to address the remaining therapy-interfering behaviors of the client and therapist that had been previously ignored. In addition to the ones mentioned for individual therapy, the client behaviors include things such as not responding, sitting facing away from the group, playing with stuffed animals in the group, and other distracting or avoidant behaviors. The therapist behaviors include pushing too hard, invalidation of the client, going too fast over the material, and a stubborn rather than cooperative attitude toward the treatment process. Although these issues are not so severe as to prevent therapy, they reduce its effectiveness and also constitute a handicap in similar settings. This goal is approached for the client by gradually shaping her away from the interfering behaviors and toward more appropriate group functioning. The therapist behaviors are dealt with in supervision as described below.

The fifth and final goal of individual DBT is to focus on client goals. These typically include quality-of-life issues such as getting off welfare and steps toward career development, interpersonal issues such as establishing intimate relationships or working out conflicted family relationships, and intrapersonal issues such as ameliorating the effects of past traumas including rape or childhood physical and sexual abuse. This final goal is again not an explicit one in the group treatment, but many client goals lend themselves to the application of the behavioral skills. To the degree that such application is possible, both client satisfaction with treatment and progress toward individual goals and skill acquisition are enhanced.

If parasuicidal and therapy-interfering behaviors have ceased, the focus in each individual therapy session is usually determined by the wants and needs of the client. The emphasis on escape behaviors and integrating skills can generally be merged with attention to the client's issues. As noted before, however, if higher priority target behaviors have not stopped, the time constraints are such that goals important to the client may be slighted. This outcome makes explicit the DBT contingency that parasuicidal behavior must stop, and the client must actively engage in therapy so that she can get on with her life. This is the fundamental dialectic, that acceptance of current life (rather than rejection by parasuicide and other avoidant behaviors) must precede its change. With progression in treatment leading to the joint cessation of destructive behaviors and acquisition of coping skills, a stable therapeutic stage has been set for the generally long-term exploration and resolution of the client goals.

Factors Affecting Treatment

Setting

For group DBT, a university clinic classroom has been well received as the therapy setting. In early pilot sessions, space in a county psychiatric hospital was used and was uniformly disliked by the clients who said that it reminded them of their hospitalizations. The switch to the nonhospital setting resulted in the group therapists reporting decreased problems with attendance and greater client satisfaction with the group. Given the aversive experiences in psychiatric hospitals that many borderline clients report and the equivocal outcomes of such hospitalizations (Hargreaves &

Shumway, 1987), the differential effect of these settings is understandable and should be a consideration for such a psychoeducational group.

The therapist's clinical practice office has routinely been the setting for individual DBT sessions and has generally been satisfactory. For a few adolescent clients who were highly ambivalent regarding therapy, however, flexibility in setting has been extremely important for therapy retention. Out-of-office sessions in places such as bowling alleys and cars were helpful in continuing contact through difficult phases. The same end might have been accomplished by simply remaining in touch until the adolescent would come for an office appointment, but with a research limit of four consecutive absences, this was not practical. It is also possible that such alternative meeting places are a more natural environment for some adolescents and as much as they can tolerate in the midst of the traumas in their lives.

Another important setting for DBT is the telephone call. Clients are encouraged to call their individual therapists when confronted with stressful situations, subject to the limits of the therapist (see *Contingency Strategies* below). The main DBT goal in encouraging these calls is to facilitate *in vivo* practice of coping skills. Thus, a telephone call is treated as a chance to reduce behavioral passivity, and the same two-step sequence of validation and problem solving described earlier under the group goals is employed. Also, for clients who frequently miss sessions, telephone calls are a means of both maintaining contact and disrupting the clients' avoidant patterns. To avoid the reinforcement of parasuicidal behavior, however, telephone calls are discouraged following self-harm (see discussion of telephone calls under *Contingency Strategies*).

Client Characteristics

A variety of client characteristics were factors in the ease of treatment. A quality needed to participate in group therapy was the ability to control hostility towards others. Groups with an overtly hostile member were greatly handicapped given the usual client combination of high emotional sensitivity and behavioral passivity. Other important characteristics were a local residence and the abilities to commit voluntarily to therapy for a year and to commit to the elimination of parasuicidal behaviors. Clients who did not live in the immediate area or who had to move to the area for therapy were more likely to terminate early. Court-ordered clients who would not agree to remain in therapy without the court order were also more likely to drop out once the order was removed. Since the primary goal of therapy was the elimination of parasuicidal behaviors, a commitment to work toward that was essential to even begin therapy. As noted above, age was sometimes an index of the readiness for therapy. Given that many clients presented a high degree of difficulty, however, it is difficult to say whether or not age itself was an important factor.

As part of the research criteria, clients were screened for active psychosis and organic mental disorders or deficits such as cerebral palsy. For a nonresearch application of DBT, this would be needed only to the degree that significant cognitive impairments such as inability to attend to or grasp somewhat abstract concepts would prevent these types of clients from benefiting from the group. The presence of drug or alcohol dependency was not grounds for exclusion except in cases where the client also wanted to be in a drug treatment program or could not benefit from other treatment before the dependency was eliminated. Since no other professional treatment was allowed at the same time for the research subjects, this was an exclusion criterion if drug treatment was ongoing or scheduled. For a nonresearch application of DBT, there is no evidence that this restriction would be necessary. For clients who were parasuicidal only when consuming drugs or alcohol, or whose lives were dominated by drugs, however, drug treatment was viewed as the treatment of choice.

Therapist Characteristics

The most important therapist characteristics for effective DBT include: compassion, sensitivity, willingness to admit and repair errors, comfort with ambiguity and paradox, flexibility, patience with frustration and extremely slow progress, and therapeutic skill (Linehan, 1989). Compassion and sensitivity are essential to deal with clients who are as sensitive to emotional and environmental stimuli, while simultaneously as constricted and limited in emotional expression, as most BPD individuals. Without these qualities, a therapist is always two steps behind the frequently very subtle reactions of clients to therapist statements, remarks of other group members, and internal or environmental cues. Although a major effort is devoted to teaching clients the skills to identify and verbalize emotions, in the earlier stages of treatment, the therapist who cannot come very close to mind reading is likely to believe that BPD clients deliberately sabotage therapy with capricious behavior. Therapists so lacking are also at greater risk of perceiving the behaviors of clients who are experiencing fear and helplessness as hostile and attacking. The consequences of these mis- or unperceived reactions for therapist attitudes about BPD clients and the therapeutic relationship are generally very negative.

Given the odds of making a mistake in the light of the preceding discussion, an overall willingness to admit and repair mistakes made in the course of the therapeutic relationship is essential. Put another way, in such a complex and difficult therapeuic endeavor, some mistakes are inevitable; what the therapist does afterwards is a better index of good therapy. Whether the mistake was smiling at the wrong moment and being perceived as mocking rather than warm, getting into power struggles, or becoming impatient with the client's slow progress and then rejecting her by not returning telephone calls and behaving coldly, the effective therapist must be able to acknowledge such actions as errors. Higher-functioning clients might be able to experience simultaneously both trust in the therapist and painful affect arising from some therapist's actions and thus not require as much "repair" work. BPD clients are not likely to be in this category, however, and the therapist becomes identified with other abusive individuals in their lives. Without therapist validation of their experience and active attempts to problem solve the situation, the therapeutic relationship becomes for the BPD client one more mistaken trust, one more failed relationship that either must be fled or hopelessly endured.

Since the dialectical emphasis in DBT is large, a therapist must be comfortable with the ambiguity and paradox inherent in DBT strategies. Individuals who need black and white conceptualizations, goals, or methods are likely to experience DBT as dissonant when confronted with the dialectic inherent in actions to control clients' destructive behaviors while also promoting growth, autonomy, and independence. Furthermore, a therapist must be patient with both frustration at clients' rejection of seemingly appropriate interventions and progress that may appear glacial. Flexibility in strategies and timing is key to any progress.

Finally, therapist skills are an important characteristic in effective therapy. Components of these skills include both the ability to conceptualize parasuicidal behavior and BPD in a dialectical manner, and the verbal and emotional skills to implement effectively the techniques described below as treatment strategies. Among the verbal and emotional skills must be the ability to simultaneously express warmth and control in the therapy settings. Much of the control in changing client behavior is achieved through the use of the relationship; without a significant level of concurrent warmth, the therapist will probably be experienced as hostile and demanding rather than caring and controlling. The distinctions and therapeutic issues involved in all these skills are likely to be overly complex for inexperienced therapists.

Supervision Issues

Supervision for both individual and group therapists is extremely important for DBT with BPD clients. For experienced licensed therapists accustomed to practicing independently, this may sound as if their qualifications are questioned. It is not. We believe that experienced therapists who have been trained in DBT to work with this population know how to perform the therapy effectively. Major issues that DBT supervision addresses are what therapists feel like doing in any given week and how well they are able to sort out the often complicated issues arising in the course of therapy. Even with an appropriate observation of limits, the lack of progress, therapist stress, and the demands of highly distressed clients in crisis are sufficient on occasion to blunt the caring of the most committed therapists. Furthermore, personal issues are often a factor, and the stress of difficult clients only exacerbates their impact. For the average therapist who is not striving for sainthood, the combination of these occasions can be all too frequent. Supervision provides a setting in which the therapist's frustrations can be appropriately voiced and in which client difficulties with the therapist can be heard from a different perspective. Additionally, issues can be problem solved, and the therapist reinforced for such a difficult undertaking.

Effective formats for supervision include group supervision to coordinate treatment between individual and group therapists and supervision in pairs to deal with issues more specific to individual therapy. An important factor is the presence of two or more people. Since dialectical issues are by definition relational, more than one person is generally needed to conceptualize and plan the therapy process and is certainly needed for a dialectical treatment of the therapist's issues with the client. The fundamental dialectic, that change is possible only with acceptance, is a basic supervision guideline. The role of the supervisor or others is to balance in time the therapist's emphasis on acceptance versus change. Another basic guideline is to promote compassion in the therapist's understanding of the client. To this end, the least prejudicial theory consistent with the behavior is advanced. In the many situations where the "true cause" of a behavior cannot be determined, an important part of DBT is to choose the explanation that will raise the likelihood of the therapist liking the client. For example, aggressive behavior is therefore more likely to be explained in DBT as arising from fear and hopelessness rather than malicious intent, manipulation, or "game-playing." Finally, the therapist's issues and difficulties are validated as well as problem solved.

Treatment Strategies

DBT is further defined by eight coordinated sets of activities, or strategies, which are employed by therapists in obtaining the goals described above. These strategies can be characterized by their relative emphasis on acceptance versus change; they are combined as needed to deal with specific problem situations. Not all strategies may be necessary or appropriate for any given session, and the pertinent combination may change over time. These are more fully described in the treatment manual (Linehan, 1984).

Dialectical Strategies

The principal dialectic is that change occurs in the context of acceptance of life as it is. The role of the therapist is to facilitate growth by bringing out the opposites appearing both in therapy and the client's life and guiding the client through synthesis after synthesis. The underlying rule is that for any statement, an opposite can be made. The emphasis on opposites is frequently over time rather than simultaneously, however. Thus, change may be facilitated by emphasizing acceptance, and acceptance by emphasizing change. The wisdom of this with BPD individuals was noted much earlier by Sherman (1961, cited in Seltzer, 1986) who commented that "whichever side the therapist aligns himself with, the patient will usually feel impelled to leave" (p, 55). Conversely, a rigid adherence to either pole of a dialectic leads to increased tension between therapist and client and decreased reconciliation and synthesis.

In addition to the focus on the dialectic in the therapist–client relationship, an explicit focus is also made on the promotion of dialectical thinking. This differs somewhat from the usual cognitive-behavioral approach, which primarily emphasizes formal, empirical logic. Empirical logic is not ignored, especially in problem solving, but it is treated as only one way to think. Specific techniques that target the therapist–client relationship and dialectical thinking follow.

Foot in the Door. This technique relates to dysfunctional beliefs that the client has expressed or problematic rules that she appears to be following. The therapist presents an extreme version of such a statement or rule and then plays the role of devil's advocate to counter client attempts to disprove the statement or rule. An example of such a client belief might be "I can't say (or do) that if anyone will be offended." The therapist might proceed by pointing out the millions of individuals around the world, a few of whom known to the client, who would be offended by such action, or indeed, any action the client might take. Anything the client proposes can be countered by this hypothesized audience until the ridiculousness of the belief becomes apparent.

Yes and No. The therapist continually stresses to the client that things can both be true and not true, that answers can be both yes and no. Rather than being drawn into one side to the exclusion of the other, the therapist emphasizes the validity of both answers. When using this, the therapist does not have to clear up the client's confusion about how both yes and no can coexist. As the client becomes more comfortable with dialectical thinking, the confusion will lessen.

Confronting Evaluations. Basic to confronting evaluations are the tenets that all evaluations are relative and a property of the evaluator rather than of the evaluated. These confrontations are necessary to deal with BPD clients' tendencies to make evaluations of events and then respond to the evaluations as if they were real, absolute properties of the events. The therapist's role is to help the client see when she is making an evaluation and also to see that this is a relative judgment. What is perceived as good or beautiful can also be bad or ugly. The previous foot-in-the-door technique can be helpful in seeing the relativity of judgments. The DBT emphasis is therefore to think nonjudgmental whenever possible. The therapist must be open, however, for the times when judgments are necessary and helpful.

Identifying and Testing Cognitive Extremes and Absolutes. We have reviewed elsewhere (Linehan & Shearin, 1988) the literature indicating that suicidal individuals think in terms of absolutes and extremes. This is always a failure in dialectical thinking, and when the evidence does not fit the conclusions drawn, it is also a failure in logical thinking. The task of the therapist is to help the client identify when she is thinking in absolutes and extremes and to help her test the validity of her thinking. A dialectical style is very important here, for the therapist must help the client expand her cognitive options rather than prove her wrong. Therefore, validation of existing viewpoints is important when suggesting that others are possible.

Myth and Parables. Parables or myths are alternative means of teaching dialectical thinking. Ones from which multiple meanings can be drawn are usually the most effective in encouraging different views of reality. The use of analogy and story telling is extremely important in DBT, since it encourages both client and therapist to look for and create alternate meanings and points of reference for events under scrutiny.

Problem-Solving Strategies

Problem solving with borderline clients is a difficult two-stage process. The first stage focuses on acceptance and employs both insight and behavioral analysis strategies, whereas the second targets change through solution analysis and environmental intervention. The dialectical view that change can only occur in the context of acceptance takes on concrete meaning when clients find the existence of some problems too painful to acknowledge. The DBT therapist must initially deal with the client's tendencies to view all problems at one moment as self-generated and therefore avoid any examination thereof because of the pain and guilt involved, and at another moment, to shift to the opposite extreme and view everyone else as the exclusive source of problems. Repeated attempts to deal with both the misconceptions leading to these positions and the emotions involved may be necessary before the client can acknowledge the existence of some problems. The irreverent communication and validation strategies described below are helpful to this end without reinforcing suicidal behavior.

Furthermore, the situation is usually complicated by the difficulty of identifying the problem(s) causing the distress that has precipitated suicidal or other maladaptive behaviors. This first stage of the problem-solving process proceeds with teaching the client to use parasuicide and other dysfunctional responses as an indication that a problem needs to be solved. A thorough behavioral analysis of these responses is then conducted. Minute attention is paid to each detail in the chain of events leading to the dysfunctional events including the reciprocal interaction between the environment and the clients' cognitive, emotional, and behavioral responses. Hypotheses regarding the putative controlling variables are generated and evaluated jointly. This strategy is repeated over time for every instance of parasuicide until the client achieves an understanding of the stimulus–response patterns involved (the insight strategy).

The second stage begins with the generation, evaluation, and implementation of alternative solutions that might have been made or could be made in the future. At this point numerous other strategies (described in the following sections) may be necessary. If it becomes clear that the client does not have the necessary skills to cope effectively with the problem, the therapist employs the capability-enhancement strategies. If the client has the needed skills but is inaccurate in the prediction of current environmental response contingencies or contingencies that favor dysfunctional over functional behaviors, the therapist uses contingency strategies. Sometimes the therapist must use the consultant strategy to enable the client to elicit needed help such as hospitalization, medication, or financial support from other community professionals. If issues in the therapist–client relationship are the problem source, the relationship strategies are employed. Finally, environmental intervention by the therapist may be needed to effect immediate changes which the client cannot yet produce.

Irreverent Communication Strategy

After the dialectical strategies, the irreverent communication strategy is the most likely to be perceived as paradoxical by the client. In employing this strategy with dysfunctional problem-solving behaviors such as suicidal, therapy-interfering, and other escape behaviors, the therapist takes a rather irreverent, matter-of-fact attitude toward *past* occurrences of these. These instances are accepted as a normal consequence of the individual's learning history and current factors operating in her life. This often comes as a surprise to the client for whom the behaviors have usually elicited a significant community response in the past. In contrast, however, the suffering that accompanied these events is never treated with an indifferent attitude (see the validation strategies). A therapist must be careful to differentiate between a particular behavior and the emotional state preceding it. Used judiciously, this strategy facilitates problem solving the events precipitating the distress without reinforcing the suicidal or other problematic behavior that was a consequence of it.

Consultant Strategy

In DBT, the therapist is a consultant for the client, not for other professionals who deal with the client. Mental health professionals are viewed as any other person in the client's life. Thus, if a client has a problem with another professional, the role of the DBT therapist is to problem solve with the client rather than the professional. The goal is to teach the client, not other professionals, effective skills for dealing with her environment. If the DBT therapist is contacted directly by other professionals, they are advised to follow their normal procedures.

Two exceptions arise for this rule. A direct intervention is made when substantial harm may come to the client from professionals who will not modify their treatment of the client unless a high-power person intervenes. Situations involving involuntary commitment and public assistance are instances in which this may be necessary. The second exception as noted above under supervison is the coordination of individual and group therapists. The differences in therapists' points of view that have traditionally led to staff splitting with borderline clients are treated as equally valid poles of a dialectic. Therapists' disagreements over a client are seen as failures in synthesis and interpersonal process rather than as a client problem.

Finally, the client's family is not seen as an exception for the consultant strategy. If the therapist thinks communication with the client's family might be helpful in resolving certain problems, particularly for younger clients, the proposal is advanced as would any other solution to a problem as something the client must choose and direct. This means that although the therapist helps the client understand the reactions of significant others, the therapist's contract is always with the client, not others. Although this approach is consistent with behavior therapy in general, it may seem somewhat inconsistent with the general systems view of DBT as it might be applied to adolescent clients. However, it is a practical limit imposed by the extremely abusive backgrounds of many of the clients.

Validation Strategies

The gist of the validation strategies is a three-step process for the active validation of client emotions, thoughts, and behaviors by the therapist and the communication thereof. The therapist first helps the client identify the response patterns in which she engages. Then the therapist communicates hearing and/or observing accurately the client's response (emotions, thoughts, perceptions, or actions). Lastly, the therapist communicates that even though information may not be available to explain all the relevant causes, the client's feelings and behavioral responses make perfect sense in the context of the client's current experience and life to date. These strategies lead the therapist to search the client's responses for their inherent validity and functionality before any consideration of a more functional approach. In contrast, the usual cognitive-therapy approach is to search for and either immediately replace dysfunctional processes (Ellis, 1962, 1973) or at least to suggest an experimental test of them (Beck, Rush, Shaw, & Emery, 1979). Although these procedures obviously work for many clients, the severity of the invalidating environment described earlier for BPD clients makes these validating strategies an essential component of DBT. The therapist must function at times for the client as the dialectically opposite pole to such invalidation.

Capability-Enhancement Strategies

Whereas the validation strategies emphasize the acceptance pole of the dialectic, the capability-enhancement strategies emphasize the change pole. During the employment of these strategies, the therapist insists at every opportunity that the client actively engage in the acquisition and practice of skills needed to cope with her life. The therapist directly, forcefully, and repeatedly challenges the borderline client's passive problem-solving style. Acting as a teacher, the therapist employs the full repertory of behavioral skill-acquisition techniques described in standard behavior therapy texts (e.g., Goldfried & Davison, 1976; Kendall & Hollon, 1979) and the DBT treatment manual (Linehan, 1984).

Relationship Strategies

The therapist–client relationship is, as implied before, the basis of DBT. It has a dual role in being so. As in behavior therapy and many other therapies, the relationship is the vehicle through which the therapist can effect the therapy (Arnkoff, 1983; Beck et al., 1979; Langs, 1977, 1982). Also as in behavior therapy and other therapies, the relationship in DBT is also the therapy. In this sense, however, the view of the relationship is close to Rogerian and other humanistic approaches (Rice, 1983). There is a dialectical tension between these two views. The latter implies that the therapy will be successful if the therapist can be a certain way, in this case, compassionate, sensitive, flexible, nonjudgmental, accepting, and patient. With the provision of a relationship having these qualities, the wounds of past experiences will heal, developmental deficiencies will be rectified, and the client's innate potential and capability for growth will be stimulated. Control over behavior and the course of therapy in general is seen as residing primarily with the client. In contrast, when the relationship is used as the vehicle to bring about therapy, the therapist controls therapy with the consent of the client. The relationship then is just the means to an end, a way of having sufficient contact and leverage with the client to cause change and growth. In this view, wounds heal only because of active exposure of the client to similar but benign situations, deficiencies are rectified by the acquisition of coping strategies, and growth occurs because it is made more rewarding than other alternatives.

In DBT, a dialectic is thus intrinsic in the relationship; the therapist must choose an appropriate balance between these two approaches for each moment. The relationship as therapy facilitates both acceptance of the client as she is and autonomy. Therapy through the relationship facilitates therapist control of behavior that the client cannot control and acquisition of skills previously unknown or insufficiently generalized.

Before either can proceed, however, there must be a therapist–client relationship. Therefore, one of the goals of the initial phase of therapy is quickly to develop the client–therapist attachment. Means of achieving this include: the emphasis on validation of the client's affective, cognitive, and behavioral experiences, the clarity of the contract (ending self-harm and building a life worth living), the focus on therapy-interfering behavior, outreach and availability through telephone calls, and problem solving of feelings regarding the relationship. Through these, the therapist nurtures the client's feelings of attachment and trust. Equally important, however, is the therapist's attachment to the client. If the therapist feels ambivalence or dislike for the client, this will be communicated through omissions, if not direct actions, and the relationship will suffer. Resolution is facilitated by the focus on self-harm (which will reduce therapist stress), therapy-interfering behaviors, and feelings about the relationship as well as supervision.

The intensity of the client–therapist relationship is different for individual versus group therapy. In order to make the time requirements for the group therapists feasible with their larger numbers of clients, the relationship in group therapy is not stressed to the same degree as in individual DBT. Telephone calls to or from group therapists are limited to issues surrounding attendance and the group. All other calls except in a backup situation are directed to the individual therapist. Relationships in the groups are also more distributed by the encouragement of group members to provide limited concrete support for each other outside of the group (such as going for a walk or sharing a meal or movie). Nevertheless, the client–therapist attachment is still quite important and must receive the same kinds of attention described above. As in individual therapy, the relationship may be the only therapeutic ingredient that keeps the client alive at times.

The relationship strategies are divided into six groups that focus respectively on relationship acceptance, reciprocal vulnerability, and relationship enhancement, problem solving, generalization, and contingency. The first two strategies are at the acceptance pole of the acceptance-change dialectic, whereas the remaining four are change-oriented. Unless the dialectical philosophy of DBT is held clearly in mind, the presence of such opposite techniques as relationship acceptance and relationship contingency in the same set of strategies will seem paradoxical indeed.

Relationship acceptance focuses on the process of the therapist's accepting the client–therapist relationship as it currently is at each moment. This includes an explicit acceptance of the stage of therapeutic progress or lack thereof. In addition to the therapist characteristics described before, a high tolerance for criticism and hostile affect as well as an ability to maintain a nonjudgmental, behavioral approach are extremely important for relationship acceptance. Reciprocal vulnerability involves the therapist's using his or her own personal experiences, either outside or within the therapy setting, as tools for therapy. For example, the therapist may share with the client in a nonjudgmental way the effect of the client's behavior on the therapist. The appropriate moments for this approach are the times when the therapist anticipates or is experiencing a negative client reaction to every possible intervention. Rather than engage in a power struggle with the client, the therapist accepts the situation and in a matter-of-fact way makes his or her own feelings of frustration or impotence part of the agenda to be discussed. Another approach in this situation would be for the therapist to share times when he or she has struggled with the same issue.

The relationship-enhancement strategy involves a focus on creating a strong client–therapist relationship. The techniques described earlier for initially developing the client–therapist relationship are basic to this end. Additionally, the therapist must clarify for the client what she can realistically expect from both the therapist and the treatment and must remain sensitive to moments when the client appears to be operating on the basis of unrealistic and probably unverbalized expectations of the therapist. The therapist needs to communicate an understanding of how the client could arrive at unrealistic expectations and, where appropriate, validate the client's need for such a relationship. The relationship problem-solving strategy is applicable when the relationship is a source of problems for either member. Unhappiness, dissatisfaction, or anger at the therapist on the part of the client or the therapist's frustration are treated as signals that the relationship needs problem-solving attention. The relationship generalization strategy is also involved as the therapist models how to work out difficult interpersonal problems in the context of a "real" relationship (Linehan, 1988). Although there are many differences between a therapeutic relationship and a "real" one, the therapist uses times of relationship problem solving to explore the similarities with relationships in the client's life and how analogous approaches in those might be productive.

The relationship contingency strategy involves the use of the contingencies inherent in the client's attachment to the therapist as the motivation for behavioral changes for which there is little or even negative reinforcement in the patient's environment (the complexity and difficulty involved in this approach are suggested by its informal label of the "blackmail" strategy). Behaviors in this category include ending parasuicide and getting off public assistance rolls. Three conditions are essential to the successful use of this strategy. Most obviously, there must be a strong client–therapist relationship. Second, both the therapist and client must be clear that the behavioral change is for the greater welfare of the client and not just for the convenience of the therapist. To achieve this clarity with the client, the therapist may have to appeal to the client's "wise" sense of what is best for her. Third, the client must have the capability to make the change. Other conditions are very important but impossible for us to state in specifics. The therapist must know the client very well, since the exact nature of the contingency depends greatly on the particular client. With some clients, conditional warmth may be key, but with others, this might be harmful. Furthermore, therapist skill is crucial, since mistakes in either timing or exact wording can have disastrous effects. We describe the technique here primarily to note its existence and importance within the therapy rather than to provide guidelines for its use.

Contingency Strategies

The contingency strategies contain both the clarification of contingencies operating within therapy and the exploration of contingencies in the client's external environment. The first incorporates what can be expected from the therapist and the treatment as noted above in the relationship strategies as well as the requirements for therapy. The latter includes giving information on what factors are known to influence behavior in general and theories and data that might be relevant to a particular client's behavior patterns. The overall contingency approach requires the therapist to tailor responses to the degree possible to reinforce adaptive, nonsuicidal behaviors while at the same time to extinguish maladaptive and harmful behaviors. Because of the life threatening nature of suicidal behavior, this is necessarily a delicate and somewhat hazardous balance as the therapist attempts neither to reinforce suicidal responses excessively nor ignore them in such a manner that the client escalates to a life-threatening level. The DBT approach requires the therapist to take some short-term risks to achieve long-term gains.

One specific instance of this application is the telephone protocol for parasuicidal behavior. The client is told in the first session to call before she reaches the point of harming herself rather than after and that she does not have to be suicidal in order to call. The generally reinforcing nature of any call is explained, and the prohibition of calls following self-injury is explained as arising both from the therapist's caring for the client as well as his or her ethical requirement to perform good therapy. To be consistent with both, the therapist must reinforce adaptive rather than maladaptive coping. The client is requested to call the crisis center or 911 if necessary to secure aid following self-injury. If the client does call the therapist following parasuicide, the interaction is limited to the time necessary to determine the medical risk of the injury. If there is none, the call is ended. If the client does not agree to seek needed medical attention or is incapable, the therapist should call the appropriate agency after informing the client of the intent. The goal is to shape the client toward asking for help while the problems are still manageable. To this end, the therapist must be careful to provide similar time and attention for less crisis-oriented moments as for peak suicidal periods.

With the considerable effort that is needed for relationships with BPD clients, therapists must both be aware of and observe their own limits. The word "observe" is used rather than "set" to imply a flexible and internal rather than arbitrary external standard for limits. Since DBT encourages rather than prohibits telephone contact, the therapists themselves must determine at what hours they can be available. Therapists who cannot accept any after-hours telephone calls probably should not have BPD clients. Beyond that, both individual client and therapist needs as well as short-term issues must be considered in determining an appropriate telephone policy. The therapist who has never placed some restrictions on telephone calls (if only that the client cannot call just to chat at 2 a.m.) has either never had a needy client or is headed for burnout and rejection of the client. In DBT, such necessary limits are explained, not as if they are good for the client, but rather as necessary in the long run for the therapist to continue to perform effective therapy. The distress and need of the client in the face of therapist limits are validated and treated as legitimate problems to be solved; the therapist's limits are seen as unfortunate and at odds with the client's needs. Therapists must be comfortable with such a dialetic in observing their limits.

Summary

In the preceding sections, we have described dialectical behavior therapy, a psychotherapy developed by Linehan and her associates for parasuicidal clients with a diagnosis of borderline personality disorder. DBT relies heavily on a dialectical format for both its theory of BPD and its methods of therapy. Consistent with behavior therapy in general, the therapy is organized around a hierarchy of behavioral goals that vary according to the mode of therapy. The individual therapy targets range from the elimination of dysfunctional behaviors to the facilitation of individual client goals, whereas the concurrent psychoeducational group spends the greatest amount of time on the teaching of more adaptive skills for interpersonal effectiveness, emotion regulation, and distress tolerance. Each therapy mode places more explicit emphasis than behavior therapy in general on the client–therapist relationship, both as a means of therapy and as the therapy itself. Techniques for achieving the specific goals are clustered into eight sets of strategies that are both acceptance- and change-oriented

Dialectical behavior therapy represents one approach to how paradoxical techniques can be conceptualized and integrated into behavior therapy. Our preference has been to emphasize the dialectical viewpoint that we believe both provides a theoretical basis for such techniques and, in addition, captures some fundamental aspects of psychotherapy. These include the puzzling relationship of acceptance to change, the variety of ways in which a relationship appears to facilitate change, and the multiple views of reality that may be held by the parties engaged in a therapeutic enterprise. The shifting and inclusive emphasis of the dialectical approach is also consistent with both systemic views of behavior and perspectives emphasizing multiple causation. Although the specific targets of DBT are appropriate primarily for suicidal borderline clients, a dialectical approach may have more general utility for psychotherapy.

Of the many aspects of DBT described above, we believe one of the most important is the emphasis on compassion and nonpejorative conceptualization. Although this ought be important for any treatment population, several reasons make it especially so in this case. For clients as challenging as most BPD individuals, such emphasis is critical for the therapeutic relationship and the motivation of the therapist. Additionally, until we have therapies that can more efficiently reduce the suffering of these clients, compassion toward the client needs to be fundamental in any approach.

Although compassion is emphasized, the needs of the therapist as a human being are also focal in DBT. Major portions of the therapy are devoted to the development of flexible, realistic limits to the therapeutic effort and to the recognition and resolution of problems within the client-therapist relationship. A basic tenet of DBT is that even the most committed therapist has circumstances under which he or she will reject the client. As a consequence, supervision plays a greater role in DBT than is probably typical in most independent therapy practices.

We recognize that whereas no chapter on psychotherapy can contain enough detail to serve as a basis for practice, the added issues and risks in working with a parasuicidal borderline population make this one particulary inappropriate as a treatment manual. With that limitation understood, however, we hope this may at least provide a fresh viewpoint on both the disorder and some possible ways of approaching it in the beginning phases of treatment.

Acknowledgments

Preparation of this article was supported in part by National Institute of Mental Health Grant MH34486 to Marsha Linehan.

References

Adams, H. J., & Durham, L. (1977). A dialectical base for an activist approach to counseling. In E. I. Rawlings & D. K. Carter (Eds.), *Psychotherapy for women* (pp. 411–428). Springfield, IL: Charles C. Thomas.

American Psychiatric Association. (1987). *Diagnostic and statistical manual of mental disorders* (3rd ed.—rev.). Washington, DC: American Psychiatric Association.

Andolfi, M. (1979). Redefinition in family therapy. *American Journal of Family Therapy, 7,* 5–15.

Arnkoff, D. B. (1983). Common and specific factors in cognitive therapy. In M. J. Lambert (Ed.), *A guide to psychotherapy and patient relationships* (pp. 85–125). Homewood, IL: Dorsey.

Basseches, M. (1984). *Dialectical thinking and adult development.* Norwood, NJ: Ablex.

Beck, A. T., Rush, A. J., Shaw, B. F., & Emery, G. (1979). *Cognitive therapy of depression.* New York: The Guilford Press.

Chase, J. L., Shea, S. J., & Dougherty, F. I. (1984). The use of paradoxical interventions within a prison psychiatric facility. *Psychotherapy, 21,* 278–281.

Coleman, M. L. (1956). Externalization of the toxic introject: A treatment technique for borderline cases. *Psychoanalytic Review, 43,* 235–242.

Coleman, M. L., & Nelson, B. (1957). Paradigmatic psychotherapy in borderline treatment. *Psychoanalysis, 5,* 28–44.

Derryberry, D., & Rothbart, M. (1984). Emotion, attention, and temperament. In C. Izard, J. Kagan, & R. Zajonc (Eds.), *Emotions, cognition and behavior* (pp. 132–166). Cambridge: Cambridge University Press.

Dyer, J. A. T., & Kreitman, N. (1984). Hopelessness, depression and suicidal intent in parasuicide. *British Journal of Psychiatry, 144,* 127–133.

Eliasz, A. (1985). Mechanisms of temperament: Basic functions. In J. Strelau, F. H. Farley, & A. Gale (Eds.), *The biological bases of personality and behavior: Theories, measurement techniques, and development* (pp. 45–49). Washington, DC: Hemisphere.

Ellis, A. (1962). *Reason and emotion in psychotherapy.* New York: Stuart.

Ellis, A. (1973). *Humanistic psychology: The rational emotive approach.* New York: Julian Press.

Fay, A. (1978). *Making things better by making them worse.* New York: Hawthorn.

Firestone, S. (1970). *The dialectic of sex: The case for feminist revolution.* New York: Bantam Books.

Frances, A., Fyer, M., & Clarkin, J. F. (1986). Personality and suicide. *Annals of the New York Academy of Sciences, 487,* 281–293.

Frankl, V. E. (1975). Paradoxical intention and dereflection. *Psychotherapy: Theory, Research, and Practice, 12,* 226–237.

Goldberg, C. (1980). The utilization and limitations of paradoxical intervention in group psychotherapy. *International Journal of Group Psychotherapy, 30,* 287–297.

Goldfried, M., & Davison, G. (1976). *Clinical behavior therapy.* New York: Holt, Rinehart & Winston.

Gunderson, J. F. (1984). *Borderline personality disorder.* Washington, DC: American Psychiatric Press.

Gunderson, J. F., & Elliott, G. R. (1985). The interface between borderline personality disorder and affective disorder. *American Journal of Psychiatry, 142,* 277–288.

Gunderson, J. F., & Kolb, J. E. (1978). Discriminating features of borderline patients. *American Journal of Psychiatry, 135,* 792–796.

Gunderson, J. F., Kolb, J. E., & Austin, Y. (1981). The diagnostic interview for borderline patients. *American Journal of Psychiatry, 138,* 896–903.

Haley, J. (1973). *Uncommon therapy: The psychiatric techniques of Milton H. Erickson, M.D.* New York: Norton.

Hargreaves, W. A., & Shumway, M. (1987, February). Effectiveness of services for the severely mentally ill. Paper presented at the National Institute for Mental Health Conference, *The future of mental health services research,* Tampa, FL.

Hellman, I. D., Morrison, T. L., & Abramowitz, S. I. (1986). The stresses of psychotherapeutic work: A replication and extension. *Journal of Clinical Psychology, 42,* 197–205.

Kastenbaum, R. J. (1969). Death and bereavement in later life. In A. H. Kutscher (Ed.), *Death and bereavement* (pp. 28–54). Springfield, IL: Charles C. Thomas.

Kendall, P. C., & Hollon, S. D. (Eds.). (1979). *Cognitive-behavioral interventions: Theory, research, and procedures.* New York: Academic Press.

Kernberg, O. F. (1984). *Severe personality disorders: Psychotherapeutic strategies.* New Haven: Yale University Press.

Kreitman, N. (1977). *Parasuicide.* Chichester, UK: John Wiley & Sons.

Kuhn, T. S. (1970). *The structure of scientific revolutions* (2nd ed.). Chicago: University of Chicago Press.

Langs, R. (1977). *The therapeutic interaction: A synthesis.* New York: Jason Aronson.

Langs, R. (1982). *Psychotherapy: A basic text.* New York: Jason Aronson.

Leff, J. P., & Vaughn, C. (1985). *Expressed emotion in families: Its significance for mental illness.* New York: The Guilford Press.

Levins, R., & Lewontin, R. (1985). *The dialectical biologist.* Cambridge, MA: Harvard University Press.

Linehan, M. M. (1979). Structured cognitive-behavioral treatment of assertion problems. In P. C. Kendall & S. D. Hollon (Eds.), *Cognitive-behavioral interventions: Theory, research, and procedures* (pp. 205–240). New York: Academic Press.

Linehan, M. M. (1981). A social-behavioral analysis of suicide and parasuicide: Implications for clinical assessment and treatment. In H. G. Glazer & J. F. Clarkin (Eds.), *Depression: Behavioral and directive intervention strategies* (pp. 229–294). New York: Garland Press.

Linehan, M. M. (1984). *Dialectical behavior therapy for treatment of parasuicidal women. Treatment manual.* Unpublished manuscript, University of Washington, Seattle.

Linehan, M. M. (1987a, November). Behavioral treatment of suicidal clients meeting criteria for borderline personality disorder. In A. T. Beck (Chair), *Cognitive and behavioral approaches to suicide.* Symposium conducted at the annual convention of the Association for Advancement of Behavior Therapy, Boston.

Linehan, M. M. (1987b). Dialectical behavior therapy for borderline personality disorder: Theory and method. *Bulletin of the Menninger Clinic, 51,* 261–276.

Linehan, M. M. (1987c). Dialectical behavior therapy in groups: Treating borderline personality disorders and suicidal behavior. In C. M. Brody (Ed.), *Women's therapy groups: Paradigms of feminist treatment* (pp. 145–162). New York: Springer.

Linehan, M. M. (1988). Perspectives on the interpersonal relationship in behavior therapy. *Journal of Integrative and Eclectic Psychotherapy, 7,* 278–290.

Linehan, M. M. (1989). Cognitive and behavior therapies in borderline personality disorder. In E. Tasman (Ed.), *American Psychiatric Press Review of Psychiatry, 8,* 84–102.

Linehan, M. M., & Shearin, E. N. (1988). Lethal stress: A social-behavioral model of suicidal behavior. In S. Fisher & J. Reason (Eds.), *Handbook of life stress, cognition, and health* (pp. 265–285). Chichester, UK: John Wiley and Sons.

Linehan, M. M., & Wagner, A. W. (in press). Dialectical behavior therapy: A feminist-behavioral treatment of borderline personality disorder. *the Behavior Therapist.*

Linehan, M. M., & Wasson, E. J. (in press). Behavior therapy for borderline personality disorder. In A. S. Bellack & M. Hersen (Eds.), *Handbook of comparative treatment.* New York: John Wiley & Sons.

Madanes, C. (1984). *Behind the one-way mirror: Advances in the practice of strategic therapy.* San Francisco: Jossey-Bass.

Main, F. O., & West, J. D. (1987). Sabotaging adolescent depression through paradox. *Individual Psychology, 43,* 185–191.

Marx, K., & Engels, F. (1970). *Selected works* (Vol. III). New York: International Publishers.

McGlashan, T. H. (1983). The borderline syndrome, II: Is it a variant of schizophrenia or affective disorder? *Archives of General Psychiatry, 40,* 1319–1323.

Miller, J. B. (1983). The necessity of conflict. In J. H. Robbins & R. J. Siegel (Eds.), *Women changing therapy* (pp. 3–10). New York: Haworth Press.

Mozdzierz, G. J., Macchitelli, F. J., & Lisiecki, J. (1976). The paradox of psychotherapy: An Adlerian perspective. *Journal of Individual Psychology, 32,* 169–184.

Nelson, M. C. (1962). Effect of paradigmatic techniques on the psychic economy of borderline patients. *Psychiatry, 25,* 119–134.

Perelman, C. H. (1982). *The realm of rhetoric.* Notre Dame, IN: University of Notre Dame Press.

Pope, H. G., Jonas, J. M., Hudson, J. I., Cohen, B., & Gunderson, J. F. (1983). The validity of DSM-III borderline personality disorder. *Archives of General Psychiatry, 40,* 23–30.

Reiser, D. E., & Levenson, H. (1984). Abuses of the borderline diagnosis: A clinical problem with teaching opportunities. *American Journal of Psychiatry, 141,* 1528–1532.

Rice, L. N. (1983). The relationship in client-centered therapy. In M. J. Lambert (Ed.), *A guide to psychotherapy and patient relationships* (pp. 36–60). Homewood, IL: Dorsey.

Roswell, V. A. (1988). Professional liability: Issues for behavior therapists in the 1980s and 1990s. *the Behavior Therapist, 11,* 163–171.

Scanlon, P. L. (1980). A gestalt approach to insight-oriented treatment. *Social Casework, 61,* 407–415.

Seltzer, L. F. (1986). *Paradoxical strategies in psychotherapy: A comprehensive overview and guidebook.* New York: John Wiley & Sons.

Selye, H. (1956). *The stress of life.* New York: McGraw-Hill.

Sherman, M. H. (1961). Siding with the resistance in paradigmatic psychotherapy. *Psychoanalysis and the Psychoanalytic Review, 48,* 43–59.

Sperry, R. W. (1988). Psychology's mentalist paradigm and the religion/science tension. *American Psychologist, 43,* 607–613.

Staats, A. W. (1975). *Social behaviorism.* Homewood, IL: Dorsey Press.

Stone, M. H. (1980). Borderline conditions: Early definitions and interrelationships. In M. H. Stone (Ed.), *The borderline syndromes* (pp. 1–43). New York: McGraw-Hill.

Strelau, J., Farley, F. H., & Gale, A. (1986). *The biological bases of personality and behavior: Psychophysiology, performance, and applications.* Washington, DC: Hemisphere.

Thomas, A., & Chess, S. (1986). The New York longitudinal study: From infancy to early adult life. In R. Plomin & J. Dunn (Eds.), *The study of temperament: Changes, continuities and challenges* (pp. 39–52). Hillsdale, NJ: Lawrence Erlbaum Associates.

Turkington, C. (1986, March). Limbic responses seen in borderline cases. *APA Monitor, 17.*

Turner, R. M. (1987, November). *A bio-social learning approach to borderline personality disorder.* Paper presented at the annual convention of the Association for Advancement of Behavior Therapy, Boston.

Watts, A. W. (1961). *Psychotherapy east and west.* New York: Pantheon.

Watzlawick, P. (1978). *The language of change: Elements of therapeutic interaction.* New York: Basic Books.

Webster's new collegiate dictionary. (1979). Springfield, MA: G. & C. Merriam Co.

Wells, H. K. (1972). Alienation and dialectical logic. *Kansas Journal of Sociology, 3*(1).

Whitaker, C. A. (1975). Psychotherapy of the absurd: With a special emphasis on the psychotherapy of aggression. *Family Process, 14,* 1–16.

Widiger, T. A., Frances, A., Warner, L., & Bluhm, C. (1986). Diagnostic criteria for the borderline and schizotypal personality disorders. *Journal of Abnormal Psychology, 95,* 43–51.

Chapter 10

Principles and Techniques of Couples Paradoxical Therapy

Philip H. Bornstein
Holly K. Krueger
Kenneth Cogswell

Paradoxical psychotherapy is a relatively recent development. As a distinct form of therapy, it is less than 15 years old; however, paradoxical techniques have been embedded and utilized in many different systems of psychotherapy (Weeks & L'Abate, 1982). In this chapter, we review first the historical precursors to couples paradoxical therapy. Emphasis is placed on theory principles and techniques of paradoxical treatment as applied in particular, to the behavioral context. Further, case examples are provided for illustrative purposes throughout the chapter.

Historical Precursors to Couples Paradoxical Therapy

Mozdzierz, Macchitelli, and Lisiecki (1976) suggest that Alfred Adler, in 1914, was the first person in Western civilization to use or write about paradox. Adler advocated avoiding power struggles with clients and suggested that therapists accept and go with the client's resistance (Weeks & L'Abate, 1982). Mozdzierz et al. (1976) call this approach a nonspecific paradoxical strategy. In addition, they delineated 12 specific paradoxical techniques that are Adlerian-based. Examples of these techniques include: (1) prescription—encouraging the patient to enact his or her symptomatic behavior; (2) permission—giving the patient permission to have his or her symptoms; (3) practice—encouraging the patient to refine the symptomatic behavior; and (4) prediction—suggesting that the patient would relapse.

Rohrbaugh, Tennen, Press, and White (1981) propose that Knight Dunlap was the theorist first responsible for systematically describing paradoxical treatment procedures. Dunlap (1930) developed a technique called "negative practice" for habit disturbances such as enuresis, stammering, and nail biting. This technique consisted of having the client practice the symptom under prescribed conditions.

The work of Victor Frankl, the developer of logotherapy, was the most explicitly paradoxical of all the historical precursors of paradoxical psychotherapy (Weeks & L'Abate, 1982). The goal of logotherapy, an existential approach to therapy, is to help the client consciously accept personal responsibility. A primary technique of logotherapy is paradoxical intention (Weeks & L'Abate, 1982). Frankl (1975) reports that he used paradoxical intention since 1929, although he did not formally describe it until 1939. According to Frankl, anticipatory anxiety characterized anxiety neurosis and phobic reactions. Paradoxical intention, therefore, was utilized to change the meaning of symptoms, which in turn interrupted the cycle for anxiety and ultimately relieved the neurotic condition. Frankl's students and followers went on to popularize the use of paradoxical intention in the United States (Weeks & L'Abate, 1982).

Another major theorist who may be credited with developing therapeutic paradox is John Rosen (Rohrbaugh et al., 1981). In his 1953 book, *Direct Psychoanalysis*, Rosen advocated a procedure he called "re-enacting an aspect of the psychosis" (p. 27). This consisted of encouraging a psychotic patient to act out or re-enact the psychotic episode. This technique is analogous to symptom prescription (Weeks & L'Abate, 1982). Rosen (1953) also utilized two other techniques, magical gestures and "misery loves company," which were paradoxical strategies. Magical gestures consisted of joining the patient in his or her psychosis and exaggerating it, whereas "misery loves company" consisted of the therapist enacting the psychotic symptoms as if the symptoms were his or her own when he or she was crazy. Both of these techniques give the patient permission to have the symptom.

Weeks and L'Abate (1982) suggest that hypnosis, in general, could be considered a precursor of paradoxical therapy. They delineated several strategies utilized by hypnotists that are paradoxical in nature. The paradoxical procedures include: (1) reframing; (2) use of double-binds; (3) emphasis of the positive; and (4) accepting the resistance.

Two relatively recent theories of psychotherapy, gestalt therapy and provocative therapy, also utilize paradoxical strategies (Weeks & L'Abate, 1982). In gestalt therapy, a technique known as exaggeration involves encouraging the client to repeat and amplify a movement or gesture. Weeks and L'Abate (1982) suggest that other gestalt techniques may be interpreted as paradoxical, although most gestalt therapists would reject the premise that they employ paradoxical procedures. In provocative therapy (Farelly & Brandsma, 1974), the goal is to produce an affective response in the client. As a means to that end, symptom exaggeration and humor are utilized to provoke the client within his or her own frame of reference.

Perhaps the most important precursor of paradoxical psychotherapy is the work of Milton Erickson and the Bateson project (Weeks & L'Abate, 1982). The members of this group, the Palo Alto group, identified the role of paradoxical communication in the families of schizophrenics (Bateson, Jackson, Haley, & Weakland, 1956). This work led to the description of the therapeutic double-bind, which is a mirror image of the pathological double-bind: "If in a pathogenic double-bind the patient is 'damned if he does and damned if he doesn't,' in a therapeutic double-bind he is 'changed if he does and changed if he doesn't'" (Watzlawick, Beavin, & Jackson, 1967, p. 241). In the therapeutic environment, the client is encouraged to enact the symptomatic behavior as a means to change. The client, therefore, gains control of the symptom either by enacting it voluntarily and intentionally or by disobeying the paradoxical injunction and giving it up (Weeks & L'Abate, 1982).

> The therapeutic situation prevents the patient from withdrawing or otherwise dissolving the paradox by commenting on it. Therefore, even though the injunction is logically absurd, it is a pragmatic reality: The patient cannot not react to it, but neither can he react to it in his usual, symptomatic way. (Watzlawick et al., 1967, p. 241)

Watzlawick, Weakland, and Fisch (1974) postulate that paradoxical injunctions, resulting in a therapeutic double-bind, create second-order change. A second-order change occurs when there is a change in the system or frame of reference itself, whereas a first-order change refers to a change that occurs within the system. The system itself, therefore, remains unchanged.

The most recent development in the evolution of paradoxical psychotherapy has been the work of the Milan group, a group of Italian psychiatrists (Weeks & L'Abate, 1982). Selvini Palazzoli, Cecchin, Prata, and Boscolo (1978), in their book *Paradox and Counterparadox*, describe their use of paradox with the families of anorexics, schizophrenics, and other psychotic patients. Their work is discussed below.

Toward a Theory of Paradox

Over the last decade, paradoxical techniques have been used in the treatment of a wide range of emotional, behavioral, and psychiatric problems (Cade, 1984). Interest in paradox has mushroomed as evidenced by the increase in books, journal articles, conferences, and seminars on paradoxical therapy (Weeks & L'Abate, 1982). Unfortunately, it remains a difficult task to explicate the principles of paradoxical work. Paradoxical psychotherapy has no unifying or underlying theory. There has been little empirical investigation on the process or outcome of paradoxical therapy, and the principles guiding the use of this approach have been poorly delineated (Weeks & L'Abate, 1982).

Tennen, Eron, and Rohrbaugh (1985) suggest that "down-playing theory in a framework of technical eclecticism offers a limited and limiting vision" (p. 190). They place paradox in the framework of a systemic theory of behavior and a strategic orientation to intervention and technique. Implicit in the systemic viewpoint is that the way a problem began is less important than the way it is maintained (Weakland, Fisch, Watzlawick, & Bodin, 1974). Strategic interventions are designed to induce change whether or not awareness, insight, or emotional release occurs (Tennen et al., 1985).

According to Tennen et al. (1985), the systemic and strategic themes converge in three interrelated models: (1) the brief, problem-focused therapy developed by the Palo Alto group; (2) the systemic family therapy developed by Selvini Palazzoli and the Milan group; and (3) the strategic-structural approach of Haley and Madanes. Together, these models define a contextual framework for paradoxical therapy. Each approach postulates that problems are maintained in cycles of interaction and are interwoven in the social context. In each, a therapeutic intervention is based on a specific plan in order to resolve the problem as efficiently and quickly as possible (Tennen et al., 1985).

A related theoretical view of paradox is the dialectical approach. Mozdzierz et al. (1976) suggest that paradox is dialectics applied to psychotherapy. Dialectical thinking appears to have influenced Adler's psychology (Ansbacher, 1972), and Watzlawick et al. (1974) maintain that their theory of second-order change is similar to a dialectical approach. Weeks (1977) postulated that dialectics serve as the theoretical foundation for paradoxical psychotherapy.

Dialectical psychology attempts to discover the complex network of connections among various social, historical, economic, and psychological phenomena (Weeks & L'Abate, 1982). Riegel (1976) proposes that human development proceeds simultaneously along four independent dimensions: (1) cultural-sociological; (2) outer-physical; (3) inner-biological; and (4) individual-psychological. A developmental crisis ensues when asynchronization occurs within or between dimensions. Crisis is resolved, therefore, by synchronizing the dimensions. Clients seeking therapeutic help are generally experiencing asynchronization (Weeks &

L'Abate, 1982), and they may require a "synchronizing reinterpretation" (Riegel, 1976). This reinterpretation involves two general components. First, all the possible dimensions and the interactions between the dimensions need to be considered. Second, the system requires a second-order solution (Weeks & L'Abate, 1982). For most families or individuals, symptom reduction, or problem solving, is generally approached in a linear fashion rather than a circular fashion. For example, if X represents a problem for an individual or a system, then not-X is seen as the solution (Watzlawick et al., 1974). According to Weeks and L'Abate (1982):

> The individual caught in this situation is in a double-bind—not the kind of double-bind that is usually described, but what we call a meta double-bind. In a double-bind, one is trapped between two unacceptable alternatives which can be stated explicitly. In a meta double-bind, the individual is bound to a frame of reference in which the solution cannot be described because it lies outside the frame of reference being used. (p. 43)

A second-order change is required to alter the frame of reference. Paradoxical injunctions, according to Watzlawick et al. (1974), produce second-order change.

Principles of Paradox

In order to work paradoxically, the therapist must conceptualize the problem systemically, considering the ecological, dialectical, and reciprocal nature of problems. In addition, the therapist must think paradoxically, which entails conceptualizing the problem in terms of the double-bind it creates for the client. Finally, intervention consists of inventing a therapeutic double-bind (Weeks & L'Abate, 1982).

Weeks and L'Abate (1982) delineated five basic principles of paradoxical psychotherapy that may be utilized with individuals, couples, or families. The first principle utilizes the symptom as an ally. The symptomatic behavior of the individual or system is not considered in negative terms. Rather, "the symptom is seen as the vehicle of change, since its function has been one of precluding change in the family system" (Weeks & L'Abate, 1982, p. 30). Principle two is only applicable to symptoms that occur within a social context and is, therefore, crucial when dealing with couples or families. Principle three places the symptom under conscious control. If the therapist is working with an individual, the client could be instructed consciously to enact and magnify the symptom. When the symptom occurs within a system of interaction, all members of the system should be included. One strategy to accomplish this would be to have the other members of the system help the identified patient have the symptom. A second strategy involves having the other members assume a paradoxical role. Weeks and L'Abate (1982) cite the following example:

> Assume the symptom is a daughter's acting-out and taking charge in a single-parent family. The daughter is told to exaggerate her taking charge of the mother. At the same time, the mother is told to assume the paradoxical role of the child. She is instructed to give up her position of authority and to pretend to be a helpless child. (p. 91)

Principle four involves blocking the reappearance of the symptom. This may be accomplished by predicting or prescribing a relapse. Finally, principle five insures the client's involvement. This may be achieved through several techniques. The client may be instructed to have the symptom whenever X occurs, or the paradoxical message may be put in writing to be read on a regular basis by the client. In addition, the task may be prescribed in a ritualized manner as suggested by Selvini Palazzoli, Cecchin, et al. (1978).

Methods of Intervention

Reframing

Reframing involves a shift in the frame or reference of symptomatic behavior. In essence, the identified patient's problem is reframed from an individual problem to a contextual or transactional problem. According to Keller and Elliot (1982), reframing procedures, also known as positive connotation:

> involve the therapist in the process of bringing the family to see the problem from an alternative perspective which places the therapist in alliance with the homeostatic tendency of the family. (p. 119)

For example, Keller and Elliot (1982) cite the case of a couple (K) who presented for marital therapy. Mrs. K relentlessly attempted to get her husband to communicate more with her. In response, Mr. K scheduled his work hours in a manner that limited direct interaction as much as possible. After assessing the individual and/or interactional dynamics that maintained the communication deficit, the therapist reframed the problem. It was stated to the couple that their caring and sensitivity in the marriage led them to intuitively sense each other's concerns. They had, therefore, caringly sacrificed open and intimate communications so as to insure that their partner's needs were met.

Relabeling

"Relabeling refers to changing the label attached to a person or problem without necessarily changing the frame of reference in the sense of moving from the individual to the dyadic or systemic level" (Weeks & L'Abate, 1982, p. 106). This technique involves changing a negative label to a positive label and generally results in the client gaining a sense of control over the symptom. Andolfi (1979) utilized this technique with the case of Mr. and Mrs. R. Mrs. R, a graduate student, spent hours each day in self-mutilating her face. She presented herself as the identified patient and carefully defined her "neurotic" symptomatic behavior. The therapist countered with "This is the first *creative* product of your curriculum vitae! It seems that in this sea of conformity the only creative thing you see or feel is what you have written on your face" (Andolfi, 1979, p. 7).

Prescriptions

Prescriptions are the most commonly utilized paradoxical strategy. Essentially, these techniques involve instructing the client to keep and/or exaggerate the symptom. There are many subtle variations of prescriptions; therefore, a few illustrative examples will follow. de Shazer (1978) described a couple seen for marital therapy because of their increasing number of uncontrollable fights. Except for the fights, both members of the couple found their marriage rewarding and exciting. After the therapist provided them with a pseudoexplanation of their fights, the couple was instructed that they needed to learn a new, more effective manner of fighting. They were assigned the following task:

> Every other day in the coming two weeks they were to set aside one hour when they must fight. To start this fight, they were to toss a coin to decide who went first, and then take turns yelling and screaming for ten-minute periods. Each was to take a turn as yeller and non-responsive listener. (de Shazer, 1978, p. 21)

This technique, referred to by de Shazer as "fighting to stop fighting," was a systemic symptom prescription designed to shift the negatives on the explicit level toward the positive (p. 23).

Selvini Palazzoli, Boscolo, Cecchin, and Prata (1978) devised a therapeutic tactic called ritualized prescription. This tactic is "aimed at breaking up those behaviors through which each parent disqualifies and sabotages the initiatives and directions of the other parent in his relation with the children" (p. 3). The case described in their 1978 article involved a family of four. The presenting patient, Carla, had been diagnosed as hebephrenic. The therapists assigned the following task: on even days of the week, Father alone would decide what to do with Carla and her symptomatic behavior. Mother would behave as if she were not present. On odd days of the week, Mother would be in control and Father would behave as if he were not there. Everyone would behave spontaneously on Sundays. According to Selvini Palazzoli, Boscolo, et al. (1978), this prescription works on several levels. First, it changes the rules of the family game. Second, it exploits the possible competition between the parents for the therapist's approval. Third, whether the family follows the prescription or not, it provides clarifying feedback regarding the family rules. In the case of Carla, the family did not follow the prescription but a family rule surfaced:

> Carla is Mother's absolute property, Father must beware of touching her. But clearly he had not given up and silently, unobtrusively acted with kindness, with understanding, with the resignation of a pitiful victim. Thus, the father passed on to Carla a powerful double-bind: "I want so much to have you on my side, for you to behave affectionately to me: but you *must not* do it because *I am afraid* of Mother, it would mean disaster for Mother and myself." (p. 7)

Another variant of symptom prescription, paradoxical intention, was utilized by Frankl (1975). He defined paradoxical intention as a process where "*the patient is encouraged to do, or wish to happen, the very things he fears* (the former applying to the phobic patient, the latter to the obsessive-compulsive)" (p. 227). Frankl (1975) cited an example provided by a reader of one of his books. The reader had to take an examination and discovered that he was literally frozen with fear. Since he knew he would fail if he felt that way during the exam, he said to himself:

> Since I am going to fail anyway, I may as well *do my best at failing*! I'll show this professor a test *so* bad, that it will confuse him for days! I will write down total garbage, answers that have nothing to do with the questions at all! I'll show him how a student *really* fails a test! This will be the most ridiculous test he grades in his entire career! With this in mind, I was actually giggling when the exam came. (p. 228)

The reader relaxed and received an A on the test.

Symptom scheduling (Newton, 1968) is a further variation of the prescription technique. The client is instructed to enact the symptom at a specified time and for a specific length of time. The enactment of the symptom should be scheduled before it occurs spontaneously if possible. Another similar technique involves extending the feeling state (Weeks & L'Abate, 1982). If, for example, a client reported feeling nervous, the therapist might instruct the client to continue to feel nervous for 20 minutes before he could allow himself to feel better.

According to Weeks and L'Abate (1982), prescriptions are essentially double-binds. To make an appropriate paradoxical prescription at the dyadic and familial level, the therapist must assess the sequences of behavior. It must be kept in mind that causality in relationships is circular. Once the assessment has been completed, the prescription is delivered to the system in a manner that precludes comment by the members of the system. "The bind must be an inescapable box requiring a 'jump' to a higher level" (p. 116).

Restraining

Restraining is a strategy that alters the therapist's actual or potential role inside a system. This intervention cautions against or discourages change in some manner (Tennen et al., 1985). Even clients voluntarily seeking therapy are resistant to change. Change involves a homeostatic imbalance, whereas permanence is a form of protection. Restraining is a method that alleviates the problem of the therapist working harder than the client, while at the same time addressing the client's ambivalence (Weeks & L'Abate, 1982).

Weeks and L'Abate (1982) describe a restraining technique that is particularly useful with problems of long duration and where resistance is high. The strategy helps to polarize and crystalize the consequences of change. Essentially, this technique involves enumerating all the "negative" consequences that would occur if the client changed. In reality, these consequences would be positive but they are reframed and presented to the client in a negative fashion. For example, Weeks and L'Abate (1982) cited the case of a depressed male. One of the negative consequences that they presented to him was that if he gave up his depression, he would be able to make friends. That would be bad because making friends is stressful and might lead to conflict and rejection. According to Weeks and L'Abate, "This procedure challenges the client to change. It is a provocative device used to increase the reactance *not* to change" (p. 128). They suggest amplifying or exaggerating the negative reframing if the client does not argue with the consequence.

Another restraining technique, inhibiting, involves instructing the client to go slower than the client states he or she would like to go (Weeks & L'Abate, 1982). Reactance is increased when the importance of making small changes is stressed (Watzlawick et al., 1974). The next level of restraining technique is to forbid change. This may be accomplished by "giving in" (Watzlawick et al., 1974). The client is instructed to stop trying to give up his or her symptoms. Rather, for a set time period, he or she is to allow the symptom to occur (Weeks & L'Abate, 1982). Another method is to instruct the client not to engage in the behavior he or she wants to change (Weeks & L'Abate, 1982). This technique is most frequently employed in sex therapy, although it is not overtly labeled paradoxical.

An extreme form of dealing with the resistance involves telling the client that change is impossible (Weeks & L'Abate, 1982). "The therapist mobilizes resistance by benevolently suggesting that change may not be feasible" (Rohrbaugh et al., 1981). Rohrbaugh et al. (1981) advocate the use of this technique with highly reactant clients who repeatedly seek help but fail to benefit.

Predicting and prescribing a relapse are two restraining techniques that are frequently utilized in paradoxical psychotherapy. According to Weeks and L'Abate (1982), predicting a relapse is an essential component of paradoxical work:

> In general, a paradoxical prescription is given first and if it is successful the symptom suddenly disappears. The next step is to predict a relapse. The client is told that the symptom will suddenly reappear. By predicting a relapse the therapist is placing the client in a therapeutic double-bind. If the symptom does occur again, the therapist predicted it, so it is under his control. If it does not occur again, it is under the clients' control. The symptom has been defined in such a way that it can no longer be perceived as uncontrolled or spontaneous. (p. 135)

Prescribing a relapse is often useful with clients who improve too quickly (Rohrbaugh et al., 1981). This technique consists of prescribing the symptom's reenactment so that it is an ordeal for all those involved and is therefore less likely to occur (Weeks & L'Abate, 1982).

A general rule regarding the use of restraining strategies, according to Weeks and L'Abate (1982), is that as soon as change begins to happen a restraining statement should be given to the client. These messages should be delivered in a concerned, empathic, and warm manner. The underlying message to the client is: to change you must stay the same.

Indirect Paradox

Cryptic messages, or indirect messages, constitute another variation of a paradox. These messages may contain ambiguous terms, contradictions, double meanings, metaphors, or other linguistic devices that make the message difficult to interpret and frequently create a sense of confusion in the client (Weeks & L'Abate, 1982). Weeks and L'Abate (1982) postulate that these messages are advantageous in several ways: (1) the messages are directed toward the unconscious; (2) they are generally not recognizable as directives; (3) they are necessary for clients who would be too threatened by straightforward confrontation or direct paradox; (4) they are beneficial with clients who intellectualize or are therapy-wise because the client cannot oppose, resist, or ignore the message; and (5) the ambiguity of the message causes the client to think about the statement and explore alternative perceptions.

de Shazer (1978) cited the case of a couple, Mr. and Mrs. C, who had been vaguely unhappy with their marriage for a long time. Mrs. C had a long list of complaints about Mr. C, whereas he accepted her criticism without complaint. After the first two sessions, the couple was still unable to establish mutual goals for therapy. Mr. C's implied goal was to "get her off my back," and Mrs. C's goal was to "fix him" (p. 24). According to de Shazer (1978):

> It seems more efficient to view this lack of goal-setting as a type of resistance, and to accept it. Therefore, the first step of therapy is to abort efforts to set a goal, to just go with the resistance, and to encourage their confusion until they demand some specific goal or direction for therapy. . . . This building up of confusion is used to promote a growing need for the couple to make sense out of the situation, and to make a clear statement about the situation and their goal(s). (p. 25)

Positioning

Positioning is a strategy where the therapist accepts and exaggerates the client's position or assertion about his or her problems or self. This technique is generally used when the client's position is maintained by an opposite or complementary reaction from others (Rohrbaugh et al.,

1981). For example, if a client's depression was assessed to be reinforced or maintained by the efforts of significant others to help the client cheer up and feel better, the therapist would attempt to exaggerate the depression by defining it as worse than the client proposed.

The Use of Paradoxical Interventions in Behavioral Marital Therapy

Behavioral marital therapy (BMT) has grown and developed steadily over the past 15 years, and its successful application with many types of couples is well documented (Jacobson & Holtzworth-Munroe, 1986). However, increasing numbers of practitioners and researchers have come to realize that the behavioral approach to marital therapy has limitations and is not optimally effective with all clients who seek marital counseling. As a result, several behaviorally oriented researchers such as Alexander, Barton, Birchler, and Weiss, are turning to other theoretical schools, looking to incorporate new ideas and approaches into the behavioral model so as to make it more flexible and effective. The systems, or strategic, approach has influenced several BMT therapists and theoreticians, and an integration of the two paradigms is growing increasingly popular (Birchler & Spinks, 1980). One of the key components of strategic marital therapy, the paradoxical intervention, has long been anathema to practitioners of BMT, but even this barrier is falling as behaviorists come to understand and employ more of the systems approach.

Why have behavioral marital therapists typically rejected the use of paradoxical interventions? One of the basic reasons is the differing views taken by strategic and behavioral therapists concerning the maladaptive behavior in question. Systems theory maintains that a couple's undesirable behavior is best seen as a metaphor serving a communicative and relationship-defining function. They assume that there is an unconscious agreement between the marital dyad that approves of the target behaviors in spite of their conscious objections. Because of this unconscious desire to maintain the symptomatic behavior, the couple will resist the therapist's effort to eliminate the behavior. This type of conceptualization, in which resistance to change is expected as a matter of course, lends itself to paradoxical interventions where the couple will either (1) obey the therapist and thus set up a collaborative relationship that will be crucial later in therapy, or (2) disobey the therapist and thus reduce or eliminate the target behavior. Behaviorists, on the other hand, maintain that a couple's presenting complaints are actually experienced as aversive and couples that ask for help generally wish to be helped. There is no assumed unconscious motive to resist change and thus no need for "covert coercion" or paradoxical interventions (Jacobson & Margolin, 1979).

The covert, deceptive nature of many paradoxical strategies is also opposed by behavioral marital therapists. They view this type of approach as incompatible with an above-board social learning paradigm and avoid such strategies at all costs. In addition, the empirical support for the effectiveness of paradoxical techniques is not strong. The groups that pioneered the use of paradox in marital and family therapy have not produced definitive studies of its effectiveness, and behaviorists traditionally endorse only those approaches that have strong data in support of their efficacy (Birchler, 1981).

A final point that helps explain the hesitance of BMT practitioners to employ paradoxical interventions is their customary view of the causes underlying resistance, or blocks, in therapy. Typically, when a couple fails to make progress in therapy, or when progress is suddenly halted, the behaviorally oriented therapist blames the situation on poor case management. The therapist will review the case in detail and look for instances where the logistics of therapy have failed, misunderstanding has occurred, conceptualization was inadequate, and so forth. The therapist will then take steps to correct the perceived problem, trusting that this will alleviate the difficulties encountered. This straightforward approach obviates the need for any paradoxical technique aimed at undermining unconscious motives (Spinks & Birchler, 1982).

Given the behaviorist's conceptualization of marital therapy in general, and resistance in particular, it may seem difficult to conceive of how paradoxical strategies could mesh with BMT. Yet, there are a few factors at work that are bringing the two increasingly closer together. Probably the most important factor is that more and more practitioners of BMT are realizing that their system is not always capable of adequately handling resistance. As Spinks and Birchler (1982) note, the behavioral approach can be "experienced as overly structured, and many therapists are uncomfortable with inattention to process and failure to deal with underlying issues. On occasion, such inattention to process issues results in the failure of otherwise very elaborate and carefully designed behavioral interventions" (p. 9). As the above suggests, behaviorists are finding that resistance cannot always be explained by poor case management techniques but, rather, is often the result of more subtle issues that must be raised if therapy is to prove successful. A second factor that is helping make paradoxical techniques more palatable to those who employ BMT is the realization that this approach does not have to be deceptive or misleading to the client. A closer look at these two factors will prove helpful.

Spinks and Birchler (1982) list four underlying causes of resistance that cannot simply be explained as poor case management. However, the authors caution that none of the four alternative conceptualizations should be invoked until a thorough review of the treatment strategy has been conducted and found satisfactory. The first possible cause of resistance may be the breaking of a family or marital rule in therapy. Either the therapist or one of the spouses may break an important, and usually implicit, rule governing the marital relationship, causing one or both spouses to resist any attempt by the therapist to induce further change. Hidden agendas may also impede therapeutic progress. Oftentimes a conflict that appears to concern money matters or disciplining the children actually reflects an underlying more basic struggle concerning power, expectations, and so forth. Indeed, until the real conflict is brought up and discussed, progress will prove difficult.

An impasse in therapy may also rise when one or both partners are aware of an important underlying issue but have catastrophic expectations about confronting the subject. This often leads to a denial of the issue or ignoring its presence, but again, it must be dealt with before therapy can continue successfully. Finally, if either member of the marital dyad perceives the cost of change as being too high, considerable resistance is likely to result.

Resistance

Spinks and Birchler (1982) also describe what they consider to be the most common signs of resistance: (1) acting out between sessions (missed appointments, tardiness, failure to complete homework assignments, etc.); (2) blocks to communication skills training when basic abilities are present; (3) regression to original or new symptoms after major progress; and (4) lack of generalization and maintenance of gains. Although resistance can be evidenced in many different ways, the authors have found the above problems to be the most frequently displayed.

Whereas Spinks and Birchler (1982) go on to detail several different options for dealing with resistance, this chapter focuses only on paradoxical techniques. Birchler (1981) outlines a system for the judicious application of paradox that is "quite compatible with the behavioral approach" (p. 92). First, he suggests that paradoxical interventions be employed only after the couple has received and successfully employed basic communication and problem-solving skills. This is to help insure that the couple will feel relatively confident that they can overcome any problems that may arise as a result of this fairly complex intervention. Birchler also advises a complete review of the case to insure that other more straightforward factors are not responsible for the resistance. Examples of poor case management are inaccurate identification of primary problem areas, lack of good rapport with clients, insufficient behavioral rehearsal or coaching, and poorly planned homework.

If the resistance continues to obstruct therapy and poor case management techniques are ruled out as a potential cause, Birchler (1981) cautiously advises considering a paradoxical intervention. If the therapist chooses to employ such a strategy, Birchler stresses that a crucial criterion for a successful intervention is that the therapist's functional analysis of the system be accurate. Paradoxical techniques are relatively complex and difficult to employ, and so a solid understanding of the interactional system is essential. Birchler then recommends that the therapist explain his or her conceptualization of the situation to the couple so that they receive a plausible rationale underlying the paradoxical assignment. This open and honest explanation is important because it is consistent with the behavioral idea that the client should not be deceived or tricked in any way. If such an approach is used, then paradoxical strategies do indeed fit into a behavioral framework, and those who practice BMT need not shy away from these techniques on theoretical grounds. Obviously, one does not tell the clients that their task is meant to have a paradoxical effect, but such is not necessary in order to maintain an honest relationship.

In describing the paradoxical assignment to the clients, it is helpful to explain its necessity in view of the past failure to progress using other techniques. It may also be helpful for the therapist to encourage the couple to view the assignment as an experiment, the results of which will provide valuable information regardless of effect. This "try it out and then we will evaluate" approach is in line with the social-learning orientation of BMT and will also help to elicit an honest effort from the couple (Birchler, 1981). These latter two suggestions serve to demystify the use of paradoxical strategies for both client and therapist.

Whereas Birchler (1981) attempts to fit paradoxical interventions into a behavioral theoretical framework, Jacobson and Margolin (1979) take a slightly different tact. They describe the basic assumption of strategic, or systems, theorists underlying the use of paradox (i.e., that the clients inevitably resist the therapist's attempts to change their behavior) and conclude that "paradox as a general strategy of marital therapy is inconsistent with a behavioral perspective" (p. 152). However, they go on to state that paradoxical techniques can be helpful at times and even "be viewed as consistent with and facilitative within a behavioral exchange framework" (p. 152). Since the authors admit that these techniques involve deceit, it is difficult to see how they fit paradox into a behavioral perspective. However, Jacobson and Margolin do note that other aspects of paradoxical interventions can be consistent with BMT.

For example, Jacobson and Margolin (1979) describe the case of a young couple who entered therapy in a state of crisis with fighting occurring frequently between sessions. Though their between-sessions battles nearly necessitated a separation, they could not fight during therapy in the presence of the therapist. The therapist, claiming that he needed first-hand information on their arguments, suggested that the couple turn on a portable cassette recorder whenever they began to fight at home. Sure enough, no more fights! Although this intervention can be viewed as paradoxical, it is also compatible with the paradigm that emphasizes the environmental control of behavior. The therapist took advantage of his own value as a discriminative stimulus for polite, rational behavior with the cassette recorder acting in his stead. This technique was deceptive in that the therapist convinced the couple he needed the information for assessment purposes, whereas his actual intent was to stop the fights. Although such a technique cannot be said to be completely consistent with behavioral principles, it incorporates some behavioral ideas and was, above all, effective.

Although Jacobson and Margolin (1979) do not supply as detailed an account of when and how to use paradoxical techniques, they do list a number of guidelines for the practitioner to follow. First, they state that paradoxical assignments must be given in a context of obvious caring and concern for the clients, since the directives often seem confusing or nonsensical. It must be clear that the therapist has the long-range goal of improving the couple's relationship. Second, they suggest that the therapist use humor along with recognition that the clients' problem is significant and troubling. It is important that the therapist does not impart the impression that he is toying with the couple; yet the appropriate use of humor can help the clients accept the therapist's suggestion. Third, the couple must be presented with a reasonable rationale for the paradoxical task (e.g., data gathering, homework assignment, etc.). This will help insure that the couple puts forth an honest effort and that the assignment will not leave them bewildered as they leave the session. Fourth, the clients must not be "debriefed" after they report improvement following the paradoxical exercise. Debriefing can lead to the couple feeling tricked or manipulated by the therapist and thereby threaten the therapeutic relationship. Further, debriefing may cause the couple to focus on the therapist as the sole agent of change rather than individuals as instigators of their own improvement. Finally, the authors urge that paradoxical strategies be used rarely and only with much forethought. As with most advocates of BMT, they see these techniques only as a final resort when all other behavioral approaches have failed.

In spite of their many warnings against employing paradoxical strategies too frequently, there are several areas in which practitioners of

BMT use this approach regularly. Jacobson and Margolin (1979) describe a four-step "behavioral" paradoxical treatment plan for couples who are experiencing conflict regarding the amount of affiliation and independence desired in the marriage. This treatment approach was formulated for marriages where one spouse depends heavily on the marital relationship for gratification. Under these circumstances, both spouses may be distressed because expectations for independence and affiliation in the marriage are being violated. Jacobson and Margolin outline a program that contains the following basic message to the affiliative spouse: "You must give your mate more breathing room, achieve more distance in your relationship if you want to become closer to your spouse." A paradoxical statement if ever there was one! As the first step in the treatment program, the therapist informs the affiliative spouse (A) that he or she must temporarily accept the independent spouse's (B) desire for more distance in the relationship. Because A's constant pleading for less independence merely drives B further away, halting this complaining will set the stage for future closeness. Next, A must temporarily reduce the rewards given to B in an attempt to seduce B into increased affiliation (i.e., cooking dinner, cleaning house, special favors, etc.). These rewards most likely irritate B because they impede B's quest for distance and also raise A's costs in the marriage.

The third step in the program involves A cultivating more interests and activities outside of the relationship. This serves not only to make A less dependent on the relationship (resulting in improved confidence and self-esteem), but it will also attract B to the relationship more since some pressure has been relieved and balance restored. In effect, moving away from the relationship will result in increased closeness. The final stage in the program consists of communication training aimed at helping both partners express their feelings in a more empathic and genuine manner. Thus, this treatment strategy effectively displays how behavioral and paradoxical strategies can coexist both theoretically and practically.

Finally, another area where practitioners of BMT frequently employ paradoxical directives relates to sexual difficulties. As Vandereycken (1982) notes, some of the techniques and strategies advocated by Masters and Johnson (e.g., avoiding coitus for a prescribed length of time) derive their power from paradoxical procedures. Even sensate focus exercises bear some similarity to paradoxical-type interventions. Here, the couple is instructed to take time each day to "pleasure" each other through touching, kissing, massage, etc. Intercourse, however, is to be avoided. The goal is to reduce the performance anxiety that often accompanies sexual interaction such that the couple can, once again, enjoy basic sensual feelings. Indeed, a frequent benefit is that after a few days couples often find this procedure affords them better communication. Correspondingly, they feel less pressure, greater intimacy, and are often able to actually enjoy intercourse—against the therapist's direction! Interventions such as these appear to redirect the couple's attention away from their obsessive focus (i.e., orgasm, premature ejaculation, etc.) onto more constructive, facilitative behaviors.

Indications and Contraindications for Paradoxical Therapy

A final consideration for the therapist employing paradox is the need to assess when paradoxical interventions are specifically indicated. Although the literature on paradoxical therapy includes numerous successful case reports, little has been written about the specific clients or situations where paradox is indicated. Conversely, there are almost no contraindications to be found in the literature (Weeks & L'Abate, 1982). Whereas paradox has been applied to a wide variety of problems (Cade, 1984), paradoxical methods may be more appropriate for certain types of cases. Weeks & L'Abate (1982) advocate assessing the applicability of paradox along two, interrelated continua: (1) the dimension of pathology, which ranges from mild (transient or neurotic disorders) to severe (psychotic); and (2) the dimension of resistance, which ranges from cooperative to difficult or impossible. Paradoxical methods appear to be most useful at the severely disturbed end of the continuum, although more rapid change may be obtained with paradox at the mildly disturbed pole (Weeks & L'Abate, 1982). In addition, Weeks and L'Abate (1982) suggest that highly resistant clients, such as "therapist-killers" or "therapy addicts" are appropriate candidates (p. 56). Therapist-killers have seen numerous therapists in the past, none of whom were successful. Therapy addicts appear to live for their therapy session but show no improvement in the long run. Both of these types appear eager for help, yet they continually sabotage it.

Weakland et al. (1974) postulate that severe and/or chronic problems have strong feedback loops that are maintained and reinforced in the social context. Paradoxical strategies are appropriate because they destroy the feedback loops.

In addition to the aforementioned guidelines, with couples or families paradoxical interventions are most appropriate when the system, or any subsystem, is in a developmental crisis-asynchronization (Weeks & L'Abate, 1982). For example, when a teenager moves from child to young adult, the family requires corresponding changes in their interactional rules (Watzlawick et al., 1974). For a couple, the birth of a child is one example of a developmental crisis that requires resolution.

Weeks and L'Abate (1982) delineated a number of dysfunctional transactional patterns found in couples or families where paradoxical strategies seem appropriate. These are: (1) expressive fighting and bickering—the members of the system relate to one another by fighting; (2) unwillingness to cooperate with each other and complete assignments—the members comply with each other verbally but defeat each other nonverbally; (3) continuation of the same patterns regardless of intervention—rigid resistance to any type of intervention; (4) divide and conquer—the child attempts to separate parents from each other; and (5) disqualifications—members disqualify communications through the use of a variety of techniques.

Although the literature provides few contraindications for paradoxical interventions, there appear to be several types of situations where paradoxical strategies are inappropriate. Fisher, Anderson, and Jones (1981) delineated the following four family patterns that contraindicate the use of paradox: (1) impulsive families that openly express hostility; (2) childlike families where the adult members are immature and looking for a parental figure in the therapist; (3) families that project responsibility onto others; and (4) chaotic families characterized by loose and vague structures that do not present a repetitive pattern of symptomatic behavior.

Weeks and L'Abate (1982) identified four additional types of cases where paradoxical interventions are contraindicated. They are: (1) cases where there is a potential for destructive behavior especially suicide or homicide; (2) sociopathic individuals; (3) paranoids who may sense the "deceit" and become more suspicious; and (4) clients who have not developed a relationship with the therapist (e.g., court-mandated clients). In the fourth case, clients who are forced into therapy may neither cooperate nor resist. Additionally, a condition for paradox and the double-bind is that a relationship must exist.

Summary

Although paradoxical techniques have been utilized in some form since the early days of psychotherapy, as a distinct form of therapy, it is less than 15 years old. The work of the Palo Alto group, which identified the role of paradoxical communication in the families of schizophrenics, may be the most important precursor of paradoxical psychotherapy (Weeks & L'Abate, 1982). This work led to the description of the therapeutic double-bind that is the foundation of paradoxical intervention (Watzlawick et al., 1967).

Although there is no underlying or unifying theory to guide paradoxical work, most therapists in this area view problems as interwoven in the social context and maintained in cycles of interaction. Tennen et al. (1985) suggest that the following three models provide a contextual framework for paradoxical therapy: (1) the brief, problem-centered therapy developed by the Palo Alto group; (2) the systemic family therapy developed by Selvini Palazzoli and the Milan group; and (3) the strategic-structural approach of Haley and Madanes.

To guide the work of therapists utilizing paradoxical strategies, Weeks and L'Abate (1982) delineated five basic principles that are applicable with individuals, couples, or families. The principles are: (1) positively reframe the symptom; (2) link the symptom to all members of the system; (3) reverse the symptom's vector; (4) prescribe and sequence paradoxical interventions over time; and (5) utilize a paradoxical intervention that will insure the client(s) will act on the task in some manner.

In the literature, the methods of intervention that are most frequently applied include: (1) reframing and/or relabeling; (2) prescriptions: (3) restraining; (4) positioning; and (5) indirect paradox. Although little has been written about the indications or contraindications for paradoxical therapy, paradoxical methods may be more appropriate for certain types of cases (Weeks & L'Abate, 1982).

In general, chronic, severe, and long-term problems may be best suited for paradoxical interventions. In addition, highly resistant clients and/or systems are appropriate candidates. Paradoxical strategies are contraindicated in the following cases: (1) when there is a potential for destructive behavior; (2) with sociopathic or paranoid individuals; (3) when a therapeutic relationship has not been formed (Weeks & L'Abate, 1982); (4) with families who project responsibility; (5) in chaotic families characterized by loose and vague structures that do not present a repetitive pattern of symptomatic behavior; (6) in childlike families where the adult members are immature and looking for a parental figure in the therapist (Fisher et al., 1981).

References

Andolfi, M. (1979). Redefinition in family therapy. *American Journal of Family Therapy, 7,* 5–15.

Ansbacher, H. (1972). Adler's "Striving for power" in relation to Nietzsche. *Journal of Individual Psychology, 28,* 12–24.

Bateson, G., Jackson, D., Haley, J., & Weakland, J. (1956). Toward a theory of schizophrenia. *Behavioral Science, 2,* 4.

Birchler, G. (1981). Paradox and behavioral-marital therapy. *American Journal of Family Therapy, 9,* 92–94.

Birchler, G., & Spinks, S. (1980). Behavioral systems marital and family therapy: Integration and clinical application. *American Journal of Family Therapy, 8,* 6–28.

Cade, B. (1984). Paradoxical techniques in therapy. *Journal of Child Psychology and Psychiatry, 25,* 509–516.

de Shazer, G. (1978). Brief therapy with couples. *International Journal of Family Counseling, 6,* 17–30.

Dunlap, K. (1930). Repetition in the breaking of habits. *Science Monthly, 30,* 66–70.

Farelly, F., & Brandsma, J. (1974). *Provocative therapy.* Fort Collins, CO: Shields Publishing.

Fisher, L., Anderson, A., & Jones, J. (1981). Types of paradoxical intervention and indication/contraindication for use in clinical practice. *Family Process, 20,* 25–35.

Frankl, V. E. (1975). Paradoxical intention and dereflection. *Psychotherapy: Theory, Research, and Practice, 12,* 226–237.

Jacobson, N. S., & Holtzworth-Munroe, A. (1986). Marital therapy: A social learning-cognitive perspective. In N. S. Jacobson & A. S. Gurman (Eds.), *Clinical handbook of marital therapy* (pp. 29–70). New York: The Guilford Press.

Jacobson, N. S., & Margolin, G. (1979). *Marital therapy: Strategies based on social learning and behavior exchange principles.* New York: Brunner/Mazel.

Keller, J. F., & Elliot, S. S. (1982). Reframing in marital therapy: From deficit to self-sacrifice as focus. *Family Therapy, 9,* 112–126.

Mozdzierz, F., Macchitelli, F., & Lisiecki, J. (1976). The paradox in psychotherapy: An Adlerian perspective. *Journal of Individual Psychology, 32,* 169–184.

Newton, J. (1968). Considerations for the psychotherapeutic technique of symptom scheduling. *Psychotherapy: Research, Theory, and Practice, 5,* 95–103.

Riegel, K. (1976). The dialectics of human development. *American Psychologist, 31,* 689–700.

Rohrbaugh, M., Tennen, H., Press, S., & White, L. (1981). Compliance, defiance, and therapeutic paradox: Guidelines for strategic use of paradoxical interventions. *American Journal of Orthopsychiatry, 51,* 454–467.

Rosen, J. (1953). *Direct psychoanalysis.* New York: Grune & Stratton.

Selvini Palazzoli, M., Boscolo, L., Cecchin, G., & Prata, G. (1978). A ritualized prescription in family therapy: Odd days and even days. *Journal of Marriage and Family Counseling, 4,* 3–9.

Selvini Palazzoli, M., Cecchin, G., Prata, G., & Boscolo, L. (1978). *Paradox and counterparadox.* New York: Jason Aronson.

Spinks, S., & Birchler, G. (1982). Behavioral-systems marital therapy: Dealing with resistance. *Family Process, 21,* 169–185.

Tennen, H., Eron, J. B., & Rohrbaugh, M. (1985). Paradox in context. In G. R. Weeks (Ed.), *Promoting change through paradoxical therapy* (pp. 187–214). Homewood, IL: Dow Jones-Irwin.

Vandereycken, W. (1982). Paradoxical strategies in a blocked sex therapy. *American Journal of Psychotherapy, 36,* 103–108.

Watzlawick, P., Beavin, J., & Jackson, D. (1967). *Pragmatics of human communication.* New York: W. W. Norton.

Watzlawick, P., Weakland, J., & Fisch, R. (1974). *Change: Principles of problem formation and problem resolution.* New York: W. W. Norton.

Weakland, J. H., Fisch, R., Watzlawick, P., & Bodin, A. (1974). Brief therapy: Focused problem resolution. *Family Process, 13,* 141–168.

Weeks, G. (1977). Toward a dialectical approach to intervention. *Human Development, 20,* 277–292.

Weeks, G. R., & L'Abate, L. (1982). *Paradoxical psychotherapy: Theory and practice with individuals, couples, and families.* New York: Brunner/Mazel.

Chapter 11

Paradoxical Procedures in Family Therapy

Barry L. Duncan

The use of paradoxical procedures in family therapy, and family therapy itself, have evolved concurrently from similar beginnings. At the time during which several independent groups were experimenting with families containing a schizophrenic member, one of these groups, the Bateson project, conducted research that led to the double-bind theory of schizophrenia (Bateson, Jackson, Haley, & Weakland, 1956). From this seminal work came the suggestion that paradoxical communication or double-binds may be therapeutically useful. The suggestion that paradoxical communication could be therapeutic when combined with communication and systems theory and the influence of Milton Erickson formed the basis for the use of paradoxical procedures in family therapy.

This chapter presents paradoxical procedures utilized with families in which the primary presenting complaint is either a parent–child difficulty or a child problem. Paradoxical methods are presented as an integral component of an overarching theoretical framework usually called strategic and more recently termed "process constructive." The assumptions of a process-constructive view are presented, and the process of integrating paradoxical interventions into behaviorally oriented therapies are explicated. An intervention typology is presented, and case vignettes illustrate each general and specific strategy.[1]

[1]Identifying information in the case illustrations has been altered to protect client confidentiality. The excerpts represent actual session dialogue, but have been edited for space considerations and clarity.

Assumptions of a Process-Constructive Perspective

The theoretical foundation of a process-constructive approach is derived from two major areas. First is the concept of "process," which has three levels of definition: (1) Buckley's (1967) process/adaptive level of system description; (2) the Mental Research Institute's (MRI) problem-formation model of interactional process that surrounds the presenting complaint (Watzlawick, Weakland, & Fisch, 1974); (3) and Held's (1986) distinction between process- and content-oriented approaches.

Constructivism is the other major theoretical component. A constructive view posits that rather than passively observing reality, individuals actively construct meanings that frame and organize their perceptions and experience.

Buckley's Process Model of Systems

Buckley (1967) classifies systems into three levels, each having a specific domain of applicability: (1) mechanical/equilibrial; (2) organismic/homeostatic; (3) process/adaptive.

The process/adaptive level is germane to family systems and has three characteristics; (1) fluid structure, ongoing process: (2) nonpurpose; and (3) evolution and elaboration. Social systems exhibit a complex interplay of widely varying degrees and intensities of association and disassociation. Structure is no more than a temporary accommodating representation of the ongoing process and is an attribution made by an observer describing the process. Process is primary over structure; structure flows from process and is only the observed intersection among time, space, and ongoing process. It is the actions and interactions among members of a system that is important at this level.

System interactions are initiated from small changes or variations from both the internal and external environment. Variation may occur from chance or from some developmental or transitional change. The variation or perturbation is information to the system, which may or may not convey a message of difference or importance. The system members interact around the variation (new information) in an attempt either to assimilate it into ongoing family patterns or to accommodate those patterns to the variation. Individual and shared meanings are constructed via the interaction surrounding the variation. The new meanings both guide and are shaped by the ongoing interaction around the new information. System purpose or function does not exist in process-level systems but, rather, is an attribution made by an observer constructing meaning from interactive process.

Process systems are fundamentally open and require variability to remain viable. Evolution and change comprise the heart of the system and are inevitable. Variation serves as a stimulus for interactional process, constructed meaning, and a continual movement toward greater complexity, flexibility, and differentiation.

An implication of this perspective is that, regardless of basic origins, problems persist only if they are maintained by ongoing current behavior of the client and others with whom he or she interacts.

The following case may illustrate: a 20-year-old young man in the process of separating from his family of origin began having symptoms that would ordinarily be described as paranoid schizophrenic. In the first interview with him, he described many somatic delusions. The major somatic delusion concerned a feeling in his face that was directed by the curvature of his spine, which either curved to God or to the devil. His hands were not there at times, and one of his legs was a woman's and one was a man's.

THERAPIST: Which leg is the woman's?
CLIENT: (*He indicated that it was his left leg.*)
THERAPIST: Have you shaved it yet?
CLIENT: (*He got a confused, then embarrassed look, and then he laughed.*) No, I'm not going to shave my leg.

The client didn't say another delusional thing the rest of the session, and the therapist began discussing how the client was going to move out on his own.[2]

This case illustrates that all behavior, normal or problematic, whatever its relationship to the past or to individual personality factors, is continually being maintained by ongoing interaction in the social system (Watzlawick et al., 1974). In this case, regardless of possible brain dysfunction or biochemical imbalances, there was an interactional nexus to the problem, which enabled the therapist to impact upon a seemingly intractable problem. This is not to say the client's schizophrenia was

[2]This intervention is an example of tracking with a delusional system and acting on the premises of the delusion to interrupt its sequence. The therapist accepted the delusion and asked a logical question, based upon the young man's delusion regarding his female leg. The question extended the delusion a bit further than the client had taken it himself, which seemed to interrupt the delusional process. Such an approach is an outgrowth of Erickson's work and the famous story concerning his treatment of a man who believed himself to be Jesus Christ. Erickson commented to the man that he had heard that he possessed carpentry skills and needed some shelves built in his office. The man was put in the position of either denying his delusion or doing something constructive for the first time during his long stay in the hospital.

"cured" but, rather, that current patterns of interaction at least maintained and perhaps exacerbated the delusional behaviors.

Problem Process

Problems occur as part of vicious cycle patterns of attempts to adjust or adapt to an internally or externally produced variation. The variation, once perceived as a difficulty, will interact with the individual and shared constructs of the system. The problem becomes not only the original difficulty, but also all the meanings it has accumulated through the course of those interacting around it. The problem itself, then, creates the system in that the meanings constructed by those involved both influence and are influenced by the problem itself.

Based on the individual and shared meanings about the problem or how to solve it, people will try variations on a theme of the same solution pattern over and over again. This may occur despite the fact that the solution pattern itself may be making the problem worse instead of better.

The MRI simply and eloquently suggests that two conditions are all that is necessary for a difficulty to become a problem: (1) the mishandling of the difficulty; and (2) when the original attempt fails, more of the same is applied (Watzlawick et al., 1974). The solution, in essence, becomes the problem.

It is, therefore, the problem process that is of importance—the process of interaction surrounding the problem, the process of meaning construction, and the interplay of both. The problem is whatever the original difficulty was plus all of the distressful meanings that have been constructed along the way.

The problem process model is a general and inclusive view of problem formation and maintenance. It posits no specific theoretical formulations of how problems occur and is therefore distinguished from what Held (1986) calls content-oriented approaches to psychotherapy.

Process versus Content

Held (1986) suggests that while the MRI does not present their approach as such, it can be argued that an MRI approach can subsume both individual and interpersonal levels of content. This can occur because the MRI proposes that change is achieved via interactive process, as opposed to the application of a given theoretical content. The problem-formation model of the MRI and the problem process described above state no specific content (e.g., fixated psychosexual development, confused hierarchy, irrational beliefs, etc.) as the true maintainer or real cause of the presenting problem (Held, 1986). In other words, no consistent precursors of either personality or circumstance are believed to necessarily cause problems or are important to problem improvement.

Because of the MRI's lack of preconceived theory regarding the "true maintainer" of the problem, Held (1986) classifies the MRI as a process approach. All models of psychotherapy have content, and it is a matter of degree rather than an either-or proposition. The distinction lies in the specificity of problem etiology and the pursuit of a particular therapeutic path based on the speculated etiology.

Based on a view that posits no specific content regarding the problem or its resolution, the therapist may pursue any content that may influence the interaction surrounding the problem or the constructed meanings it has acquired. Such a freedom of action is critical to the design of paradoxical interventions. The therapist's flexibility with regard to content is based in the belief in a constructed reality versus an objective one, that is, based in constructivism.

Constructivism

Constructivism states that individuals do not discover reality, they invent it (Watzlawick, 1984). This view suggests that reality does not exist separate from the constructs of the observer–describer. Experience does not directly reflect what is "out there," but is an ordering and organizing of it. Reality, then, develops as an emergent process around an individual's interaction with the environment.

The construction of reality or the ascription of meaning by individuals is a creative process that is limited somewhat by prevailing sociocultural limits and expectations. The creation of meaning frames and organizes perceptions and experience into predictable, rule-governed patterns with which individuals may predict, describe, and direct their lives. Meaning, therefore, is not simply in some external event or behavior, or solely in some internal state of the individual, but rather, it is the interaction and relationship between the two (Buckley, 1967).

Adding Paradoxical Interventions to Behavior Therapy

Behaviorally oriented clinicians may recognize many inherent similarities between a process-constructive or strategic perspective and a behavioral view (Duncan, Rock, & Parks, 1987): (1) both are symptom-oriented;

(2) conceptually and practically, both models focus on present patterns of observable behavior that precipitate and maintain problems: (3) intrapsychic variables and the role of the past are not necessarily important to problem resolution; (4) both models seek behavior change; insight is not viewed as necessary for problem resolution but is often a useful consequence of behavior change; (5) homework and behavioral assignments are utilized; (6) concrete observable behavior and specificity of information from interview data are required for intervention; (7) both are directive, active approaches; (8) both are brief approaches utilizing focused intervention; (9) both share a constructive bias in that they rely significantly on understanding and changing the client's construct of the situation; and (10) neither have a theoretical view of health or normality (Duncan et al., 1987).

In addition to the similarities, the two approaches are complementary in terms of their domains of expertise. Given the behavioral insistence on empirical support for technique, skill acquisition can be argued to characterize the domain of expertise or major strength of a behavioral approach.

The strategic approach, on the other hand, is widely recognized for its view of resistance as a naturally occurring process variable inherent to the therapeutic context. The MRI clearly delineates strategies (see below) that enhance compliance with therapists' suggestions and utilize the "resistance" to change. In essence, the major limitation of each aaproach (compliance in the behavioral approach and skill acquisition in the strategic approach) represents the domain of expertise of the other.

Given the similarities and the complementarity domains of expertise, the addition of paradoxical procedures to the repertoire of behaviorally oriented clinicians may, hopefully, be seen as an approachable task. Behavioral clinicians need not abandon their current theoretical orientations or embrace an orientation that runs counter to their adherence to strictly observable behavior. Rather, paradoxical strategies may be used simply in an additive fashion (Duncan et al., 1987).

Paradoxical Interventions with Families

Two classes of paradoxical interventions are discussed and exemplified below. *General* interventions, developed by the MRI (Fisch, Weakland, & Segal, 1982), are tactics that can be applied to nearly all cases and thus are not client- or problem-specific interventions. General interventions represent a well-delineated methodology for the therapist of any orientation to use to enhance compliance, minimize "resistance," and encourage client movement. *Specific* interventions are those in which the therapist designs or constructs client-specific treatment strategies based on the client's presentation of the presenting problem (Duncan, Parks, & Rusk, in press).

General Interventions

There are two types of general interventions: (1) restraining; and (2) therapist-style. In retraining, the therapist discourages change and may even deny that change is possible. There are many different variations of the restraining interventions that can be used at different points in the therapeutic process to help facilitate or to maintain the changes that have already been made. Therapist-style interventions represent the manner in which the therapist approaches the client and the methods by which the client's beliefs and values are incorporated and respected by the therapist.

Restraining

The therapist may want to use a retraining strategy early in the therapeutic process in order to avert the seemingly inherent therapeutic dilemma that faces many clients; that is, clients seek therapy voluntarily and most often with every intention to try and change their problem, but they are also quite ambivalent about changing and may even be fearful of the loss of security or permanence. No matter how much pain is currently experienced, the draw toward the familiar and hesitance to confront the unknown seem always to be present to some degree. The restraining interventions directly address this ambivalence and align with that part of the client that may be afraid or reluctant to change. A general message of "go slowly" will often be a most welcome and empathetic stance for the client uneasy about change.

Go Slowly

Of all paradoxical procedures, the injunction to clients to "go slowly," in their resolution of the problem is perhaps the most frequently used. The client is essentially instructed to do nothing about the problem. Most of this restraining intervention consists of offering valid rationales for going slowly in terms of resolving the presenting complaint.

The "go slowly" injunction is especially useful and typically is delivered in the first session for clients who present as trying too hard to resolve a problem or for clients who press the therapist with urgent demands for problem improvement. This stance is perhaps most applicable when the client, after being given a specific suggestion or task, has returned reporting some definite improvement in the presenting complaint. Rather than celebrating the change, the therapist might convey concern and explain that, welcome as the change may be, it is too fast and such quick improvement makes the therapist uneasy. The client is then encouraged to hold back on any further improvements (Fisch et al., 1982).

"Go slowly" may be helpful as a technique because it portrays the therapist as uncommitted to changing the client, certainly quickly, and therefore applies implicit pressure on the client to cooperate with any suggestions the therapist may subsequently give. It also removes a sense of urgency for the client, which perhaps has helped maintain the problem through the client's overinvolvement in repetitive unsuccessful solution attempts. The mandate to go slowly may enable such clients to relax their problem-maintaining efforts if they are told that satisfactory resolution of the problem may depend on proceeding slowly. Finally, when the therapist takes the position of conservatism regarding change, clients are allowed the freedom of exploring and expressing the risks associated with change.

Example. The S family was a blended one in which there were three children: Sue, the 16-year-old identified client and two brothers, ages 11 and 7, were the children of the mother. Because of Sue's recent runaway, the court had removed her from the home and placed her in temporary custody of a relative. She reported to the authorities that she had run away because of an intolerable (not abusive) relationship with her stepdad. Mom was very anxious to get Sue back in the home and seemed to feel exceedingly guilty about the entire situation. Both her mom and stepdad were very angry with the court system for removing Sue from the home and for mandating family therapy. Both seemed to possess an urgency for immediate reunification, which, of course, Sue opposed adamantly.

To the parents, the following go slowly injunction was delivered:

THERAPIST: In many ways, it is not surprising that you are encountering this problem given all the changes that your family has had to adjust to over the last couple of years. First and foremost, you are a blended family, a situation in which parental conflict regarding discipline is a natural consequence of bringing an outsider of sorts into an already established family. Kids have to adjust to the new disciplinarian and usually resist the efforts of the stepparent attempting to fulfill the role of a parent. Often, kids will also try to place the natural parent in between their conflict with the stepparent and in doing so create tension and conflict between the parents. You two are also still

> adjusting to each other and to being married, which is in and of itself a difficult transition to make. Finally, besides being a newly blended family, you have an adolescent who is apparently having great difficulty adjusting to the notion of a stepparent while at the same time trying to emancipate herself or mature into an adult. I'm not even commenting on the recent job change and subsequent move you all are just recovering from. All this is to say that I guess I'm surprised that the situation is not worse and that Sue's relationship with you [stepdad] is as good as it is. Therefore I suggest that you proceed very cautiously and slowly in attempting to work out this problem with Sue and get her back into the house. Besides being another change to contend with, my greatest concern is that Sue would be forced back before she is really ready. This, of course, would likely result in another blow-up and another runaway, which, as you know, would be a difficult situation to deal with. The reunification process, by definition, needs to be slowly worked through step-by-step for success to occur because there is a fair amount of "bad blood" between Sue and stepdad. For these reasons, I am requesting that you make no attempt with the courts or Sue to get her back. Please hold back and do very little to work on this issue.

The family returned and had in large part complied with the injunction to go slowly. They had stopped pressuring both Sue and the court system and had enjoyed a relaxing week. They had, however, called Sue and asked her to participate in a family picnic, and to their amazement, she not only agreed but also was quite pleasant. To this, the therapist expressed bewilderment and a concern that they were moving a bit quickly for his own comfort level. The go slowly message continued to be given throughout the course of therapy.

Dangers of Improvement

A variation of restraining and an extension of the injunction to go slowly is to ask clients if they can recognize the dangers inherent in resolving the problem. Some therapists may relate this tactic to opening the issue of secondary gain for discussion. This intervention addresses the client's ambivalence about change and helps clarify the consequences of change in the hopes of motivating the client to behave differently with regard to the presenting problem. The "dangers" of improvement may be used in most cases but is especially helpful in cases for which previous therapy has failed or the problem is one of long duration. The "dangers of improvement" concept is also useful in situations in which there has been initial noncompliance with a suggestion because it places subtle pressure on the client to comply with subsequent suggestions. The "dangers" intervention also aligns the therapist with that ambivalent side of the client that can free the client to choose to make a change (Fisch et al., 1982).

In most cases, clients will reply that there could be no danger and that nothing could make them happier than to resolve their problem. The therapist, however, can always begin the discussion with some possible drawback, if not for the client, then for someone else, or for the entire family. If the client sees merit in even one suggested drawback, it legitimizes the therapist's position that there are indeed dangers and risks associated with improvement or change. Once legitimized, the "dangers" intervention can be utilized to extend the go slowly injunction, since it is difficult to go any more slowly than deliberating about making any change at all. The technique can also be used to increase motivation by having the therapist comment on the deleterious effects that change would have on someone about whom the client(s) is not too fond.

In some cases, this restaining tactic may promote a significant change, particularly with problems of anxiety or of great urgency. If clients can see that improvement is frought with difficulties as well, they will will feel less compelled to harass themselves or others to change and may thus relax current ineffective solution attempts. In some ways, this intervention challenges clients to change. If the client agrees with the dangers, then the therapist can amplify them and ask whether or not there should be any more attempts at change, given the risks involved. If clients disagree and maintain that even considering the risks they want to improve the problem, then it is likely that compliance with treatment will occur (Fisch et al., 1982).

Example. The D family consisted of mom, dad, and one son, aged 8 years. Matt was the identified client and was an encopretic of the secondary type. He soiled only at home and not at school. Mom and dad were very concerned and embarrassed about the problem. Mom was particularly frustrated and felt as though she was at her wits' end in dealing with him. Mom did not work outside the home, and dad worked long hours in a mid-level management position. Matt had been a very sickly child, and mom had been through many illnesses and doctors.

After a review of the problem, the parents were instructed in a positive reinforcement plan largely consisting of token reinforcement of nonencopretic behaviors. The instructions were delivered in a one-down, qualified manner (see *Therapist-Style Interventions* below), and the token program was presented as a simple, painless method of eliminating a problem through the systematic reward of competing behaviors. The parents gave verbal agreement to the plan and seemed to be enthused about its possibilities.

On the next visit it became evident that little follow-through had occurred. The chart had been made, but dad had not entered the data with Matt onto the chart. Mom replied that dad had essentially not been home much and when he had, he had admonished Matt for soiling rather than ignoring it and merely allowing Matt to clean himself and his clothes. Mom admitted that she also had spent much time discussing the problem with Matt and had done little to implement the plan agreed upon.

The therapist decided to intervene with dangers of improvement to enhance compliance to subsequent suggestions and to motivate the parents to take different action regarding the encopresis.

THERAPIST: No need to apologize for not following the token reinforcement plan—I was undoubtedly moving much too fast and had not considered the difficulties for your family in attempting to resolve this problem of yours. It may be that your inability to follow through on the plan was a clear indicator that there may be risks for each of you personally, as well as collectively, in resolving the soiling. Sometimes there are disadvantages or drawbacks to getting over a problem, like a whole new set of issues to deal with, which may even be more troublesome than the original problem. Let me ask you then, can you see any danger in Matt resolving his soiling problem?

CLIENT: I don't know what you mean. How can there be any danger? It would be great if we did not have to deal with this. Can you tell us what kind of danger?

THERAPIST: Well, without much thought—well maybe I can just give you a couple off the top of my head. One danger might be that if Matt got over this problem, then you two would not have a "neutral issue" to focus your time on and therefore may have more conflict about dad's lack of time for home activities. Not to make a big deal of that, but mom does seem to be pretty frustrated with the split-up of parental responsibilities, and Matt's problem keeps all centered on him and not on other things.

CLIENT: We have been avoiding discussion of his work and avoiding spending quiet time together in general.

THERAPIST: Another one may be that if Matt continues to soil, then he will essentially never grow up and can always remain the real baby of the family. This type of dependency tends to make parents feel very needed and such a feeling would be difficult to let go of. If he stops soiling, then mom, you may have to come to grips with the fact that your baby is growing up and doesn't need you anymore, which may be a bitter pill for you to swallow. I don't know if that applies—do you see any other risks involved?

The discussion of dangers continued throughout the session. After the discussion, both parents reported that despite the noted drawbacks, they truly wanted to help Matt resolve his problem and that if it caused marital problems, they would just have to deal with them. Reluctantly, the therapist suggested that mom withdraw from the problem and allow dad to solve it in any manner he saw fit. Dad implemented the token plan and spent less time at work. The encopresis subsided to an occasional accident, which was tolerable to everyone involved.

The dangers of improvement intervention seemed to facilitate cooperation with this family and motivated the father to take corrective action about Matt's soiling problem.

Predicting or Prescribing Relapse

The last restraining intervention to be discussed is that of predicting or prescribing a relapse after an improvement in the problem has been reported by the client. Predicting relapse begins with the therapist acknowledging that improvement has occurred but then adding that, desirable as the change is, it has occurred more rapidly than the therapist would like. The client is instructed to make no further improvement for the time being. The therapist adds that such rapid change is more often than not quite tenuous and that the problem will very likely recur.

By predicting a relapse, the therapist is placing the client in a win-win situation. If the problem does occur again, the therapist has predicted it, and therefore the problem is often experienced with less intensity. If it does not occur, the client has essentially prove the therapist wrong by maintaining his or her gains (Fisch et al., 1982).

A further step is prescribing a relapse, usually with a rationale that it brings the problem further under control or that relapse is a necessary part of the change process that must occur if change is to solidify. The therapist may prescribe the relapse by suggesting that it would be beneficial if the client could find some way of creating an exacerbation of the problem, at least temporarily.

In this intervention, clients are implicitly told that they have done unexpectedly well in therapy, so well that they should not make any further gains right away. Since a relapse has been prescribed and the client is asked to bring about some intensification of the problem, should the relapse occur, it will have already been defined as a success rather than a failure to sustain improvement.

In other words, this intervention anticipates that problem improvement can increase apprehension about change and meets this danger by relabeling any relapse as a step forward rather than backward. The obvious purpose of all this is to minimize recurrence of the problem by undercutting fears associated with preventing a relapse. Such a prescription sometimes prevents clients from overinterpreting relapse as meaning that everything is out of control once again.

Example. The G family consisted of mom, dad, and 15-year-old Andrea. The presenting problem was loud uproars between dad and Andrea, usually related to times in which dad requested that Andrea pitch in and help around the house. After a few sessions, the arguments had dwindled and ultimately stopped. The parents reported that everything was not perfect but that many things, particularly the arguments, were greatly improved. The therapist predicted that additional fights were bound to happen given the age of Andrea and the likelihood that dad would not be able to keep his temper in check indefinitely. The therapist cautioned the parents and Andrea about making any more changes as he gets quite nervous when families report that they are "getting along" with their teenagers.

The family returned still reporting that no big blow-ups had occurred and that Andrea was pitching in a bit more. The therapist was amazed and puzzled and prescribed the relapse in the following way.

THERAPIST: I am pleased for you that there have been no big uproars and that there seems to be a bit less tension around the house. But frankly, I'm also quite worried that the changes you've made are not going to last and that the slightest blow-up may plummet you all back down to the depths of despair you were in a couple of months ago. In other words, I believe that the true test of whether dad can hold his temper and Andrea can hold her mouth and continue to pitch in will not be passed until a fight has occurred. The question is, how will the family deal with it? Will it create the whole mess all over again or will the family withstand the argument and bounce back to generally cooperating with one another? For this reason, to esssentially solidify the changes, I would suggest that dad engineer a fight by somehow picking at Andrea and that Andrea escalate the fight by behaving obnoxiously. Only then will it be clear whether or not any lasting gains have been made.

The family returned for the last session and reported that a fight had indeed occurred, but it was a minor one that had lasted only an hour and that by the time dinner was served, everyone was talking once again. They also reported that they understood that fights with adolescents were bound to occur and that they believed their family could handle it.

Therapist-Style Interventions

Therapist-style interventions are those in which the subtle use of the self is employed to enhance compliance and minimize resistance to change. Therapist-style interventions represent a way of interacting with clients in therapy rather than a specified technique used in specific instances. Such a style devalues the therapist as an expert and tends to be more conversational and collaborative (Duncan et al., 1987). Therapist-style interventions also offer a way in which to utilize the clients' values and perceptions regarding themselves and their problems. There are two types of therapist-style interventions: (1) taking a one-down; and (2) utilizing client position.

Taking a One-Down

Success in therapy depends greatly on the ability of the therapist to obtain clear information from clients and to elicit their compliance in carrying out suggestions or tasks (Fisch et al., 1982). Some people may respond well to authority or expertise, but generally, compliance is reduced markedly if the therapist is seen in a one-up or power position. Such a position can intimidate clients who may already be embarrassed to talk about their problem. Consequently, some information may not be shared with the therapist because of clients' fear that they will be demeaned even further.

The therapist–client relationship inherently conveys a position of presumed power. As such, taking a one-down requires some effort, based not on the notion that one-downness is particularly influential but, rather, is the clearest way of avoiding the one-up stance. Taking a one-down, therefore, does not interfere with those persons who are ready to cooperate. It prevents the implication that the client has failed in not seeing the appropriate solution already, or that any cooperation will be regarded as following orders (Fisch et al., 1982).

Another aspect of taking a one-down is the use of qualifying language. Qualifying language enables a therapist to maintain a one-down stance and retain credibility at the same time. At many points in therapy, the therapist may want to offer some specific intervention or a particular way of looking at the client problem (see below), or some assignment, but is uncertain whether the strategy is one that will work or will be accepted by the client. Therefore, the therapist does not want to convey the intervention from the position of an expert or want his or her credibility to depend on the success or failure of the intervention (Fisch et al., 1982).

For these reasons, the suggestion or way of looking at the problem may be couched in qualified language. Rather than saying, "I've seen many cases like this, and I have a suggestion that will help you improve your relationship with your daughter," a qualified statement would be, "I have a suggestion to make, but I'm not sure how helpful it will be—it will depend on your willingness to take a risky step toward improvement and your ability to be creative." Words such as not sure, how, depends, ability, willingness, may, seems, and so forth, constitute qualified statements. The qualifications convey a one-down position and imply that the suggestion is appropriate, but the outcome depends on the client's efforts, thus protecting therapist credibility.

This is not to say that a therapist should never assume a one-up and unqualified stance. If a client seems to respond well to an authority stance, then such a position would be appropriate. If it is not clear at the onset which position would be better, it is easier to shift from a one-down to a one-up; therefore, a one-down stance enables more maneuverability (Fisch et al., 1982).

Examples. The following are several brief illustrations of the subtle but powerful utilization of the therapist's personal style as a tool to facilitate cooperation.

THERAPIST: Conflict resolution training may or may not help your relationship with your son. Its success will depend on your ability to recognize when it may be of benefit and your readiness to try a risky step toward improvement. It, of course, also depends on your creativity in arranging your schedule to practice and implement it.

THERAPIST: I'm sorry, I'm a bit confused. I'm a pretty concrete person, and it would help me understand your problem if I could get an example.

THERAPIST: I don't know whether this is on target or not, but some therapists may say that by continuing your periodic drinking problem you are carrying on the family legacy and demonstrating the most ultimate kind of respect.

THERAPIST: I want to apologize about our last session. After thinking about it this week, I came to the conclusion that I was really on the wrong track with you and had not been considering the point that you brought up. I'm sorry for leading us in the wrong direction and am glad you voiced your concern about our direction.

Utilizing Client Position

Utilizing client position is a central component to nearly all paradoxical procedures and is the hallmark of an MRI approach. Utilizing position is the implementation of the famous Erickson adage, "Accept what the client offers." Position is defined as those strongly held beliefs, values, and attitudes that influence a client's behavior in relation to the presenting problem (Fisch et al., 1982). Knowing a client's position about the problem itself, and therapy as well, allows the therapist to formulate how to frame a suggestion or alternative meaning in a way that the client is most likely to accept. Just as the presenting problem offers in a concise package what the client is wanting to address, client position indicates a belief system within clients that can be utilized to enhance the acceptance and carrying out of therapist directives.

Client position is most helpful in understanding the presenting problem and the client's attitude about therapy itself. Determining position does not require great attentiveness or a search for a hidden clue, since the most useful positions are those that are strongly held. Such strong positions are likely to be expressed over and over again, and a therapist could miss them only by active disregard.

To utilize position, a therapist must accept the client's statement, recognize the values it represents, and avoid making inflammatory or noncredible comments (Fisch et al., 1982). Successful utilization of position requires the therapist to overcome the temptation to confront, reason, or argue with the client. Restraint from attempting to help by direct educative methods can reduce resistance by not creating an unnecessary values conflict between the therapist and client.

Examples. Consider the following two sets of parents who have basically the same problem with their adolescent daughters. Both have a position regarding the nature of the problem and its cause, as well as some notion of how it can best be treated.

FAMILY 1: We have entered family therapy because we are worried sick about our 16-year-old daughter. She is having problems with adjusting to our recent move and to the new school, and this seems to be expressed by her missing school and being nasty to us at times. We believe that her self-esteem has suffered greatly, and we fear that she may be headed for a serious depression or even suicide.

FAMILY 2: We have entered family therapy because we are at our wits' end with our 16-year-old daughter. She is skipping school, she curses at us both, and, well, she is just out of control. We believe that she has no respect for anything or anyone and somehow we need help in ways to shake some sense into her head. We fear that she may be headed for jail.

The treatment goals for both families may be very similar. Both are requesting school attendance and less parent–child conflict. In addition, the recommended strategy may also be very similar. The framing or rationale for the recommendation, however, will be quite different. Although both sets of parents have similar goals, they hold different viewpoints or positions about how they can be helped.

Regardless of the specific recommendation chosen in this example, the therapist will need to deliver it to family 1 framed as "therapeutic for the child" and to family 2 as "helping to establish proper parental respect and control." In other words, the interventions chosen will be suggested in light of the therapist's respect for client position. Such a respect tends to enhance compliance with treatment and minimize the possibility of unnecessary resistance or power struggles with clients.

Utilizing client position underlies nearly all paradoxical work with individuals or families. In the next section, the application of position to the construction of client-specific interventions will be discussed and illustrated by clinical example.

Specific Interventions

This discussion of client-specific intervention strategies will largely be taken from three sources: (1) the brief therapy of the MRI (Fisch et al., 1982; Watzlawick et al., 1974); (2) the brief therapy of the Brief Therapy Center of Milwaukee (de Shazer, 1982, 1985, 1988); and (3) the process-constructive approach of the Dayton Institute for Family Therapy (Duncan & Parks, 1988; Duncan & Solovey, 1989; Duncan et al., in press).

Four categories of paradoxical procedures will be described[3]: (1) ascribing different meanings to problem situations; (2) prescribing different behaviors based on an accepted client meaning; (3) prescribing current behavior in new contexts and tasks; and (4) empowering client-ascribed meaning.

Ascribing Different Meanings to Problem Situations

In addition to the general utilization of position discussed earlier, it is often helpful to use clients' observations about themselves (self-awareness) combined with the particulars (specific situation and historical presentation of the problem) to design interventions. The use of client position, self-awareness, and problem specifics is most obvious in the technique of reframing. To reframe means "to change the conceptual

[3]The intervention typology evolved from the training and teaching experiences of the faculty of the Dayton Institute for Family Therapy, Greg Rusk, Paul Bruening, and Andy Solovey. It represents an attempt to broadly classify strategic interventions in a practical conceptual framework.

and/or emotional setting or viewpoint in relation to which a situation is experienced and to place it in another frame that fits the facts of the same concrete situation equally well or even better, and thereby changes its entire meaning" (Watzlawick et al., 1974, p. 95). Simplified, the therapist ascribes an alternative meaning to the problem, solutions, and/or circumstances related to the problem in the hope of influencing the client to take different immediate action regarding the presenting problem (Duncan & Solovey, 1989).

Ascribing different meanings to problem situations, or more simply, therapist-ascribed meaning, sometimes resembles what many therapists call interpretation. To understand this class of intervention, it may be helpful to compare therapist-ascribed meaning with the traditional intervention of interpretation. Interpretation can be defined as "a statement that refers to something the patient has said or done in such a way as to identify features of his behavior that he has not been fully aware of (Weiner, 1975, p. 115). Interpretation is intended to expand clients' awareness of their thoughts and feelings and thereby enhance their understanding of themselves (Weiner, 1975).

There are two major differences between therapist-ascribed meaning and interpretation (Duncan & Solovey, 1989). Interpretation offers clients a *way* of looking at their dilemma that is based on the therapist's frame of reference or theoretical orientation. A psychodynamic therapist may interpret unresolved conflict, a cognitive therapist may interpret irrational and self-defeating thoughts, a transactional analysis therapist may interpret client games and ego states, and a transgenerational family therapist may interpret the family ledger or legacy. Implicit to the notion of interpretation is its representation as a more accurate way for clients to perceive their problems (Duncan & Solovey, 1989).

Therapist-ascribed meaning is not intended to offer a better way of understanding the client problem, nor a true meaning of the situation because the ascribed meaning is not based on the adherence of the therapist to any particular orientation. Thus, a process-constructive perspective is interested in pursuing alternative meanings to problem situations rather than correct or true meanings. No inherently correct meaning is pursued, because of a belief that there is no "true maintainer" of the presenting problem, that is, no specific preconceived ideas that account for problematic behavior. Reiterating, this approach is a "process" view that asserts no particular "content" as an explanatory scheme for client problems (Held, 1986). Change occurs via interactive process in current communication sequences, rather than through the pursuit of a particular content. In much the same fashion, a behavioral approach may also be argued to be a process-based one.

Since no particular theoretical or content path must always be followed, the therapist may ascribe many different meanings to problem situations. The therapist is therefore free to select and offer "true" meanings from any approach that seems to fit the client predicament. This creative selection of content from other approaches to construct client-specific interventions is the major thrust of a process-constructive approach (Duncan, 1984; Duncan & Parks, 1988; Duncan et al., in press).

In addition to the true versus different meanings distinction, interpretation and therapist-ascribed meaning are different in terms of goals. The *immediate* objective of interpretation is promoting insight or increasing client understanding and self-awareness. The immediate or short-term goal is insight, and it is expected that behavior change will then ultimately occur. Although the ultimate or long-range goal may be behavior change, the pursuit of understanding is sometimes a long-term process and an end in and of itself.

Therapist-ascribed meaning, conversely, is primarily and specifically designed to act as an immediate stimulus for the client to behave differently in relation to the presenting problem. Therapist-ascribed meaning is therefore different from interpretation in that the immediate goal of the former is behavior change, as opposed to the long-term goal of interpretation. If the problematic behavior persists despite the different meaning ascribed by the therapist, that particular meaning is not considered useful and another one may be offered. It is the behavioral outcome that determines the utility of an ascribed meaning rather than the client's verbal acceptance; increased awareness is only helpful if it leads to a change in the presenting problem (Duncan & Solovey, 1989).

Ascribing different meanings to problem situations can occur as an intervention in itself, or as a rationale to present a suggestion or homework assignment.

Example. The P family, an intact family of three, sought therapy because of 10-year-old Robby's "school phobia." He had not attended school for more than one time per week for 4 weeks. The parents were very concerned and were worried about Robby's self-esteem. The mother had returned to work outside the home just 1 year prior, but as many women do, still attempted to maintain her home responsibilities as well. She was also clearly the primary caregiver for Robby. Father was supportive and warm, but generally peripheral with regard to home and child responsibilities.

With anger in her voice, the mother reported the typical morning scene. Mom got up before everyone and did chores she didn't have time for the day before. She made breakfast for dad and Robby. Dad, in the meantime, got up, ate breakfast, and went to work. Mom got Robby up and got him ready for school. Mom then went to work, leaving Robby to wait for the bus alone for a half-hour. Robby would call mom within that half-hour and report that he was sick to his stomach, and mom would leave work and return home to comfort Robby. On some occasions, Robby would throw up his breakfast.

This case can easily be conceptualized as the mother maintaining and exacerbating the problem through her very efforts to help it. Equally plausible is a view that sees the problem as being reinforced and therefore becoming a more strengthened response. With the goal of interrupting the attempted solution and changing the reinforcement contingency, the therapist decided to ascribe a different meaning to Robby's school phobia based on certain aspects of the mother's presentation regarding her work load and child-care responsibility.

THERAPIST: There are certainly a lot of ways to look at a problem like this. Some therapists might say, and this may sound a bit crazy so please bear with me, that Robby's school phobia problem, his getting sick to his stomach in the morning, is a metaphorical expression of unexpressed anger between the parents.

MOTHER: What do you mean? (*looking interested*)

THERAPIST: Well, again, this is just one way of looking at this problem—that Robby gets sick in the morning preventing him from going to school, is a metaphorical expression of mom being *sick* and tired of carrying the whole load. After all, both of your jobs are equally important, yet it is always mom who must interrupt her work routine and come home, while dad is able to work and not be bothered. Not to mention that it is mom who must also be responsible for keeping the house, fixing the meals, etc. In essence then, and this may seem far-fetched, when Robby throws up, he's doing it more for mom than for himself.

MOTHER: That's great! (*laughing hysterically for a while*) You know, I haven't told Dan about my resentment for all this.

DAD: What should we do?

THERAPIST: To let Robby see that he is no longer needed to express mom's unexpressed resentment, it may be helpful for you, Dan, to help a bit more around the house—but more importantly, it may more strongly convey the message to Robby if you are the one that he calls in the morning when he is sick. Are you willing to try that?

DAD: Of course, anything that will help.

The therapist brought Robby back in the session and instructed him to call his dad from now on in the morning if he is sick and cannot get on the bus, to which Robby replied, "I guess I won't be staying home from school anymore."

In this case the therapist utilized the mother's obvious burdensome workload, the father's somewhat minimal involvement, and the mother's apparent frustration to construct a client-specific intervention. The ascribed meaning itself was adopted from the work of Madanes (1981), not because the therapist believed it to be true, but rather, because such a frame or meaning seemed best to match the clients' presentation.

Prescribing Different Behaviors Based on an Accepted Client Meaning

This class of intervention is a client-specific extension of utilizing position. Reiterating, client position represents the beliefs, values, and attitudes that clients have regarding the problem and its resolution. The therapist then utilizes the client's position to frame interventions in such a way that compliance is enhanced. For example, should a parent express an attitude of pessimism, "Johnny's grade problem has gone on for so long, and we've tried so many things, including other therapists, but the school counselor recommended you highly," the therapist may engender significant "resistance" by responding in a way that indicates a position of optimism.

Despite the positive intention of a position of optimism, when such a position contradicts the client position, it may hinder progress, especially if the client has already been discouraged by previous therapy attempts that began on an optimistic note, only to terminate with no improvement (Fisch et al., 1982). The therapist may instead match the client's position by saying, "I understand your hope that I will be of some help to you, but considering all you've tried so far and the longstanding nature of the problem, it may be better to start treatment this time with a healthy sense of skepticism." In making this comment, the therapist is recognizing the client's discouragement and its validity, and is not attempting to patronize the client with false hope.

While all clients express some general position, some clients have such a strong position about the problem or its resolution that such a position must be accepted and not challenged by the therapist. An extreme example is the client with a firm delusional system. If the therapist confronts or challenges the delusional system, or attempts to reason or offer a more realistic view, it is likely that such a denial of the experience of the client will tend to further entrench the delusion and alienate the client. This is, of course, what others in the social network of the delusional person have done, and it has likely escalated the delusional process.

A far more useful stance for the therapist is to respect the client's beliefs and prescribe different behaviors based on those beliefs. In other words, the therapist can utilize such strong beliefs to build new and competing (e.g., not delusional) behaviors in the process surrounding the client problem. The competing behaviors may generate the construction of a new meaning system that does not include the presenting problem.

Although not delusional, many clients hold similarly strong beliefs or meaning systems that must be attended to by the therapist if compliance to suggestions is going to occur. In many ways, such strong beliefs or values offer the therapist a good indication of what path to pursue; thus, the therapist can align with the beliefs or meaning that the client holds regarding the problem and make all suggestions in light of that meaning. In other words, the therapist can offer even opposite behaviors as suggestions as long as the client meaning or position is validated.

Example. A very strong belief emerged in the case below that the therapist chose not to confront or counter, largely because the meaning of the problem as the client understood it was so intensely and unequivocally presented. It sometimes takes great restraint by the therapist to resist the temptation to confront clients in these circumstances.

The C family entered family therapy at the suggestion of Mrs. C's psychiatrist. The presenting problem was 9-year-old Amy's "depression." Mr. C did not say much, except to agree with Mrs. C, and Mrs. C wanted suggestions about how to handle Amy's depression.

CLIENT: I'm really worried about Amy. She's so depressed. She gets very upset when kids at school tease her and sometimes she even takes it out on me at home. She complains about being bored all the time and mopes around all day when she can't play with one of her friends. . . . You see, I'm depressed and have been seeing a psychiatrist, Dr. B, for 10 years, and I understand that I have a chemical imbalance and will need to take antidepressants for probably the rest of my life. I've been depressed all my life, and I remember being very sad as a child. My mother is also depressed and takes antidepressants. My doctor told me it was genetic, and I'm sure that Amy is just like my mother and me and probably needs to be on medication of some kind. I was hoping that she was going to be okay, chemically, you know, but the genetics were just too strong.

Mrs. C. had total confidence in her psychiatrist and was convinced that Amy's behavior was an early expression of a "genetic depression." The therapist decided to utilize the client meaning of genetic depression to prescribe different behaviors in the hope of interrupting the parents' current solution attempts, which were reinforcing Amy's problem behaviors. The problem behaviors were described as a general negative attitude, complaining, boredom, and sadness when unable to find a friend with whom to play. The parents' current solution attempts largely revolved around long discussions that resembled lectures, in which both parents, particularly the mother, would attempt to comfort and reason with Amy and talk her out of her negativism. The mother would also go to great lengths to help Amy not be bored or sad. For example, Mrs. C at times called Amy's friends to invite them over to play; she invented games for Amy to play; and, in general, spent much of her time monitoring Amy's "depression" and trying to help her overcome it. Also, at times, Mrs. C would take Amy shopping when she appeared sad.

The mother's intense involvement in responsibility for the problem, combined with her specific behaviors designed to help Amy, perpetuated the very problem she was attempting to solve. From a behavioral view, it is not difficult to see the reinforcement contingency that strengthened Amy's problem behaviors. The therapist hypothesized that the attributed meaning of genetic depression to Amy's behaviors must be respected, given how strongly the mother held this belief. Mrs. C's statement in the first interview, "Doctor, I need for you to verify what Dr. B has told me and what I already know in my heart, that Amy is depressed like me and my mother," provided a snapshot of both the nature of the problem and what Mrs. C wanted from therapy.

THERAPIST: After spending some alone time with Amy and viewing the tape from our first session, I have come to the conclusion that you are absolutely correct in your estimation of Amy's problem—she is indeed depressed—and given her family history of depression in both her mother and her grandmother, it seems very likely that she is genetically predisposed to depression.

CLIENT: I knew it all along, but it is nice to get confirmation. But, is there anything else I can do?

THERAPIST: Well, that's what I wanted to discuss with you today. Because she is genetically predisposed to depression, what happens in the environment is particularly important to the manifestation of the depression. Although the predisposition to depression is always there, the depression may or may not be expressed, depending on what happens in her environment and how she learns to cope. For these kinds of special kids, it takes a special kind of parenting, and frankly, a special kind of committed parent. Not all parents can demonstrate the level of involvement necessary to help a depressed child. What I'm getting at is a way to help Amy cope with her depression and learn how to control its expression. You can help do that by validating her concerns, boredom, and sadness when she expresses it, and then after that validation, drop the conversation so that she will learn to deal with her feelings. For example, if Amy says, "I'm bored, there's nothing to do around here; I hate it when no one is around to play," what I am suggesting that you say in return is, "Yes, it must be tough to be all alone in the house with nobody to play with." By validating her concern, she will feel understood, and the ball will essentially be back in her court for her to deal with the boredom. The hard part for parents, especially parents of depressed kids, and as I said earlier many cannot do it, is to resist the temptation to cheer up, entertain, or otherwise coerce the kid to feel better. Of course, all this accomplishes is making the parents feel like they have done everything they could. Another way of looking at the validation procedure is to, in general, respond to "gloom and doom" comments with agreement and even with a slight exaggeration of her original complaint. For example, to the comment, "I hate school," you may respond, "School can certainly be a bummer, and the worst of it is there's so much more to go." At other times when she is not complaining, or glooming and dooming, spend those times having discussions, playing games, and going shopping. In essence, you are accepting her depression by validating it and teaching her how to cope with it by allowing her some time and space to deal with it.

This intervention was specifically designed to influence the parents, particularly the mother, to back off from Amy and lessen her involvement in Amy's everyday activities. The therapist believed that directly suggesting that Mrs. C withdraw her involvement from her depressed child would be met with noncompliance and would also lessen the therapist's credibility. The therapist did not assess anything other than normal 9-year-old behavior from Amy, but the therapist also did not believe that Mrs. C would respond to a suggestion that Amy was normal and not depressed, and therefore could be left to her own devices. Amy reported to the therapist that her mother drove her "crazy" by asking her whether or not she was depressed about something.

From a behavioral view, once again, the reinforcement contingency is apparent. The unwanted behaviors were reinforced with entertainment, attention, and shopping, and therefore Amy learned to express negative statements.

Accepting Mrs. C's meaning of her daughter's behavior enabled the therapist to prescribe different behaviors based on that meaning. Such an acceptance and utilization of a strongly held client meaning not only provides the direction for intervention but also enhances compliance and therefore the likelihood of outcome success.

The C family returned for two more sessions following the intervention described above. Both parents reported that Amy seemed happier and that she was complaining less. Mrs. C reported that although it was difficult for her, she was not attempting to rescue Amy from her depression any more. Instead, she was responding to Amy's comments with concern and leaving it at that. The therapist responded with restraining techniques, described earlier, and terminated the next session.

Prescribing Current Behavior in New Contexts and Tasks

Symptom prescription, or prescribing current behavior in new contexts, is the most common form of specific intervention. This intervention has many variations, but implicitly, there are two messages in prescriptions: (1) in order to lose your symptom, keep it and/or exaggerate it; and (2) will or force your uncontrollable problem to occur voluntarily. By virtue of prescribing the symptom or current problematic behavior, the context in which it occurs is changed. The prescription may be offered for a multitude of reasons, but the goal is to set up an experience that interrupts the current solution attempts that are maintaining the problem. Prescriptions, therefore, are intended to provide a competing experience to the presenting problem, so that current solution attempts are interrupted and/or the client ascribes a different meaning to the problem. Sometimes, prescribing behaviors in a new context enables clients to find an alternative solution to the problem on their own because of the new meanings constructed.

For example, a mother brought her 7-year-old son to therapy because of his temper tantrums. The temper tantrums occurred every day when the mother picked him up at his grandmother's after work. Usually, the mother would sit and chat with her mother while Jimmy played quietly until it was time to leave, and then he would yell and cry at the top of his lungs. The mother was exasperated because all her attempts to stop the tantrums had failed, and she was beginning to feel guilty about them. Her fear was that they were related to her recent divorce. She also reported that these nightly tantrums tended to spoil the rest of the evening for her and her son.

The therapist prescribed the symptom in the following way to the son and his mother together:

THERAPIST: The tantrums seem to be a very important way for Jimmy to make his point about not wanting to leave grandma's house. The tantrums also seem to help grandma feel loved, since Jimmy always puts up such a fuss about leaving. For these, as well as other reasons, perhaps it may be that the tantrums should continue. What I am suggesting is that Mom, you should ensure that the tantrum occurs in the proper intensity. Every day, precisely 10 minutes before leaving grandma's, remind Jimmy that it is time to have his tantrum. If he resists, firmly encourage him to have it. When he starts the tantrum, model for him and coach him in the proper manner so he doesn't slack off in his responsibility by having a low-level or quiet tantrum.

The mother returned in 2 weeks and reported that encourage though she did, Jimmy didn't have any temper tantrums. After a few days, he asked her to stop, in a somewhat angry fashion, because he wasn't going to "act like a baby" anymore. The mother also reported that their overall relationship had improved as well and that she was enjoying him much more than before.

Prescribing tasks is similar to symptom prescription in that tasks are intended to provide a new experience that either behaviorally, affectively, or cognitively competes with the presenting problem and enables a different meaning to be constructed by the client.

For example, a task often given to parents who are trying to force an unruly child to comply with their demands by argument and threats is to ask them to, when the presenting problem situation occurs, observe the child without intervention and in the natural environment so that the therapist can learn baseline information. Such an intervention may interrupt the current problem-maintaining behaviors of the parents and thus enable a different and perhaps more compliant response from the child. The parents may in the process learn something themselves concerning their part in the problem.

Task prescriptions can take many forms and are only limited by the creativity of the therapist. Tasks can be general and vague, as in the example above, or can be very specific to the particular case under scrutiny, as in the example below. Tasks enable clients to confront limitations of the meanings attributed to problems and form different and perhaps more adaptive ways of perceiving themselves or their problems. The importance of client-ascribed meaning will be discussed in the next section.

Example. A case of an adolescent's flying phobia illustrates both prescribing current behaviors in new contexts, as well as task prescription. The therapist received a call on Tuesday from a very worried mother. Her 18-year-old daughter was due to fly the coming Sunday to her college entrance interviews at three prestigious universities. The problem was that the daughter had a flying phobia and had refused to fly on a recent trip home, which had resulted in the parents having to drive 400 miles to pick her up. Two appointments were set. After a discussion of the phobia and an assessment of the solution strategies employed by all involved and the accompanying meaning system around the problem, the parents and daughter were interviewed separately. The daughter's primary solution was putting the fear outside of her mind and trying to avoid thinking about it, to the extent that she would leave the room if flying was mentioned on the news. She attempted to control her fears by willing them away. The parents tried various forms of comforting and reassurance, largely concerning the safety of flying, and how she would eventually get over her fear once she got a few flights "under her belt." The meaning system surrounding the problem was that flying was "no big deal" and should be taken in stride, and the daughter's problem was clearly an overreaction.

In the first session, the therapist normalized the phobia, commenting that as far as he was concerned, hurling through space at 600 miles an hour at 30,000 feet in a 30-ton metal cylinder was a pretty frightening thing to think about. Although it may be statistically safer than driving, added the therapist, the problem with flying is that one time is all it takes to be fatal; there are not any fender benders. The therapist continued expressing a belief that it was somewhat Pollyanna-ish not to be afraid of flying and that most people indeed were afraid. The therapist ended the first session with both a task and symptom prescription directed at the daughter:

THERAPIST: My greatest concern here is that you are minimizing the extent to which flying is inherently a frightening and nerve-racking experience. For that reason, there are two suggestions that I would like you to consider. First, I am suggesting that you go out to the airport tonight and observe people waiting to get on airplanes. Observe 10 people for 10 minutes each and rate their anxiety levels on a scale of 1 to 10, where 10 is extremely nervous and 1 is not nervous at all. Observe the nonverbal signs of anxiety that we discussed earlier. The other suggestion is that, once you arrive back home, I am suggesting that you spend at least 15 minutes, but not more than 30 minutes, considering the dangers of flying so that you experience your fears intensely, and thereby avoid minimizing the magnitude of this situation. Do you understand what I am suggesting?

The family returned for session two, and again they were separated for discussion. The daughter had complied with both suggestions and reported that she couldn't believe how nervous everyone was at the airport. In fact, seven out of the 10 people observed had ratings of 6 or more. She also added that she was glad to see that not everyone took flying in stride, as she used to think.

She was able to think about the dangers associated with flying and reported that the fears didn't seem as strong. The therapist expressed concern that she was minimizing, but the client disagreed. The therapist also taught the young woman a relaxation exercise that was presented as possibly, but probably not, helpful to her problem. The therapist suggested that the parents help the daughter by expressing their own concerns about flying and encourage her to express her very valid feelings of fear. The session was ended with the therapist expressing concern about taking flying too lightly and with a further extension of the symptom prescription and task:

THERAPIST: I would suggest that between now and Sunday you spend time each night, just as before, considering the inherent dangers of flying and experiencing your feelings to the fullest. You may want to do that just before you board the plane. Finally, when you board the plane, observe at least 10 people and rate their anxiety levels on that same 1 to 10 scale.

The prescription of the symptom and the task had two purposes: (1) to create an experience that interrupted the current solution or problem process and/or competed affectively, behaviorally, or cognitively; and (2) to create a new context that enabled the clients to shift their view or ascribe a different meaning to the problem. In this case, the daughter's solution attempts of avoidance and willpower were interrupted, and she was able to give new meaning to her situation that allowed her to accept her fear as expected anxiety. By telephone follow-up, the therapist learned that although she had felt anxious, the daughter flew to and from the interviews. The daughter also added that she did not need to think about the dangers before boarding and that she used the relaxation technique with some success.

Empowering Client-Ascribed Meaning

As discussed above, tasks and prescriptions are designed in part to encourage the client to ascribe a new and helpful meaning to the presenting problem. To enhance this process, it is sometimes useful to prescribe a task or symptom without the benefit of a therapist-ascribed meaning, or frame. Such tasks are usually prescribed for "information purposes" or some other vaguely defined reason (e.g., the observe-without-intervention suggestion discussed above).

Sometimes a hoped for, but puzzling phenomenon occurs: clients report new insights that apparently come to them as an outgrowth of following or attempting to follow a homework assignment. It seems particularly confusing when such client-ascribed meaning appears to have little logical connection to the task or prescription and perhaps to the presenting problem itself. In these instances, the client report of enhanced self-awareness and/or increased knowledge about the problem is strikingly similar to what other therapies would call insight.

Two distinctions, however, have been identified between client-ascribed meaning and insight (Duncan & Solovey, 1989). Insight occurs as the result of the gradual accumulation of many interpretations offered by the therapist. Over time, the therapist builds his or her case, carefully selecting interpretations on the basis of depth, focus, and connotation. The therapist therefore generates or promotes the insight based on his or her frame of reference.

Client-ascribed meaning, on the other hand, is client-generated as opposed to therapist-generated. Clients are offered an ambiguous and often confusing assignment and are then faced with creating or constructing their own meanings for the task. The therapist has no particular meaning in mind that he or she is hoping to promote. Client-ascribed meanings seem to occur spontaneously and serendipitously in response to ambiguous tasks that start the change process in motion. The new client-ascribed meaning reinforces or enables continued change, and vice versa.

Besides the therapist- versus client-generated distinction, the time at which the "insight" occurs is another difference between client-ascribed meaning and insight. Insight-oriented approaches tend to view insight as a necessary precondition for change and believe that change occurring without insight is spurious or short-lived. Client-ascribed meaning, conversely, occurs either during the process of change or as a postcondition of it. Reacting to the ambiguity of the task, and to the seemingly spontaneous change that has occurred, clients will ascribe a meaning that makes sense to them about why the task was assigned and why they were able to make a change in their problem. These ascribed meanings are viewed as very important by the therapist, because the client will likely take ultimate responsibility for the change. Therapeutic movement is thus further amplified as the therapist expands the meaning of the change and the client feels still more empowered to progress toward problem resolution (Duncan & Solovey, 1989). The following case illustrates client-ascribed meaning and its strategic use in empowering continued change.

Example. The Z family sought therapy for their 13-year-old daughter, Mary, who had superficially cut her wrist after an argument with her parents. The parents were very concerned, and described Mary as an overemotional child who was very different from her two older sisters. Her sisters were academically successful, attractive, and quite popular. Mary was not attractive, according to the parents, and not motivated at school. The primary concern was, of course, the wrist-cutting episode, but the parents also identified the loud arguments and crying that had been occurring on a regular basis (two to four times per week) as important as well. It seemed to the therapist that the parents believed Mary couldn't do anything right, although he found Mary to be both bright and charming.

At the end of the first session to all three family members, the therapist asked the parents to observe Mary closely and note the things they observed that they would like to see continue (de Shazer, 1985). The parents were instructed not to make comment on the things they noticed, but simply note them to discuss with the therapist. The task was given for informational purposes.

The family returned in 3 weeks and responded to the question of what they had observed with a long list of positive events and attributes. The therapist went through each item on their list and encouraged discussion while expressing amazement and confusion at each break between items. Mary was then asked to wait in the next room.

THERAPIST: I'm amazed at all the positive things and all these changes. But frankly, I'm also quite confused. Can you fill me in on what's going on here?

MOTHER: Well, Mary just seemed to turn around and be more cooperative—we didn't have any major fights, a couple of disagreements, but they didn't turn into any big deal.

THERAPIST: What do you attribute the turn of events to?

DAD: That assignment you gave us, well I think I know what you were driving at. I was also surprised at all the good things that Mary does. I don't know, I guess we were just always focusing on the bad things about her—how she's not as attractive or popular as her sisters.

THERAPIST: I'm sorry, I'm not understanding very well.

MOTHER: Well, we have probably been a little harsh on Mary. She's different than her sisters, and I think I've not been able to accept that until now. I was always comparing her with them and not seeing her strengths.

THERAPIST: What strengths are you talking about?

MOTHER: She's a lot more sensitive and affectionate than the other girls. She seems more concerned about people than clothes or boyfriends. Do you know what I mean?

THERAPIST: I think I'm sorta understanding a little better, but I'm still puzzled and amazed about how you were able to overcome the temptation to argue with Mary and dwell on the problems that she has been having.

DAD: I decided that I was going to back off and when I did, well, I found out that she can be a pretty neat kid. I also found out that I like myself better as a parent when I'm not so critical.

This case illustrates the use of client-ascribed meaning to empower and encourage change. A task was suggested without a therapist-ascribed meaning as a rationale. The parents gave meaning to the task and were able to do something different (back off, appreciate Mary's strengths) in relation to the problem. After making changes in the way they interacted with Mary, they continued to ascribe meaning to the task and to the changes she was making

Once clients make a change or experience a serendipitous change and ascribe a new and seemingly helpful meaning to the problem or themselves, the therapist's task is one of empowerment. The therapist punctuates the change that has occurred by asking questions that encourage the clients to articulate and embellish the reasons behind their puzzling change of circumstances or heart. The client gains momentum for change by describing the change and how it came about, often ascribing more and more positive meaning to the change. The client essentially gets on a role of positive ascriptions and is thereby empowered for further change without the therapist taking responsibility for the change or assuming a cheerleading position. In essence, then, the use of client-ascribed meaning to promote change is fundamentally a growth-enhancing intervention (Duncan & Solovey, 1989).

Paradox: Caveats for Practice

Almost all publications addressing the use of paradox contain some discussion regarding when and when not to use paradox. Many assert that only if resistance is high and motivation low is there any need to abandon direct interventions and "resort" to paradox (Papp, 1979; Stanton, 1981). In addition, the authors often provide a list of types of problems and/or clinical situations in which the use of paradox is contraindicated (Weeks & L'Abate, 1982). Usually such lists include crisis situations, situational violence, grief, suicide, and psychosis, to mention a few.

It is the position of this author, however, that such contraindications belie a misunderstanding of paradox and that, furthermore the use of paradox is rarely, if ever, contraindicated. Although somewhat of a radical stance at first glance, this position stems from the assumption that paradox is not an entity in and of itself but, rather, is relative to the frame of reference of the observer (Dell, 1981; Cronen, Johnson, & Lannamann,

1982). Paradox exists only in the eyes of the observer and not inherently in the situation under observation. In other words, the phenomenon of paradox requires the beliefs, values, opinions, expectations, and common sense of the observer. Action deemed paradoxical by an observer may not seem so to those involved in the event under observation.

Paradox is not something a therapist does to manipulate or trick people out of their problem. It is exactly the view that paradox is a thing to do to "resistant" clients that results in contraindication lists. It is also this view of paradox that can lead to the arrogances of power and control. Dell (1981, p. 132) states, "The use of therapeutic 'paradoxes' is offensive precisely when such 'paradoxes' are wielded with an unseemly excitement by an insensitive therapist who has succumbed to the lust for power and control." Dell makes a strongly worded yet crucial point. It is perhaps the abuse of so-called paradoxical methods, by therapists intrigued with such power positions and the authority they represent that requires a caveat for responsible practice.

To hold paradox in abeyance until "resistance" rears it's ugly head precisely illustrates this point. Resistance in psychotherapy is an expected phenomenon that has as much to do with the therapist and his or her orientation as it does with the client or family. If resistance is high and motivation low, then it may be related to a therapist's choice of intervention and style of presentation rather than some quality attributable to the client.

As has been conveyed through example in this chapter, seemingly paradoxical interventions are offered with great respect to the client's values and beliefs to prevent impasses in treatment and enhance compliance rather than as a form of therapeutic chicanery.

A Final Example: Constructive Payback

To tie together many of the above points, as well as convey the sense of collaboration with clients that often occurs within this clinical perspective, one final example is presented below:

Rita and Steve entered therapy shortly after their 18-year-old son, Hank, quit school and got a job as a motorcycle mechanic. He was failing in school anyway, and the parents were exasperated with him for many reasons. The problems were Hank's "thoughtless" and irresponsible behaviors. Examples included things such as not picking up his dirty clothing, being late for dinner, leaving for the evening just as dinner was being served, or insisting that family meals conform to his spur-of-the-moment plans, and staying out past curfew or all night without calling. Steve and Rita felt as if they had tried everything and stated that rewards and punishment didn't work with Hank. The following excerpts are from the end of the first session and the beginning of the second:

RITA: We are feeling abused and taken for granted on a daily basis. His thoughtlessness really hurts me.

STEVE: It really makes me mad. What should we do?

THERAPIST: I have an idea, but it's one that I am usually reluctant to offer, until I'm sure that two things are in the situation. The first is that the parents have to be real frustrated and even angry, because it takes a lot of effort to enact the suggestion.

RITA: Oh we are . . . we both are.

STEVE: We're beyond frustration and anger, I'm ready to strangle the kid.

THERAPIST: Good! It takes that kind of determination. Second, it is a special tactic that is especially for the kid who is really on a self-defeating path and definitely has a wrong attitude about many aspects of life. This method is for the kid who is completely out of touch with other's feelings and is stuck in a way of perceiving the world that is thoughtless, disrespectful, and unconcerned about the effects of his behavior on others as well as his own future. It is for the situation in which it is clear that the kid is obviously caught in the wrong frame of mind.

RITA: That fits him to a tee. He isn't concerned with anyone or anything else but himself and is so self-absorbed that it seems we are servants in the house rather than parents.

STEVE: Look, we're ready to try anything. Hank is definitely on the wrong track with his thinking and something has to change.

THERAPIST: Well, O.K., I can see how your situation is one in which the tactic could apply—but I'm also hesitant to suggest this because it sounds so crazy that the benefits sometimes are hard to see. Something so crazy takes more determination to apply than many parents are able or willing to put forth. . . . As I was saying, your son seems to have a frame of mind that is inherently self-defeating for him. The tactic that is sometimes helpful to try is called constructive payback, and it is intended to shake him up and essentially turn the tables on him so that he becomes confused. He is perceiving his parents in a disrespectful manner and needs to reorient his thinking. What needs to happen first is that Hank needs to be stopped cold in his tracks and made to become seriously confused. In other words, he needs to become disorganized to be able to reorganize his thinking in a more constructive and appropriate manner. Confusion is the precursor to change in many instances. It is often the uncomfortable psychological state that one will work very hard cognitively to get out of. Through confusing him, he may shift his focus off of himself and onto the effects of his behavior on others. Let me stop here. Sometimes I ramble and don't make any sense.

RITA: I understand what you're saying (*looking intrigued*), but how do we confuse him so he will have to reorganize his thinking? (*Husband nods head in agreement.*)

THERAPIST: Well, this is the crazy part. Constructive payback is the method of confusion. It entails "benignly sabotaging" the adolescent shortly after the thoughtless or irresponsible behavior occurs. In other words, it means that you pay him back for his inappropriate behavior—but for constructive purposes. For example, if he fails to consider your needs by failing to inform you that he will be late for dinner, you may accidentally over- or undercook his food or put debris in his food (*some laughter from both parents*), or you may run the vacuum while he's on the telephone. It can really be anything that you know will be an annoyance to him, and it can take whatever creative and situation-specific form you can come up with. After you have constructively paid him back and he confronts you with the evidence and inquires what in the hell is going on, it is quite important to this particular tactic to respond in a way that conveys a very humble apology and a sense of helplessness and hopelessness. In other words, things like, "I'm so sorry, I don't know what's gotten into me lately, I haven't been myself," or "I must be losing my mind, how can I make it up. I've been depressed lately, and it must be affecting my mind." "I'm sorry, I feel so stupid," or anything in that vein. Basically, the position you want to convey is that you're terribly sorry and that you're either incompetent, stupid, senile, or crazy. It is often appropriate to be disgustingly sorry and self-effacing. Remember, I warned you that it's crazy, and I wouldn't blame you if you left here today and never came back.

RITA: No, no, it sounds great. I can get rid of a lot of hostility this way (*laughing*).

STEVE: Once we do this, what happens next?

THERAPIST: Well, that's a good question. I'm not, of course, completely sure. What may happen is that Hank will become real confused about why in the hell are mom and dad acting so weird, and what is going on. It will likely make him put some effort into trying to figure what is happening and may shake him enough to get him on the right track. Earlier I said that constructive payback requires a good bit of anger to implement, but it also is an effective and harmless method of discharging your anger in a way that may be helpful. One last thing. If you think this over and decide to do it, it must be carried out without sarcasm or other clues that you are purposely hassling him.

STEVE: I don't think we need to think about it. I'm ready for it. (*Rita nods.*)

This intervention is based on a tactic called benign sabotage developed by the MRI. The only difference with constructive payback is that the therapist encourages the clients to be creative and come up with their own ways of payback that fit their particular situation. The primary purpose of this intervention is to interrupt the current problem-solving attempts and construct an experience for the parents and the child or adolescent that may enable both to ascribe a different meaning to their situation. The parents in this case had been attempting to influence their adolescent by lecturing, coercion, exhortation, and confrontation. Constructive payback is a way of interrupting these solution attempts and can be helpful in giving parents some feeling of power and control and enables them to impose consequences for misbehavior (Fisch et al., 1982). The avoidance of the confrontive solutions undercuts the provocative and rebellion-inducing behavior the parents were unwittingly using. Three weeks later, Steve and Rita returned; both greeted the therapist with big smiles on their faces.

THERAPIST: You two seem in a good mood today. How's it going?

RITA: It's going great. We;ve been having lots of fun constructively paying back Hank for his inappropriate behaviors. I've been looking forward to this session for about a week because I couldn't wait to tell you about it. Steve, do you want to tell him or should I?

STEVE: Go ahead, you did most of it (*with excitement in his voice*).

RITA: Well, we used the tactic with success for about 2 weeks, concentrating on the daily hassles over laundry and meals. For example, we went out to dinner, "forgetting" to tell Hank. When he came home late, the house was dark and the pots were cold (*laughing*). Convenient microwave fare was missing from the refrigerator because I had "neglected" to stock up. How stupid of me! Remember about those last-minute demands for meals? Well, those dinners prepared quickly at his last-minute insistence were accidentally raw or overdone. Of course, I apologized profusely. Laundry not picked up by him was regrettably overlooked by "mom," with the consequence of his having nothing clean to wear. Since he would then wear the dirty clothes with no apparent problem, I began remembering to wash them, but unfortunately would neglect to transfer them to the dryer. Even *he* wouldn't wear wet clothes! So much for some Monday through Friday irritations. One source of real worry for us was his frequent neglect to call us by a 1:00 a.m. deadline if he were going to stay over at some friend's house on a weekend night. [The 1:00 a.m. time had been negotiated with him previously.] After a long Saturday discussion with him, we were at a loss when Sunday morning arrived with his bed empty—again. We decided this situation needed some creative constructive payback. But how? We chose to take the happy position that he was indeed a man of his word. He had just agreed to call us by 1:00 a.m. if he were not coming home. Since no call was received, we reasoned he *must* be home. Our ruse was aided by two unrelated happenstances: a recent rash of crank telephone calls, of which Hank was aware, and the date—April first. As usual, Hank called about noon Sunday to tell us where he was. His carefree "Hi, mom," was greeted by a swift disconnect on my end. Seconds later, instant replay. On the third call, he yelled an exasperated, "Wait, mom, don't hang up." I responded, "Please, whoever you are, stop harassing us with these silly crank calls," and again hung up on him. The fourth call brought a pleading to be recognized as our son. With all the annoyance I could muster, I snapped that our son was still in bed and so couldn't possibly be on the phone, and furthermore, these nuisance calls were likely to wake him up. Click! Now Hank enlisted the help of the friend with whom he had spent the night. The next call began with a rapid, "Mrs. D, this is Scott. Don't hang up!" There followed a testimony that the previous calls were truly from our son, who was being repeatedly frustrated in his efforts to let us know his whereabouts. I resisted entreaties to check his room by saying I didn't want to wake him and expressed shock that Scott was a party to all of the crank calls we had received for weeks. Scott became defensive, forgetting his mission of aiding our son and transferring his efforts to extricating himself from suspicion. I finally forgave him his "prank" with a grudging acknowledgment that it was a good try at an April Fool's joke. Helpless silence followed and the telephone pleadings ended. Steve and I spent several amused hours gloating over our coup. We knew where Hank was and we had totally frustrated him. We laughingly pictured him in his exasperation. Hours later, Hank came home "unnoticed" by us and was greeted with, "Well, you finally decided to get up." No response. He immediately went to the laundry room for the first time in my memory to transfer his clothes from the washer into the dryer. His only comment was, "Mom, I'm really worried about you; you're losing it; you're getting senile." Mission accomplished. *He* was worried about *me*.

THERAPIST: This is quite remarkable. I am really impressed by your ability to creatively apply constructive payback. What I'm really surprised and somewhat confused about, though, is your change of mood. I mean, I understand your response in regard to having some constructive fun with Hank, but something else? . . .

STEVE: Well, tension around our house has been relieved incredibly—tension between Hank and us and also tension between Rita and me. We were beginning to argue a bit about Hank, and it was good to agree about a plan of attack.

RITA: Yes, I agree with that, but also I feel like, well, I don't feel as burdened by this whole situation any more.

THERAPIST: What do you mean? I think I'm understanding, but can you help me out?

RITA: Well, this technique that you suggested not only helped us shake up Hank, it also altered our attitude as well. Well, it's like the freedom and fun of our new helplessness and incompetence helped us change from overly responsible nags to more carefree happy parents.

The therapist continued to empower the client-ascribed meaning and then predicted a relapse. In the following termination session, the therapist ended treatment with a prescription of relapse. This case illustrates many of the interventions presented in this chapter, both general and specific. It hopefully illustrates the collaborative nature of this approach and the usefulness of constructing experiences for clients that offer competing behaviors to their current solutions and enable new meaning to be ascribed.

Summary

Because of the MRI's position regarding problem formation and its lack of a preconceived explanatory scheme to account for problem behavior, the therapeutic focus is on current interactional patterns around the presenting problem and how to intervene to interrupt that process. Much like a behavioral view, then, a strategic approach emphasizes the contingencies surrounding the problem and how they might be changed, rather than the pursuit of a particular or perceived reason of why the problem exists. Many other process and conceptual similarities are easily identified. Because of these similarities, and the complementary nature of their respective domains of expertise, behavioral and strategic approaches can be integrated in an additive fashion.

General interventions from the MRI that can be used adjunctively with any orientation, offer a well-defined methodology for the clinician who wishes to enhance compliance and avoid "resistance" to treatment suggestions. Specific interventions, or those that are constructed to be problem- and client-specific, can be utilized in an additive fashion with other approaches and may also be used in isolation. Specific interventions were described as methods of: altering the premises that clients hold about problems; altering the behaviors based on the client's current premise; creating experiences for clients that compete on an affective, behavioral, or cognitive level with their current solution attempts and self-limiting premises; and finally, empowering any helpful client-ascribed meaning that may occur.

Behavioral and strategic approaches constitute a natural fit and may be integrated flexibly to achieve a variety of therapeutic objectives. This chapter has sought to provide the behaviorally oriented clinician with practical guidelines for utilizing paradoxical interventions with families.

Acknowledgments

The author wishes to thank Steve Drewry and Greg Rusk for their invaluable comments and critiques and Alice Penney for her unending patience in preparing the manuscript.

References

Bateson, G., Jackson, D. D., Haley, J., & Weakland, J. (1956). Toward a theory of schizophrenia. *Behavioral Science*, 1, 251–264.

Buckley, W. (1967). *Sociology and modern systems theory*. Englewood Cliffs, N.J.: Prentice-Hall.

Cronen, V. E., Johnson, K. M., & Lannamann, J. W. (1982). Paradoxes, double binds, and reflexive loops. *Family Process, 21*, 91–112.

Dell, P. (1981). Paradox redux. *Journal of Marital and Family Therapy, 7*, 127–134.

de Shazer, S. (1982). *Patterns of brief family therapy: An ecosystemic approach*. New York: The Guilford Press.

de Shazer, S. (1985). *Keys to solutions in brief therapy*. New York: W. W. Norton.

de Shazer, S. (1988). *Clues: Investigating solutions in brief therapy*. New York: W. W. Norton.

Duncan, B. L. (1984). Adopting the construct of functionality when it facilitates system change: A method of selective integration. *Journal of Strategic and Systemic Therapies, 4*, 58–63.

Duncan, B. L., & Parks, M. B. (1988). Integrating individual and systems approaches: Strategic-behavioral therapy. *Journal of Marital and Family Therapy, 14*, 151–161.

Duncan, B. L., Parks, M. B., & Rusk, G. (in press). Eclectic strategic practice: A process constructive perspective. *Journal of Marital and Family Therapy*.

Duncan, B. L., Rock, J. W., & Parks, M. B. (1987). Strategic-behavioral therapy: A practical alternative. *Psychotherapy, 24*, 196–201.

Duncan, B. L., & Solovey, A. (1989). Strategic brief therapy: An insight-oriented approach? *Journal of Marital and Family Therapy, 15*, 1–9.

Fisch, R., Weakland, J., & Segal, L. (1982). *The tactics of change: Doing therapy briefly*. San Francisco: Jossey-Bass.

Held, B. S. (1986). The relationship between individual psychologies and strategic/systemic therapies reconsidered. In D. E. Efron (Ed.), *Journeys: Expansion of the strategic-systemic therapies*. New York: Brunner/Mazel.

Madanes, C. (1981). *Strategic family therapy*. San Francisco: Jossey-Bass.
Papp, P. (1979). Paradoxical strategies and countertransference. *American Journal of Family Therapy, 7,* 11–12.
Stanton, M. D. (1981). Strategic approaches to family therapy. In A. S. Gurman & D. P. Kniskern (Eds.), *Handbook of family therapy*. New York: Brunner/Mazel.
Watzlawick, P. (1984). *The invented reality*. New York: W. W. Norton.
Watzlawick, P., Weakland, J., & Fisch, R. (1974). *Change: Principles of problem formation and problem resolution*. New York: W. W. Norton.
Weeks, G. R., & L'Abate, L. (1982). *Paradoxical psychotherapy*. New York: Brunner/Mazel.
Weiner, I. B. (1975). *Principles of psychotherapy*. New York: John Wiley & Sons.

Chapter 12

Child-Focused Paradoxical Psychotherapy: Reframing the Behavioral Picture for Therapeutic Change

Steven A. Szykula

A good deal of confusion and antagonism exists regarding "paradoxical" psychotherapy. Some mental health professionals espouse paradoxical approaches for their profoundly positive and impactful results. Other mental health professionals have condemned paradoxical therapies as being unethical, dishonest, sneaky, bizarre, or even dangerous. Both extreme views are probably based on hearsay, miscommunication, exaggeration, misinformation, or an uninformed prejudice for or against the term "paradoxical." Unfortunately, then, the term loses its meaning or its meaning becomes contorted.

Although some readers of this book may not yet be ready to integrate paradoxical interventions into their own work, it is my intention to help demystify and clarify paradoxical therapy approaches. Hypotheses are presented on why paradoxical approaches facilitate therapeutic change. Furthermore, I offer operational definitions of clinically important therapist and client communications and case examples with concurrent explanations of the in-session processes. This will give readers a sense of when and how to apply paradoxical techniques with children. My goal is to help insure that these methods, which represent only a fraction of what is available to psychotherapists, are understood and deliverable to children and their family members in a clinically sensitive way. These methods reduce resistance, increase cooperation, and induce therapeutic improvement.

Outline of Hypotheses

Paradoxical interventions are effective, I believe, because they serve to decontextualize a person's problem (Dowd & Brockbank, 1985). This decontextualization *changes the rules governing the problem and its solution.* I assert that paradoxical interventions primarily impact on clients' "rules." These rules include clients' beliefs about themselves and others regarding values, identity, and power (see *Client Statements* below for clarification). These rules are referred to as "core human processes" that are critical to either indirectly or directly influence a client's improvement (Mahoney, in press). This chapter posits that a person's rules can more powerfully influence behavior than can immediate contingencies and situations.

Paradoxical therapies may work where other therapies have failed. This is so primarily because paradoxical interventions can better match a child's or parent's personal and interpersonal rules of behaving than can interventions from other orientations. This enables a child to change even chronic and longstanding dysfunctional patterns. In other words, traditional behavioral methods or other techniques, even when appropriately delivered, may not address these dysfunctional core change factors adequately (that is, the client's personal and interpersonal rules) and thus may fail. Clinical studies have documented that a variety of clinical subsamples (referred for psychological treatment) engage in behavior consistent with the "rules" hypothesis (Devaney, Hayes, & Nelson, 1986; Dumas & Wahler, 1983; Hayes, 1987).

The most powerful rules are those that relate to the self and to significant others. Rules that developed during contexts of trauma or distress are especially potent. This hypothesis is based in part on an evolutionary epistemology. That is, if one "survives" a situation or experience even though one behaved in a maladaptive way and received a negative outcome, an emotional and personal rule that is consistent with the former pattern of behavior may form. This maladaptive rule then governs future behavior in stressful situations.

During therapy sessions, children and parents articulate, imply, and enact patterns of behavior. These patterns communicate to the therapist which personal and interpersonal rules are operative within the various target problem contexts presented for treatment (as well as those that are operative in the context of therapy itself). The therapist probes for, listens to, and observes the contextual detail and the explicit and implicit rules presented during therapy sessions and guides child patients and their parents to reduce or eliminate the target complaints. The therapist accomplishes this by: (1) expanding the detail of the context surrounding the problem so that rule-governed and previously contextually bound maladaptive patterns are replaced and discontinued because of the client's increased awareness (see Case 1); or (2) presenting the maladaptive patterns and raising a concern to the child or parents that the action they are taking is incongruous to their context and that the action also contradicts personally held rules regarding their senses of power, identity, or values (see Cases 2-A and 2-B below); or (3) exposing operative client-held rules as dysfunctional, superstitiously held, or of lesser importance than another personally held rule that may prove to influence more adaptive behavior (see Case 3).

After a brief explanation of salient client communications, clinically important paradoxical therapist communications are defined. The bulk of this chapter is then devoted to exploring clinical case examples that illustrate the techniques included in the three methods delineated above. Following each illustrative client or therapist communication (or series of communications), explanations are given to illustrate how therapeutic techniques and/or communications and client verbalizations are used to facilitate change.

Centrally Important Client and Therapist Communications

Client Statements

The most important, clinically relevant child and parent statements made during therapy are those that reflect clients' positions on their world view about self and others. Research has provided documentation of the clinical importance of such statements (Szykula, Laylander, Czajkowski, & Sayger, in press; Szykula, Morris, Butler, & Lambert, 1988). The statements may directly reflect or indirectly imply personal rules. These rule communications are statements, questions, or implications that indicate the speaker's perception of a personal and/or interpersonal rule of identity, power, values, or a conditional situation.

1. *Identity rule.* Statement of a general trait, ability, or personal "style"—not a statement of situation. "I am. . . ," "He is always. . . ," "She's the kind of person that. . . ," "He is not. . . ."
2. *Power rule.* Evidence of control or self-efficacy. "I can/cannot. . . ," "He never could. . . ," "I am able to. . . ," "She has control over. . . ."
3. *Value rule.* Perception of speaker's general worth and expectations. May be established or justified on the basis of religion,

morality, societal norms, ethics, etc. May be articulated in terms such as good/bad, right/wrong, should/ought, or must.

4. *Conditional rule.* May include any of the above rule types, but is qualified by the speaker to occur only in a specific context or situation; it occurs when a client explains or predicts someone's behavior given a certain set of conditions.

Therapist Statements

The following 11 types of paradoxical or strategic therapist statements are only a sampling of the many types that exist.

Engagement

The therapist interprets and/or encourages the therapeutic relationship, therapy, or self (therapist) in ways that motivate the client to be cooperative and less defensive. In paradoxical or strategic methods, this is accomplished by assessing the personal and interpersonal rules a child or child's family member maintains regarding therapy and/or the therapist.

Probes

A therapist requests or elicits information regarding the client's personally held rules about his or her own and family members' values, power, and identity as they relate to the details of the problem and problem context. Probes are usually, and simply, questions, and they occur more frequently during early sessions of therapy. A probe is usually used after the therapist asks open-ended questions that bring into focus the child's or parents' referral problem or goal. Other probes are designed to identify the sequence of events leading to the problem's occurrence, the context including who is involved, and the consequences that those involved with the problem experience. Probes "set the stage" for paradoxical interventions.

Framing

The therapist interprets and explains how or why a problematic pattern developed or is being maintained. The therapist frames interventions in ways that are consistent with the child's or family members' personally held rules.

Reframing

The therapist interprets an interpersonal pattern, situation, or a client's significant other's action in a way that alters the client's viewpoint and feelings about it. Reframing is related to the client's negative rules that focus on others' and one's own identity, power, or values. A negative rule is an obstacle to interpersonal compromise and problem resolution; it must be successfully reframed if improvements are to occur.

Paradoxical Injunctions

The therapist suggests to a child or parent that he or she do something that, at face value, does not appear to be a solution to the problem presented. Paradoxical injunctions may be indirectly, oppositionally, or directly related to the problem of focus, and they are almost always accompanied by a framing that justifies the prescription as fitting with the clients' personal rules. This framing increases a client's understanding of a motivation to engage in the prescription. It is important to remember that *paradoxical injunctions must be tailored to the person to match his or her rules as well as the problem.* (See case examples for illustrations of this.) Some examples of specific paradoxical injunctions include:

1. The therapist advises a parent to tell the child to have a symptom at the parent's request. The child is then not "rescued" by the parent when the symptom is exhibited. The goal here is for the intervention to inhibit the occurrence of the symptom.
2. The therapist directly instructs a child client to experience, for example, his or her anxiety (which the client reports having no control over) at times that just precede the time the client would normally experience the anxiety. Again, the intervention inhibits the occurrence of the symptom.
3. The therapist directs the child client to actually experience the symptoms or problems the client wishes to eliminate or reduce under his or her own volition or control. The goal here is for the symptom to occur but under the regulation of the child.

Benevolent Sabotage

The therapist may, for example, instruct parents to allow their child to experience negative consequences as a result of the parents performing the child's responsibilities ineptly. For example, instead of nagging a child to clean his or her bedroom and getting locked in a power struggle, the parents clean the room, making it impossible for the child to find valued objects.

Benevolent Doubt

A therapist challenges, in a positive way, a child's, teen's, or parents' positive personally held rules. This may challenge a client's implied or proclaimed certainty ("I can do it!") to perform particular acts. This serves to increase the probability that the act or behavior will occur.

Affective Focus

The therapist reveals to a client a personal emotion of the therapist in response to the client's manner of interacting in a session. The therapist may or may not point out how this may serve a similar function outside of therapy with persons other than the therapist.

Eavesdrop Inductions

A therapist requests that parents purposefully allow their child to overhear an intervention strategy. For example, two parents discuss with each other, with their child in the next room listening in, that if the child cleans up the bedroom by lunchtime, they would be happy to give him or her a surprise treat later on.

Pretending

Pretending is a strategic technique that enables a person to experience behaviors that formerly were inhibited by a personal negative rule of power, "I couldn't do that," or identity, "I'm not the kind of person who does that, even though I want to."

Problem-Solution Rut Analysis

The therapist advises the clients that their solution is responsible for getting them the exact opposite results from what they desire and encourages them to think of another way.

Again, children and parents who participate in therapy imply or express rules regarding other family members and themselves. If a rule is detected by the therapist to be maladaptive, his or her objective is to alter the client's rule and/or to reframe it so that its maladaptive behavioral and cognitive expression changes to adaptive response patterns. The most important therapist verbalizations are those that are designed to elicit, clarify, alter, or reinterpret the maladaptive rules held by children and parents. These interventions are essential to the effective alteration of rule-bound maladaptive patterns observed or reflected on during child-focused therapy sessions in which paradoxical psychotherapy techniques are delivered. (Other therapy orientations may also employ some of these general therapist verbalizations. However, these methods would be delivered with content that matches the "orientation" [i.e., behavioral, cognitive, psychodynamic, etc.] as opposed to content that matches the clients' rules.)

Clinical Case Examples

The case examples that follow illustrate the way paradoxical interventions are used to alter clients' dysfunctional rules and thus alter behavior. The first example deals with the method of therapeutic change in which the application of uncommon therapy expands the detail of the context surrounding the problem. Rule-governed and previously contextually bound maladaptive patterns are then replaced or discontinued.

Case 1: Erik

Ten-year-old Erik was referred for treatment by his parents. Their main concerns were his "bad attitude," disobedience, and inability to take "no" for an answer to his requests or to his desires for extra privileges.

THERAPIST: Hi, Erik. As I said, my name is Steve. Please sit down. (*Erik sees an interesting toy across the room.*) Have you every played with one of those space warp roller coasters?

The therapist–child interchanges noted here depict the therapist employing the therapeutic elements of *engagement* and *probes.*

ERIK: Nope. I haven't ever seen one. How's it work?
THERAPIST: Come over here, I'll show you. (*Erik approaches the toy. The therapist demonstrates how the toy works. As the toy is operating, the therapist begins his intervention.*) What did your mom explain to you about coming here to see me?
ERIK: She said I was going to the doctor.
THERAPIST: What for?

ERIK: Well, she thinks I've got a bad attitude.
THERAPIST: What do you think about your attitude?
ERIK: It's O.K.
THERAPIST: Your mother probably told you that I'm a psychologist and that I talk with kids to try to help them with things they wish to change about themself or about their family. (*Pause*) If you could change something about yourself, what would you wish to change?
ERIK: My temper.

In this therapy sequence, the therapist *frames* his role and function and then makes a *probe* that focuses on the potential identified problem. In the next series of interchanges, the therapist *paraphrases* what the client child is communicating and *probes* for more detail about the problem and its context.

THERAPIST: So, you think you lose your temper too much? I know your mother thinks this is a big problem, too. (*Pause*) What usually happens to make you lose your temper?
ERIK: My mom tells me I can't do something I want to do and stuff.
THERAPIST: I see. So that makes you angry and you lose your temper, argue with your mom, and smart mouth her. Is that how it goes?
ERIK: Yeah.
THERAPIST: O.K. Then what happens? Do you get your mom to give in, does she then let you do what you want?
ERIK: No.
THERAPIST: Does your mother then punish you?
ERIK: Yeah. Sometimes she grounds me to the house for a couple of days.
THERAPIST: So, tell me if I have this right. Your mom tells you that you can't do something. Then you get angry and there's a hassle between you and your mom. Then your mom punishes you on top of telling you that you can't do something you want to do. Is that right?
ERIK: Yeah.
THERAPIST: And this happens over and over again?
ERIK: Uh huh.
THERAPIST: About how many times a week do you think this happens?
ERIK: I don't know. (*Pause*) Once or twice.
THERAPIST: So your not controlling your temper causes you to lose something twice, about two times a week?
ERIK: Yeah, I guess so.
THERAPIST: I can see why you would want to make some changes in your temper. Would you agree to let me try to help you with your temper problem?
ERIK: I guess so.

The therapist used an *engagement strategy* by taking a one-down position and asking the child if the child would agree to allow the therapist to help.

THERAPIST: We (that is, if you let me help you) need to learn a bit more about this out-of-control type anger. To do this, I want you *not* to change at all this week. I'll tell your mother to remind you every so often by telling you, "Remember what the doctor said, Erik." So, this next week I suggest you go ahead and lose your temper as usual, but try to remember everything that happens when you lose your temper—you know, getting double punished and stuff. Got the idea?

The therapist provides a *paradoxical injunction* that instructs the child not to change in spite of the apparent knowledge that was gained through the interview that specified two negative consequences that had occurred because of Erik's temper problem. This is sometimes called a *restraining technique* by strategic therapists. A restraining technique is a form of *paradoxical intervention* that functions to raise the consciousness of the client; then, once the consciousness is raised, the client presumably will find it most difficult to avoid responding more adaptively because he or she is more cognizant of the details of the context that requires the adaptive response.

ERIK: I think so.

THERAPIST: Well, let's be sure. What do I suggest for you to do this week?

ERIK: Um, I'm not supposed to change, and, um, I'm supposed to remember what happens when I lose my temper.

THERAPIST: Yes, that's perfect. Any questions? Well then, let's make an appointment for next week. Let's get your mom now.

ERIK: Can I see how the toy works again?

THERAPIST: Sure, go ahead and turn it on. I'll tell your mother to remind you with "the doctor said" stuff.

The client provides *detail* about his understanding of the therapeutic assignment, and the therapist makes additional *probes* focused on that understanding that further elucidate the problem sequence for both Erik's and the therapist's awareness.

The following week, the therapist interviews Erik's mother, who reports that Erik hasn't lost his temper once during the last week, even though he had plenty of chances to lose control. The therapist then invites Erik in for his session. An abbreviation of the interview is presented next.

THERAPIST: Erik, your mom tells me that your anger problem didn't happen this week. Is this true?
ERIK: Yeah.
THERAPIST: You didn't lose your temper at all?
ERIK: Nope. I don't think I did.
THERAPIST: What happened?
ERIK: I dunno.
THERAPIST: What do you remember about what I suggested you do about your temper?
ERIK: You told me to go ahead and lose my temper just like before.
THERAPIST: What else?
ERIK: I don't know.
THERAPIST: To remember everything that happens.
ERIK: Oh, yeah.
THERAPIST: Why do you think you could control your temper this last week?
ERIK: I didn't want to get double punished, I guess.
THERAPIST: Yup, that's probably it. But, how are you going to remember that—even when you're not coming in to see me?

The therapist and client continue this session with an interchange that includes therapist *probes* and client articulation of detail. Finally, the therapist articulates a probe that asks the client how he will maintain his therapeutic accomplishments.

ERIK: I don't know. I'll just try to remember, I guess.
THERAPIST: Well, let me have your mom come in to help with this. (*Pause. Erik listens in.*) Mrs. Jones, I want you to help Erik learn to remember to control his temper in the future in a special way.
MOTHER: How's that?
THERAPIST: I want you to, every 10 days or so, deny Erik a privilege or a request on purpose, for no real good reason. But never tell Erik if it's a "regular time" or an "on-purpose" time. That way, every time you deny Erik a privilege he will even better learn how to control his temper, so that he doesn't get punished twice. And, even if you begin to forget to do this on purpose in a week or two, it will serve the same function. Do you think you can follow through on this?

The therapist employs a *paradoxical injunction*. Embedded in the injunction is a *framing* of the intervention justifying its use.

MOTHER: Yes, I don't see any reason why I wouldn't, but I don't think it's fair that I would be doing this on purpose.

THERAPIST: On the contrary, you will be more than fair to Erik, because not only will you be reminding him to learn to control his temper, you will be preparing him for the certain unfairness he will face in his life. You will be preparing him to face unfair and tough times, because at school or later on at work, Erik will be denied privileges because of circumstances that have very little to do with him personally.

The therapist continues to frame the intervention to further justify its use. This particular framing is matched to the mother's question about the fairness of the intervention, fairness being a value rule of the mother, and implied is the value and identity rule combined, "I am a fair mother."

MOTHER: I never thought of it that way.

THERAPIST: Erik, in the next week or so, do you think you can hold your temper even if your mom is sometimes going to tell you on purpose that you can't do something you want to do?

ERIK: Yeah, I think so.

THERAPIST: O.K. Mrs. Jones, if you feel like you're being too unfair, you don't need to follow through—follow through when you know it's best, but also when you think Erik will think it's at least a little unfair. Is this more doable for you?

MOTHER: Yes, as long as I don't have to be too unfair, I think I can do it.

The therapist continues to frame the context of how and when the paradoxical injunction is to be delivered in a way that is more consistent with the mother's values. The way the therapist words this intervention allows the possibility of the mother unintentionally forgetting to do the therapeutic assignment and only naturally denying privileges whenever the occasion is appropriate from her perspective. The previous interchanges are also embedded in a technique known as an *eavesdrop induction*. Erik overhears how privilege denials will be made by his mother, and the intervention is hypothesized to, once again, serve to raise Erik's consciousness about the double jeopardy that he exposes himself to when he loses his temper.

At 6-month follow up, Erik's mother reported him to be doing very well. She said that he still lost his temper at times, but he would catch himself, say he was sorry, and accept her parenting including the occasional denials of his requests that he received from her. His mother also indicated that his temper outbursts were less frequent and much less intense.

In the above case example, the therapist worked to expand the child's consciousness of the detail surrounding the problem to induce change. In addition, paradoxical prescriptions were also delivered to further heighten Erik's awareness of the problem context and its sequence. Finally, a paradoxical prescription was used to continue Erik's awareness and improved anger control.

The following two cases, Cases 2-A and 2-B, also use the technique of paradoxical prescription. In Case 2-A, the therapist uses a paradoxical prescription to alter Amanda's action or behavior, which in turn alters her personally held power rule: "I can't control my fear." In Case 2-B, the therapist presents the maladaptive patterns and raises a concern to the child, Kevin, that the action the child is taking is incongruous to the context and actually gets the child the opposite from what the goal of his rule is directed toward. The therapist indicates that the results of the child's behavior contradict a personally held rule.

Case 2-A: Amanda

Amanda, age 11, was referred by her parents who report that she recently experienced significant changes and stressors. Her grandmother had died, the family moved to a new neighborhood, she began attending a new school, and a child two doors down in the new neighborhood was struck by a car and hospitalized for 3 weeks. Amanda did not witness the accident but heard the tire screech as the driver attempted to avoid hitting the child. These incidents were related to the therapist over the phone as probable causes for Amanda's recent exhibition of extreme fearfulness, nightmares, and anxiety when left with a babysitter or alone in the house for short periods of time. Her parents reported that Amanda is a pleasant, cooperative child who has many friends, does well in school, and who has had no significant emotional or behavioral problems in the past. In the therapist–client interchanges to follow, the therapist makes several probes, and the client responds by providing descriptive detail of her problem. In the first response, the child articulates a personal rule of "I can't sleep" as a general and unconditional-type rule. The interchange also implies that Amanda can't stop worrying.

THERAPIST: Amanda, I've just talked with your dad; thanks for waiting in the lounge. Um, your dad says that you've been having some problems lately. He tells me that you have nightmares and that you're scared a lot, and it's hard for you to, I guess, see your parents go away from you—like when they go out together as a couple, or when your dad leaves town for work, then it's real hard for you. But what I'd like to hear is what you describe in your own words. What are you experiencing difficulties with?

AMANDA: Well, I can't sleep. I wake up in the middle of the night, afraid.

THERAPIST: And this fear—is it the same kind of fear, the same kind of worry, when your parents go away from you?

AMANDA: Uh huh, I sort of feel, it seems worse at night, but it's the same kind of feeling during the day when they leave, when they go, you know, somewhere and leave me home.

THERAPIST: How many times a week do you experience this kind of thing when you're feeling this worry and anxiety and fear?

AMANDA: Well, oh lately it's been more and more often, maybe two or three times a week, I guess.

THERAPIST: And have you tried to do anything about it to make it not happen so often, or make it not so bad?

AMANDA: My mom and dad tell me not to worry, that everything will be all right, and just to think about something else, but it doesn't really help when they say that. . . .

THERAPIST: Have you tried that?

AMANDA: I've tried. But it doesn't work too well.

THERAPIST: O.K. I was wondering, you're here today talking to me. . . . I was wondering if you would like me to try to help you not worry so much and not be so scared; maybe it would help with the nightmares. Would that be O.K. with you?

The therapist uses an engagement strategy of asking permission to help, often referred to by strategic therapists as taking the "one-down" position. The interchange continues with the therapist probing and the child/client responding by providing descriptions, some of which continue to indicate that she cannot control her fear and worry, a power rule.

AMANDA: Uh huh, that would be O.K. I don't like feeling afraid, I would like to not feel afraid.

THERAPIST: And it's O.K. if I try to help you?

AMANDA: Sure, it's O.K.

THERAPIST: How do you feel when you feel this worry and fear—do you feel like it's something that's in your control, or is it out of your control—how does it happen?

AMANDA: Well, it just happens. The nightmares just happen, and they just come during the night and wake me up, and I'm just scared.

THERAPIST: What about during the day?

AMANDA: Well, when my parents leave for a little while, and I'm alone, I get real worried and scared, and I don't know why that happens, but it happens a lot. I just can't stop being scared.

THERAPIST: I understand. You feel out of control, it happens automatically . . . this scared feeling.

AMANDA: Uh huh . . .

THERAPIST: It happens out of your control . . .

AMANDA: Yeah . . .

THERAPIST: And you can't seem to stop it . . .

AMANDA: I don't want to worry but I just do. I can't make it stop.

THERAPIST: Do you get any other feelings in your body when you become scared?

AMANDA: Yeah, sort of—I can't eat when I get worried, and I get shivery and kind of nervous inside.

THERAPIST: O.K. What do you think about when you're having these fears and these worries, and you have these feelings come on you?

AMANDA: (*Pause*) I just feel like maybe something bad's going to happen to my mom and dad when they go out of the house. (*Pause*) When I have nightmares I usually have nightmares about something bad happening to them.

THERAPIST: When we're talking here, Amanda, do you sort of know that probably nothing bad is going to happen to them . . . I mean, you could still feel scared like when you have your problem, but you sort of know that they're going to be okay, that they're going to go somewhere and come back safe?

AMANDA: Yeah. 'Cause every day, you know, they go places and come back when they say they will. I know that probably nothing is going to happen to them.

THERAPIST: O.K. I guess what I'd like to do is to help you get control of these feelings of worry and fear, and to do that, I'd like to try something right here in my office. I'd like you to try, as hard as you can, to bring on the feelings that you have—the fearful feelings and the nervous feelings that you have.

The therapist invites the client to try as hard as she can; this is a direct invitation to engage in the therapeutic process. Also in this first therapist verbalization is the core of a *paradoxical prescription*. During the next series of interchanges, the therapist continues to describe the specifics of the paradoxical prescription and also provides a frame for how the symptom prescription will bring the child's worry under her control.

AMANDA: What do you mean, bring on?

THERAPIST: Before you do this, I want to explain the whole thing to you.

AMANDA: O.K.

THERAPIST: What I mean by bringing the fear or scared feeling on is to go ahead and bring on, under your own influence, on purpose under your own control—you know, go ahead and think about something that would make you feel worried or scared like you do at night or like when your mom and dad are leaving to go to, let's say, a movie on the weekend. I want you to try to do that on purpose, right here and right now. The reason I want you to do this is because if you do this on purpose it will be under your control this time—it won't be something that happens, BAM!—automatically. It will be something that happens because you are doing it on purpose, then you can make it go away on purpose. So are you willing to try it?

AMANDA: O.K., I'll try.

THERAPIST: O.K.

AMANDA: Do you want me to do it right now?

THERAPIST: Yes, that would be nice. Thank you. O.K., Amanda, when you've tried for a while to bring on those feelings, and you've given it a good try, I want you to just look over at me and tell me that you tried and that you want to do something else. It might help you now to look away from me or close your eyes while you try to bring on the feelings. Go ahead now.

AMANDA: (*Tries for a few minutes, then turns to the therapist.*) Um, I want to do something else now.

THERAPIST: Were you able to bring on those feelings, Amanda?

AMANDA: I couldn't.

THERAPIST: You couldn't bring on those feelings?

AMANDA: No.

THERAPIST: O.K. Um, well, that's good, that's good. Sometimes what happens is, that because you try to bring it on, it won't come—by trying to bring them on on purpose, you made those feelings that were out of your control, under your control and not necessary to happen.

AMANDA: Oh!

Here the therapist reframes the experience of Amanda's not being able to bring on the symptom as a positive one that enables her to control the nonoccurrence of her worry and fear.

THERAPIST: So what I'm going to suggest that you do every morning, every noontime, right after school, before dinner, and at bedtime (that's five times a day) is for you to go ahead and try to bring those worried and scared feelings on, on purpose, just like you tried a few minutes ago. And if they do come, you can make them go away, just like you made them come on—and if they don't come, like a few minutes ago, eh, that's okay, too! If they don't come after a few minutes, then you just go on with whatever else you need to do. Does that sound like something that you can do?

The therapist provides a paradoxical homework assignment, or "worry homework," which is to serve the function of a paradoxical prescription that prevents the worry from coming. The remainder of the interchange is a series of frames by the therapist and questions by Amanda.

AMANDA: I think I can try it. (*Pause*) Should I go in my bedroom or where should I do it at home?

THERAPIST: Wherever you feel comfortable doing it would be okay. It could be at your desk at school, it could be on the playground by yourself for a while, or at home in your room or in the TV room, wherever you feel comfortable doing it. What I think I'd like to do is to have your dad come in now, so that he understands what you're going to be doing and why you're going to be doing it. Sound O.K. to you?

AMANDA: Sure.

THERAPIST: Is there anything else, Amanda, that you think we should be talking about before I bring your dad in?

AMANDA: (*Pause*) Um, what happens when I wake up in the middle of the night with nightmares, then what do I do?

THERAPIST: Well, I'm thinking that if you do this "worry homework"—that's what we'll call it—that maybe your nightmares won't come as much, and maybe they won't even come back at all. But if they do, we can work on it the next time you come in. O.K.?

AMANDA: O.K.

THERAPIST: Let's call your dad in now.

The therapist talks with Amanda's father with Amanda still there. The therapist then suggests that the intervention be implemented once the father understands the reason for the assignment (to put the uncontrollable feelings under Amanda's control). The therapist offers an open invitation for the parents or Amanda to call him during the week if there are any problems with the assignment, and an appointment is scheduled for 10 days following the session above.

Ten days later, Amanda and her father return to the office. The therapist invites both Amanda and her dad into the inner office and asks how the last couple of weeks have been in regard to her problem. Amanda's father answers that things have been much better, that

Amanda is worried a lot less during the day, and that she has been able to not be emotional when she is left with a sitter or alone for short periods of time. Amanda nods. The father also relates that the nightmares have ceased.

THERAPIST: Amanda, what have you done over the last 10 days to help yourself with the problem of worry and fear?

During this follow-up therapy sequence, the therapist's primary goal is to discover what has occurred since the last therapy visit. After establishing the success of the initial intervention, the paradoxical prescription, the therapist moves the focus of therapy toward maintenance of the therapeutic benefit. This is accomplished through several probes and a prescription to resume the paradoxical prescription as advised.

AMANDA: Um, well, I did what you said I should—I tried to practice, um, in the morning before I go to school, and right before I go to lunch, and after dinner I try to worry for a little while, and I can't worry very much.

THERAPIST: How about this last week?

AMANDA: Well, I haven't done it as much as I did right at first—I do it, um, about two times every day.

THERAPIST: Well, that's O.K., Amanda. I'm glad that for the first few days you did your homework every day, three or four or five times, but now it seems that twice a day is all you need to do it. Maybe for the next couple of weeks, you'll only need to do your worry homework once or twice a day—then sometimes only once or twice a week for the next few weeks. Do you think that you could do that?

AMANDA: Yeah, I could do it that much.

THERAPIST: Now, what happens 6 months from now, Amanda, what happens if 6 months from now for some reason you get real scared and start to worry again—what do you think you'll do?

AMANDA: (*Pause*) Um, I'd go back to doing my worry homework five times a day again.

THERAPIST: (*To father*) It might be a good idea if, for the next 6 or 7 weeks or so, that you remind Amanda about her worry homework—that she might want to take 1 day every couple of weeks and go ahead and set that aside for doing the worry homework assignment a few times that day.

Two months later, Amanda's parents were called by the therapist. The parents reported that Amanda was doing well and had not relapsed in any way with regard to her worrying.

Case 2-B: Kevin

Ten-year-old Kevin would have crying fits and stomachaches each day before school. This would result in severe conflict with his mother, a single parent. She would attempt to get him to go to school and would reassure him that everything would be okay, that there was nothing to be afraid of, to no avail. The family history showed that one day the previous year Kevin's mother had been suddenly hospitalized after she sent him off to school in the same manner saying: "Have a nice day, and don't worry about me, sweetheart." (She had been ill for some time.)

Kevin's mother provided the therapist with background information that indicated that Kevin was somewhat timid at school; however, he had friends there, and there was no evidence of conduct problems. He also earned good grades. Recently, though, Kevin's grades had declined because of absenteeism resulting from his mother's not being able to get him to school on time or there at all on some days. The core of the intervention is illustrated below during the second half of the second session.

THERAPIST: This is the second time that I've met you, Kevin, and I've finished talking with your mom, and she says that you're really not doing much better; it's still real hard for you in the mornings, that you're not getting to school on time. Is that right?

This sequence depicts an interchange consisting primarily of probes and descriptions of detail. The child articulates a conditional rule that if he stays home his mother will be okay, and he will not worry about her.

KEVIN: Uh huh. (*Pause*) Some mornings I'm late; some days I stay home.

THERAPIST: And, do you know why you become so upset?

KEVIN: I just worry about my mom, um, when I have to go to school.

THERAPIST: Do you sometimes feel like she's going to be safer if you stay home?

KEVIN: Well, I just know if I stay home I don't worry about her like I do when I go to school. Um, I guess if I stay home with her I feel like she'll be O.K.

THERAPIST: All right. Well, do you know your mom has been sick in the past and is still trying to get over her illness?

KEVIN: Yeah, she was really sick last year. I came home from school and she wasn't there; they put her in the hospital.

THERAPIST: And she still sometimes goes to the doctor for her illness?

KEVIN: Yeah, she goes about once a month to the doctor's now.

THERAPIST: Well, I'm concerned because your mom has a kind of sickness that gets worse with stress. Like when she's nervous or tense and has too many things to do or too many worries, her sickness gets worse. When I talked to her, she told me that her biggest worry is that she feels she's not being a good mother because she's not able to get you to go to school.

KEVIN: She's worried about that?

THERAPIST: She worries about that a lot—that's her biggest worry right now. And, I'm afraid that if she worries too much, and you and she have lots of problems over this, that she's just going to make herself sicker.

In response to the child's contextual and conditional rule, the therapist reframes the child's actions as inconsistent or incongruent with his rule—by indicating that the child's staying home from school is causing anxiety and worry that exacerbates his mother's illness. The remainder of this sequence consists of the therapist's reframing and engagement strategies based on the child's core conditional rule.

KEVIN: Well, I don't want my mom to get sicker.

THERAPIST: I know you don't, but I just wanted to have you understand that she is very, very worried about you, and . . . I don't know what else to say, other than I know you'll try as hard as you can to get yourself to school so that your mom is not going to be worried.

KEVIN: Well, I want my mom to be all better—so I'll try.

THERAPIST: That's very thoughtful. Well, how about if we set up an appointment for next week, and we'll see how this next week goes for you. We'll see if things get better between you and your mom in the mornings . . .

The following week, Kevin's mother reports that he has gone to school every day without a hassle and is very curious to know what the psychologist said to make this happen. The therapist explained that Kevin was following a personal, conditional rule: "If I stay home, my mother will not become ill." The therapist explained his communication about how worried and stressed the mother got when Kevin did not attend school or get there on time, and how this might erode her health. Thus, Kevin's rule was modified to be, "I must go to school to keep my mom from being stressed and getting sicker."

In this therapy case example, a reframing of how the mother's illness functions in relationship to her child's behavior caused the child to alter his personal conditional rule.

It may have been more consistent with the author's theory to have delivered this intervention more cautiously; that is, that it be reviewed with a parent first, prior to discussing the intervention with the child. However, this case example is presented verbatim, in the order the interventions occurred.

Case 3: Terry

This case example illustrates how a therapist might expose the client-held rules that are operative as being dysfunctional, superstitiously held, or of lesser importance than another personally held rule that may influence more adaptive behavior.

Terry, a 15-year-old sophomore in high school, was referred to treatment by her parents because she was not attending some of her classes, was missing practices for her singing group, and anticipated missing performances in the near future. She remained isolated after school and had very few friendship contacts during the week. During the previous year, Terry had been very active socially and had had many friendship contacts with a variety of peers. Terry, in an initial interview with the therapist, discussed a fight that she had had with a friend of hers who formed a coalition with another friend, and Terry was very hurt. She had then isolated herself from further friendship contact. Since that time, she has been very anxious about receiving the same sort of rejection. She feels that she is not acceptable, that she might be rejected by peers, and that she does not measure up to standards that the other kids might have.

THERAPIST: Thanks for coming in today, Terry. If today's appointment is to be worthwhile to you, what would you want to accomplish?

TERRY: Today, um, well, today I would like to find out how I can . . . well, my mom wants me to go to school every day, too, except that I feel . . . I feel kind of funny going to school.

THERAPIST: You feel "kind of funny" going to school. . . . Can you describe to me what that feeling is?

TERRY: Well, I don't feel funny about going to all of my classes . . . there's a couple of classes where my friend, well, she isn't really my friend anymore—I feel funny about going to those classes where she is.

THERAPIST: This is the friend that you had a big fight with a few months ago?

TERRY: Yes, she's the same one . . . I just don't want to be around her. I don't know.

THERAPIST: She also participates in the singing group that you're in, is that right?

TERRY: Yes, she's been in it at the same time that I've been.

THERAPIST: So when you feel funny about going to class, do you miss class, or what?

TERRY: Sometimes I skip. I go late a lot. But when I go, it just feels like I'm not really there.

THERAPIST: About your old friend you had a fight with, does she have lots of friends?

TERRY: Oh yes, she's real popular, she's got so many friends—she's kind of, you know, she gets to do lots of things, and her parents kind of let her go out a lot, so she gets to be with friends a lot.

THERAPIST: Do you think that other kids like her more than you?

TERRY: Well, I guess . . . she has a lot more friends than I do . . . I think, I think other people like her more. There are some people who used to be my friends, and now they're just her friends, and they're not my friends.

THERAPIST: I'm not sure, Terry, but I think your not being around your friends a lot is part of the problem. Do you think that you give people a fair chance to get to know you and like you?

The therapist primarily relies on probes, and the client responds by answering the questions that fill in the detail about her problem. Moreover, in the paragraphs above and the next sequence, the therapist employs probes and reframes that expose the client's behavior (avoidance) as a form of her rejecting others or a way of making herself more rejectable. The therapist also makes an assumption that fairness is a value rule for Terry and frames her avoidant pattern as being unfair to others.

TERRY: Well, . . . I don't know. Do you . . .

THERAPIST: I guess I ask that because if you miss classes and your singing group it might be that you're not giving people a chance.

TERRY: I don't know, I think I sort of give people a chance. It's just that they don't seem to like me. I don't know, they don't want to be around me.

THERAPIST: You know, that's interesting that you say that because when you describe how you're not going to class and you're not participating with other kids in school, I get the feeling that sometimes you're not giving them a fair chance to get to know you and get to like you. I think that maybe what's happening is that because you're not giving them that chance that they think you're stuck up—they think that you might think you're too good for them.

TERRY: You know . . . some kids have called me stuck-up and conceited.

THERAPIST: Is that the way that you want to come across? Do you think you're too good for other kids?

TERRY: Oh, no! I don't think that . . . (*Pause*) I think maybe I'm not good enough for them, that they won't like me.

The client communicates an identity rule that she's not good enough for her peers.

THERAPIST: So it's really just the opposite—you kind of worry about whether you measure up, and yet, what you might be communicating to other kids is that you're stuck-up, and they don't measure up. So stuck-up is what you might be communicating—by not participating more with your peers. But I can understand that it's difficult for you; it's hard to participate because of these feelings you have . . .

The therapist *reframes* the client's action as not fitting her identity rule.

TERRY: I feel like. . . . (*Pause*) Maybe I'm just not good enough; so I stay home and stay in my room and do things by myself most of the time.

THERAPIST: What's the feeling like when you actually push yourself to try to go ahead and go to a class or go to the singing group? What's the feeling like?

TERRY: Um, I feel real, um, scared . . . kind of nervous, and I feel like everybody, like all the other girls are, um, you know, more popular than I am and they, you know, just seem to not have any problems making friends.

Further probing indicates that Terry has an interpersonal identity rule that other teenagers are not like her because they do not have problems making friends.

THERAPIST: So it seems to you that it's easy for the other girls to make and keep friends.

TERRY: Uh uh, they don't seem to have any trouble . . .

THERAPIST: O.K. What classes are you taking this semester?

The therapist probes about Terry's school schedule to gain information to use in forming a paradoxical prescription, and Terry shares detail.

TERRY: I've got biology, and English, and my music class—choir—um, and then, my math class, and you know, I'm just sort of starting out on my requirements.

THERAPIST: O.K. In English, do you ever have to do any kind of writing or reports or anything like that?

TERRY: Oh, yeah . . . about once a week the teacher gives us an assignment to write—she calls them theme papers.
THERAPIST: And do you get to pick the topics for the papers?
TERRY: Sometimes. Sometimes she gives us a topic, but once in a while we get to pick what we want to write about.
THERAPIST: Well, do you remember when you used to be a young, young child and you used to pretend to be a princess or a grown-up or whatever? Did you ever pretend when you were real young?

The therapist probes about the concept of pretending, again further formulating a potential uncommon prescription.

TERRY: Oh, sure, I used to pretend.
THERAPIST: So you still remember that kind of thing when you had fun pretending?
TERRY: Yeah, I remember some of it.
THERAPIST: O.K. Well, I have this idea about what you might try, and I think it might help you. I suggest you talk to your English teacher and see if you could write a theme paper about, I don't know, maybe you could call it "teenagers today" or something like that. What I want you to do is to pretend you're a reporter for the school newspaper, and I want you to write an article about what's most difficult about being a teenager. And what I'd like you to do is to interview kids in your classes, especially those classes that you feel scared to go and to participate in. . . .

The therapist introduces a paradoxical prescription for Terry to pretend to be a reporter for the school newspaper. This indirectly facilitates the client's beginning to interact with her peers on a personal level.

TERRY: Um, you want me to just interview girls?
THERAPIST: No, girls and guys. Especially guys.
TERRY: I get, um, a little nervous when I have to go up to a boy and talk.
THERAPIST: You don't really have to be nervous with this because you'll be pretending—you'll be pretending that you're a reporter, so it'll be like you won't really be you, and you won't be because the reason you'll be talking to them won't be any personal reason. It will be because you're doing this darned report, and so that will make it a lot easier to talk with boys. I think it's important that you understand what's most difficult for teenagers. You think you could do this?

The therapist frames the therapy assignment as one that Terry does not need to become worried or fearful of because the pretending and the class assignment emotionally distances her (initially) from the interactions with her peers and effectively reduces or eliminates her fear of personal rejection. Any rejection that may be felt can be interpreted by Terry as rejection of the "reporter" or the "class assignment."

THERAPIST: At least, are you willing to give it a try?

TERRY: I'm willing to try. There's a couple of people I could ask. I know they'd answer the questions, but I don't know about the other ones.

THERAPIST: Um, which ones?

TERRY: Well, you know, the ones that are always, they're always talking with other people all the time, and I'd feel funny going up to them . . .

THERAPIST: I want you to write some of their names down, and after you get through interviewing the people you're comfortable with, I want you to go ahead and interview a couple of those kids you're not so comfortable with.

TERRY: Do I have to do this at school, or can I call 'em up at home; can I do it on the phone?

THERAPIST: You should not do it over the phone, but you could do it after school—you need to do this in person. O.K.?

TERRY: Um hum.

THERAPIST: Do you see anything that would stop you from, from doing this?

TERRY: Well, um, I guess the only thing that would stop me would be, you know, if someone didn't want to answer the questions, but I guess most people would just do it—especially if it was an assignment, and I was going to get graded on it.

THERAPIST: Well, very good. Remember, sometimes other kids might think you're stuck-up when you're really not, when you're just kind of nervous and scared about participating—um, what was the other thing we talked about? Oh, yeah, that you think other kids don't have any trouble making friends. Your doing this report and interviewing people may help you learn something that may surprise you about how other kids view themselves and their friends. So let's schedule an appointment for, say, 2 weeks from now . . .

The sequence ends with the therapist reminding Terry of her behavior as being a potential communication to others that she thinks she is better than they are and is misconstrued as rejecting of them first. The therapist also reminds her, indirectly, of her interpersonal rule that others don't have trouble making friends.

TERRY: Do I have to get this assignment done by the time I come back?

THERAPIST: Oh, why don't you get started on it. Talk to your teacher and get the project approved so you could get a good grade for doing it, and, uh, I at least want you to get started on it. You might find that you like doing it, and you can do as much as you like after you get started. O.K.?

TERRY: O.K.

Terry's personal rule is an identity rule that she is not acceptable to others. The frame of the intervention is that it encourages her to perform behaviors that do not fit her rule. However, she is able to carry these out because she doesn't have to be herself—she can pretend. The therapist also hypothesizes that Terry will discover that her power rule about other teens making and keeping friends easily is not true. The therapist also frames Terry's social-avoidance behavior as a rejecting and conceited communication to peers. It is assumed this is something she wishes to avoid communicating, as she fears rejection by peers.

During the next session, the therapist interviews Terry and discusses with her how she was able to carry out the assignment and talk to her peers whom she had previously avoided. Terry reports that she finished her theme paper and that the interviewing went well, even with those kids whom she was fearful of approaching. The therapist points out that she pretended to be a reporter and that she was doing an assignment; however, the therapist also points out to her that she was the one who was doing the pretending, which places Terry in conflict with regard to her rule about not being acceptable; the therapist reframed again that Terry (not the so-called reporter) was the one who was accepted by other people while she did the interviews. One of the delightful experiences that came about in these interviews was that Terry was able to talk about her own anxieties and about her fear of being rejected by peers. She even disclosed that she felt badly because she was shy and sometimes that caused her to be misperceived by other kids as being stuck-up. She also discovered that the major problem that teenagers talked about was about making and keeping friends, and about not being rejected by peers of the same or opposite sex.

The end result of this intervention was that Terry learned that others were also worried about their ability to make and keep friends; this countered her negative rules of identity. This, in turn, reduced her anxiety that she was not like her peers and reduced her anxiety about being rejected.

Appropriate Application of Paradoxical Therapy

In my own clinical experience, I have found paradoxical intervention methods to be effective even when the client and his or her family are aware of why paradoxical techniques are being used (e.g., as in Case 2-A). In other words, there seems to be no advantage to "sneak" a paradoxical technique into the therapy process. This has also been shown to be true in clinical research (Ascher & Turner, 1980). Advising and educating the client about how a paradoxical technique functions does not seem to decrease its potency.

Paradoxical therapy may be used effectively with clients who exhibit high reactance (resistance to therapy or therapist—see Dowd & Brockbank, 1985, for details) and who exhibit symptoms that are experienced as not being under their own power or control. Reactance may be exhibited by a child in response to attempts at control by the child's parents or in response to the therapist's in-session communications. Reactance may also be demonstrated by an entire family in the therapy context or by parents in response to the therapist's suggestions. Such reactance is motivated by clients' personal and interpersonal rules as were discussed earlier.

Other good candidates for paradoxical therapy are those children who have entered into treatment for the second, third, or fourth time. In these cases, detailed interviewing may determine which possible solutions to the referral problem were unsuccessfully attempted during past treatment and are now to be avoided and what factors caused these attempts to fail. If usual, common, and straightforward therapeutic interventions failed, then it is likely that these will fail again and that a more unusual, paradoxical, rule-focused, and rule-justified therapy intervention would be more effective.

Finally, when a therapist interprets problems and justifies particular interventions, this must be based on in-therapy child's or parents' interactions and statements (reflecting clients' world views and personal rules). Most salient here are the rule-oriented statements and implications communicated by the client about others and about himself or herself. The task of the therapist is to provide a therapeutic probe, frame, reframe, or prescription that helps to create an alternate, more adaptive pattern of thought, emotion, or behavior as it relates to the target problem or its context.

Contraindications for the Use of Paradoxical Interventions

There are several situation-specific contraindications that argue against the use of "paradox." First, the use of paradoxical approaches in psychotherapy should not be attempted prior to the establishment of a trusting therapeutic relationship. There is no set time, or number of sessions, involved in determining this qualitative aspect of the therapy relationship. It must be determined on a case-by-case, moment-by-moment basis. The clinician must be sensitive to the client's level of trust, openness, and engagement during psychotherapy.

Paradoxical interventions should be avoided when the therapist can determine through clinical interviews that the client does not learn from experience (Dowd & Brockbank, 1985). Indeed, these clients are poor candidates for most kinds of therapy. Some clients, when engaging in various thoughts, behaviors, and emotions, do not have a conscious awareness of what they have experienced and consequently fail to learn the consequences of their behaviors.

Destructive behaviors are also classified in a category that would be highly suspect (though not unheard of) for the application of paradoxical interventions. Destructive behaviors would include suicidal ideation and intentions as well as intentions to do physical or emotional harm to animals, oneself, others, or property.

There are occasions when the use of paradoxical interventions is mediated and delivered by clients to their significant others or by parents to a child. It is important to realize that mediation of paradoxical interventions attenuates the amount of control that the therapist has over the quality of the implementation of such interventions. Therefore, when the therapist asks a client to deliver a paradoxical intervention to a family member or friend, for example, it is important to be sure that the client is able to deliver the intervention in a caring, sincere, and accurate manner. Persons in high degrees of distress who are confused and live chaotic lifestyles are poor candidates for the use of indirect or mediated paradoxical interventions.

I also caution therapists about the use of paradoxical interventions in certain contexts or service delivery systems. Our clients and communities from which they come are sometimes not as understanding of the psychotherapy profession as we wish them to be. Even though paradoxical interventions have been detailed and demonstrated to be effective with children (Szykula, Sayger, Morris, & Sudweeks, 1987; Szykula & Morris, 1985, 1986; Szykula, Morris, & Turner, 1986), they sometimes do not meet the "common sense" standards that are often established by the professional community in psychology and psychiatry. Paradoxical interventions may be viewed as "odd" by a number of professionals and lay community members. Therefore, when providing a paradoxical intervention, it is important to realize the ramifications of such interventions within the community system. For example, some clients who go from therapist to therapist, defeating every intervention suggested to them, seek out therapists who will take their side against all other previous forms of therapy and therapists. When one uses a paradoxical approach with this type of client, it may later be used against the therapist in the community, simply because it is different. The method may be misrepresented by the client to other professionals and nonprofessionals in the community in a way that allows people to believe that the therapist and therapy are weird or even unethical.

Summary and Conclusions

Preliminary conclusions based on our clinical experience and research data (see Szykula & Morris, 1985, 1986; Szykula et al., 1986, 1987) support the idea that, in the therapeutic context, human change processes are facilitated by at least some specific therapist verbalizations used in response to some specific types of client verbalizations and communications. As depicted in this chapter, these paradoxical therapist verbalizations are designed to change behavior by reframing or altering the personal rules of power, identity, and values that are communicated by clients and that determine their behavior.

At times, I have observed common behavioral interpretations and interventions to be effective in treating referred children and their parents. At other times I have observed their failure. This also holds true for paradoxical interpretations and interventions. Empirical, scientific investigations of both paradoxical and common behavioral therapies are currently being analyzed in our research (Szykula et al., 1988). Our goal is to clarify what specific effects are determined as a function of the therapy communications between therapists and clients (children and parents).

We should no longer accept, at face value, that a certain type of therapy is effective; empirical process-to-outcome investigations will help make it possible for practicing clinicians to match in-session interventions to a client's in-session as well as out-of-session responding. In the meantime, clinical and research literature on psychotherapy must take increasing care to detail therapy processes and procedures as well as outcomes.

As clinicians, we are being held more and more accountable, both ethically and financially, for what we actually do and accomplish when we provide psychotherapy. As our specific interventions move closer to their targets and are based on each client's rules and behaviors (and not on general assumptions of what works for most people), we will increasingly become more accountable—to ourselves and to others. Most importantly, we will be more helpful to the distressed children and parents who visit us with hope.

Acknowledgments

Acknowledgments are extended to Julia Laylander and Stephen B. Morris for their editorial and inspirational contributions to the preparation of this chapter. Special appreciation is also extended to Bernie Grosser, M.D., Chair, Department of Psychiatry, for his support.

References

Ascher, L. M., & Turner, R. M. (1980). A comparison of two methods for the administration of paradoxical intention. *Behaviour Research and Therapy, 18,* 121–126.

Devaney, J. M., Hayes, S. C., & Nelson, R. O. (1986). Equivalence class information in language abled and language disabled children. *Journal of the Experimental Analysis of Behavior, 46,* 243–257.

Dowd, E. T., & Brockbank, L. (1985). *Compliance-based and defiance-based strategies in the treatment of free and unfree behaviors.* Paper presented at the American Psychological Association Convention, Los Angeles.

Dumas, J. E., & Wahler, R. G. (1983). Predictors of treatment outcome in parent training: Mother insularity and socioeconomic disadvantage. *Behavioral Assessment, 5,* 301–313.

Hayes, S. C. (1987). A contextual approach to therapeutic change. In N. S. Jacobson (Ed.), *Psychotherapists in clinical practice: Cognitive and behavioral perspectives* (pp. 327–387). New York: The Guilford Press.

Mahoney, M. J. (in press). *Human change processes: Notes on the facilitation of personal development.* New York: Basic Books.

Szykula, S. A., Laylander, J. L., Czajkowski, L., & Sayger, T. V. (in press). "Consciousness streaming": A single-subject, within session analysis of therapeutically-relevant verbalizations. *Journal of Cognitive Psychotherapy: An International Quarterly.*

Szykula, S. A., & Morris, S. B. (1985). *Strategic therapy with children: Some applied behavior analyses and case studies.* Paper presented at the Association for Advancement of Behavior Therapy, Houston.

Szykula, S. A., & Morris, S. B. (1986). Strategic therapy with children: Single-subject case study demonstrations. *Psychotherapy, 23,* 174–180.

Szykula, S. A., Morris, S. B., Butler, P., & Lambert, M. A. (1988). *Child-focused family therapies: Mechanisms of change as identified through a process rating system.* Panel discussion presented at the convention of the Society for Psychotherapy Research, Santa Fe.

Szykula, S. A., Morris, S. B., & Turner, C. W. (1986). *Child-focused behavioral therapy and strategic therapy: A look at differential potencies.* Paper presented at the Association for Advancement of Behavior Therapy, Chicago.

Szykula, S. A., Sayger, T. V., Morris, S. B., & Sudweeks, C. (1987). Child-focused behavioral and strategic therapies: A preliminary report of outcome comparisons. *Psychotherapy, 24,* 546–551.

Index

C

D

H

I

J

L

M

N

O

P

R

S